iPhone 4S Made Simple

Martin Trautschold and Rene Ritchie
with
Gary Mazo

Apress®

iPhone 4S Made Simple

ISBN-13 (pbk): 978-1-4302-3587-3

ISBN-13 (electronic): 978-1-4302-3588-0

Trademarked names, logos, and images may appear in this book. Rather than use a trademark symbol with every occurrence of a trademarked name, logo, or image we use the names, logos, and images only in an editorial fashion and to the benefit of the trademark owner, with no intention of infringement of the trademark.

The use in this publication of trade names, trademarks, service marks, and similar terms, even if they are not identified as such, is not to be taken as an expression of opinion as to whether or not they are subject to proprietary rights.

President and Publisher: Paul Manning
Lead Editor: Steve Anglin
Development Editor: James Markham
Editorial Board: Steve Anglin, Mark Beckner, Ewan Buckingham, Gary Cornell, Morgan Engel, Jonathan Gennick, Jonathan Hassell, Robert Hutchinson, Michelle Lowman, James Markham, Matthew Moodie, Jeff Olson, Jeffrey Pepper, Douglas Pundick, Ben Renow-Clarke, Dominic Shakeshaft, Gwenan Spearing, Matt Wade, Tom Welsh
Coordinating Editor: Laurin Becker
Copy Editor: Mary Behr, Mary Ann Fugate, Heather Lang, Patrick Meader, Ralph Moore, Kim Wimpsett
Technical Reviewer: Leanna Lofte
Compositor: MacPS, LLC
Indexer: BIM Indexing & Proofreading Services
Artist: MacPS, LLC and Rod Hernandez
Cover Designer: Anna Ishchenko

Distributed to the book trade worldwide by Springer Science+Business Media, LLC., 233 Spring Street, 6th Floor, New York, NY 10013. Phone 1-800-SPRINGER, fax (201) 348-4505, e-mail orders-ny@springer-sbm.com, or visit www.springeronline.com.

For information on translations, please e-mail rights@apress.com, or visit www.apress.com.

Apress and friends of ED books may be purchased in bulk for academic, corporate, or promotional use. eBook versions and licenses are also available for most titles. For more information, reference our Special Bulk Sales–eBook Licensing web page at www.apress.com/info/bulksales.

The information in this book is distributed on an "as is" basis, without warranty. Although every precaution has been taken in the preparation of this work, neither the author(s) nor Apress shall have any liability to any person or entity with respect to any loss or damage caused or alleged to be caused directly or indirectly by the information contained in this work.

This book is dedicated to our families.

*Without their love, support, and understanding,
we could never take on projects like this one.
Now that the book is done, we will gladly share
our iPhones with them—for a little while!*

Contents at a Glance

Contents.. vl

About the Authors..xxii

About the Technical Reviewer xxiii

Acknowledgments xiv

Part I: Quick Start Guide 1

Getting Around Quickly.. 3

Part II: Introduction 27

Introduction.. 29

Part III:You and Your iPad 33

Chapter 1: Getting Started... 35

Chapter 2: Typing, Copy, and Search 69

Chapter 3: Sync with iCloud, iTunes, and More..................................... 97

Chapter 4: Connect to the Network 133

Chapter 5: AirPlay and Bluetooth 157

Chapter 6: Icons and Folders... 169

Chapter 7: Multitasking and Siri 179

Chapter 8: Personalize and Secure 189

Chapter 9: Using Your Phone... 207

Chapter 10: SMS, MMS, and iMessage.. 243

Chapter 11: Video Messaging and Skype 259

Chapter 12: Playing Music 275

Chapter 13: iBooks and E-Books 301

Chapter 14: Newsstand and More 319

Chapter 14: Viewing Videos... 331

Chapter 15: Safari Web Browser 345

Chapter 16: Communicate with Email 365

Chapter 17: Contacts and Notes... 407

■Chapter 18: Calendar and Reminders.. 431

■Chapter 19: Working with Photos.. 459

■Chapter 20: Maps 485

■Chapter 21: iTunes on Your Device.. 505

■Chapter 22: The Amazing App Store.. 523

■Chapter 23: Games and Fun 541

■Chapter 24: Social Networking.. 551

■Chapter 25: Troubleshooting 567

Index.. 583

Contents

Contents at a Glance iv

About the Authors xxii

About the Technical Reviewer xxiii

Acknowledgments xxiv

Part I: Quick Start Guide 1

■ Getting Around Quickly 3

Learning Your Way Around 4

    Keys, Buttons, and Switches 4

    Switching Apps (AKA Multitasking) 5

    Using Siri (Your Personal Assistant) 6

    Using Voice Dictation 7

    Music Controls and Portrait Screen Rotation Lock 8

    Starting Apps and Using Soft Keys 8

    Menus, Submenus, and Switches 9

    Reading the Connectivity Status Icons 10

Flying on an Airplane—Airplane Mode 11

Touch Screen Basics 13

    Touch Screen Gestures 13

Tapping and Flicking 14

Swiping 15

    Scrolling 16

    Double-Tapping 17

    Pinching 17

App Reference Tables 18

    Getting Started 19

    Stay Connected and Organized 20

    Be Entertained 22

    Stay Informed 24

    Network Socially 25

    Be Productive 26

Part II: Introduction **27**

■**Introduction** **29**

Congratulations on Your New iPhone 4S! 29

How This Book Is Organized 30

Quickly Locating Tips, Cautions, and Notes..31

iPhone Video Tutorials 32

Part III: You and Your iPhone 4S...**33**

■**Chapter 1: Getting Started** **35**

Getting to Know Your iPhone 35

What Is Included in the Box 35

Removing or Installing the SIM Card...37

Charging Your iPhone and Battery Life Tips 38

Setting up Your iPhone 43

Knowing If You Need to Set Up Your iPhone 43

Setting up Your iPhone Over-the-Air Using iCloud.....................................43

Setting up a New iPhone Using iCloud..45

Creating a Free Apple ID 46

Configuring iCloud Options 47

Restoring Your iPhone Using iCloud..47

Setting up Your iPhone Using iTunes 48

Restoring Your iPhone From a Previous Backup.....................................49

Maintaining Your iPhone 50

Cleaning Your iPhone Screen...50

Cases and Protective Covers for Your iPhone 50

Where to Buy Your Covers 51

What to Buy...51

iPhone Basics 53

Powering On/Off and Sleep/Wake...53

Assistive Touch Accessibility 53

Slide to Unlock and Quick Camera and Media Access..................................54

Moving Around Inside Apps and Your Settings Screens 55

The Home Button 55

Start Siri by Pressing and Holding the Home Button 56

Access the Fast App Switcher by Double-Clicking the Home Button 56

Volume Keys for Ringer and Audio/Video Playback 56

Locking Your Screen in Portrait (Vertical) Orientation 58

Adjusting or Disabling the Auto-Lock Time-Out Feature 58

Adjusting the Date, Time, Time Zone, and 24-Hour Format.........................59

Adjusting the Brightness...61

Notifications...61

Lock Screen Info 62

In-App Notifications 63

The Notification Center 64

Configuring Notification Center..65

Accessibility Options For Notification Center 67

Chapter 2: Typing, Copy, and Search 69

Typing on Your iPhone 69

 Typing on the Screen with Two Thumbs...............................70

 Type Quick Phrases with Shortcuts 71

 Saving Time with Auto-Correction 72

Spell Checker..74

Accessibility Options..75

 Getting Your iPhone to Speak To You (VoiceOver) 75

 Speak Selection and Speak Auto-text 77

 Using AssistiveTouch 77

 Using Zoom to Magnify the Entire Screen............................78

 White on Black 79

 Triple-Click Home Button Options...80

Using the Magnifying Glass for Editing Text or Placing the Cursor...........81

Typing Numbers and Symbols 82

 Touch and Slide Trick 83

 Press and Hold Keyboard Shortcut for Typing Symbols and More 84

Caps Lock 85

Quickly Selecting and Deleting or Changing Text 85

Keyboard Options and Settings...86

 Setting Auto-Correction to ON or OFF 86

 Auto-Capitalization..86

 Enabling Caps Lock...87

 The ".." Shortcut..87

Typing in Other Languages—International Keyboards 87

 Adding a New International Keyboard 87

 Editing, Re-Ordering, or Deleting Keyboards 88

Copy and Paste...90

 Selecting Text by Double-Tapping It.....................................90

 Selecting Text with Two-Finger Touch 91

 Selecting a Web Site or Other Non-Editable Text with Touch and Hold........92

 Cut or Copy the Text..92

 App Switching and Multitasking 93

 Pasting the Text 93

 Shake to Undo...94

Finding Things with Spotlight Search 94

 Activating Spotlight Search 95

 Searching the Web or Wikipedia...96

 Customizing Spotlight Search..96

Chapter 3: Sync with iCloud, iTunes, and More............ 97

iCloud..97

Setting up iCloud...98

Managing iCloud Storage and Backup 99

Buying More iCloud Storage 101

iTunes in the Cloud 101

iCloud on the Computer 102

Syncing with iTunes..104

Prerequisites 104
Syncing iTunes with an iPod or iPad *and* Your iPhone? 105
There Are Other Sync Methods—Should I Use iTunes? 105
Set Up Your iTunes Sync 107
The iPhone Summary Screen 107
Getting to the Sync Setup Screen (Info Tab) 109
Sync Your Contacts 110
Syncing Your Calendar 112
Syncing Email Accounts 113
Syncing Bookmarks and Notes 114
Syncing Your iPhone with iTunes 114
Sync Apps in iTunes 114
Move Apps, Work with Folders, or Delete App Icons 115
Removing or Reinstalling Apps 116
Syncing Media and More 116
Syncing Ringtones 117
Syncing Music 117
Syncing Movies 118
Syncing TV Shows 119
Syncing Podcasts 120
Syncing iBooks and Audiobooks 121
Sync Photos 122
Troubleshooting iTunes and the Sync 123
Check Out the Apple Knowledgebase for Helpful Articles 123
iTunes Locked Up and Will Not Respond (Windows Computer) 124
iTunes Locked Up and Will Not Respond (Mac Computer) 125
Updating Your iPhone Operating System 126
Other Sync Methods 127
Setting Up Your Google or Exchange Account on Your Device 128

■ **Chapter 4: Connect to the Network** **133**
What Can I Do When I'm Connected to a Wi-Fi or 3G Network? 133
Wi-Fi Connections 134
Connecting to a Wi-Fi Network 135
Connecting at a Public Wi-Fi Hotspot with Web Login 135
Secure Wi-Fi Networks—Entering a Password 136
Switching to a Different Wi-Fi Network 137
Verifying Your Wi-Fi Connection 138
Advanced Wi-Fi Options (Hidden or Undiscoverable Networks) 138
Why Can't I See the Wi-Fi Network I Want to Join? 139
Reconnecting to Previously Joined Wi-Fi Networks 140
Cellular Data Connection 142
Select and Monitor Your Cellular Data Usage 143
International Travel: Things to Do Before You Go 144
Avoiding a Shockingly Large Bill 144
Step 1: Call Your Phone Company 144
Step 2: Check If You Can Use an International SIM Card 145
Step 3: Do Any Data Intensive Stuff Prior to Leaving 146
Flying on an Airplane: Airplane Mode 146

International Travel: When You Arrive..147
   Step 1: Make Sure the Time Zone Is Correct 147
   Step 2: Buy and Insert Your International SIM Card..147
   Step 3: Reset Your Data Usage When You Land 147
   Step 4: Turn Off Data Roaming If It's Too Expensive 148
   Step 5: Use Wi-Fi When Possible 149
International Travel: Returning Home 149
   Step 1: Make Sure the Time Zone Is Correct 150
   Step 2: Turn Off Your Special International Rate Plan 150
Personal Hotspot...150
   Personal Hotspot vs. Tethering...150
   Step 1: Contact Your Phone Company 151
   Step 2: Enable Personal Hotspot on Your iPhone..151
   Step 3: Connect to Your iPhone Personal Hotspot 153
   Step 4: Set Up Networking on Your Computer 153
VPN: Virtual Private Network 153
   Getting Connected 153
   Knowing When You Are Connected to a VPN Network..156
   Switching VPN Networks 156

Chapter 5: AirPlay and Bluetooth **157**
Understanding AirPlay 157
   AirPlay Devices That Work with the iPhone 157
Setting Up and Using AirPlay 157
   AirPlay Mirroring 159
Understanding Bluetooth 160
Understanding Bluetooth 160
   Bluetooth Devices that Work with the iPhone 160
Pairing with a Bluetooth Device 160
   Turning On Bluetooth 161
   Pairing with a Headset or Any Bluetooth Device...161
   Using the Bluetooth Headset 163
Bluetooth Stereo (A2DP) 165
   Connecting to a Stereo Bluetooth Device 165
Disconnecting or Forgetting a Bluetooth Device..167

Chapter 6: Icons and Folders... **169**
Moving Icons to the Bottom Dock 170
   Starting the Move 170
Moving Icons to a Different Icon Page 171
Deleting Icons 172
Resetting All Your Icon Locations (Factory Defaults) 174
Working with Folders 175
   Creating the Folder 175
   Moving Folders 176

Chapter 7: Multitasking and Siri **179**
Fast App Switching...179
   Jumping Between Apps...180
   Killing Apps from the Fast App Switcher Bar..180

Media Controls and the Screen Portrait Orientation Lock..181
Volume Controls and AirPlay..182
Siri: Your Virtual Assistant 182
Enabling and Configuring Siri 183
Using Siri..184
What You Can Ask Siri 184
Changing Names and Setting up Relationships 186
Taking Dictation 188
What Siri Can't Do 188

■Chapter 8: Personalize and Secure 189
Changing Your Lock Screen and Home Screen Wallpapers..189
Changing Wallpaper from Your Settings App...190
Using Any Photo As Wallpaper...192
Downloading Great Wallpaper from Free Apps..193
Using the Wallpaper App..193
Using Your Newly Saved Wallpaper 194
Adjusting Sounds on Your iPhone 195
Keyboard Options..197
Securing Your iPhone with a Passcode 197
Setting a Simple Four-Digit Passcode 197
Setting a More Complex Password 198
Adjusting Your Passcode Options 199
Setting Restrictions...199
Restricting Apps..200
Allowing Changes 202
Restricting Content 204
Restricting Game Center..206

■Chapter 9: Using Your Phone... 207
Getting Started with the Phone Features...207
Finding Your Phone Number 207
Using the iPhone Headset...208
Connecting to a Bluetooth Headset or Car Stereo 208
Dialing a Number from the Keypad...209
Different Phone Views..210
Using Favorites (Speed Dials) 210
Using Recents (Call Logs) 214
Placing Calls from Contacts..215
Calling Any Underlined Phone Number 217
Creating a New Contact from an Underlined Phone Number...218
Voice Dialing using Siri 218
Functions While on a Call...218
Using the Keypad...220
Muting the Call..220
Using the Speakerphone...221
Putting a Caller on Hold 221
Browsing Your Contacts..222
FaceTime Video Call..223

Setting up and Using Voicemail 223
    Setting Up Voicemail 224
    Changing Your Voicemail Password 225
    Playing Your Voicemail 226
    Deleting a Voicemail Message 227
Conference Calling 228
    Initiating the First Call 228
    Adding a Second Caller 228
    Merging Calls 229
    Talking Privately with or Disconnecting from Individuals 230
Phone Options and Settings 231
    Call Forwarding 231
    Call Waiting 233
    Show or Block (Hide) Your Caller ID 233
    Setting up Security on Your SIM Card 233
    TTY for Deaf People 235
    Switching Between Wireless Carriers 235
    Carrier Services 236
Ring Tones, Sounds, and Vibration 237
Assigning Unique Ringtones to Contacts 237
    Giving a Contact a Unique Ringtone 237
Purchasing a Tone from the iTunes App 238
Creating Custom Ringtones 239
    The Free, But More Challenging Way to Create Ring Tones 239
    Syncing the Ringtone to Your iPhone 241
    Using Your New Custom Ringtone 241

Chapter 10: SMS, MMS, and iMessage 243
SMS/MMS vs. iMessage 243
Does iMessage Count As Text or Data? 244
How Will Messages Send? 244
Enabling iMessage and Adjusting Settings 245
Text Messaging on your iPhone 246
    Composing Text Messages 246
    Composing a Text Message from the Messages App 246
    Options After Sending a Text 248
    Composing a Text Message from Contacts 250
    Replying to a Text Message 250
    Viewing Stored Messages 251
    Text Tone and Sound Options 252
MMS—Multimedia Messaging Service 253
    Sending a Picture or Video with Messages 253
    Choosing a Picture from Photos to Send via Messages 256
    Sending Multiple Pictures 257

Chapter 11: Video Messaging and Skype 259
Video Calling 259
    Video Calling with FaceTime 260
Making Phone Calls and More with Skype 263

Downloading Skype to Your iPhone 264

Creating Your Skype Account 264

Log into the Skype App 265

Finding and Adding Skype Contacts 265

Making Calls with Skype on Your iPhone..267

Receiving Calls with Skype on Your iPhone...268

Chatting with Skype 269

Adding Skype to Your Computer 270

Video Recording...271

Starting the Video Recorder..271

Chapter 12: Playing Music 275

Your iPhone as a Music Player..275

The Music App 276

Playlists View 278

Creating Playlists on the iPhone 278

Searching for Music 279

Changing the View in the Music app 280

Viewing Songs in an Album 280

Navigating with Cover Flow 281

Playing Your Music 283

Pausing and Playing..283

To Play the Previous or Next Song...284

Adjusting the Volume 284

Double-Click the Home Button for Media Controls 285

Repeating, Shuffling, Moving around in a Song...286

Moving to Another Part of a Song 286

Repeat One Song or All Songs 287

Shuffle 287

Now Playing 288

Viewing Other Songs on the Album 288

Adjusting Music Settings 289

Using Sound Check (Auto Volume Adjust)..290

EQ (Sound Equalizer Setting) 290

Volume Limit (Safely Listen to Music at a Reasonable Level)..291

Using Home Sharing 291

Showing Media Controls When Your iPhone is Locked..293

Listening to Free Internet Radio (Pandora) 293

Getting Started with Pandora...294

Pandora's Main Screen..295

Thumbs Up or Thumbs Down in Pandora...296

Pandora's Menu 297

Creating a New Station in Pandora 297

Adjusting Pandora's Settings—Your Account, Upgrading, and More..................................298

Chapter 13: iBooks and E-Books 301

Downloading iBooks 302

The iBooks Store..302

Using the Search Button 305

Switching Collections (Books, PDFs, More) 305
Reading PDFs 306
Reading iBooks 307
    Customizing Your Reading Experience: Brightness, Fonts, and Font Sizes............307
    Grow Your Vocabulary Using the Built-In Dictionary...309
    Setting an In-Page Bookmark 309
    Using Highlighting and Notes...310
    Using Search..312
Moving and Deleting Books 313
Other E-Book Readers: Kindle and Kobo...313
    Download E-Reader Apps 314
    The Kindle Reader...314
    The Kobo Reader...317

▓ **Chapter 14: Newsstand and More** **319**
Newsstand 319
Buying and Subscribing to Periodicals 320
Newspapers...321
    The New York Times app 322
    Moving Through and Enjoying Content 323
Magazines..323
    The Zinio Magazine App—A Sampler 324
Comic Books 325
The iPhone as a PDF Reader 328
    Transferring Files to your iPhone 328
    Connecting to Google Docs and other Servers with GoodReader 330

▓ **Chapter 15: Viewing Videos**.. **331**
Your iPhone as a Video Player 331
    Loading Videos onto Your iPhone 332
    Watching Videos on the iPhone 332
    Video Categories...332
    Searching for Videos...332
Playing a Movie..333
    Fast-Forward or Rewind the Video 333
    Using the Time Scrubber Bar 334
    Changing the Size of the Video (Widescreen vs. Full Screen)...............................334
    Using AirPlay...335
    Using the Chapters Feature 336
    Viewing the Chapters 336
Watching a TV Show 336
Watching Podcasts 337
Watching Music Videos...338
Video Options...338
    The Start Playing Option 339
    Closed Captioning 339
Deleting Videos 339
YouTube on your iPhone 340
    Searching for YouTube Videos...340

Using the Bottom Icons..340

Playing Videos..341

Video Controls..341

Checking and Clearing your History..343

■Chapter 16: Safari Web Browser 345

Web Browsing on the iPhone...345

An Internet Connection Is Required 346

Launching the Web Browser...346

Layout of the Safari Web Browser Screen...347

Typing a Web Address 348

Moving Backward or Forward Through Open Web Pages 348

Using the Open Pages Button 349

Zooming In and Out in Web Pages 349

Activating Links from Web Pages 350

Working with Safari Bookmarks 350

Adding a New Bookmark 350

Using Bookmarks and History 351

Managing Your Bookmarks 352

Reading List 354

Safari Reader 355

Safari Browsing Tips and Tricks 356

Jumping to the Top of the Web Page...356

Emailing or Tweeting a Web Page 357

Printing a Web Page...357

Watching Videos in Safari...357

Saving or Copying Text and Graphics 358

Saving Time with AutoFill 359

Adding a Web Page Icon to Your Home Screen 361

Adjusting the Safari Browser Settings 361

Changing the Search Engine...362

Enabling AutoFill 362

Adjusting Privacy Options 363

Adjusting Security Options..364

■Chapter 17: Communicate with Email 365

Getting Started with Mail 365

A Network Connection Is Required 365

Setting up Email on the iPhone...366

Entering Passwords for Email Accounts 366

Adding a New Email Account on the iPhone 367

The Mailboxes Screen—Inboxes and Accounts 371

Adding or Editing Email Folders or Mailboxes 371

Inbox, Flagged (Marked) and Threaded Messages 373

Viewing an Individual Message 374

Composing and Sending Emails 375

Composing a New Email Message...376

Addressing Your Message—Choose the Recipients..376

Changing the Email Account to Send From 378

Typing Your Subject...379

Typing Your Message..379

Keyboard Options...381

Auto-Correction and Auto-Capitalization 381

Send Your Email...382

Checking Sent Messages..383

Reading and Replying to Mail 383

Marking Messages as Unread or Flagged...384

Zooming In or Out..385

Email Attachments...385

Knowing When You Have an Attachment..385

Receiving an Auto-Open Attachment..386

Opening Email Attachments..386

Opening and Viewing Compressed .zip Files 389

Replying, Forwarding, or Deleting a Message 391

Replying to an Email 392

Using Reply All 392

Using the Forward Button 392

Cleaning up and Organizing Your Inbox 393

Deleting a Single Message 393

Deleting, Moving or Marking Several Messages...393

Deleting from the Message Viewing Screen..393

Moving an Email to a Folder While Viewing It..394

Copy and Paste from an Email 395

Searching for Email Messages 396

Activating Email Search..396

Fine Tuning Your Email Settings 397

Automatically Retrieve Email (Fetch New Data) 397

Adjusting Your Mail Settings...399

Changing Your Email Signature 400

Changing Your Default Mail Account (Sent From)..401

Toggling Sounds for Receiving and Sending Email 402

Advanced Email Options...402

Removing Email Messages from Your iPhone After Deletion.......................................403

Using SSL and Authentication..403

Deleting from Server...403

Changing the Incoming Server Port 404

Troubleshooting Email Problems 404

E-Mail Isn't Being Received or Sent...405

■ Chapter 18: Contacts and Notes 407

Loading Your Contacts onto the iPhone 407

When Is Your Contact List Most Useful? 408

Improving Your Contact List...408

Adding a New Contact on Your iPhone 408

Start the Contacts App 409

Adding a New Phone Number 410

Adding Email Addresses 411

Custom Ringtone or Text Tone..411

Entering Web Site Addresses..411
Adding the Street Address 412
Adding New Fields 412
Adding a Photo to Contacts..413
Searching Your Contacts 415
Quickly Jump to a Letter by Tapping and Sliding on the Alphabet 416
Search by Flicking 416
Search Using Groups 416
Adding Contacts from Email Messages 417
Sending a Picture to a Contact 419
Sending an Email Message from Contacts 420
Showing Your Contacts Addresses on the Map 420
Changing Your Contact Sort and Display Order 422
Searching for Global Address List (GAL) Contacts 422
Contacts Troubleshooting 422
When Global Address List Contacts Don't Show Up (For Microsoft Exchange Users)...........423
The Notes App..423
Sync Notes 424
Getting Started with Notes..424
How Are My Notes Sorted? 425
Adding a New Note 426
Adding a Title to the Note 426
Viewing or Editing Your Notes 427
Using Voice Dictation for Your Notes 428
Deleting Notes 428
Emailing or Printing a Note 429
Data Detectors - Cool Things With Underlined Words...429

Chapter 19: Calendar and Reminders...................................... 431
Calendars, Reminders and Siri 431
Managing Your Busy Life on Your iPhone 432
Syncing or Sharing Your Calendar and Reminders..432
Today's Day and Date Shown on the Calendar Icon 433
Viewing Your Appointments and Getting Around in Calendar 433
The Four Calendar Views 434
Working with Several Calendars 436
Adding New Calendar Events..438
Adding a New Appointment 438
Recurring Events..440
Calendar Alerts 441
Second Alert 441
Choosing a Calendar 442
Availability 442
Adding Notes to Calendar Events 443
Using Copy and Paste Between the Email and Calendar Apps 443
Editing Appointments..445
Editing a Repeating Event 446
Switching an Event to a Different Calendar 446
Deleting an Event..447

Meeting Invitations 447
Calendar Options...448
Changing the Default Calendar 449
Reminders...449
Reminder Views 450
Adding a New Reminder 451
Adding Reminder Details 452
Setting Due Dates and Locations 452
Recurring Reminders 453
Changing Lists 454
Adding Notes to a Task 455
Completing Reminders..455
Editing Reminders...456
Deleting a Reminder 456
Adding a New List...456
Moving and Deleting Lists...457
Reminders Options..457
Changing the Default List...458

■Chapter 20: Working with Photos.. 459
Taking Photos Quickly...459
Using the Camera App 460
Geo-Tagging 461
Taking a Picture 461
Viewing Pictures You Have Taken..464
Editing Photos 465
Getting Photos onto Your iPhone 466
Viewing Your Photos 469
Launching from the Photos Icon 470
Choosing a Library 471
Managing Libraries 471
Working with Individual Pictures 472
Moving Between Pictures 473
Zooming in and out of Pictures 473
Double-Tapping 473
Pinching 474
Viewing a Slideshow 475
Using a Picture As Your iPhone Wallpaper...476
Emailing or Tweeting a Picture 476
Share, Copy, Print, or Delete Several Pictures at Once..477
Assigning a Picture to a Contact...478
Viewing a Photo on Your Apple TV 480
Deleting a Picture 480
Downloading Pictures from Web Sites...482
Finding a Picture to Download 482

Chapter 21: Maps 485

Getting Started with Maps 485
    Determining Your Location (the Blue Dot)...........................486
Changing Your Map Views 486
    Checking Traffic...488
Searching for Anything 488
    Google Maps Search Tips 489
Mapping Options...490
    Working with Bookmarks...491
    Adding a Mapped Location to Contacts 492
    Searching for Establishments Near You 493
    Zooming In and Out...494
    Dropping a Pin 494
    Using Street View..496
Getting Directions 497
    Tap the Current Location Button First.............................497
    Choosing Start or End Location.....................................498
    Looking at the Route...499
    Switching Between Routes 501
    Switching Between Driving, Transit, and Walking Directions 501
    Reversing the Route..502
Maps Options...502
Using the Digital Compass 503
    Calibrating and Using the Digital Compass..........................503

Chapter 22: iTunes on Your Device............................. 505

Getting Started with iTunes 505
    A Network Connection Is Required 506
    Starting iTunes..506
    Navigating iTunes 507
Customizing iTunes Soft Keys..507
Finding Music with New Releases, Top Tens, and Genres 508
    Top Tens: The Popular Stuff..509
    Genres: Types of Music...509
    Browsing for Videos (Movies) 510
    Finding TV Shows 511
    Audiobooks in iTunes...512
iTunes U: Great Educational Content 513
Download for Offline Viewing 513
Searching iTunes 514
Purchasing or Renting Music, Videos, Podcasts, and More.........................515
    Previewing Music...515
    Check Out Customer Reviews...516
    Previewing a Video, TV Show, or Music Video........................516
    Purchasing a Song, Video, or Other Item 517
Podcasts in iTunes..518
    Downloading a Podcast 518
    The Download Icon: Stopping and Deleting Downloads 519

Where the Downloads Go...519

Redeeming an iTunes Gift Card 520

Ping...521

■ Chapter 23: The Amazing App Store.. 523

Learning More About Apps and the App Store...523

Where to Find Apps News and Reviews 524

App Store Basics..525

A Network Connection Is Required 525

Starting the App Store...525

The App Store Home Page 525

Viewing App Details 527

Finding an App to Download 528

Viewing the New Apps 529

Viewing What's Hot..529

Genius..530

Categories..531

Looking at the Top 25 Charts 532

Searching for an App 533

Downloading an App 534

Finding Free or Discounted Apps 535

Redeeming Gift Cards or iTunes Codes..535

Maintaining and Updating Your Apps 535

Redownloading Apps 537

Automatic Downloads 538

Other App Store Settings 538

■ Chapter 24: Games and Fun 541

Using the iPhone As a Gaming Device 541

Acquiring Games and Other Fun Apps 543

Reading Reviews Before You Buy..545

Looking for Free Trials or Lite Versions 545

Being Careful When You Play...545

Two-Player Games..546

Online and Wireless Games 546

Other Fun Stuff: Baseball...547

AirPlay Mirroring 548

■ Chapter 26: Social Networking.. 551

Facebook 551

Different Ways to Connect to Facebook..552

The Facebook App 553

Facebook Notifications 556

LinkedIn 558

Downloading the LinkedIn App 558

Twitter...560

Setting up Twitter 561

Using Twitter..562

Refreshing Your List of Tweets 563

Your Twitter Profile 564

The Compose Button..564

Options within Tweet..565

■Chapter 27: Troubleshooting 567

Basic Troubleshooting 567

What to Do If the iPhone Stops Responding 567

How to Hard-Reset Your iPhone 570

How to Soft-Reset Your iPhone..570

No Sound in Music, Video, Alerts or Phone Ringer 571

If You Can't Make Purchases from iTunes or the App Store 573

Advanced Troubleshooting 573

When Your iPhone Does Not Show Up in iTunes..573

Synchronization Problems 574

Reinstalling the iPhone Operating System (with or Without a Restore)....................575

Additional Troubleshooting and Help Resources 579

On-Device iPhone User Guide 579

The Apple Knowledgebase...580

iPhone-Related Blogs..580

Index.. 583

About the Authors

Martin Trautschold is the founder and CEO of Made Simple Learning, a leading provider of Apple iPad, iPhone, iPod touch, and BlackBerry books and video tutorials. He has been a successful entrepreneur in the mobile device training and software business since 2001. His newest venture, 1 800 Notify, offers automated appointment reminder services to physicians and is being very well received. With Made Simple Learning, he has helped to train thousands of iPhone, iPad, and BlackBerry smartphone users with short, to-the-point video tutorials. Martin has now co-authored seventeen "Made Simple" guide books. Prior to this, Martin spent 15 years in technology and business consulting in the US and Japan. He holds an engineering degree from Princeton University and an MBA from the Kellogg School at Northwestern University. Martin and his wife, Julia, have three daughters: Sophie, Olivia, and Cece. He enjoys rowing and cycling. Martin can be reached at martin@madesimplelearning.com.

Rene Ritchie is editor-in-chief of TiPb.com, one of the largest and most influential iPhone, iPod touch, and iPad web sites in the world. Part of the Mobile Nations network, TiPb provides daily news, how-tos, and app and accessory reviews to help you get the most out of your iOS devices. Rene is also co-host over several Mobile Nations shows, including iPhone Live, iPad Live, Iterate for mobile design and development, ZENandTECH to help center your inner geek, and Superfunctional to keep you healthy and moving. Prior to this, Rene worked in product marketing, design, and web development. He can be reached on Twitter @reneritchie or by email at rene@mobilenations.com.

Gary Mazo is Vice President of Made Simple Learning. He is also a writer, college professor, gadget nut, and ordained rabbi. Gary joined Made Simple Learning in 2007 and has co-authored the last thirteen books in the Made Simple series. Along with Martin and Kevin Michaluk from CrackBerry.com, Gary co-wrote *CrackBerry: True Tales of BlackBerry Use and Abuse*—a book about BlackBerry addiction and how to get a grip on one's BlackBerry use. The second edition of this book will be published by Apress this fall. Gary also teaches writing, philosophy, technical writing, and more at the University of Phoenix. Gary has been a regular contributor to CrackBerry.com, writing product reviews and adding editorial content. He holds a BA in anthropology from Brandeis University. Gary earned his M.A.H.L (Masters in Hebrew Letters), as well as ordination as Rabbi, from the Hebrew Union College-Jewish Institute of Religion in Cincinnati, Ohio. He has served congregations in Dayton, Ohio; Cherry Hill, New Jersey; and Cape Cod, Massachusetts. Gary is married to Gloria Schwartz Mazo, and they have six children. Gary can be reached at gary@madesimplelearning.com.

About the Technical Reviewer

 **Leanna Lofte** is the App Editor for the iPhone, iPad, and iPod touch blog, TiPb, whom she has been for writing since 2009. She is responsible for TiPb's app content, including news, updates, giveaways, and reviews. Leanna also has a master's degree in Mathematics from the University of Denver and teaches college-level mathematics.

Acknowledgments

A book like this takes many people to successfully complete. We would like to thank Apress for believing in us and our unique style of writing.

We would like to thank our editors, Jim and Kelly, and the entire editorial team at Apress.

We would also like to thank our families for their patience and support in allowing us to pursue projects such as this one.

Part I

Quick Start Guide

In your hands is one of the most exciting devices to hit the market in quite some time: the iPhone 4S. This Quick Start Guide will help get you and your new iPhone 4S up and running in a hurry. You'll learn all about the buttons, switches, and ports, and how to use the responsive touch screen, multitask and be introduced to Siri, the amazing voice-activated personal assitant. Our App Reference Tables introduce you to the apps on your iPhone—and serves as a quick way to find out how to accomplish a task.

Getting Around Quickly

This Quick Start Guide is meant to be just that—a tool that can help you jump right in and find information in this book, as well as learn the basics of how to get around and enjoy your iPhone right away.

We'll start with the nuts and bolts in our "Learning Your Way Around" section, which covers what all the keys, buttons, switches, and symbols mean and do on your iPhone. In this section, you'll see some handy features such as multitasking by double-clicking the **Home** button. We will also introduce you to Siri, the amazing new personal assistant function on your iPhone. You'll also learn how to interact with the menus, submenus, and set switches—tasks that are required in almost every application on your iPhone. You'll also find out how to read your connectivity status and what to do when you travel on an airplane.

> **TIP:** Check out Chapter 2: "Typing, Copy, and Search" for great typing tips and more.

In the "Touch Screen Basics" section, we will help you learn how to touch, swipe, flick, zoom, and more.

Later, in the "App Reference Tables," section, we've organized the app icons into general categories, so you can quickly browse through the icons and jump to a section in the book to learn more about the app a particular icon represents. This guide also includes several handy tables designed to help you get up and running with your iPhone quickly:

- Getting Started (Table 2)
- Stay Organized (Table 3)
- Be Entertained (Table 4)
- Stay Informed (Table 5)
- Network Socially (Table 6)
- Be Productive (Table 7)

Let's get started!

Learning Your Way Around

To help you get comfortable with your iPhone, we will start with the basics—what the buttons, keys, and switches do—and then move onto how you start apps and navigate the menus. Probably the most important status indicator on your iPhone, besides the battery, is the one that shows network status in the upper-left corner. Understanding what these status icons do is crucial to getting the most out of your iPhone.

Keys, Buttons, and Switches

Figure 1 shows all the things you can do with the buttons, keys, switches, and ports on your iPhone. Go ahead and try out a few things to see what happens. Swipe left to search, swipe right to see more icons, try double-clicking the **Home** button to bring up the multitasking **App Switcher** bar, and then press and hold the **Power/Sleep** key to power your phone on or off. Have some fun getting acquainted with your device.

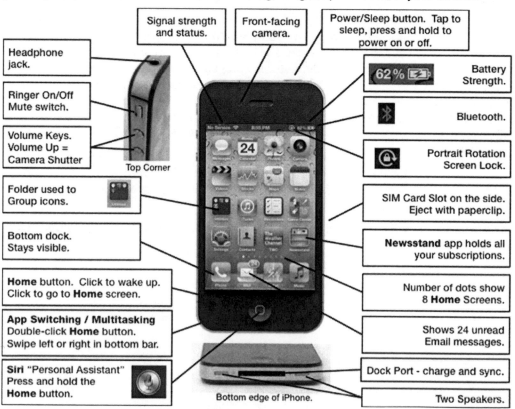

Figure 1. *The iPhone's buttons, ports, switches, and keys*

Switching Apps (AKA Multitasking)

One of the great new features introduced with the iPhone 4 is the ability to multitask or jump between applications (see Figure 2).

Double-click the **Home** button to bring up the **App Switcher** bar in the bottom of the screen. Next, swipe right to see more icons and tap any icon of any app you want to start. If you don't see the icon you want, then single-click the **Home** button to see the entire **Home** screen. Repeat these steps to jump back to the app you just left. The nice thing is that the app you just jumped from is always shown as the first app on the **App Switcher** bar.

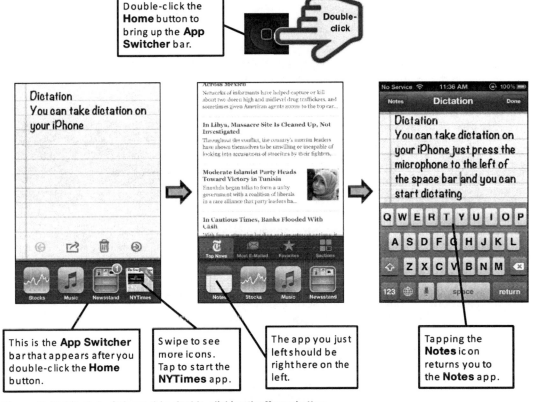

Figure 2. *Multitask (switch apps) by double-clicking the **Home** button.*

Using Siri (Your Personal Assistant)

There are two ways to launch Siri, your personal digital assistant. First, you can press and hold the **Home** button. Alternatively, if your iPhone is on and you've enabled the feature in Settings (see Chapter 7: "Multitasking and Siri"), simply bring the device to your ear.

Your **Home** screen will slide up to reveal a silver **Microphone** icon. Wait for Siri to beep before you begin to speak, and then speak in a clear voice, at a moderate speed, just as you'd speak to another person. When you're done speaking, wait for Siri to beep again. Then the fun begins.

Apple recommends you talk to Siri the way you'd talk to another person. Don't try to remember a set list of commands or queries—there are far too many types and variations. Instead, just ask for what you want. Here are some examples of what Siri can do for you:

- Set up reminders, calendar appointments, and clock alarms and timers.

- Send texts, iMessages, and emails.

- Play music.

- Search for location-based information like restaurant and business listings, and then search for directions to those (and other) locations.

- Respond to silly questions such as asking your iPhone to marry you!

The fun really begins when you combine these functions together into interactions. Siri can read a message requesting a dinner date, search for a restaurant, get directions, send back a confirmation message, and add an appointment for the dinner—all as part of an interactive confirmation. Check out Chapter 7: "Multitasking and Siri" for more details.

Using Voice Dictation

New to the iPhone Keyboard is a small **Microphone** button immediately to the left of the **Space Bar**.

Tap it and your screen will slide up to reveal a glowing, purple microphone. Speak to it as you would to Siri; and when you're finished, tap the **Done** button. Everything you said will be transcribed and entered as text.

While no text-to-speech engine is perfect, Siri does a pretty good job of transcribing what you said. If it makes any mistakes, just edit it as you would text you typed with the keyboard. Learn more in Chapter 7: "Multitasking and Siri."

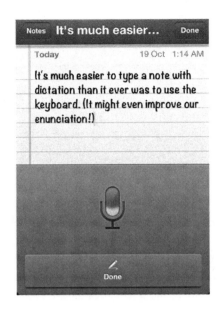

Music Controls and Portrait Screen Rotation Lock

You will see a few more icons if you swipe from left to right in the **App Switcher** bar. You can lock the screen rotation by tapping the leftmost icon, and the middle buttons control the currently playing music or video. The last icon on the right will start your **Music** app (see Figure 3).

Figure 3. *The Screen Rotation Lock button, Music app controls, and Music icon in the App Switcher bar*

Starting Apps and Using Soft Keys

Some apps have soft keys at the bottom of the screen, such as the **Music** app shown in Figure 4.

To see and use the soft keys in the **Music** app, you must have some content (e.g., music, videos, and podcasts) on your iPhone. See Chapter 3: "Sync with iCloud. iTunes and More" for help with syncing your music, videos, and more to your iPhone. Follow these steps to launch the **Music** app and become familiar with using the soft keys to get around:

1. Tap the **Music** icon to start the **Music** app.

2. Touch the **Songs** soft key at the bottom to view your albums.

3. Touch the **Playlists** soft key to view a list of your artists.

4. Try all the soft keys in **Music.**

5. In some apps, such as the **Music** app, you will see the **More** soft key in the lower-right corner. Tap this key to see additional soft keys or even rearrange your soft keys.

TIP: You know which soft key is selected because it is highlighted—usually with a color. The other soft keys are gray, but can still be touched.

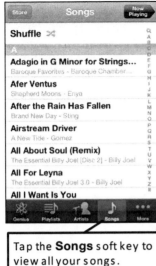
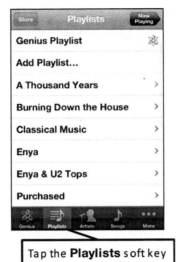
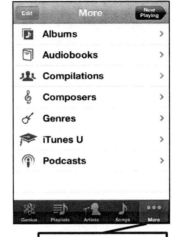

Tap the **Songs** soft key to view all your songs.

Tap the **Playlists** soft key to view your playlists.

Tap **More** to see additional soft keys.

Figure 4. *Working with soft keys in apps*

Menus, Submenus, and Switches

Once you are in an app, you can select any menu item by simply touching it. Using the **Settings** app as an example, tap **Sounds**, and then tap **Ringtone**, as shown in Figure 5.

Submenus are any menus below the main menu.

> **TIP:** You know there is a submenu or another screen if you see the **Greater Than** symbol next to the menu item (>).

How do you get back to the previous screen or menu? Tap the button in the top of the menu. If you're in the **Ringtone** screen, for example, you simply touch the **Sounds** button.

You'll see a number of switches on the iPhone, such as the one next to **Airplane Mode** shown in Figure 5. To set a switch (e.g., change the switch from **OFF** to **ON**), just touch it.

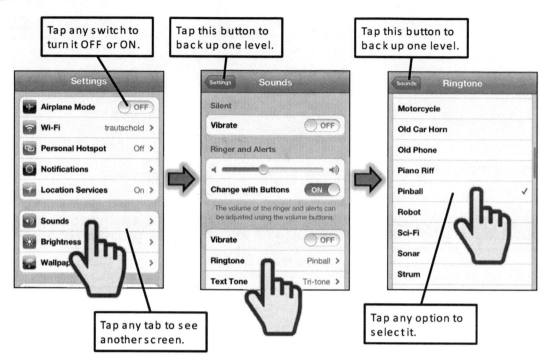

Figure 5. *Selecting menu items, navigating submenus, and setting switches*

Reading the Connectivity Status Icons

Most of the functions on your iPhone work only when you are connected to the Internet (e.g., email, your browser, the App Store, and the **iTunes** app), so you need to know when you're connected. Understanding how to read the status bar can save you time and frustration:

Cellular Data Signal Strength (1-5 bars):

Strong ▮▮▮▮   Weak ▮▮..   Radio Off – Airplane Mode ✈

Wi-Fi Network Signal Strength (1-3 symbols):

Strong 📶   Weak 📶   Off ▮

You can tell whether you are connected to a network, as well as the general speed of the connection, by looking at the left end of your iPhone's **Top** status bar. Table 1 shows typical examples of what you might see on this status bar.

Table 1. *How to Tell When You Are Connected*

In the upper left corner, if you see letters and symbols...	Cellular Data Connection	Wi-Fi Connection	Speed of Data Transfer
.ıll. AT&T 3G	✓	✗	HIGH
.ıl.. AT&T 📶	✓	✓	HIGH
.ıll AT&T E	✓	✗	MEDIUM
.ıll AT&T 0	✓	✗	LOW
✈ (Airplane Mode without Wi-Fi)	✗	✗	No connection
✈ 📶 (Airplane Mode with Wi-Fi)	✗	✓	HIGH

Chapter 4: "Connect to the Network" shows you how to connect your iPhone to a Wi-Fi or 3G Cellular Data Network.

Flying on an Airplane—Airplane Mode

Often when you are flying on an airplane, the flight crew will ask you to turn off all portable electronic devices for takeoff and landing. Then, when you get to altitude, they will say "all approved electronic devices" can be turned back on.

> **TIP:** Check out the "International Travel" section of Chapter 4: "Connect to the Network" for many money saving tips you can take advantage of when you travel overseas with your iPhone.

If you need to turn off your iPhone completely, press and hold the **Power** button on the top right edge, and then **Slide to Power Off** with your finger.

Follow these steps to enable **Airplane Mode**:

1. Tap the **Settings** icon.

2. Set the switch next to **Airplane Mode** in the top of the left column to **ON.**

3. Notice that the Wi-Fi is automatically turned **Off** and that the **Phone** will not work.

> **TIP:** Some airlines have in-flight Wi-Fi networks. On those flights, you may want to turn your Wi-Fi back **On** at the appropriate time.

You can turn your Wi-Fi connection **Off** or **On** by following these steps:

1. Tap the **Settings** icon.

2. Tap **Wi-Fi** near the top of the screen.

3. To enable the Wi-Fi connections, set the switch next to **Wi-Fi** at the top of the page to **ON**.

4. To disable the Wi-Fi, set the same switch to **OFF**.

5. Select the Wi-Fi network and follow the steps the flight attendant provides to connect to in-flight Wi-Fi.

Touch Screen Basics

In this section, we will describe how to interact with the iPhone's touch screen.

Touch Screen Gestures

The iPhone has an amazingly sensitive and intuitive touch screen. Apple—renowned for making its iPad, iPod touch, and iPod devices easy-to-use—has come up with an excellent, even higher resolution, highly responsive touch screen.

If you are used to a physical keyboard and a trackball or trackpad, or even an iPod's intuitive scroll wheel, then this touch screen will take a little effort to master. With a little practice, though, you'll soon become comfortable interacting with your iPhone.

You can do almost anything on your iPhone by using a combination of the following:

- Touch screen "gestures"
- Touching icons or soft keys on the screen
- Clicking the **Home** button at the bottom

The following sections describe the various gestures you can use on your iPhone 4.

Tapping and Flicking

To start an app, confirm a selection, select a menu item, or select an answer, simply tap the screen. To move quickly through contacts, lists, and the music library in **List** mode, flick from side to side or up and down to scroll through items. Figure 6 shows both of these gestures.

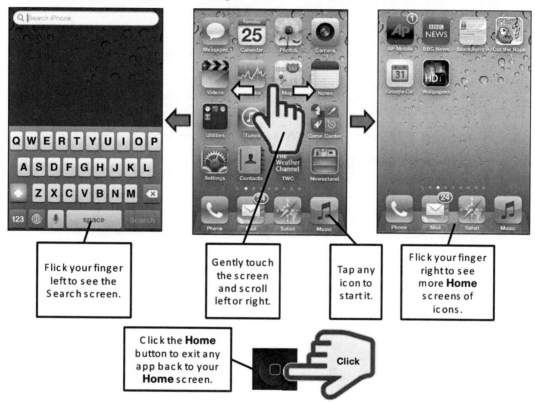

Flick your finger left to see the Search screen.

Gently touch the screen and scroll left or right.

Tap any icon to start it.

Flick your finger right to see more **Home** screens of icons.

Click the **Home** button to exit any app back to your **Home** screen.

Click

Figure 6. *Basic touch-screen gestures*

Swiping

To swipe, gently touch and move your finger as shown in Figure 7. You can also do this to move between open **Safari** web pages and pictures. Swiping also works in lists, such as the **Contacts** list.

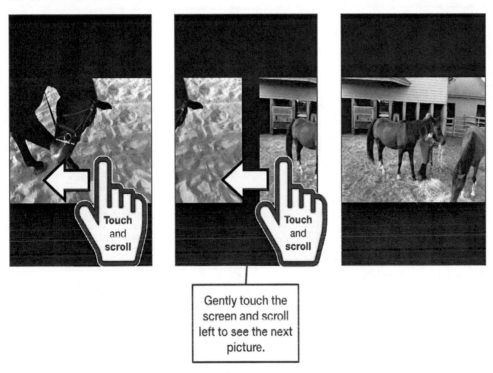

Gently touch the screen and scroll left to see the next picture.

Figure 7. *Touch and swipe to move between pictures and web pages.*

Scrolling

Scrolling is as simple as touching the screen and sliding your finger in the direction you want to scroll (see Figure 8). You can use this technique in messages (email), newspaper and magazine apps, the **Safari** web browser, menus, and more.

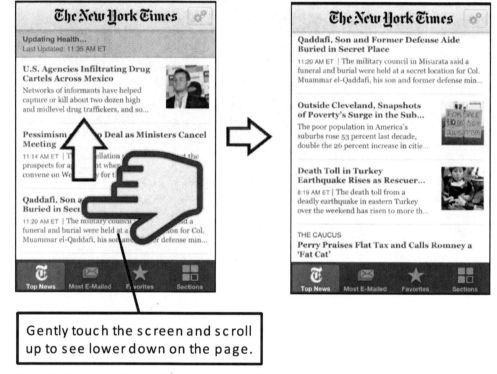

Gently touch the screen and scroll up to see lower down on the page.

Figure 8. *Touch and slide your finger to scroll around a web page, a zoomed picture, and more.*

Double-Tapping

You can double-tap the screen to zoom in and then double-tap again to zoom back out. This works in many places, such as web pages, mail messages, and pictures (see Figure 9).

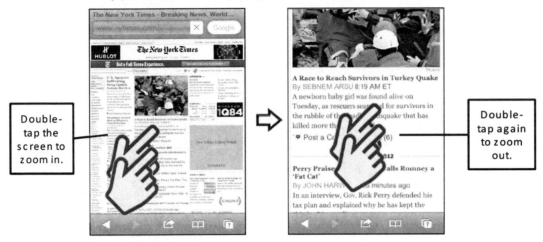

Figure 9. *Double-tapping to zoom in or out*

Pinching

You can also pinch open or closed to zoom in or out. This works in many places, including web pages, mail messages, and pictures (see Figure 10). Follow these steps to zoom in using the *pinching* feature:

1. To zoom in, place two fingers that touch each other on the screen:

2. Gradually slide your fingers open. The screen zooms in.

Follow these steps to zoom out using the pinching feature:

1. To zoom out, place two fingers with space between them on the screen.

2. Gradually slide your fingers closed, so they touch. The screen zooms out.

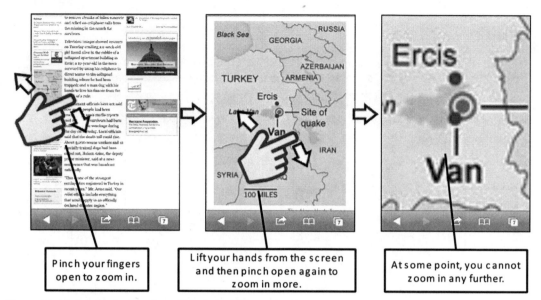

Pinch your fingers open to zoom in.

Lift your hands from the screen and then pinch open again to zoom in more.

At some point, you cannot zoom in any further.

Figure 10. *Pinch open to zoom in and pinch closed to zoom out.*

App Reference Tables

This section gives you a number of handy reference tables that group the various apps that are pre-installed on your iPhone by their functionality. Also included in the tables are other useful apps you can download from the App Store. Each table gives you a brief description of the app and tells you where you can find more information about it in this book.

Getting Started

Table 2 provides some quick links to help you connect your iPhone to the Web (using Wi-Fi or 3G); buy and enjoy songs or videos (using the **iTunes**, **Music** and **Video** apps); make your iPhone sleep or power off; unlock your iPhone; use the electronic **Picture Frame**; and more.

Table 2. *Getting Started*

To Do This...	Use This...		Where to Learn More
Turn the iPhone on or off.		The **Power/Sleep** button: Press and hold this key on the right of the top edge of the iPhone.	Getting Started – Ch. 1
Adjust settings and connect to the Internet (via Wi-Fi or 3G).		**Settings > Wi-Fi** or **Settings > General > Network**	Connect to the Network – Ch. 4
Return to the **Home** screen.		The **Home** button	Getting Started – Ch. 1
Unlock the iPhone.		Slide your finger to unlock your iPhone.	Getting Started – Ch. 1
Completely power down your iPhone.	Press and hold the **Power** key	Slide this button to power the device off.	Getting Started – Ch. 1
Back up all your content wirelessly.		iCloud Backup	iCloud Sync – Ch. 3
Wirelessly sync all your content.		iCloud Sync	iCloud Sync – Ch. 3

Stay Connected and Organized

Table 3 provides links for everything from organizing and finding your contacts to managing your calendar, working with email, sending messages, getting driving directions, calling people, and more.

Table 3. *Staying Connected and Organized*

To Do This...	Use This...		Where to Learn More
Manage your contact names and numbers.		**Contacts**	Contacts and Notes – Ch. 18
Manage your calendar.		**Calendar**	Calendar and Reminders – Ch. 19
Surf the Web.		**Safari**	Safari – Ch. 16
Call your friends.		**Phone**	Phone – Ch. 9
Use video conferencing.		**FaceTime**	Video Messaging and Skype – Ch. 11
Use your personal assistant: **Siri**. (Press and hold the **Home** button or hold your device up to your ear.)		**Siri**	Multitasking and Siri – Ch. 7

To Do This...	Use This...		Where to Learn More
Send text, picture, and video messages.		**Messages**	SMS, MMS, and iMessage – Ch. 10
View and send email.		**Mail**	Email – Ch. 17
Find just about anything, get directions, avoid traffic, and more.		**Maps**	Maps – Ch. 21

Be Entertained

You can have lots of fun with your iPhone; Table 4 shows you how. For example, you can use your iPhone to buy or rent movies, check out free Internet radio with **Pandora**, or buy a book and enjoy it in a whole new way using **iBooks**. If you already use a Kindle, you can sync all your Kindle books to your iPhone and enjoy them right away. You can also choose from hundreds of thousands of apps from the App Store to make your iPhone even more amazing, fun, and useful. You can also rent a movie from Netflix or iTunes, downloading it immediately for later viewing (say on an airplane or train).

Table 4. *Being Entertained*

To Do This...	Use This...		Where to Learn More
Buy music, videos, podcasts, and more.		**iTunes on your Device**	iTunes on Your Device – Ch. 22
Browse and download apps right to your iPhone.		**App Store**	App Store – Ch. 23
See playlists, artists, songs, albums, audiobooks, and more.		**Music**	Playing Music – Ch. 12
View videos and movies.		**Videos**	Viewing Videos– Ch. 15
Listen to free Internet radio.		**Pandora**	Playing Music – Ch. 12
Read a book anytime, anywhere.		**iBooks**	iBooks & E-Books – Ch. 13

To Do This...	Use This...		Where to Learn More
Read your Kindle books.		**Kindle**	iBooks & E-Books – Ch. 13
Take pictures and videos with your iPhone.		**Camera**	Working with Photos – Ch. 20
Look at, zoom in on, and organize your pictures.		**Photos**	Working with Photos – Ch. 20
Watch a video from YouTube.		**YouTube**	Viewing Videos– Ch. 15
Play a game.		**Games Icons**	Games & Fun – Ch. 24
Interact with comics in a whole new way.		**Marvel Comics**	Newsstand and More – Ch. 14

Stay Informed

You can also use your iPhone to read your favorite magazine or newspaper with up-to-the-minute vibrant pictures and videos (see Table 5). Or, you can use it to check out the latest weather reports.

Table 5. *Staying Informed*

To Do This...	Use This...		Where to Learn More
Check out your favorite radio news program.		**NPR News**	App Store – Ch. 23
Organize your newspapers and magazines.		**Newsstand**	Newsstand and More – Ch. 14
Read the newspaper.		**New York Times**	Newsstand and More – Ch. 14
Check the weather.		**The Weather Channel**	App Store – Ch. 23
Check out the latest headlines.		**AP Mobile**	App Store – Ch. 23

Network Socially

You can also use your iPhone to connect and stay up-to-date with friends, colleagues, and professional networks using the social networking tools on your iPhone (see Table 6).

Table 6. *Networking Socially.*

To Do This...	Use This...		Where to Learn More
Call or message with Skype.		**Skype**	Video Messaging and Skype – Ch. 11
Network on LinkedIn.		**LinkedIn**	Social Networking – Ch. 25
Stay connected with friends on Facebook.		**Facebook**	Social Networking – Ch. 25
Follow your favorites on Twitter.		**Twitter**	Social Networking – Ch. 25

Be Productive

An iPhone can also help you be more productive. You can use it to access and read just about any PDF file or other document with the **GoodReader** app. You can take notes with the basic **Notes** app or step up to the advanced **Evernote** app, which has amazing capabilities for integrating audio, pictures, and text notes, and as well as syncing everything to a web site. You can also use your iPhone to set an alarm, calculate a tip, see what direction you are walking in, and record a voice memo (see Table 7).

Table 7. *Being Productive.*

To Do This...	Use This...		Where to Learn More
Access and read almost any document .	GoodReader	**GoodReader**	Newsstand and More– Ch. 14
Keep on top of your to-do lists.	Reminders	**Reminders**	Calendar and Reminders – Ch. 19
Take notes, store your grocery list, and more.	Notes	**Notes**	Contacts and Notes – Ch. 18
Use folders to organize your icons.	Utilities	**Folders**	Icons and Folders – Ch. 6

Part II

Introduction

Welcome to your new iPhone 4S—and to the book that tells you what you need to know to get the most out of it. In this part we show you how the book is organized and where to go to find what you need. We even show you how to get some great tips and tricks sent right to your iPhone 4S via short e-mail messages. If you are a visual learner, we also point out a resource for learning your iPhone using short, to-the-point video tutorials produced by one of the authors.

Introduction

You hold in your hands perhaps the most powerful and elegant smartphone available!

Congratulations on Your New iPhone 4S!

Your iPhone 4S is more than a powerful smartphone; it is also a media player, e-book reader, gaming machine, life organizer, and just about everything else available today.

The iPhone 4S can do more than just about any other smartphone on the market. In a beautiful and elegantly designed package, your iPhone 4S will have you surfing the web, checking email, and organizing your busy life in no time.

> **NOTE:** Take a look at Chapter 11: "Video Messaging and Skype," where we show you how to use the **Skype** iPhone app and the new **FaceTime** video chat feature!

With your iPhone 4S, you can view your photos and interact with them using intuitive touch-screen gestures. You can pinch, zoom, rotate, and email your photos—all by using simple gestures.

Your phone lets you interact with your content like never before. For example, news sites and web sites look and read like never before due to the incredibly clear and crisp retina display. You can flip through stories, videos, and pictures, and even interact with your news.

For the first time, it's possible to really feel as though you are reading a book when you read content on an electronic device. Pages turn slowly or quickly—and you can even see the words on the back of the pages when you turn them.

Your phone also lets you manage your media library like never before. The **iTunes** app features a beautiful interface, letting you choose music, watch videos, organize playlists, and more—all in an effortless and fun way on the iPhone 4S's high definition–quality screen.

Do you have a Netflix account? If so, you will soon be able to organize your instant queue, and stream high-quality movies and TV shows right on your iPhone 4S.

Hulu + is also available now. This app allows you to watch complete seasons of your favorite TV shows right on your iPhone (see Chapter 15: "Viewing Videos" for more information).

You can also update your Facebook status and receive push alerts, as well as stay connected to the Web and your email with your phone's built-in Wi-Fi connection or the 3G connection. All the latest high-speed protocols are supported, so you can always be in touch and get the latest content. The iPhone 4S also includes a horizontal keyboard to type out emails and notes when you use the device in Landscape mode.

Getting the Most out of *iPhone 4S Made Simple*

You can read this book cover-to-cover if you choose, but you can also peruse it in a modular fashion, by chapter or topic. Maybe you just want to check out the **App Store** app, try **iBooks**, set up with your email or contacts, or just load up your phone with music. You can do all this and much more with this book.

You will soon realize that your iPhone 4S is a very powerful device. There are, however, many secrets "locked" inside—secrets we will help you "unlock" throughout this book.

Take your time—this book can help you understand how to best use, work, and have fun with your new iPhone 4S. Think back to when you tried to use your first Windows or Mac computer. It took a little while to get familiar with how to do things. It's the same with the iPhone 4S. Use this book to help you get up to speed and learn all the best tips and tricks more quickly.

Also, remember that devices this powerful are not always easy to grasp—at first.

You will get the most out of your iPhone 4S if you can read a section and then try out what you read. We all know that reading and then doing an activity gives us a much higher retention rate than simply reading alone.

So, in order to learn and remember what you learn, we recommend the following:

Read a little, try a little on your iPhone 4S, and repeat!

How This Book Is Organized

Knowing how this book is organized will help you quickly locate things that are important to you. Here we show you the main organization of this book. Remember to take advantage of our abridged table of contents, detailed table of contents, and our comprehensive index. All of these elements can help you quickly pinpoint items of interest to you.

A Day in the Life of an iPhone 4S User

Located inside the front and back covers, the "Day in the Life of an iPhone 4S User" reference is an excellent guide to your phone's features, providing ideas on how to use your iPhone and lots of easy-to-access, cross-referenced chapter numbers. So, if you see something you want to learn, simply thumb to that page and learn it—all in just a few minutes.

Part 1: Quick Start Guide

Touch Screen Basics: This book's many practical and informative screen shots will help you quickly learn how to touch, swipe, flick, zoom, and more with your iPhone 4S touch screen.

App Reference Tables: Quickly skim the icons or apps grouped by category. Also get a thumbnail view of what all the apps on your iPhone 4S do. Finally, this section includes pointers to the relevant chapter numbers, so you can jump right to the details of how to get the most out of each app covered in this book.

Part 2: Introduction

You are here now...

Part 3: You and Your iPhone 4S

This is the meat of the book, organized in 26 easy-to-understand chapters, all of them packed with loads of pictures to guide you every step of the way.

Quickly Locating Tips, Cautions, and Notes

If you flip through this book, you can instantly see specially formatted **TIPS**, **CAUTIONS**, and **NOTES** that highlight important facts about using the iPhone 4S. For example, if you want to find all the special tips relevant for using the iPhone's **Calendar** app, you can flip to Chapter 19: "Calendar and Reminders" to search for these highlighted nuggets of information.

> **TIP: TIPS**, **CAUTIONS**, and **NOTES** are all formatted like this, with a gray background, to help you see them more quickly.

iPhone Video Tutorials

Finally, check out the author's web site at www.madesimplelearning.com for a set of short, three minute video tutorials to help you or your entire organization master your iPhone. Learning in small chunks is a great way to master your iPhone 4S!

Part **III**

You and Your iPhone 4S...

This is the heart of *iPhone 4S Made Simple*. In this section, you'll find clearly labeled chapters—each explaining the key features of your iPhone. You'll see that most chapters focus on an individual app or a specific type of application. Many of the chapters discuss applications that come with your iPhone, but we also include some fun and useful apps you can download from the App Store. Sure, the iPhone 4S is for fun, but it's for a whole lot more, too. We finish with some handy troubleshooting tips that can help if your iPhone isn't working quite right.

Getting Started

In this chapter, we will take you on a step-by-step tour of your new iPhone and everything you get in the box. We will also look at the ins and outs of charging it and how to make your battery last longer. In order to get started with your iPhone, you need to connect it to iTunes to get it activated and registered. In our "iPhone Basics" section at the end of this chapter, we will show you the basics of how to maneuver on your iPhone, so you can get up and running quickly.

Getting to Know Your iPhone

In this section, we will show you how to use everything you get in the box with your iPhone. We also give you some iPhone battery and charging tips, talk about how to determine if your iPhone is already activated, and discuss the **Slide to Unlock** feature.

What Is Included in the Box

The box your iPhone comes in may seem skimpy if you're new to iPhones. However, it does contain everything you need to get started and enjoy your iPhone—except for a good manual, which is why we wrote this book! Here is what your box contains:

- **iPhone**: On the very top, as soon as you open it, you will see your new iPhone.

- **Paper folder**: Under the plastic holder for the iPhone, you will find a paper folder that contains the following:

  - **Finger Tips**: A 4.5" x 2.5" small fold-out booklet with 19 panels of basic information about your iPhone.

  - **iPhone Product Information Guide**: A 4.5" x 2.5" booklet with font that is way too small to read. This book contains all the legal terms, conditions, warnings, and disclaimers related to your iPhone.

  - **Apple Logo Stickers**: Two of those nice white Apple logos that you sometimes see on car windows. Enjoy!

In the bottom of the box, you will find the items shown in Figure 1–1: a headset, a USB cable, and a wall plug adapter.

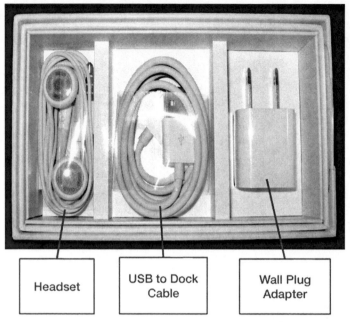

| Headset | USB to Dock Cable | Wall Plug Adapter |

Figure 1–1. *The headset, USB cable, and wall plug adapter in the bottom of your phone's box*

iPhone Headset

The headset consists of two white earphones for listening to music, videos, or phone calls, as well as a small controller attached to the wire of the right earphone. Plug this into the hole on the top-left edge of your iPhone. Make sure you insert it all the way—it can be a little tough to press in.

As the image here shows, the controller has **Plus** (+) and **Minus** (-) keys, as well as a **Center** button. You can increase or decrease volume with the (+) and (-) keys and use the **Center** button to answer or hang up phone calls.

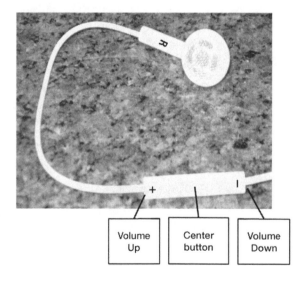

| Volume Up | Center button | Volume Down |

NOTE: You can move between songs with two or three clicks of the **Center** button. Double-click to go to the next track. Triple-click to go to the previous track.

The included headset also contains a small microphone for phone calls.

USB to Dock Cable

The USB to dock cable connects your iPhone to your computer; it also doubles as your power cable.

Wall Plug Adapter

The wall plug adapter has a USB socket on one end and a plug on the other end that you insert into an electrical socket. Just connect the USB cable to your iPhone and the other end to a wall plug to charge your iPhone from the wall.

Removing or Installing the SIM Card

In order to place or receive phone calls on an AT&T/GSM iPhone (currently any iPhone except the Verizon iPhone), you need to have a SIM card (Subscriber Identity Module card). Every new GSM iPhone should already have a SIM card pre-installed.

NOTE: Like the iPad and iPhone 4, iPhone 4S uses the new MicroSIM standard—not the MiniSIM that you find on most other phones.

There may be times when you want to remove and replace the SIM card. For example, you might want to do this if you are travelling internationally, or if you just received a replacement IPhone and want to use the SIM card from your old one.

Follow these steps to eject and remove your iPhone's SIM card:

1. Insert the paperclip into the hole on the right side of your iPhone.Press the paperclip straight into the hole until the SIM card tray pops out.

2. Remove the tray, so you can remove or replace the SIM card.

3. When inserting a SIM card, make sure the SIM card is installed with the notch facing the top right of the holder. It should sit flush in the holder with the metal contacts facing the bottom of the holder.

4. Slide the SIM card tray back into the iPhone until it clicks into place.

Charging Your iPhone and Battery Life Tips

Your iPhone may already have some battery life, but you might want to charge it completely, so you can enjoy uninterrupted hours of use after you get it set up. This charging time will give you a chance to check out the rest of this chapter, install or update the **iTunes** app, or check out all the cool iPhone apps available (see Chapter 23: "The Amazing App Store").

Charging from a Power Outlet

The fastest way to charge your iPhone is to plug it directly into a wall outlet. You use the same USB connection cable you use to connect your iPhone to your computer. As shown here, plug the wide end of the cable into the port at the bottom of your iPhone (next to the **Home** button) and the end of the USB cable into the wall plug adapter. Finally, plug the adapter into any wall outlet.

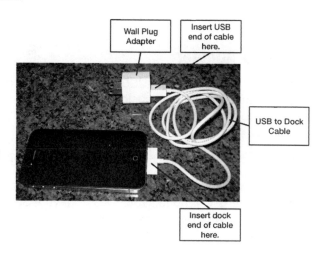

Wall Plug Adapter

Insert USB end of cable here.

USB to Dock Cable

Insert dock end of cable here.

You can tell your iPhone is charging by looking at the screen. You will see a lightning bolt or plug icon inside the battery indicator in the upper-right corner.

The **Main Battery** icon will show your charge level. The image to the right shows a charging iPhone with an almost full battery.

The lightning bolt or plug icons show charging.

This shows the battery level is almost full.

> **TIP:** Some newer cars have built-in power outlets (just like in your home) that you can use to plug in your iPhone power cord. Some also have a dock option that allows you to control the **iPod** app from your car radio headset. These outlets are sometimes buried in the middle console behind the front seat.

Charging from Your Computer

You can also charge your iPhone when you plug it into your computer, albeit a little more slowly than when you connect it directly to a wall charger.

> **TIP:** Try using different USB ports on your computer. Some USB ports share a bus and draw less power, while others have their own bus and draw more power.

For optimal charging, you should have your computer plugged into the wall outlet. If your computer is not connected to the wall outlet, your iPhone will charge, but at a slower rate. Keep in mind that, if your laptop computer goes to sleep or you close the screen, your iPhone will stop charging.

> **TIP:** You can show the actual percentage of battery life remaining. To do this, tap your **Settings** icon ➤ **General** ➤ **Usage**. Finally set **Battery Percentage** to **ON**.

Charging from Other Accessories

Some accessories designed to work with your iPhone will also charge it. The most common of these are iPhone/iPod music docks. These are speaker systems that you plug into your iPhone to listen to music. The only time your iPhone will not charge is when you see the following warning message on your screen: "Charging is not supported with this accessory." This occurs on older accessories or those not designed specifically for your iPhone.

> **TIP: A Case and External Battery Combined**
>
> Some cases actually have external batteries built into the case. There are several manufacturers available. One provider, mophie (www.mophie.com), has such cases for the iPhone 4 and iPhone 4S models called a *juice pack air* and *juice pack plus*.

Expected Battery Life

Apple says the iPhone with its bigger battery and advanced technology should last longer than the iPhone 3Gs (see Table 1–1).

Table 1–1. *Battery Life Specifications from Apple*

Talk Time	8 hours of talk time on 3G
(Talking on the phone or using **FaceTime** video chat)	14 hours of talk time on 2G (GSM)
Internet Use	6 hours of Internet use on 3G
(Browsing the Internet with **Safari**)	9 hours of Internet use on Wi-Fi

Video Playback	10 hours of video playback
Audio Playback	40 hours of audio playback
Standby Time	200 hours when in Sleep mode

These battery life durations are in ideal conditions with a new, fully charged battery. You will notice that, over time, your actual battery life will diminish.

Battery and Charging Tips

The key question is this: how do you get the most out of your battery life and make sure your iPhone is charged and ready for you when you need it? In this section, we will cover a few tips to help you accomplish this.

Getting More Out of Each Charge

To extend your battery life, try some of the following tips:

- **Lower your screen brightness**: Tap **Settings ➤ Brightness**, and then use the slider bar to lower your brightness to a level less than halfway across that still works for you.

- **Turn off Location Services**: If you don't need your actual location to be transmitted to your apps, you can turn this off. Tap **Settings ➤ General ➤ Location Services**, and then set **Location Services** to **OFF**. If you go into an app that wants your location, you will be reminded to turn it back on.

- **Set a Shorter Auto-Lock**: This feature shortens the time your iPhone takes to enter Sleep mode (i.e., turn off the screen) when it's not being used. Shortening this time can help save your battery life. To do this, tap **Settings ➤ General ➤ Auto-Lock**, and then set **Auto-Lock** to as short a value as possible—you can set it to as short as **1 minute** if you like.

- **Turn off push email and push notifications.**

- **Turn off Siri's Rasie to Speak Feature**. Tap **Settings ➤ General ➤ Siri** and set **Raise to Speak** to **OFF**.

You can learn more battery life tips by visiting the Apple web site at www.apple.com/batteries/iphone.html.

Making the Battery Last Longer

The iPhone uses a rechargeable battery that has a limited number of cycles during its useful life; in other words, it will gradually lose its ability to maintain a charge over time. You can extend the life of your iPhone battery by making sure you run it down completely at least once a month. The rechargeable battery will last longer if you do this.

Finding More Places to Charge Your Phone

No matter what you do, you will want to find more places and more ways to charge your iPhone if you really use it a lot. Besides using your power cord or connecting your iPhone to your computer, you can take advantage of the charging tips described in Table 1–2.

Table 1–2. *Other Places and Ways to Charge Your iPhone*

Airport Charging Station	Today most airports have wall sockets available where you can top off your iPhone while you are waiting for your flight. Some airports have labeled *charging stations*, while others simply have wall sockets that may even be hidden behind chairs or other objects. You may have to do a bit of hunting to beat out all those other power-hungry travelers!
External Battery Pack	This accessory allows you to extend the life of your iPhone battery by five times or more. You can buy such an item for about US $40–65. Do a web search for "external iPhone battery" to find all the latest and greatest options.
Car Charger	If you are using your iPhone heavily for phone calls during the day, you may want to invest in a car charger or another way to give your iPhone a little more juice in the middle of a long day. These chargers plug directly into the cigarette lighter socket in your car. These run about US $15–25.
Car Power Inverter	If you are taking a long car trip, you can buy a power inverter to convert your 12V car outlets into a power outlet where you can plug in your iPhone charger. Do a web search for "power inverter for cars" to find many options for under US $50. This is a small price to pay for hours of enjoyment on your iPhone!
Charge in Other Accessories	As mentioned earlier, you can also charge your iPhone by docking it in many accessories designed to do other things, such as play your music over speakers. You need to look for the **Plug** or **Lightning Bolt** icons to make sure your iPhone is charging in these accessories.

Setting up Your iPhone

At this point, you know some of the basics about your iPhone and how to get the most out of your battery. Now you are ready to start enjoying it! Setting up your iPhone is the next step.

Knowing If You Need to Set Up Your iPhone

If you see a **Welcome** screen similar to the one shown here, you will need to set up your iPhone before you can use it. With iOS 5, you can set up your iPhone in a couple of ways. First, you can do so with over-the-air (OTA) using your Wi-Fi network and iCloud. Or, you can plug your phone into your PC using the USB dock cable and activate it with the iTunes service.

If this is your first iPhone or you want to set it up as a new iPhone, you probably want to use iCloud OTA.

If you are upgrading from an iPhone 4 or previous iPhone model, you probably want to restore from a backup using the iTunes service.

Setting up Your iPhone Over-the-Air Using iCloud

With iOS 5, Apple has finally cut the iTunes cord. This means you no longer need to connect your iPhone to your PC to activate it or set it up. Instead, you can activate it directly from your iPhone OTA using Apple's new *iCloud* service.

> **NOTE:** During the initial set up process, you will be able to connect to any available Wi-Fi network which will be needed to set up your iPhone OTA using iCloud. If your home, work, or school Wi-Fi network isn't available, and you don't have a public access point like Starbucks handy, then you will need to activate your iPhone later. (You could choose to set up your iPhone via iTunes on your PC instead; however, you will still need Internet access to connect to Apple's activation servers.)

Follow these steps to set up your iPhone with iCloud, as shown in the **Welcome** screen pictured earlier:

1.   Swipe to set up by touching the **Arrow** button and pulling it across the screen in the direction indicated.

2.   Choose the language you want to use with your iPhone. Apple will present you with the most common options based on where you bought your iPhone; however, you can also tap the **Down Arrow** for more language choices.

3.   When you've chosen your preferred language, tap the blue **Next** button at the top right of the screen.

4.   Choose your Country or Region. Again, Apple will provide you with a default choice based on where you bought your iPhone; however, you can tap **Show More...** to expand the list. Tap the blue **Next** button to continue.

5.   Decide if you would like to enable or disable Location Services, and then tap the blue **Next** button to continue.

> **NOTE:** *Location Services* use GPS, cell-tower triangulation, and Wi-Fi router mapping to determine the approximate location of your iPhone. This feature is used for turn-by-turn navigation (like TomTom), check-in games (like Foursquare), social networks (like Facebook), geo-tagging (in the **Camera** app), and utilities (like Find my iPhone). Unless you have a particular need to globally disable all location services, you probably want to turn on the Location Services feature right now. You can selectively disable or enable these services later in the **Settings** app (e.g., turn off your **Camera** app's geo-tagging, but leave on TomTom's turn-by-turn navigation).

6.   Choose your Wi-Fi network, enter your network password, and then tap the blue **Next** button to continue.

7.   Your iPhone will now connect to Apple for activation. This can take a few seconds or up to a few minutes, depending on how fast your connection is and how busy Apple's servers are.

8.   Once activation is complete, you'll be given the option to set up your phone as a new iPhone, restore it from an iCloud backup, or restore it from iTunes.

Setting up a New iPhone Using iCloud

If this is your first iPhone—or if you simply want a clean, fresh start—choose **Set up as a new iPhone**.

TIP: Restoring from backups—especially from backups of different devices (e.g., restoring an iPhone from an iPad backup)—can sometimes lead to problems like more frequent app crashes or lower battery life. If you're experiencing problems after restoring from a previous backup, you might want to try setting your phone up as a new iPhone. You'll have to redo all your settings and accounts from scratch, and you'll lose any saved app and game data; however, it's sometimes your only option if your iPhone is no longer stable enough for everyday use.

To set up your phone as a new iPhone, you'll either need to sign in with an existing Apple ID or create a new, free Apple ID. Apple IDs can be any of the following:

- **iTunes ID**: This is the e-mail address and password you use to log into iTunes and buy music, TV shows, movies, App Store apps and games, and iBooks.

- **Free Apple ID**: This is the e-mail address and password you use to log into Find my iPhone, FaceTime, Game Center, iCloud, or any other recent, free Apple service. This can also be the same ID you use to shop at the online Apple Store.

NOTE: If you've been using Apple products and services for a while, it's not uncommon for one person to have multiple Apple IDs. For example, you might have an iTunes ID and old MobileMe accountand an Apple Store ID. Unfortunately, at the time of writing, Apple doesn't allow IDs to be combined, so you'll have to choose which one you want to use with iCloud.

If you have an old MobileMe account, Apple will migrate it to iCloud for you. Visit `http://www.me.com/move` to begin the process

Otherwise, the authors recommend you use your iTunes ID because it will have all your music, media, app, and games purchases tied to it, and you'll be able to use iCloud's re-download feature to easily restore these purchases to your new devices now and in the future.

If you have an Apple ID, log in with it now, accept the terms and conditions, and then skip ahead to the "Configuring iCloud Options" section. If you don't have an Apple ID, create one now.

Creating a Free Apple ID

If you've never used iTunes and don't have an Apple ID, then you'll need to create one. This can be done quickly, right on your iPhone:

1. Tap Create a new Apple ID.

2. Enter your birthday by spinning the Year, Month, and Day rollers to represent the proper date, and then tap the blue Next button.

3. Enter your first and last name in the appropriate fields, then tap the blue Next button.

4. Choose whether you want to use an existing e-mail address (e.g., a Gmail, Hotmail, Yahoo!, or personal e-mail address) or create a new iCloud e-mail address (@me.com). If you don't want to be bothered remembering a new e-mail address, you'll probably want to use an existing one. If you like keeping your e-mail separate, then you'll probably want to create a new one.

5.   If you're creating a new iCloud @me.com address, enter your password and click Verify. Your password must be "strong"; that is, it must contain uppercase and lowercase letters, at least one number, and be at least eight characters long.

6. Pick a Security Info question. This is something that should be easy for you to remember, but difficult for anyone else to guess easily (which means no one else should be able to find the answer just by looking at your blog or Facebook, Google, Yahoo!, or other online profile page).

7. Choose whether you want to receive e-mail updates from Apple at this new address. If not, set this option to OFF.

8. You'll need to accept the Terms and Conditions twice, first by tapping the blue Agree button at the bottom left, and then by tapping the translucent Agree button when the pop-up confirmation appears. Again, it might take a few moments to verify.

9. Apple will then set up your new Apple ID. This can take a few moments.

Configuring iCloud Options

Once you've logged in with your Apple ID, it's time to configure your iCloud settings:

1. If you want to use the Set Up iCloud feature— and we recommend you do this because it's free and provides a host of useful backup and syncing features—then leave the **iCloud** option set to **ON** and tap the blue **Next** button.

2. Choose whether you want to use the iCloud Backup service to wirelessly back up your iPhone over-the-air to Apple's data center or to your computer over USB with iTunes. Again, we recommend using setting **iCloud** to **ON** because it's automatic, and you won't have to remember to do it.

3. The Find my iPhone service is a free part of iCloud that shows you the approximate location of your phone (you'll be able to tell whether it's at your house or at the office, but not the specific room), make it ring so you can find it even if it's fallen under the car seat or behind the sofa, or even wipe out all your personal data if it's lost or stolen. If you want to use this feature, leave this option set to **ON.**

4. That's it! Your iPhone is now set up, and you can start using it.

Restoring Your iPhone Using iCloud

If you've previously used iCloud to back up your iPhone, you can restore from that backup over-the-air right from your device:

1. Tap Restore from iCloud backup.

2. Enter your iCloud Apple ID e-mail address and password.

3. Select which backup you'd like to restore from. Typically, this will be the most recent backup available.

4. Your iPhone will reboot, download the backup, and restart. This process can take a few minutes, especially if you have a lot of data to restore.

5. Once your iPhone has been restored, your apps will begin to download and install. iCloud can download and install multiple apps at once, and you can use your iPhone while the restore process is going on.

Setting up Your iPhone Using iTunes

If you don't want to use iCloud or you have a previous iTunes back up you'd like to restore from, then you can still set up your iPhone over USB with your PC.

If you do not have iTunes loaded on your computer, then open a web browser and go to www.itunes.com/download. Download the software from the link provided.

If you already have iTunes installed on your computer, you should check to see if an updated version is available. Version 10.5 was the latest version at the time of publishing. Follow these steps to update your version of **iTunes**:

1. Start the **iTunes** app.

2. If you are a Windows user, select **Help** from the menu, and then **Check for Updates**.

3. If you are a Mac user, select **iTunes** from the menu, and then **Check for Updates**.

4. If an update is available, then follow the instructions to update **iTunes**.

Restoring Your iPhone From a Previous Backup

The first time you connect your new iPhone to iTunes, you will see the screen shown in Figure 1–2.

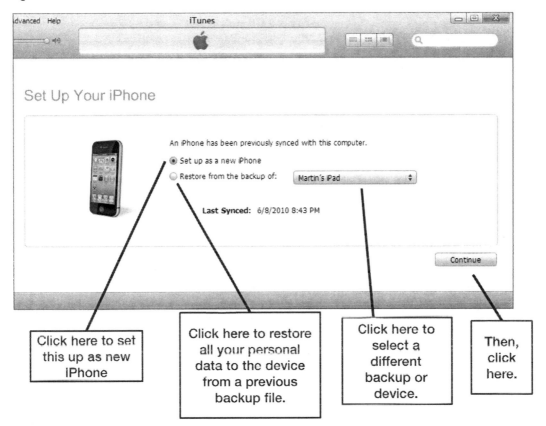

Figure 1–2. *Setting up your iPhone screen*

> **CAUTION:** We have heard of people experiencing problems (e.g., lock-ups and lower battery life) when they restore a backup from a non-iPhone (i.e., an iPad or iPod touch) to the iPhone. Also, selecting **Restore** assumes you have first made a backup of your old device; otherwise, there is no information to restore to your new iPhone.

Do the following to restore from the backup of another iPhone or device:

1. Click the radio button to the left of **Restore from the backup of**:

2. Select the particular backup file from the drop-down menu.

3. Click the **Continue** button to restore data to your iPhone from the backup file. You are now done with the initial setup of your iPhone.

> **NOTE:** You will still have to sync any apps, games, music, and other media you want to use on your new iPhone.

Maintaining Your iPhone

Now that you have set up your iPhone with iTunes, you will want to know how to safely clean the screen and keep it protected with various cases.

Cleaning Your iPhone Screen

After using your iPhone a little while, you will see that your fingers (or other fingers besides yours) have left smudges and oil on the formerly pristine screen. You will want to know how to safely clean the screen. One way to keep the screen cleaner throughout the day is to place a protective screen cover on the iPhone, which may also have the added benefit of cutting down on glare (discussed in the next section).

We also recommend the following steps:

1. Turn off your iPhone by pressing and holding the **Sleep/Power** key on the top edge, and then use the slider to turn it off.

2. Remove any cables, such as the USB sync cable.

3. Rub the screen with a dry, soft, lint-free cloth (like a cloth supplied to clean eyeglasses or something similar).

4. If the dry cloth does not work, then try adding a very little bit of water to dampen the cloth. If you use a damp cloth, try not to get any water in the openings.

5. Another option is the *iKlear* screen cleaner from Klear Screen. This product works on your iPhone and other devices such as your computer, laptop or iPad screen.

> **CAUTION:** Never use household cleaners, abrasive cleaners such as SoftScrub, or ammonia-based cleaners such as Windex, alcohol, aerosol sprays, or solvents.

Cases and Protective Covers for Your iPhone

Once you have your iPhone in your hands, you will notice how beautifully it is constructed. You will also notice that it can be fairly slippery, rock around a bit, or have the back get scratched when you are typing on it.

We recommend buying a protective case for your iPhone. Average cases run about US $10–40, and fancy leather cases can cost US $100 or more. Spending a little to protect your iPhone, which costs $200 or more, makes good sense.

Where to Buy Your Covers

You can purchase an iPhone protective cover at any of the following locations:

- Amazon.com (www.amazon.com)
- The Apple Accessory Store (http://store.apple.com)
- iLounge (http://ilounge.pricegrabber.com)
- TiPB – The iPhone + iPad Blog Store (http://store.tipb.com/)

You might also do a web search for "iPhone cases" or "iPhone protective covers."

> **TIP:** You *may* be able to use a case designed for another type of smartphone for your iPhone. If you go this route to save some money, just make sure your iPhone fits securely in the case or cover you choose.

What to Buy…

The following sections list some types of cases available for your iPhone and the price ranges you can expect to pay.

Rubber / Silicone Cases ($10–30)

Rubber and silicone cases provide a cushioned grip, absorb iPhone bumps and bruises, and isolate the edges of the phone (antennas) from your fingers.

Pros: These cases are inexpensive, colorful, and comfortable to hold. They also prevent your fingers from interfering with the iPhone antennas, which are the metal edges of the phone.

Cons: They are not as professional as a leather case.

Combined Cases with External Battery Packs ($50-80)

Cases combined with external battery packs serve a couple purposes: they combine the protective features of a hard shell case with a rechargeable external battery pack. Manufacturers such as Mophie and Case-Mate are busy working on iPhone versions of their cases; with some luck, they will be available by the time you read this book.

Pros: These cases protect your iPhone and provide a tremendous boost in your battery life—in some cases, they boost battery life by more than 50%.

Cons: They add weight and bulk to the phone.

Waterproof Cases ($10–40)

Waterproof cases protect for your iPhone from water, allowing you to safely use the device in the rain, at the pool, at the beach, on a boat, and so on.

> **TIP:** If you like to row or paddle, then you will want a waterproof case. Check out the **SpeedCoach Mobile** app, which you can buy for about $65 from the App Store.

Pros: These cases provide good protection from various sources of water.

Cons: They can make the touch screen harder to use, and they usually do not protect from drops or bumps.

Hard Plastic / Metal Case ($20–40)

Hard plastic and metal cases provide solid protection against scratches, bumps, and short drops.

Pros: These cases provide superior protection for your phone.

Cons: They add some bulk and weight. Also, you may need to remove such cases when charging your iPhone, or it might overheat.

Leather or Special Cases ($50–100+)

Leather and other special cases provide more of a luxury feel and protect the iPhone.

Pros: These cases add a touch of luxury to your phone, while also protecting the front and back of the device.

Cons: They are more expensive and add bulk and weight.

Screen Protectors ($5–40)

Screen and back glass protectors help you protect the screen and back of the iPhone from scratches.

Pros: These cases help prolong the life of your iPhone by protecting it against scratches; most such cases also decrease screen glare.

Cons: Some of these cases may increase glare or affect the touch sensitivity of the screen.

iPhone Basics

Now that you have your iPhone charged, with a clean screen, and decked out with a new protective case—let's look at some of the basics for getting around its software.

Powering On/Off and Sleep/Wake

To power on your iPhone, press and hold the **Power/Sleep** button on the top edge of the iPhone for a few seconds.Simply tapping this button quickly won't power on the iPhone if it is completely off—in that case, you need to hold the button until you see the iPhone power on.

When you are no longer using your iPhone, you have two options: you can either put it into Sleep mode or turn it off completely.

The advantage of Sleep mode is this: when you want to use your iPhone again, simply tap the **Power/Sleep** button or the **Home** button to bring your iPhone back awake. If you want to maximize your battery or if you know you won't be using your iPhone for quite some time—say when you go to sleep—you should turn it off completely. The way to do this is to press and hold the **Power/Sleep** button until you see the **Slide to Power Off** bar appear. Just slide the bar to the right and the iPhone will power off.

Assistive Touch Accessibility

As part of its excellent Accessibility features, Apple includes the Assistive Touch feature for people with special physical or motor skills needs. These include touch screen versions of the hardware buttons, as well as common and custom gestures.

Follow these steps to enable the Assistive Touch feature:

1. Tap the **Settings** icon.

2. Tap **General**.

3. Tap **Accessibility** near the bottom of the page.

4. Tap **Assistive Touch**.

5. Set the **Assistive Touch** switch to **On**.

6. Tap the **Assistive Touch** overlay icon when it appears at the bottom right of your screen.

7. Tap **Home** to simulate a physical press of the hardware **Home** button.

8. Tap **Device** to get access to other hardware button simulators, including **Rotate Screen**, **Lock Screen, Muted/Unmuted, Volume Up, Volume Down**, and **Shake**.

9. Tap **Gestures** or **Favorites** (favorite gestures) to access Pinch, Swipe, and any custom gestures that have been set up.

10. Tap the center of the overlay menu to return to the previous menu or to exit Assistive Touch.

> **NOTE:** Assistive Touch also allows for sophisticated gestures, including custom gestures.

Slide to Unlock and Quick Camera and Media Access

Once your iPhone has been activated, you will see the **Slide to Unlock** screen, as shown in Figure 1–3.

Double-click the **Home** button to see media control when you have music playing and, more importantly, get instant access to your camera for those times when you want to grab a quick picture. Tap the camera icon next to the slider at the bottom.

To get into your **iPhone**, touch your finger to the screen and follow the path of the arrow to move the **Slide to Unlock** button to the right. Once you do that, you will see your **Home** screen.

Notice the four icons in the Bottom Dock. The items in this dock do not move, while the rest of the icons can move back and forth in *pages*. You can learn how to move your favorite icons into the Bottom Dock in the "Moving Icons" section of Chapter 6: "Icons and Folders."

Figure 1–3. *Slide to Unlock,* Quick Camera and Media Access and your *Home* screen.

Moving Around Inside Apps and Your Settings Screens

Getting around the screens inside the apps on your iPhone is as simple as tapping the screen:

1. Tap the **Settings** icon to start the **Settings** app.

2. Touch **General** to see General settings.

3. Touch **Network** to see Network settings.

4. You can toggle any switch by tapping it. For example, touching the **OFF** switch next to **Data Roaming** will toggle it to **ON**.

5. To go back a level in the screens, touch the button in the upper-left corner. In this case, you would touch the **General** button to leave the **Network Settings** screen.

The Home Button

The button you will use most often is your **Home** button. This button will initiate everything you do with your iPhone. If your iPhone is sleeping, press the **Home** button once to wake up your iPhone (assuming it is in Sleep mode).

Pressing the **Home** button will also take you out of any application program and bring you back to your **Home** screen.

Start Siri by Pressing and Holding the Home Button

Start your personal assistant by pressing and holding the Home button. Then simply speak to your iPhone. If you have enabled **Raise to Speak**, you can also simply raise your iPhone to your ear and start speaking to Siri. We show you all about Siri in Chapter 7.

Access the Fast App Switcher by Double-Clicking the Home Button

Accessing the Fast App Switcher is as simple as double-clicking the **Home** button.

1. While in any app or from the **Home** screen, double-click the **Home** button .

2. The screen will slide up and you will see a small bar of icons appear in the bottom row. These represent the apps that you have started since you powered on your iPhone.

3. Tap any icon to switch back to that app.

4. Swipe your finger to the left to see more apps.

5. Swipe your finger to the right to see the orientation lock and media controls.

6. Swipe your finger to the right again to see the volume control and AirPlay button.

Follow these steps to access the Fast App Switcher from a given app:

Volume Keys for Ringer and Audio/Video Playback

On the upper-left side of the iPhone (see Figure 1–4), you can see some simple **Volume Up/Volume Down** keys that you will find very handy.

Ringer Volume

If you are not playing a song, video, or other content, pressing these **Volume** keys will adjust the volume of your phone ringer.

> **TIP:** When you're in the **Camera** app, the **Volume Up** button becomes a camera shutter, allowing you to quickly snap a picture.

Muting the Phone Ringer

You have a switch just above the **Volume** keys on the left side of your iPhone. Slide the **Ringer Mute** switch to the back of the iPhone set it to **ON**. You will see a little orange light next to the switch when your sound is muted. To turn off the mute, simply slide the switch back toward the front of the iPhone (see Figure 1–4).

Adjusting Playback or Phone Voice Volume

You can use the **Volume** keys to raise or lower your phone's volume when you are listening to music or a video, enjoying other content, or even on a phone call. When listening to music or a video, you can also use the on-screen slider bar to adjust volume (see Figure 1–4).

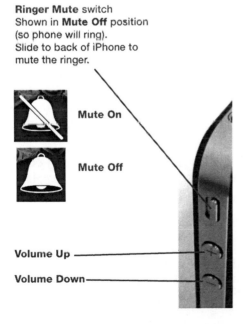

Ringer Mute switch
Shown in **Mute Off** position
(so phone will ring).
Slide to back of iPhone to
mute the ringer.

Mute On

Mute Off

Volume Up

Volume Down

Figure 1–4. *Adjusting the volume on your iPhone or muting the phone ringer*

Locking Your Screen in Portrait (Vertical) Orientation

If you tilt your iPhone on its side, you will notice that its screen rotates to Horizontal (Landscape) orientation in some apps. You might want this behavior, so you can see the larger **Landscape** keyboard for typing. However, there may be times when you don't want your screen to rotate from Portrait orientation when you turn your iPhone on its side. For these occasions, you can lock the screen in Portrait orientation.

1. Double-click the **Home** button.

2. Swipe left to right to see the media and screen lock controls.

3. Touch the **Portrait Orientation Lock** button in the icon on the left.

4. To disable the lock, tap the same button again.

> **TIP:** The orientation lock feature can be a great way to read iBooks in bed. If you prefer the larger page view in Portrait mode, enable the Portrait Orientation Lock feature. This way, when you set your iPhone on your lap or hold it almost flat, the screen will not accidentally rotate to Landscape mode. For more information, check out Chapter 13: "iBooks and e-Books."

Adjusting or Disabling the Auto-Lock Time-Out Feature

You will notice that your iPhone will auto-lock and go into Sleep mode (i.e., the screen will go blank) after a short amount of time. You can change how long it takes your phone to enter Sleep mode or even disable this feature altogether inside the **Settings** app. Follow these steps to do so:

1. Touch the **Settings** icon from your **Home** screen.

2. Touch **General**.

3. Touch **Auto-Lock**.

4. You will see your current sleep interval setting next to the **Auto-Lock** option on this page. The default setting is that the iPhone locks after three minutes of sitting idle (to save battery life). You can set this interval to **1 Minute**, **2 Minutes**, **3 Minutes**, **4 Minutes**, **5 Minutes**, or **Never**.

5. Touch the desired setting to select it—you know it's selected when you see a checkmark next to it.

6. Finally, touch the **General** button in the upper-left corner to get back to the **General** screen. You should now see your change reflected next to the Auto-Lock setting.

> **BATTERY LIFE TIP:** Setting the Auto-Lock feature to a shorter interval (e.g., **1 Minute**) will help you save battery life.

Adjusting the Date, Time, Time Zone, and 24-Hour Format

Usually, the date and time is either set for you or adjusts when you connect your iPhone to your computer; you can learn more about this in in Chapter 3: "Sync with iCloud, iPhone and More." However, you can manually adjust your date and time quite easily. You may want to do this when you are traveling with your iPhone and need to adjust the time zone when you land. Follow these steps to do so:

1. Touch the **Settings** icon.

2. Touch **General**.

3. Scroll down and touch **Date & Time** to see the **Date & Time** settings screen.

4. If you prefer to see **09:30** and **14:30** instead of **9:30 AM** and **2:30 PM**, respectively, then tap the **24-Hour Time** option to set its switch to **ON**.

5. To set the date and time manually, you have to turn off the automatic time setting feature. Tap the switch next to **Set Automatically** to set this option to **OFF**.

6. To set your time zone, tap **Time Zone** and type in the name of a major city in your time zone. The iPhone will show you matching city names as you type.

7. When you see the correct city in your time zone, tap it to select it. In the image here, we typed the first few letters of "Chicago" until we saw it appear. Next, we tapped **Chicago, U.S.A.** to select it.

8. After selecting the city, you are brought back to the main **Date & Time** screen with your selected city shown next to the **Time Zone** option.

9. Tap **Set Date & Time** to adjust your date and time.

10. On this screen you can set the date and time. To adjust the date, tap the **Date** button shown at the top of the screen.

11. To adjust the time, tap the **Time** button shown at the top of the screen.

12. You can then adjusting the date and time by touching and sliding the **Date** and **Time** wheels up or down, as shown in the image here.

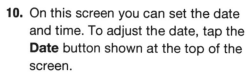

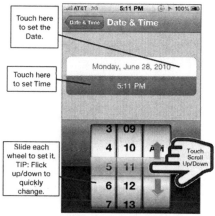

13. When you are done, tap the **Date & Time** button in the upper-left corner.

Adjusting the Brightness

Your iPhone has an Auto-Brightness control available; this feature is turned on by default. This feature uses the built-in light sensor to adjust the brightness of the screen. When it is darker outside or at night, then the Auto-Brightness control will dim the screen. When it is bright and sunny, the screen will be automatically brightened, so it is easier to read. Generally, we advise that you keep this feature set to **ON**.

If you want to adjust the brightness, use the controls in your **Settings** app. Follow these steps to do so:

1. From your **Home** screen, touch the **Settings** icon.

2. Touch **Brightness** and move the slider control to adjust the brightness.

3. Click the switch next to **Auto-Brightness** to toggle it **ON** or **OFF**.

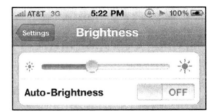

TIP: Setting the **Brightness** option to a lower value will help you save battery life. A little less than halfway across seems to work fine.

Notifications

New to iOS 5, the Notication Center introduces a better, less obtrusive, less interruptive way to organize and handle all the phone, e-mail, SMS, Twitter, Facebook, calendar, and other alert messages you receive during the day.

Notifications can appear in several ways:

- As *Lock* screen info, so you can glance at important alerts without having to unlock your phone. (This option does sacrifice some privacy.)

- As *in-app notifications*, which display as brief, rotating alerts across the top of the screen whenever a new message is received.

- In the **Notification Center** pull-down menu, which you can access with a single swipe anywhere, at any time, when your iPhone is unlocked.

If you've had an iPhone before or used an iPad or iPod touch prior to iOS 5, then Notification Center adds to the previous options of sound/vibrate, number badges, and pop-up alerts. Because they're non-interruptive, alerts won't stop your game of **Angry Birds** or the e-mail message you're composing, forcing you to dismiss or open them before you can continue playing or writing. However, you still have the option to handle things you absolutely don't want to miss, such as alarms.

Lock Screen Info

Notifications on the **Lock** screen are displayed in two different ways: as a popup with the single, newest notification and as a pull-down list of all recent notifications.

If you receive a single notification while your iPhone is locked, the screen will turn on, and it will appear in a black box in the center of your **Lock** screen. It will also show an icon on the left that represents the app associated with that type of notification. For example, an e-mail message will show the **Mail** app icon to the left; an SMS text message will show the **Messages** icon; a missed call will show the **Phone** icon; a Facebook notice will show the **Facebook** icon; and so on. There are several things you can do from here:

- Ignore the notification. This will cause your alert to fade away, and your iPhone's screen will go back to sleep.

- Grab the handle (the three gray lines right below the time and date) and drag it down to see a list of all the notifications you've received since the last time you unlocked your iPhone. The list will be sorted by notification type, so all e-mail messages will be grouped together, as will all calendar events, all missed phone calls, and so on. To the left of each notification, you will also see the appropriate icon for each alert.

NOTE: If you don't see the handle, it's because you don't have any recent notifications.

■ From either the single notification box or the list, tap the icon to the left of the notification and **Slide to Read** (or listen) to the notification, just as you would normally **Slide to Unlock** your iPhone. In most cases, you'll be taken straight to the appropriate app with the full notification displayed. For example, touching the **Mail** app icon and sliding it will unlock your iPhone, switch to the **Mail** app, and load up the e-mail you just received.

NOTE: A few notifications—such as alarms and system messages like iTunes sync failures—might also show you a button to the left of the notification, such as **Snooze** for the alarm or **OK** for the sync failure. Tap the button to delay or dismiss the notification.

TIP: If you're concerned about privacy and don't like the idea of anyone being able to see your personal e-mails, texts, and other messages or alerts on your **Lock** screen, then you can turn them off in the **Settings** app (see the "Configuring Notification Center" section later in this chapter).

In-App Notifications

When your iPhone is unlocked and you're busy using it, a new notification that comes in will animate briefly at the top part of the screen, and then rotate down to display the notification. This will happen no matter
where you are, from the **Home** screen, to the built-in **Phone** app, to your favorite video game. The notification covers only a few pixels at the very top, so it shouldn't get in the way of what you're doing (or playing). There are two things you can do with an in-app notification:

■ Ignore it and it will rotate back up and disappear. (Don't worry: You can see the notification again by clicking the **Notification Center** pull-down menu, as described later in this chapter.)

■ Tap the notification and you'll be taken straight to the associated app to see the full message. For example, it will take you to the **Mail** app to read an e-mail or the **Messages** app to reply to an SMS text.

The Notification Center

Any time your iPhone is unlocked, you can swipe down from the very top of the screen to pull down the **Notification Center** options. Notification Center combines a very limited number of *widgets* (two at the time of writing) and a list of notifications similar to what you see on the **Lock** screen.

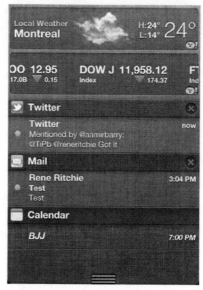

To get rid of Notification Center, swipe back up from the bottom of the screen.

The two widgets available at the time of writing are **Weather** and **Stocks**:

- The **Weather** widget displays the local weather for an area (if location-based weather is enabled) or whatever city you have set as first in the built-in **Weather** app (if location-based weather is turned off or unavailable). It also shows the high, low, and current temperature for the day. Tapping anywhere on the widget will take you to the **Weather** app.

- The **Stocks** widget shows a ticker of the stocks you follow, along with their recent market cap and an arrow showing recent losses or gains. The ticker will contain all stocks you currently have set up in the built-in **Stocks** app. Tapping anywhere on the widget will take you to the **Stocks** app.

Notification Center listings are available for the following apps and services:

- **Calendar**
- **Reminders**
- **Phone** (missed calls, voice mail)
- **Messages** (SMS/MMS/iMessage)
- **Mail**
- Game Center

■ Any additional apps or services you install that use notifications (e.g., social networks like Twitter, breaking news apps like **CNN**, and task managers like OmniFocus)

The notification list is divided by app, with a header bar for each app. On the left of the header bar is the *app icon*, followed by the *app name*. At the right of the header bar, you can see an **X** icon. Tapping the **X** icon clears all notifications for that app. For example, tapping the **X** to the right of the **Mail** icon will clear all e-mail notifications; however, this won't clear any other notifications.

Below a header, you will see all current (unread) notifications for that app, along with the time they were received, who they came from (if applicable) and a preview of their contents. For example, you might see a list of recent Facebook messages or Game Center challenges. Tapping anywhere on any of the notifications in the list will switch you to the associated app and show you the full message.

Configuring Notification Center

Notification Center can be easily configured via the **Settings** app:

1. Tap the **Settings** app icon on the **Home** screen.

2. Tap **Notifications**.

Notification Center can organize notifications **By Time** (widgets on top, then in order of the most recent notifications), or you can organize them **Manually**. Follow these steps to manually reorganize your notifications:

1. Under **Sort Apps**, tap **Manually**.

2. At the top right of the screen, tap the **Edit** button.

3. Handles in the form of three gray, horizontal stripes will appear to the right of each app. Grab the handles and drag the apps up or down to put them in the order you like best.

4. When you've got all the apps in just the order you want them, tap the blue **Done** button at the top right of the screen.

To show or hide the **Weather** or **Stock** widget, tap either widget to toggle it **ON** or **OFF**, as desired.

To choose how the notification lists work, follow these steps:

1. Tap the app you want to edit (e.g., **Mail**).

2. Switch the **Notification Center** toggle to **OFF** to remove the app from Notification Center completely. Toggle it to **ON** to put it back.

3. Choose to **Show** the number of notifications you prefer in the list. At the time of writing, the choices were limited to **1 Unread Item**, **5 Unread Items**, and **10 Unread Items**.

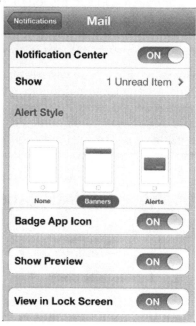

4. Choose the **Alert Style** of the in-app notification you'd prefer.

   a. **None** means you'll never see an alert.

   b. **Banner** means you'll get the subtle, animated notification at the top of the screen that won't interrupt you. This option lets you ignore the notification, if you so desire, which is useful for most communication notifications like e-mail, SMS, Facebook, and so on.

   c. **Alert** means you'll get a pop-up box that you can't ignore. You will either have to manually dismiss it or act on it right away. This is useful for alarms, appointments, and other urgent matters.

You can also set several other options related to notifications:

- **Badge App Icon**: This option adds a little red circle to the top right of **Home** screen icons. This red circle indicates how many unread notifications each app contains. For example, the number 10 on the **Mail** icon means you have 10 unread e-mail messages waiting for you. You can toggle this feature to **OFF** if you would rather not see them or to **ON** if you want them displayed.

- **Sounds**: This option lets you turn audio (and vibration) alerts for incoming notifications on or off. If a notification is urgent, like SMS, you might want to keep sounds toggled **ON**.

- **Show Preview**: This option adds the first few lines of a message associated with a notification, so you can get the gist of it at a glance. This feature enables you to see a notification's contents without sliding to tap through to the app, so you can read the whole thing. If privacy is more of a concern, you might want to toggle this feature to **OFF**.

■ **View in Lock Screen**: This option allows you to turn notifications on or off from the **Lock** screen. Again, if privacy is an issue, you might want to toggle this feature to **OFF**.

> **NOTE:** Not all apps have the same options in Notification Center. For example, some may offer sound alerts, while others do not.

When you turn off notifications for a specific app, it gets put in a separate list under **Settings** called *Not in Notification Center*. This lets you easily see which apps are—and aren't—sending you notifications.

Accessibility Options For Notification Center

Apple provides various Accessibility options for people with special visual or hearing needs, including Custom Vibrations and LED Flash for Alerts.

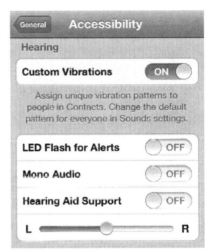

Follow these steps to enable Accessibility options for Notifications:

1. Tap the **Settings** icon.

2. Tap **General**.

3. Tap **Accessibility** near the bottom of the page.

4. Toggle **Custom Vibrations** to **ON** to assign unique vibration patterns to your Contacts (patterns can be created in the **Sound Preferences**).

5. Toggle **LED Flash for Alerts** to **ON** to make the camera flash go off when a notification comes in.

Chapter 2

Typing, Copy, and Search

In this chapter, we will show you some good ways to type on your iPhone and save valuable time when doing so. Along the way, we'll show you how to use the **Portrait** (vertical/smaller) and **Landscape** (horizontal/larger) keyboards. We will also teach you how to select different language keyboards, how to type symbols, and other tips.

Later in this chapter, we will tell you about the Spotlight search and the Copy and Paste function. The Copy and Paste function will save you lots of time, as well as increase your accuracy when working with your iPhone.

Typing on Your iPhone

You will quickly find two on-screen keyboards on your iPhone: the smaller **Portrait** keyboard that's visible when you hold your iPhone in a vertical orientation and the larger **Landscape** keyboard that's visible when you hold the iPhone in a horizontal orientation. The nice thing is that you can choose whichever keyboard works best for you.

Typing on the Screen with Two Thumbs

You will find when you first start out with your iPhone that you can most easily type with one finger— usually your index finger—while holding the iPhone with the other hand.

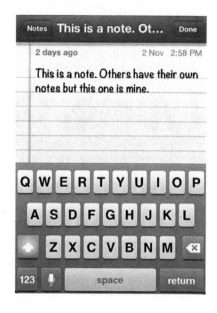

After a little while, you should be able to experiment with thumb typing (as you see so many people doing with other phones, such as the BlackBerry smartphones). Once you practice a little, typing with two thumbs instead of a single finger will really boost your speed. Just be patient: it does take practice to become proficient typing quickly with your two thumbs.

You will actually notice after a while that the keyboard touch sensitivity assumes you are typing with two thumbs. What this means is that the letters on the left side of your keyboard are meant to be pressed on their left side, and the keys on the right are meant to be pressed on their right side.

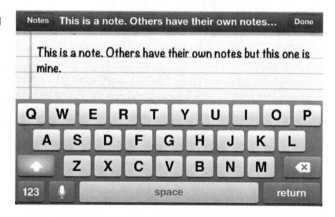

Simply turning the iPhone sideways in many apps will cause the keyboard to change to the larger **Landscape** keyboard, which makes it easier to type.

> **TIP:** If you have larger hands and find typing on the smaller, vertical keyboard challenging, then flip your iPhone on its side to get the larger, **Landscape** keyboard.

Type Quick Phrases with Shortcuts

One nice feature on your iPhone is the ability to set up shortcuts for typing common phrases or even a few sentences like directions to your home or office.

> **TIP:** Use Shortcuts to save time when typing common phrases on your iPhone. You can even use Shortcuts to type a few sentences like steps to get to your home or something you type frequently.

Access shortcuts in the Settings app. Tap the Settings icon, then General, then Keyboard and swipe to the bottom of the screen to see available Shortcuts.

Apple has supplied you with an example shortcut for "omw." When you type omw on your iPhone, you will see that the pop-up shows the phrase "On my way!"

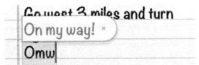

Tap Add New Shortcut to create a new one.

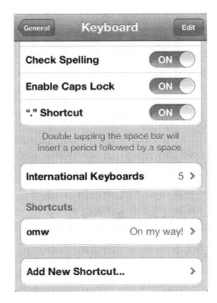

Type the **Phrase** which will replace the shortcut, then type the **Shortcut** itself. In this example, we want a shortcut to type directions to our home. So our **Shortcut** is "dirh" and the Phrase is step by step directions to get to our house. Save your new shortcut and give it a try.

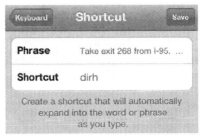

Saving Time with Auto-Correction

After you have been typing for a while, you will begin to notice a little pop-up window directly below some of the words you are typing—this feature is called *Auto-Correction*. Any **Shortcuts** that you have defined will also appear as the pop-up suggestion.

> **NOTE:** If you never see the **Auto-Correction** pop-up window, then you will have to enable the Auto-Correction feature by going into your **Settings** app ➤ **General** ➤ **Keyboard**, and then setting **Auto-Correction** to **ON**.

You can save yourself time when you see the correct word guessed by just pressing the **Space** key at the bottom of the keyboard; doing so will select that word.

In the next example, we start typing the word "especially"; and when we get to the "c" in the word, the correct word appears below in a pop-up window. To select it, we simply press the **Space** key at the bottom (see Figure 2–1).

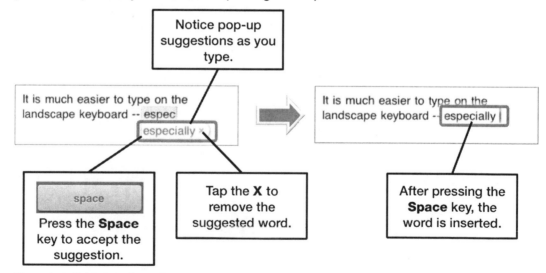

Figure 2–1. *Using Auto-Correction and suggested words*

Your first inclination might be to tap the pop-up word, but that simply erases the suggested word from the screen. It is ultimately faster to keep typing or press the **Space** key when you see the correct word pop up. In most situations, the word will either be correct or will become correct as you keep typing—and this means less finger travel in the long run.

> **TIP:** The Auto-Correction feature also looks through your **Contacts** list to make suggestions. For example, if Martin Trautschold were in your **Contacts** list, you would see "Trautschold" come up as an Auto-Correction suggestion after typing "Trauts."

After you learn to use the **Space** key, you will see that this pop-up guessing can be quite a time saver. After all, you were going to have to type a space at the end of the word, anyway.

Sometimes you accidentally accept an incorrect Auto-Correction word; in this case, you simply need to press the **Backspace** key. Doing so will make a pop-up window appear that contains the original word before the Auto-Correction feature changed it. You will also see other suggested replacements (see Figure 2–2).

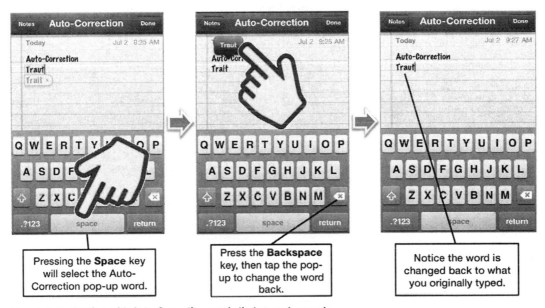

Pressing the **Space** key will select the Auto-Correction pop-up word.

Press the **Backspace** key, then tap the pop-up to change the word back.

Notice the word is changed back to what you originally typed.

Figure 2–2. *Dealing with Auto-Correction words that are not correct*

TIP: With Auto-Correction, you can save time by avoiding typing the apostrophe in many common contractions, such as "wont" and "cant." Auto-Correction will show you a little pop-up window with the contraction spelled correctly; all you need to do to select the highlighted correction is press the **Space** key.

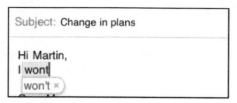

With some words, you have to add an extra character for the Auto-Correction feature to figure out what you mean:

- Type "Weree" to get "We're."
- Type "Welll" to get "We'll."

Hearing Auto-Correction Words Out Loud

You can set your iPhone to speak the Auto-text and Auto-Correction words as they appear. This might help you to select the correct word. Follow these steps to enable this type of speaking:

1. Tap the **Settings** icon.

2. Tap **General**.

3. Tap **Accessibility** near the bottom of the page (you need to swipe down).

4. Set the switch next to **Speak Auto-text** to **ON**.

After you enable this feature, you will hear the Auto-Correction word that pops up spoken aloud as you are typing. If you agree with the word you hear, press the **Space** key to accept it; otherwise, keep typing. This can save you some time from looking up from the keyboard.

Spell Checker

Working together with the Auto-Correction feature is your built-in iPhone Spell Checker. Most of the time, your misspelled words will be caught and corrected automatically by Auto-Correction. Other times, a word will not be corrected, but it is still misspelled. You will see any words that the iPhone thinks are misspelled underlined with a red dotted line, as shown in Figure 2–3.

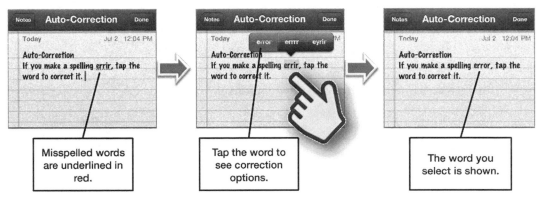

Figure 2–3. *Using the built-in Spell Checker feature*

TIP: If your Spell Checker has too many incorrect words, then you can give it a fresh start by clearing out all the custom words. Follow these steps to do so:

1. Tap your **Settings** icon.

2. Tap **General**.

3. Tap **Reset** near the bottom.

4. Tap **Reset Keyboard Dictionary**.

5. Tap **Reset Dictionary** to confirm.

Following the preceding steps will clear out all custom words that have been added to your iPhone's dictionary.

Accessibility Options

There are a number of useful features on the iPhone to help with accessibility. For example, the VoiceOver option will read various things displayed on the screen to you. It will tell you what elements you tap, what buttons are selected, and all the options available. It will read entire screens of text, as well. If you like to see things larger, you can also turn on the Zoom option, as described in the "Using Zoom to Magnify the Entire Screen" section later in this chapter.

Getting Your iPhone to Speak To You (VoiceOver)

One cool iPhone feature is the VoiceOver option. Turning this on will make your phone speak anything displayed on the screen. You can even get it to read to you from any e-mail, text document, or even an **iBook** page.

> **TIP:** Use your headphones when the **VoiceOver** option is set to **ON** and you are in a public place; this will help you hear what is said more easily, but avoid bothering others.

Follow these steps to enable the VoiceOver feature:

1. Tap the **Settings** icon.

2. Tap **General**.

3. Tap **Accessibility** near the bottom of the page.

4. Tap **VoiceOver**.

5. Set the **VoiceOver** switch to **ON**.

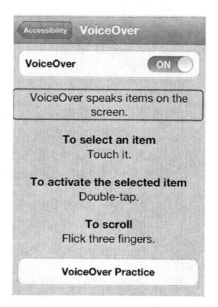

> **CAUTION:** As shown on the screen to the right, the VoiceOver gestures are different from the normal gestures. Tap the **Practice VoiceOver Gestures** button to get used to them.

Here are some additional tips for using the VoiceOver feature:

- Scroll down the **VoiceOver** screen to see more settings.

- Adjust whether or not hints are spoken by changing the setting for the **Speak Hints** option.

- When you type with VoiceOver, by default every character you type will be spoken. You can change this by tapping **Typing Feedback.** On the next screen, you can set this option to **Characters**, **Words**, **Characters and Words,** or **Nothing**.

- Adjust the **Speaking Rate** by sliding the bar beneath this option.

- Adjust whether **Phonetics** and **Pitch Change** are used by setting the switches.

To have an entire page read to you in the **Notes** or **iBooks** app, you need to simultaneously tap the bottom and top of the block of text on the screen. If you tap in the text with one finger, only a single line is read to you.

Speak Selection and Speak Auto-text

The **Speak Selection** feature is similar to **VoiceOver**, but it ties into the Copy and Paste feature, adding a **Speak** option to the selected text pop-up menu. The Speak Auto-text feature will say out loud any text that is automatically capitalized or corrected by the spelling dictionary.

With the Speak Selection feature, you can adjust the Speaking Rate using the same type of slider that the VoiceOver feature uses. The Speak Auto-text option can only be toggled ON or OFF.

Using AssistiveTouch

If you have difficulty touching the screen or have a special accessory that helps you with the touch screen, you will want to turn on AssistiveTouch. You do this in the same Accessibility section of **Settings**.

Once you turn it on, you will see a small white circle in the lower right corner of your screen. Tap the small circle to bring up the **AssistiveTouch** menu.

Assistive touch will allow you to do the following:

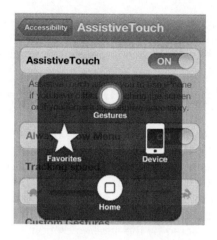

- Tap **Gestures**, to simulate, 2, 3, 4 or 5 finger gestures.

- Tap **Favorites** to access your custom gestures.

- Tap **Device** to access common device commands such as screen rotation, mute, volume, shake and lock screen.

- Tap the **Home** icon to simulate actually clicking the **Home** button.

You can even set up custom gestures to access from the Favorites menu.

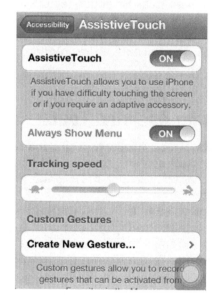

Tap **Create New Gesture**, then use your fingers to make an on-screen gesture by moving your fingers on the screen. You will see white lines follow the location of your finger tips.

Then, tap the **Stop** button.

Press **Play** to see if your gesture is correct and finally, tap **Save** at the top and give your new gesture a name.

You will then see your new gesture appear in the **Favorites** menu in AssistiveTouch.

Using Zoom to Magnify the Entire Screen

You may want to turn on the Zoom feature if you find the text, icons, buttons, or anything else on the screen a little too hard to see. With the Zoom feature turned on, you can zoom the entire screen to almost twice its normal size—everything is much easier to read.

> **NOTE:** You cannot use VoiceOver and Zoom at the same time; you need to choose one or the other. Instead of magnifying the entire screen, you can also increase just the font sizes for your major apps using the Large Text feature. We will show you how in the "Use Larger Text Size for Easier Reading" section.

Follow these steps to enable the **Zoom** feature:

1. Tap the **Settings** icon.

2. Tap **General**.

3. Tap **Accessibility** near the bottom of the page.

4. Tap **Zoom**.

5. Set the switch next to **Zoom** to **ON**.

Similar to VoiceOver, Zoom uses three-fingered gestures. Make sure to study these before you leave this screen.

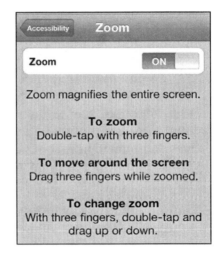

White on Black

If the contrast and colors on your screen are difficult to see, then you might want to set the **White on Black** setting to **ON**. Follow these steps to do so:

1. Go to the **Accessibility** screen in the **Settings** app, as shown previously.

2. Set the **White on Black** switch to **ON**. With this option set to **ON**, everything that was light on the screen becomes black, and everything that was dark or black becomes white.

Use Larger Text Size for Easier Reading

You can really expand the size of your fonts in the **Contacts, Mail, Messages,** and **Notes** apps by using the Large Text feature. Follow these steps to do so:

1. Tap the **Settings** icon.

2. Tap **General**.

3. Tap **Accessibility** near the bottom of the page (you need to swipe down).

4. Tap **Large Text**. You will then see a screen of font size options: **Off, 20pt text, 24pt text, 32pt text, 40pt text, 48pt text,** and **56pt text**. Tap the size you want to use. The image shown to the right uses the 48pt font.

5. Tap the **Accessibility** button in the upper-left corner to return to the previous screen, then tap the **Home** button to exit **Settings**.

Triple-Click Home Button Options

You can set a triple-click of the **Home** button to do various things related to accessibility. Follow these steps to adjust these options:

1. Go to the **Accessibility** screen in the **Settings** app, as shown previously.

2. Tap **Triple-click the Home Button** near the bottom of the page.

3. Choose from **Off, Toggle VoiceOver, Toggle White on Black,** or **Ask**.

Using the Magnifying Glass for Editing Text or Placing the Cursor

How many times have you been typing something and wanted to move the cursor precisely between two words or letters?

This can be hard to do until you figure out the Magnifying Glass trick. What you do is this: Touch and hold your finger on the place where you want the cursor (see Figure 2–4). After a second or two, you will see the **Magnifying Glass** icon appear. Then, as you hold your finger on the screen, slide it around to position the cursor. When you let go, you will see the **Copy and Paste** pop-up menu, but you can ignore it.

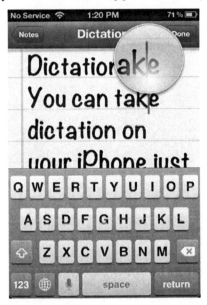

Figure 2–4. *Touch and hold the screen to see the* **Magnifying Glass** *icon and place the cursor.*

Typing Numbers and Symbols

How do you type a number or a symbol using the iPhone's on-screen keyboard? When you are typing, tap the **123** key in the lower-left corner to see numbers and common symbols such as $! ~ & = # . _ - +. If you need more symbols, from the **Numbers** keyboard tap the **#+=** key just above the **ABC** key in the lower-left corner (see Figure 2–5).

Figure 2–5. *Switching between the **Letters**, **Numbers**, and **Symbols** keyboards*

> **TIP:** After you type a number or symbol, notice that the **Numbers** keyboard will stay active until you either hit the **Space** key or press the key for another keyboard, such as the **ABC** key for the **Letters** keyboard.

Touch and Slide Trick

One cool technique that you can apply in various areas is the touch-and-slide trick. We'll cover what this is and how you can take advantage of it in the next couple of sections.

Typing Uppercase Letters

To type uppercase letters, you would normally press the **Shift** key, and then press the desired letter.

The faster way to type single uppercase letters and symbols that require the **Shift** key is to press the **Shift** key, keep your finger on the keyboard, slide over to the key you want, and then release.

For example, to type an uppercase "D," press the right **Shift** key, then slide over to the **D** key and release.

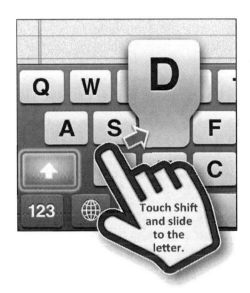

Rapidly Typing a Single Number

If you have to type just a single number, then press the **123** key and slide your finger up to the number. However, to type several numbers in a row, it's best to press the **123** key, let go, and then press each number.

Press and Hold Keyboard Shortcut for Typing Symbols and More

You might wonder how you can type symbols not shown on the keyboard.

> **TIP:** You can type more symbols than are shown on the screen.

All you do is press and hold a letter, number, or symbol that is related to the symbol you want.

For example, if you want to type the YEN symbol (¥), you press and hold the **$** key until you see the other options. Next, slide up your finger to highlight the YEN symbol, and then let go.

This tip also works with the **.com** key in the **Safari** web browser and when typing e-mail addresses by pressing and holding the **Period (.)** key. You can get additional web site suffixes by pressing and holding the **.com** or **Period** keys.

The preceding figure shows the **.co**, **uk**, **.ie**, **.de, .ca,** and **.eu** keys. These keys are not displayed on the standard US keyboard, but they are present in this case because we have installed additional international keyboards. You will learn how to enable international keyboards in the "Typing in Other Languages—International Keyboards" section later in this chapter.

> **TIP: A Few More Useful but Hidden Symbols**
>
> There is a good bullet point character on the **Symbols** keyboard just above the **Backspace** key. You can also get a degree symbol if you press and hold the **Zero** key (**0**). Also, you can press and hold the **?** and **!** keys to get their inverted Spanish cousins.

Caps Lock

You double-press the **Shift** key to turn on the Caps Lock feature. You know it's turned on when the **Shift** key turns blue.

To turn off Caps Lock, simply press the **Shift** key again.

Quickly Selecting and Deleting or Changing Text

You may need to quickly change or delete some text you are typing. Follow these steps to do so:

1. Select a part of the text you want to change or delete by double-tapping it.

    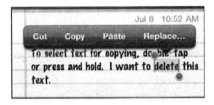

2. Adjust the selection by dragging the blue handles.

    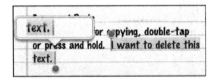

3. To erase the selected text, press the **Backspace** key.

4. To replace the text, simply start typing. The text will be instantly replaced by the letters you type.

Keyboard Options and Settings

There are a few keyboard options to make typing on your iPhone easier. These keyboard options are located in the **General** tab of your **Settings** app. Follow these steps to access them:

1. Tap the **Settings** icon.

2. Tap **General**.

3. Swipe up, then tap **Keyboard** near the bottom of the page.

Setting Auto-Correction to ON or OFF

As noted earlier in this chapter, the Auto-Correction feature will use the iPhone's built-in dictionary to automatically make changes to commonly misspelled words. You need to make sure it is **ON** if you want this feature to work. (This is the default setting.)

Auto-Capitalization

When you start a new sentence, words will automatically be capitalized if the **Auto-Capitalization** option is set to **ON**.

This feature will also correctly capitalize common proper nouns. For example, if you type "New york," then you will be prompted to change it to "New York"—again, just pressing the **Space** key will implement the correction. If you backspace over a capital letter, the iPhone will assume the new letter you type should be capitalized, as well. This feature is also set to **ON** by default.

Enabling Caps Lock

Sometimes you may want to type only capital letters; to do so, simply double-tap the **Caps** key.

This feature is set to **OFF** by default.

The "." Shortcut

If you double-press the **Space** key, it will automatically put in a period at the end of a sentence; this feature is set to **ON** by default.

Typing in Other Languages—International Keyboards

At the time of writing, the iPhone enables you to type in more than a dozen different languages, including everything from Dutch to Spanish. Some of the Asian languages, such as Japanese and Chinese, offer two or three keyboards for different typing methods.

Adding a New International Keyboard

Follow these steps to enable various language keyboards:

1. Tap the **Settings** icon.

2. Tap **General**.

3. Tap **Keyboard** near the bottom of the page.

4. Tap **International Keyboards**.

5. Tap **Add New Keyboard**.

6. Tap any keyboard or language listed to add it. You will now see the keyboard appear on the list of available keyboards.

7. There is a good bullet point character on the **Symbols** keyboard just above the **Backspace** key. You can also get a degree symbol if you press and hold the **Zero** key (**0**). Also, you can press and hold the **?** and **!** keys to get their inverted Spanish cousins.

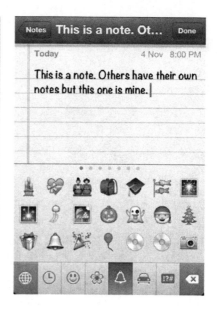

TIP: iOS 5 includes a built –in Emoji keyboard. Emoji is an extensive collection of Japanese symbols, including various smiley and frowny faces, holiday images, buildings and vehicles, and much more. While their meanings are more specific in Japan, people around the world have begun using them in SMS, Twitter, and other online messaging services.

The Emoji keyboard can be added in Settings just like any other keyboard.

Editing, Re-Ordering, or Deleting Keyboards

You may want to adjust options for a keyboard, re-order how the keyboards appear in a list, or simply remove a keyboard that you no longer use. Follow these steps to do so:

1. Follow Steps 1–4 under the "Adding a New International Keyboard" section earlier in this chapter; this will let you view the list of international keyboards.

2. To adjust options for a specific keyboard, tap it in the list of keyboards. In our example, we tapped **French (Canada)**.

3. Change the **Software Keyboard Layout** by tapping the choice in that section.

4. Adjust the **Hardware Keyboard Layout** by tapping a choice in that section.

5. Tap the **Keyboards** button in the upper-left corner to save your choices and return to the list of keyboards.

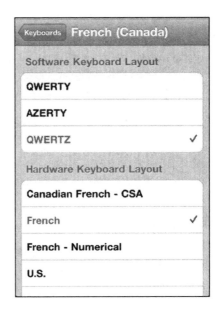

6. To re-order or delete a keyboard, tap the **Edit** button in the upper-right corner.

7. To change the order of keyboards, touch and drag the right edge of the keyboard with the three gray bars up or down.

8. To delete a keyboard, tap the **Red Minus Sign** so it swings to the vertical position, then tap **Delete.**

9. To finish editing your keyboards, tap the **Done** button in the upper-right corner.

You will notice a little **Globe** key appears when you install at least one international keyboard. Press the **Globe** key to cycle between all the languages.

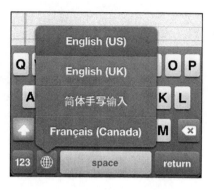

> **TIP:** You can press and hold the **Globe** key to see a list of available keyboards. This will enable you to quickly select the keyboard you wish to use. If

Japanese, Chinese, and some other languages provide several keyboard options to meet your typing preferences.

In some of the languages (such as Japanese), you will see the letters typed change into characters, or you can draw the characters yourself. You may also see a row of other character combinations above the keyboard. When you see the combination you want, tap it.

Copy and Paste

The Copy and Paste feature is very useful for saving time and increasing your typing accuracy. You can use this feature to take text from your e-mail (such as meeting details) and paste it into your calendar. Or you may want to simply copy an e-mail address from one place in a form into another to save yourself the time required to retype it. (We show you this technique in the "Setup Exchange/Google Account" section of Chapter 4: "Other Ways to Sync.") There are many places to use Copy and Paste; the more comfortable you are with it, the more you will use it. You can even copy text or images from your **Safari** web browser and paste them into a **Notes** or **Mail** message.

Selecting Text by Double-Tapping It

If you are reading or typing text, you can double-tap it to start selecting some text to copy. This works well in the **Mail**, **Messages**, and **Notes** apps.

You will see a box with blue dots (handles) at opposite corners.

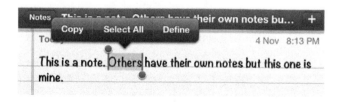

Just drag the handles to select the text you wish to highlight and copy.

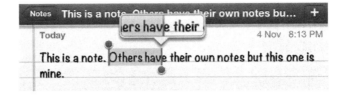

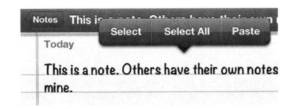

> **TIP:** If you want to select all the text, tap the cursor or double-tap the screen above or below the text. This will display a pop-up window that shows you **Select** and **Select All** options. Tap **Select** to select a word or tap **Select All** to highlight all the text.

Selecting Text with Two-Finger Touch

The other way to select text requires that you touch the screen simultaneously with two fingers. This seems to work best if you are holding your iPhone with one hand and use your thumb and forefinger from your other hand to touch the screen. You can also set the iPhone down on the table and touch the screen with a finger from both hands. Follow these steps to use this approach:

1. Touch the screen simultaneously at the beginning and end of the text you want to select. Don't worry if you cannot get the selection exactly on the first touch.

2. After the two-finger touch, use the blue handles to drag the beginning and end of the selection to the correct positions.

Selecting a Web Site or Other Non-Editable Text with Touch and Hold

In the **Safari** web browser and other places where you cannot edit the text, hold your finger on some text and the paragraph will become highlighted with handles at each of the corners.

Next, drag the handles if you want to select even more text.

> **NOTE:** If you drag smaller than a paragraph, the selector will switch to fine-text mode and give you the blue handles on both ends of the selection to pick just the characters or words you want. If you drag your finger beyond a paragraph, you get the gross-text selector, which you can drag up or down to select whole reams of text and graphics.

Cut or Copy the Text

Once you have highlighted the text that you wish to copy, just touch the **Copy** tab at the top of the screen. The tab will turn blue, indicating that the text is on the clipboard.

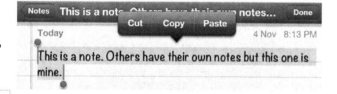

> **NOTE:** If you have previously cut or copied text, then you will also see the **Paste** option, as shown to the right.

App Switching and Multitasking

After you copy text, you may want to paste it into another app. For example, you might want to copy some text from Safari and paste it into Notes or a Mail message. The easiest way to jump between apps is to use the **App Switcher** app. Follow these steps to paste text from one app into another:

1. Copy or cut your text.

2. Double-tap the **Home** button to bring up the **App Switcher** app on the bottom of your screen

3. If you just left an app running in the background, you will be able to find it in the App Switcher bar.

4. Swipe right or left to find the app you want and tap it.

5. If you don't see the app you want in the App Switcher bar, then tap the **Home** button and start it from the **Home** screen.

6. Now, paste the text by pressing and holding the screen, and then selecting **Paste** from the pop-up window.

7. Double-tap the **Home** button again and tap the app you just left to jump back to it.

Pasting the Text

Pasting the text into the same app is easy. For example, simply follow these steps to paste the text into the same **Notes** or **Mail** message:

1. Use your finger to move the cursor to where you want to paste the text. Remember the **Magnifying Glass** trick we showed earlier in this chapter; this can help you position the cursor.

2. Once you let go of the screen, you should see a pop-up window asking whether you to **Select**, **Select All**, or **Paste**.

3. If you don't see this pop-up window, then double-tap the screen.

4. Select **Paste** to paste your selection.

Shake to Undo

One of the great features of the iPhone is the ability to undo typing, copy and pasting, even Siri dictations you just completed.

All you have to do is shake the iPhone after the paste. A new pop-up window will appear that gives you the option to undo what you have just done.

Tap **Undo Typing** or **Undo Paste** to correct the mistake.

TIP: Delete Text Quickly

If you ever want to delete a number of lines of text, a paragraph, or even all the text you just typed quickly with only one or two taps, this tip is for you. First, use the techniques described

previously to select the text you want to delete. Next, simply press the **Delete** key [⌫] in the lower-left corner of the keyboard to delete all the selected text.

Finding Things with Spotlight Search

The Spotlight Search is a great feature on your iPhone that helps you find information. This is a proprietary search method from Apple for performing a global search on your iPhone. You can use this feature to search for a name, event, or subject.

The concept is simple. Let's say you are looking for something related to Martin. You cannot remember if it was an e-mail, a document in **Notes**, or a Calendar event; however, you do know it was related to Martin.

This is the perfect time to use the Spotlight Search feature to find everything related to Martin on your iPhone.

Activating Spotlight Search

First, you need to bring up the **Spotlight Search** page, which resides to the left of the first page of the **Home** screen.

On the left side of the first circle (indicating the first page of your **Home** screen), you can see a very small **Magnifying Glass** icon.

Swipe your finger from left to right on the first page of icons to see the **Spotlight Search** page. You can also press the Home button from your first screen of Icons to see this same search page.

Follow these steps to perform a search with this feature:

1. On the **Spotlight Search** page, type in one or more words as your search parameters.

2. Tap the **Search** button in the lower-right corner to execute your search.

> **TIP:** If you are looking for a person, type his full name to more accurately find items from only that person (for example, "Martin Trautschold"). This will eliminate any other Martins who might be in your iPhone, enabling you to find items only related to Martin Trautschold.

3. In the search result, you'll see all e-mails, appointments, meeting invitations, and contact information the search finds. Swipe down to see more results.

4. Tap one of the results in the list to view its contents.

Your search results stay there until you clear them. This means you can return to the **Spotlight Search** page to view your prior search results simply by swiping to the right from your **Home** screen.

To clear the **Search** field, just touch the **X** in the Search bar. To exit the **Spotlight Search** page, just press the **Home** key or swipe to the left.

Searching the Web or Wikipedia

After you perform a Spotlight Search, you will see two options beneath your results: **Search Web** and **Search Wikipedia**.

Tap either of these options to execute your search on the Web or in Wikipedia.

Customizing Spotlight Search

You can customize your Spotlight Search by removing certain apps or types of data from the search. You can even change the order in which each type of data is searched. This might be useful if you want to search only your **Contacts** and **Mail** messages—and nothing else. Or, if you know that you always want to search **Mail** first, then **Calendar**, and then **Music**—you could set those items in the proper order. Follow these steps to do so:

1. Tap the **Settings** icon.

2. Tap **General**.

3. Tap **Spotlight Search**.

4. To change the order of the items searched, touch and drag the right edge of the item with the three gray bars up or down.

5. To remove a specific item from the search, tap it to remove the **Checkmark** icon next to it. Unchecked items are not searched by Spotlight Search.

6. Tap the **General** button in the upper-left corner to return to the **Settings** app.

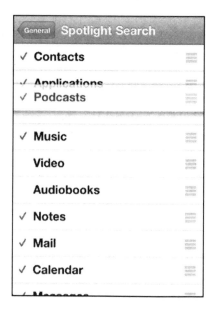

Chapter 3

Sync with iCloud, iTunes, and More

In this chapter, we will show you how to set up or adjust your storage and push your information to Apple's new iCloud service, as well as how to synchronize information between your iPhone and your Windows or Mac computer using iTunes.

With iCloud, you can wirelessly sync your mail, contacts, calendars, reminders, bookmarks, notes, photos, and documents and data, as well as back up your iPhone wirelessly over-the-air (OTA). With iTunes, you can sync or transfer contacts, calendar, notes, apps, music, videos, iBooks, documents, and picture libraries, as well as back up your iPhone.

And, because nothing ever works right all the time, we'll show you a few simple troubleshooting tips. Finally, we'll show you how to check for updates and install updated operating system software for your iPhone.

iCloud

iCloud is free, easy to set up, and easy to use. In most cases, it is the best way to sync your personal information, music, TV shows (U.S. only), and apps. It is also the best way to handle backups and to restore your phone. Unless you have very specific reasons not to, we highly recommend using iCloud for most of your syncing needs, but the **iTunes** app for anything iCloud doesn't yet handle (like movies).

iCloud also lets you re-download previous iTunes, iBookstore, and App Store purchases, but your iCloud ID can also be used with iMessage, FaceTime, and other free Apple services.

> **NOTE:** Apple is very careful not to use the word *sync* when it comes to iCloud. Instead, it says *store* and *push*. The difference is largely technical and has to do with how Apple is moving your data around.
>
> The important thing to remember is that, when you change something on your iPhone, Apple copies the change to its servers and then sends copies back down to all your other iCloud-enabled iOS devices, as well as to your Windows or Mac PC.

Setting up iCloud

In Chapter 1: "Getting Started," we showed you how to enable iCloud while setting up your new iPhone or restoring from a previous iCloud backup. Once iCloud is enabled, you can easily turn various services on or off.

Start by launching the **Settings** app and scrolling down to iCloud.

Mail, Contacts, Calendars, Reminders, Bookmarks, Notes, and **Find my iPhone** can easily be toggled to **ON** or **OFF** directly from this screen.

For the **Photo Stream option**, you need to tap the tab first to get to the **On/Off** toggle.

> **NOTE:** At the time of writing, Photo Stream is an all-or-nothing service. If Photo Stream is turned on, Apple will keep 1000 of your most recent photos for up to 30 days on its servers, copying them to your iPad, Apple TV, Mac, or Windows PC. Anything logged into iCloud will get a copy of your Photo Stream. If you take photos of a sensitive or personal nature, you might want to set the **Photo Stream** option to **Off**.

Likewise, you can tap **Documents and Data to toggle** this option **ON or OFF.** You also have the option to set the **Use Cellular option to ON**. This will make sure your documents stay up to date even when you're out and connected to a 3G data network.

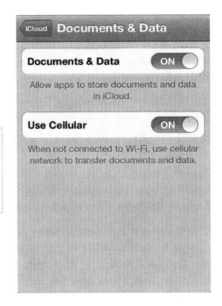

> **NOTE:** If you're on a limited data plan or are roaming while traveling, then you might want to turn this feature off to avoid costly overage charges.

Managing iCloud Storage and Backup

iCloud comes with 5GB of free storage. Music from iTunes, apps, iBooks, and your Photo Stream don't count against your 5GB, so most people will still have plenty of space left over for app data, documents, and backups.

To check your iCloud Storage, scroll down to the bottom and tap **Storage and Backup**.

The **Storage** section shows you **Total Storage**, or the full size of your iCloud account; and **Available Storage** shows how much total storage you have left.

At the bottom of the screen, you can toggle **iCloud Backup** to **ON** or **OFF**.

> **NOTE:** For most users, most of the time, we strongly recommend the **iCloud Backup** option be toggled to **ON** and left that way.

You can tap the **Back Up Now** button if you ever need to back up your iPhone immediately. You might do this if you want to reinstall your iPhone, switch to a replacement or new iPhone, or intend to go on a trip and want to make sure your phone is backed up before you leave.

To see how your iCloud storage is being used, tap **Manage Storage**.

At the top of the **Manage Storage** screen, you'll see a list of devices currently backed up to iCloud. This will include your iPhone and any other iOS devices you might own, like an iPad or iPod touch.

Tap the device you want to look at and you'll be taken to the **Info** screen, which shows when your **Latest Backup** took place and the **Backup Size**.

The **Backup Options** section lets you individually toggle different types of backups on or off , including the **Camera Roll** and any apps you might have installed that sync their settings or data with iCloud. This section also tells you how much storage each app is using.

Initially, you'll only see a few apps. Tap **See All Apps** for the full list. Setting an app to **OFF** means you'll save on storage space, but your data will no longer be synced between your iOS devices, nor will it be restored if you ever reinstall your device or the app.

> **TIP:** Your iPhone's big, 8 megapixel, 1080p camera means that backing up the **Camera Roll** can quickly eat up a lot of storage, especially if you have only the free 5GB plan. The Photo Stream feature already backs up your photos; if backing up your video isn't a concern, then you can toggle **Camera Roll** backups to **OFF** to save space.

Buying More iCloud Storage

You might find yourself constantly running out of iCloud storage, decide you want to start backing up more photos and videos, or discover you need to back up multiple iOS devices. If so, you can buy more iCloud Storage from Apple.

Simply tap any of the **Buy More Storage** buttons peppered throughout the iCloud's **Settings** screens. At the time of writing, additional iCloud storage costs were as follows:

- 10GB for US $20/year

- 20GB for US $40/year

- 50GB for US $100/year

iTunes in the Cloud

iCloud also includes the *iTunes in the Cloud* feature, which lets you re-download previously purchased apps. In some countries, it even lets you re-download iBooks, music, and even TV shows. This means you can download them to your iPhone whenever you like, delete them when you no longer need them, and then re-download them again when you want them back.

To learn more about re-downloading files from iTunes, see Chapter 22: "iTunes on Your Device," Chapter 23: "The Amazing App Store," and Chapter 13: "iBooks and E-Books."

You can also set up your iPhone to automatically download any new apps, iBooks, subscription Newsstand issues, music, and TV shows purchased on any device or computer associated with your iTunes account. If you buy a new song on your PC or a new app on your iPod touch, then that song or app will immediately download and show up on your iPhone, as well.

Follow these steps to turn on automatic downloads:

1. Launch Settings.

2. Tap Store.

3. Toggle Music, Apps, and Books to ON.

4. If you want to enable automatic downloads on 3G as well, then toggle Use Cellular Data to ON.

5. If you want to enable automatic Newsstand subscription downloads, then toggle the switch next to the name of the newspaper or magazine to ON.

NOTE: At the time of writing, Apple's 20MB download limit for 3G networks also applied to the iTunes in the Cloud feature. This means that, if you're away from Wi-Fi, you won't be able to automatically download or re-download any apps or files more than 20MB in size until you return to a Wi-Fi connection. This limitation applies to iBooks, music, TV shows, and so on.

iCloud on the Computer

iCloud doesn't just sync your information between your iPhone and Apple's servers or between your iOS devices. It can also sync information between your iPhone and your Windows or Mac PC.

If you're a Windows user, you can turn syncing on or off for several apps and services in the **iCloud Control Panel for Windows** (see Figure 3–1). Apps and services you can sync with include **Mail**, **Contacts**, **Calendars & Tasks**, and **Reminders**, among others.

Figure 3–1. *iCloud Control Panel for Windows*

If you're a Mac OS X user, you can turn these options on or off in the OS X 7.2 **Lion iCloud Systems Settings** panel (see Figure 3–2).

Figure 3–2. *The Mac's* **Lion iCloud Systems Settings** *panel (OS X 7.2)*

Automatic app, books, music, and other downloads can be turned on or off in the **iTunes** app via the **Store Preferences** screen (see Figure 3–3).

Figure 3–3. *The iTunes' Store Preferences screen*

Syncing with iTunes

There are a few things you need before you can start using **iTunes** to sync. In the upcoming sections, we will cover the prerequisites and answer a few common questions about the reasons to use iTunes. We will also help you understand what happens if you own another Apple device, such as an iPad or iPod, and start syncing with your iPhone.

Prerequisites

There are just a few things you need to do before you sync your iPhone with **iTunes**:

> **TIP:** If you followed all the steps in Chapter 1: "Getting Started," chances are you've already completed the steps listed below and the initial sync of your contacts, calendar, bookmarks, notes, and email accounts to your iPhone. If so, you may want to skip ahead to the "Apps: Sync and Manage Them" section later in this chapter.

1. Make sure you've installed version 10.5 or higher of the **iTunes** app on your computer. For help with installing or updating **iTunes**, see Chapter 22: "iTunes on Your Device."

2. Make sure you have your iTunes account ID handy. This is the email address and password you use to buy music, apps, and other content from iTunes.

3. Get the white sync cable that came with your iPhone. One end plugs into the bottom of your iPhone near the **Home** button, and the other plugs into the USB port on your computer.

Syncing iTunes with an iPod or iPad *and* Your iPhone?

You might wonder whether you can sync iTunes with multiple devices, such as your iPod or iPad and your iPhone. Yes, you can! As long as you are syncing to the same computer, you can sync several Apple devices (Apple says up to five, but we've heard of people syncing more) to the same iTunes account on a single computer.

> **CAUTION:** You can't sync the same iPhone, iPad, or iPod to two different computers. If you attempt to do this, you'll see a message like this: "Would you like to wipe this device (iPhone, iPad, iPod) and resync the new library?" If you answer **Yes**, any music and videos on the device will be erased.

There Are Other Sync Methods—Should I Use iTunes?

iCloud is both free and the easiest way to keep your iPhone in sync with your other devices, while **iTunes** is there to help you with large files, movies, and other content that iCloud doesn't yet handle. You can also use other approaches to synchronize certain data, such as your personal information and email (including Exchange/Google). Keep in mind, however, that even if you choose one of these other approaches, you'll still need to use iCloud and/or **iTunes** to accomplish the following:

- Back up and restore files and data on your iPhone

- Update the iPhone operating system software

- Sync and manage your applications (apps)

- Sync your music library and playlists

- Sync movies, TV shows, podcasts, and iTunes U content

- Sync books

- Sync photos

Table 3–1 summarizes your synchronization options. What method you choose to use for synchronization should be driven by where you currently store your email, contacts, and calendar; your environment; and whether you want to have a wireless sync.

> **NOTE:** Some environments let you wirelessly sync your contacts and calendars to your iPhone.

Table 3–1. *Synchronization Options for Your Personal Information*

Your Environment	Wireless Sync Using	Desktop Sync Using	Notes
Google for email, calendar, and contacts	**Settings ⇧ Mail, Contacts, Calendar ⇧ Add Account ⇧ Microsoft Exchange**	iTunes	This is free.
Google for email, calendar, notes	**(Cannot wirelessly sync contacts this way)** **Settings ⇧ Mail, Contacts, Calendar ⇧ Add Account ⇧ Gmail**	iTunes required to sync Google Contacts	This is free.
Email, calendar and contacts on Microsoft Exchange Server	**Settings ⇧ Mail, Contacts, Calendar ⇧ Add Account ⇧ Microsoft Exchange**	iTunes	This is free.
Email, calendar and contacts in Yahoo!	Wireless sync for email, calendar, notes (not for contacts): **Settings ⇧ Mail, Contacts, Calendar ⇧ Add Account ⇧ Yahoo!**	iTunes required to sync Yahoo! Contacts	This is free.
Email, calendar, contacts, settings, backups, music, TV shows (US only), and apps in iCloud .	**Settings ⇧ Mail, Contacts, Calendar ⇧ Add Account ⇧ iCloud**	iCloud	This is free.
Email, calendar, and contacts in AOL	Wireless sync for email, calendar, notes (not for contacts): **Settings ⇧ Mail, Contacts, Calendar ⇧ Add Account ⇧ AOL**	iTunes required to sync AOL Contacts	This is free.
LDAP (Lightweight Directory Access Protocol) contacts	**Settings ⇧ Mail, Contacts, Calendar ⇧ Add Account ⇧ Other ⇧ Add LDAP Account**	Not available.	This is free.
CalDAV calendar account	**Settings ⇧ Mail, Contacts, Calendar ⇧ Add Account ⇧ Other ⇧ Add CalDAV Account**	Not available.	This is free. You must a username, password, and access to a CalDAV account in this format: `cal.server.com`.

Your Environment	Wireless Sync Using	Desktop Sync Using	Notes
Subscribed calendar at your work	Settings ⇨ Mail, Contacts, Calendar ⇨ Add Account ⇨ Other ⇨ Add Subscribed Calendar	Not available.	This is free. You must have access to a subscribed calendar (web address, username, and password) and access to a server is in this format: `myserver.com/cal.ics`

Set Up Your iTunes Sync

Next, we will show you all the steps for using the **iTunes** app to perform both automated syncs and manual transfers of information to your iPhone.

The iPhone Summary Screen

The iPhone's **Summary** tab in **iTunes** is where you see and update your version of your iPhone operating system software. It also contains an important switch related to syncing music, video, and other content. This tab is also where you can choose to automatically open **iTunes** (to sync) whenever you connect your iPhone to your computer.

Once you connect your iPhone to your computer, you can see important information, like your iPhone's memory capacity, installed software version, and serial number (see Figure 3–4). You can also check for updates to the software version, restore data to your iPhone, and choose from the several options available on this screen.

In particular, you can decide whether you want to **Manually manage music and videos** using the checkbox at the bottom of this screen.

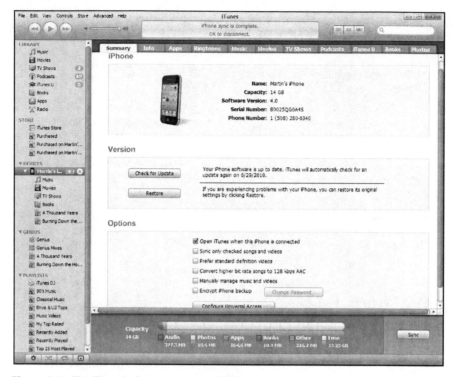

Figure 3–4. *The iPhone's* ***Summary*** *screen in* ***iTunes***

Follow these steps to see the **Summary** screen:

1. Start the **iTunes** software on your computer.

2. Connect your iPhone to your computer with the white USB cable supplied with the device. Plug one end into the bottom of the iPhone near the **Home** button and the other end into a USB port on your computer.

3. If you've successfully connected your iPhone, you should see your iPhone listed under **DEVICES** in the left nav bar.

4. Click your iPhone in the left nav bar, and then click the **Summary** tab on the top-left edge of the main window.

5. If you want to be able to drag and drop music and videos onto your iPhone, check the box next to **Manually manage music and videos**.

6. If you want to have **iTunes** open and sync your iPhone automatically whenever you connect it to your computer, check the box next to **Open iTunes when this iPhone is connected**.

> **TIP:** Note that the **iTunes** software might not be installed on your primary computer (the one you use for syncing). For example, it might be installed on a second computer that you use for charging your iPhone. If so, you should check the box next to **Manually manage music and videos** and uncheck the box next to **Open iTunes when this iPhone is connected**.

Getting to the Sync Setup Screen (Info Tab)

Let's assume you want to get to the **Info** tab, which is the setup screen for syncing your contacts, calendar, email, and so forth. To do so, you follow the same steps described previously for getting to the **Summary** screen, except now you click the **Info** tab at the top to see the Contacts (and other sync settings) in the main **iTunes** window (see Figure 3–5).

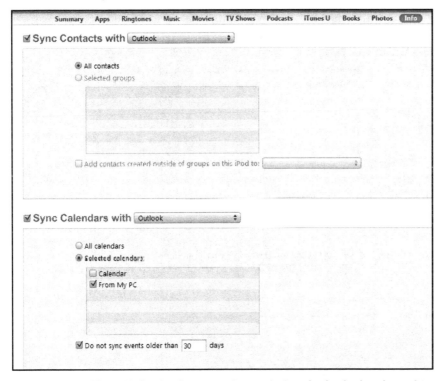

Figure 3–5. *The **iTunes' Info** tab, where you set up contacts, calendar, bookmarks, and more*

> **NOTE:** If you are already set up to sync your information using iCloud, you will see this warning and not be able to use iTunes, because iCloud already is syncing your information. If you see this warning, then you can skip syncing Mail, Contacts and Calendars using iTunes.

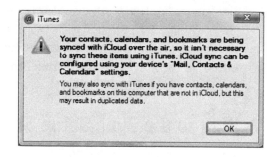

Sync Your Contacts

Let's start by setting up syncing for your contacts. The first step is to choose a service to sync with. To do so, check the box next to **Sync Contacts with** and adjust the pull-down menu to the software or service where your contacts are stored. At publication time, you have several syncing options on a Windows computer: Outlook, Google Contacts, Windows Contacts, and the Yahoo! Address Book.

> **CAUTION:** Whenever you switch between a software or service (called the *sync provider*) in these sync settings screens, it affects every one of the mobile devices connected to your iTunes account. For example, if you sync contacts to your iPad or iPod touch, these changes will also affect MobileMe. You will be changing the way contacts sync for any other devices connected to your iTunes account.

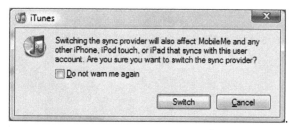

Syncing with Google Contacts

If you select **Google Contacts**, you'll be prompted to enter your Google ID and password.

To change your Google ID or password, click the **Configure** button next to the **Sync Contacts with** option you saw at the top of this section.

Syncing with the Yahoo! Address Book

If you select **Yahoo! Contacts**, you'll be prompted to enter your Yahoo! ID and password.

To change your Yahoo! ID or password, click the **Configure** button next to the **Sync Contacts with** option you saw at the top of this section.

> **NOTE:** The options you see in this and other drop-down boxes on the **Info** tab will vary slightly, depending on the software installed on your computer. For example, on a Mac the contacts sync does not have a drop-down list; instead the other services, such as Google Contacts and Yahoo!, are shown as separate checkboxes.

Once you select a service or app to sync with, you're ready to follow through on syncing your contacts:

1. Select which contacts you will sync with from either of these options:

    a. **All Contacts:** Sync all contacts in your address book (this is the default).

    b. **Selected Groups:** Sync contacts only within specific groups that you check in the window below.

2. You will see a checkbox that says **Add contacts created outside of groups on this iPhone to** (select a group from the drop-down list). This option lets you specify a new group for any new contacts you add on your iPhone that you don't explicitly assign to a group.

3. Scroll down the page to continue setting up your calendar, email, and more.

4. If you don't want to set up anything else for syncing, click the **Apply** button in the lower-right corner of the **iTunes** screen to start the sync.

> **NOTE:** Depending on how many contacts you have, the initial sync could take longer than 10 minutes, and may even require 30 or more minutes. So you may want to do this sync when you can let your iPhone sit for as long as it takes (e.g., during lunch or after dinner).

Syncing Your Calendar

Syncing your calendar is similar to syncing your contacts. Follow these steps to do so:

1.   Within the same **Info** tab, scroll down to see the calendar sync set up.

2.   Check the box next to **Sync Calendars with** and adjust the pull-down menu to the software or service that stores your calendars. This might be **Outlook** or another application on a Windows computer, and **iCal** on a Mac.

3.   Select either of these options:

     a.   **All Calendars:** Syncs all calendars (this is the default).

     b.   **Selected Calendars**: Syncs only calendars you've checked in the window below.

4.   If you want to save space on your iPhone, click the checkbox next to **Do not sync events older than 30 days.** You can adjust the days up or down to fit your needs.

5.   Scroll down the page to continue setting up email accounts, bookmarks and more.

6.   If you don't want to set up anything else for syncing, click the **Apply** button in the lower-right corner of the **iTunes** screen to start the sync.

NOTE: If you're a Mac user who uses **Microsoft Entourage**, you'll need to enable **Entourage** to sync with **iCal**. To do this, go into the **Preferences** settings in **Entourage**, and then go to **Sync Services** and check the boxes for synchronizing with **iCal** and the **Address Book**.

NOTE: At the time of writing, **Entourage**, unlike **iCal**, can't handle multiple calendars.

Syncing Email Accounts

Scroll down the page to sync email account settings.

> **NOTE:** After syncing the email account settings to your iPhone, you'll still have to enter your password for each email account in **Settings ⟡ Mail, Contacts, Calendar**. You have to do this only once on your iPhone for each account.

Follow these steps to do so:

1. Scroll down below the **Calendar** settings on the same **Info** tab in **iTunes** to see the **Mail** account settings.

2. Check the box next to **Sync Mail Accounts from** and adjust the pull-down menu to the software or service that stores your email (see Figure 3–6). This might be **Outlook** on a Windows computer, or **Entourage** or **Mail** on a Mac.

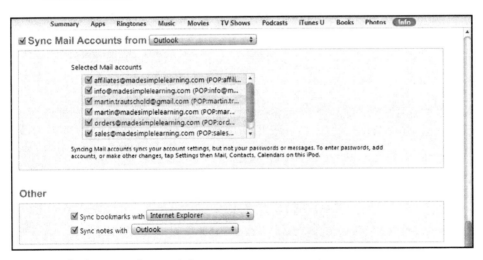

Figure 3–6. *Setting up email accounts to sync*

3. Scroll down the page to continue setting up bookmarks, notes, and more.

4. If you do not want to set anything else up for sync, then click the **Apply** button in the lower-right corner of the **iTunes** screen to start the sync.

Syncing Bookmarks and Notes

One great feature of the iTunes sync is that you can sync the browser bookmarks from your computer to your iPhone. This allows you to start browsing on your iPhone with all your favorite sites immediately. You can also sync your notes from your computer to your iPhone and keep them up-to-date in both places using **iTunes**.

> **NOTE:** At the time of writing, **iTunes** supports only two web browsers for synchronization: **Microsoft Internet Explorer** and **Apple Safari**. If you use **Mozilla Firefox** or **Google Chrome**, you can still sync your bookmarks, but you'll have to install free bookmark syncing software (such as **xmarks** from www.xmarks.com) to sync from **Firefox** or **Chrome** to **Safari** or **Explorer**. Once you install this software, you can sync your browser bookmarks in a simple, two-step process. **Firefox**'s **Home** app is a nice option for syncing bookmarks for **Firefox** users (visit http://itunes.apple.com/ca/app/firefox-home/id380366933?mt=8 for more information).

Syncing Your iPhone with iTunes

The syncing process is normally automatic when you plug in your iPhone to your computer's USB port. The only exception is if you have disabled the automatic sync feature.

Sync Apps in iTunes

Follow these steps to sync and manage apps with the **iTunes** app:

1. As you did to set up the sync previously, connect your iPhone to your computer, start **iTunes**, and click your iPhone in the left nav bar.

2. Click the **Apps** tab on the top of the main window.

3. Click the checkbox next to **Sync Apps** to see all apps stored on your iPhone and your **Home** screens, as shown in Figure 3–7.

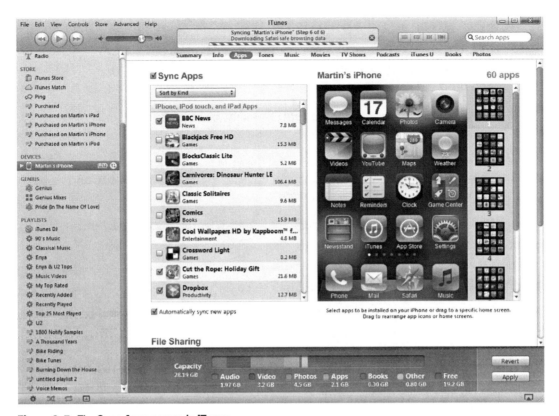

Figure 3–7. *The Sync Apps screen in iTunes*

Move Apps, Work with Folders, or Delete App Icons

It is very easy to move around and organize your application icons in **iTunes' Sync Apps** screen (again, see Figure 3–7). Try these actions to accomplish various tasks:

- **Move an app within a screen**: Click it and drag it around the screen. If you want to select more than one app at a time, you can press and hold the Ctrl key (Windows) or Command key (Mac) and click to select.

- **Move an app between Home screen pages:** Click and drag it to the new page in the right column. The new page will expand in the main screen. Drop the icon onto the main screen.

- **Dock an app on the bottom dock:** Click and drag it down to drop it on the Bottom Dock. If there are already four icons on the bottom dock, you'll need to drag one off to make room for the new icon. Only four icons are allowed.

- **Create a new folder:** Drag and drop one icon onto another icon.

- **Move an app into an existing folder:** Drag and drop the icon onto the **Folder** icon.

- **Move an app out of a folder:** Click the folder to open it. Next, drag and drop the icon outside of that folder.

- **View another Home screen page:** Click that page in the right column.

- **Delete an app:** Click it, and then click the little **x** in the upper-left corner. You can only delete apps you have installed. You won't see an **x** on preinstalled apps like **iTunes**.

- **Delete a folder:** Remove all apps from that folder (drag them out) and it will disappear.

Removing or Reinstalling Apps

To remove an app from your iPhone, simply uncheck the box next to it and confirm your selection.

> **TIP:** Even if you delete an app from your iPhone, you can still reinstall that app by rechecking the box next to it, as long as you have chosen to sync apps. The app will be reloaded onto your iPhone during the next sync.

Syncing Media and More

Now let's look at how to set up an automatic sync for music, movies, iBooks, iTunes U content, and more.

> **CAUTION:** Make sure you're logged into **iTunes** with the same iTunes account you want to use on your iPhone as Digital Rights Management (DRM)-protected content (e.g., music, videos, and so on). Your content won't sync unless both accounts match. You can log out and log into the iTunes service on both your desktop and your iPhone if you have to make sure you are logged into the right accounts.

Syncing Ringtones

When you click the **Ringtones** tab, you can choose to sync your entire ringtone library or selected items:

1. Connect your iPhone to your computer, start **iTunes**, and click your iPhone in the left nav bar.

2. Click the **Ringtones** tab at the top of the main window.

3. Check the box next to **Sync Ringtones,** as shown to the right.

4. The default is to sync **All ringtones**. To sync only specific ones, click the radio button next to **Selected ringtones**.

5. When you are done with your selections, click the **Apply** button to start the ringtone sync.

> **TIP:** Learn how to assign ringtones to your contacts, purchase custom ringtones, and create your own ringtones from your music in Chapter 9: "Using the Phone."

Syncing Music

When you click the **Music** tab, you can choose to sync your entire music library or selected items.

> **CAUTION:** If you have manually transferred some music, music videos, or voice memos to your iPhone already, you'll receive a warning message that all existing content on your iPhone will be removed and replaced with the selected music library from your computer.

To sync music from your computer to your iPhone, follow these steps:

1. Connect your iPhone to your computer, start **iTunes**, and click your **iPhone** in the left nav bar.

2. Click the **Music** tab on the top of the main window.

3. Check the box next to **Sync Music**.

4. Click next to **Entire music library** only if you are sure your music library will not be too large for your iPhone.

5. Click next to **Selected playlists, artists, and genres** if you are unsure whether your music library is too large, or if you want to sync only specific playlists or artists:

    a. You can choose whether to include music videos and voice memos by checking those boxes.

    b. You can also automatically fill free space with songs.

> **CAUTION:** We don't recommend checking this option because it will take up all the space in your iPhone and leave no room for all those cool apps!

    c. Now check off any of the playlists or artists in the two columns on the bottom of the screen. You can even use the **Search** box at the top of the **Artists** column to search for particular artists.

6. When you are done with your selections, click the **Apply** button to start the music sync.

Syncing Movies

When you click the **Movies** tab, you can choose to sync specific, recent, or unwatched movies—or all of them.

To sync movies from your computer to your iPhone, follow these steps:

1. Connect your iPhone to your computer, start **iTunes**, and click your iPhone in the left nav bar.

2. Click the **Movies** tab on the top of the main window.

3. Check the box next to **Sync Movies** (see Figure 3–8).

4. If you'd like to sync recent or unwatched movies, check the box next to **Automatically include** and use the pull-down menu to select **All, 1 most recent, All unwatched, 5 most recent unwatched**, and so on.

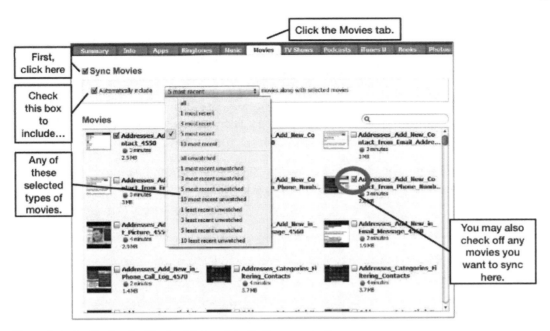

Figure 3-8. *Configuring the **Movies** tab to automatically sync selections*

5. If you selected any item besides **All**, you have the choice to sync specific movies or videos to your iPhone. Simply check the boxes next to the movies you want to include in the sync.

6. When you are done choosing movies, click the **Apply** button to save your settings and start the sync.

Syncing TV Shows

When you click the **TV Shows** tab, you can choose to sync specific, recent, or unwatched TV shows—or all of them.

To sync TV shows from your computer to your iPhone, follow these steps:

1. Connect your iPhone to your computer, start **iTunes**, and click your iPhone in the left nav bar.

2. Click the **TV Shows** tab on the top of the main window.

3. Check the box next to **Sync TV Shows**.

4. If you'd like to sync recent or unwatched TV shows, check the box next to **Automatically include** and use the pull-down menu to select **All, 1 newest, All unwatched, 5 oldest unwatched, 10 newest unwatched**, and so on.

5. Choose **All Shows** or **Selected Shows** next to **episodes of**.

6. If you choose **Selected Shows**, you can choose individual shows and even individual episodes in the two sections in the middle of the screen.

7. If you have playlists of TV shows, you can select those for inclusion by checking the boxes in the bottom section of the screen.

8. When you are done choosing individual TV shows, click the **Apply** button to save your settings and start the sync.

Syncing Podcasts

When you click the **Podcasts** tab, you can choose to sync specific, recent, or unplayed podcasts—or all of them.

> **TIP:** Podcasts are audio or video shows that are usually regularly scheduled (e.g., daily, weekly, or monthly). Most are free to subscribe to in the iTunes Store. When you subscribe and set up the auto sync as shown in this section, you'll receive all your favorite podcasts on your iPhone.
>
> Many of your favorite radio shows are recorded and broadcast as podcasts. We encourage you to check out the **Podcast** section of the iTunes Store to see what might interest you. You'll find podcasts of movie reviews, news shows, law school test reviews, game shows, old radio shows, educational content, and much more.

To sync podcasts from your computer to your iPhone, follow these steps.

1. Connect your iPhone to your computer, start **iTunes**, and click your **iPhone** in the left nav bar.

2. Click the **Podcasts** tab on the top of the main window.

3. Check the box next to **Sync Podcasts**.

4. If you'd like to sync recent or unplayed podcasts, check the box next to **Automatically include** and use the pull-down menu to select **All, 1 newest, All unplayed, 5 newest, 10 most recent unplayed**, and so on.

5. Choose **All Podcasts** or **Selected Podcasts** next to **episodes of**.

6. If you choose **Selected Podcasts**, you can choose individual podcasts and even individual episodes in the two sections in the middle of the screen.

7. If you have playlists of podcasts, you can select those for inclusion by checking the boxes in the bottom section of the screen.

8. When you are done choosing podcasts, click the **Apply** button to save your settings and start the sync.

> **TIP:** After you sync these podcasts, you can enjoy them by navigating to the **Podcasts** section of the **Music** app on your device.

Syncing iBooks and Audiobooks

When you click the **Books** tab, you can choose to sync all or selected books and audiobooks.

> **TIP:** Books on the iPhone are electronic versions of their paper cousins. They are in a specific electronic format called *ePub*. You can buy them in the iBookstore on the iPhone or acquire them from other locations and sync them to your iPhone using the steps described here. Books you acquire elsewhere must be unprotected or "DRM-free" in order to sync them to your iPhone. You read these books in the **iBooks** app or in other book reader apps on your iPhone. See Chapter 13: "iBooks and E-Books" to learn more.

To sync books or audiobooks between your computer and your iPhone, follow these steps:

1. Connect your iPhone to your computer, start **iTunes**, and click your **iPhone** in the left nav bar.

2. Click the **Books** tab on the top of the main window.

3. Check the boxes next to **Sync Books** and **Sync Audiobooks**.

4. If you'd like to sync all books, leave the default **All books** selection unchanged.

5. Otherwise, choose **Selected books** and make your choices by checking specific books in the window.

> **TIP:** In order to sync iBooks, PDF files, and other, similar documents to your iPhone, you need to first drag and drop your file from your computer into your iTunes library. Grab the file from any folder on your computer and drag and drop it right onto your library in the upper-left column in **iTunes**.

6. If you would like to sync all audiobooks, leave the default **All audiobooks** selection unchanged.

7. Otherwise, choose **Selected audiobooks** and make your choices by checking off specific audiobooks in the window below this selection item.

8. When you are done choosing individual books and audiobooks, click the **Apply** button to save your settings and start the sync.

> **TIP:** After you sync these books, you can enjoy them in the **iBooks** app on your device. You can listen to audiobooks in the **Music** app, where the **Audiobooks** tab is on the left side.

> **NOTE:** Audiobooks from Audible require that you first authorize your computer with your Audible account before you can sync them to your iPhone from your computer.

Sync Photos

When you click the **Photos** tab, you can choose to sync photos from all folders or selected folders, and you can even include videos.

> **TIP:** You can create a beautiful electronic picture frame and share your photos on the iPhone's stunning screen (see Chapter: 20: "Working with Photos"). You can even use your photos to set the background wallpaper and screen-lock wallpaper—see Chapter 8: "Personalize and Secure" for more information.

To sync photos from your computer to your iPhone, follow these steps:

1. Connect your iPhone to your computer, start **iTunes**, and click your iPhone in the left nav bar.

> **TIP:** Mac users can also sync photos using various criteria in **iPhoto**, including Events (time-based sync), Faces (person-based sync), and Places (location-based sync).

2. Click the **Photos** tab on the top of the main window.

3. Check the box next to **Sync Photos from**.

4. Click the pull-down menu next to **Sync Photos from** and select a folder from your computer where your photos are stored. If you want to grab all your photos, go to the highest folder level possible (e.g., **C:** on your Windows computer or your hard disk root directory "**/**" on your Apple Mac).

5. If you'd like to sync all photos from the selected folder on your computer, select **All folders**.

> **CAUTION:** Because your photo library on your computer may be too large to fit on your iPhone, be careful about checking **All folders**.

6. Otherwise, choose **Selected folders** and make your choices by checking specific folders in the window below.

7. You can also include any videos in the folders by checking the box next to **Include videos**.

8. When you are done choosing your photos to sync, click the **Apply** button to save your settings and start the sync.

9. When the sync starts, you'll see the status in the middle-top status window in **iTunes**.

Troubleshooting iTunes and the Sync

Sometimes **iTunes** does not behave exactly as you'd expect it to, so here are a few simple troubleshooting tips.

Check Out the Apple Knowledgebase for Helpful Articles

The first step when you're having a problem is to check out Apple's support pages, where you'll find lots of helpful information. On your iPhone or computer's web browser, go to this web page:

www.apple.com/support/iPhone/

Next, click a topic shown in the left nav bar.

iTunes Locked Up and Will Not Respond (Windows Computer)

Sometimes, **iTunes** will lock up and be completely unresponsive. Follow these steps if this happens on a Windows computer:

1. Bring up the **Windows Task Manager** by simultaneously pressing **Ctrl** + **Alt** + **Del** keys on your keyboard. The **Task Manager** should look something like Figure 3–9.

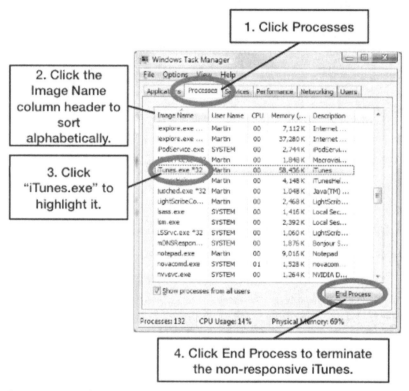

Figure 3–9. *Locating* iTunes.exe *in the **Windows Task Manager**, so you can terminate it*

2. To end the process, click **End process** from the pop-up window.

3. Now, **iTunes** should be forced to close.

4. Try restarting **iTunes**.

5. If **iTunes** will not start or locks up again, then reboot your computer and try again.

iTunes Locked Up and Will Not Respond (Mac Computer)

If you're using a Mac, then follow these steps if the **iTunes** app locks up and is completely unresponsive:

> **TIP:** Pressing **Command** + **Option** + **Escape** is the shortcut to bring up the **Force Quit Applications** window (see Figure 3–10).

1. Click the **iTunes** menu at the top.

2. Click **Quit iTunes.**

3. If that doesn't work, go to any other program and click the small **Apple** logo in the upper left corner of your Mac.

Click **Force Quit** and the list of running programs will be displayed.

4.

5. Highlight **iTunes** and click the **Force Quit** button.

6. If this does not help, try restarting your Mac.

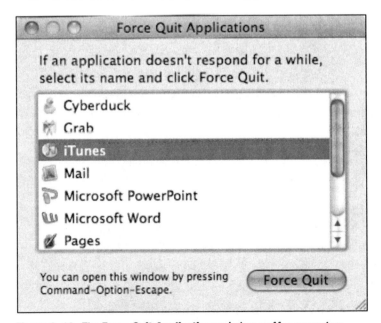

Figure 3–10. *The **Force Quit Applications** window on Mac computers*

Updating Your iPhone Operating System

With iOS 5 you can now update your iPhone operating system on-device. There are faster, more efficient update methods for doing this, and we recommend you use them whenever possible. If you need to re-install the entire OS, however, or want to upgrade via **iTunes** instead, this section will explain how to do so.

> **NOTE:** Do this update when you won't mind being without your iPhone for 30 minutes or more, depending on the amount of information on your iPhone and the speed of your computer and Internet connection.

Normally, **iTunes** will automatically check for updates on a set schedule, about every two weeks. If no update is found, **iTunes** will tell you when it will check for another update. Follow these steps to use **iTunes** to manually update your iPhone:

1. Start **iTunes**.

2. Connect your iPhone to your computer.

3. Click your iPhone listed under **DEVICES** in the left nav bar.

4. Click the **Summary** tab in the top nav bar.

5. Click the **Check for Update** button in the center of the screen in the **Version** section.

6. If you have the latest version, you'll see a pop-up window saying something like this: "This version of the iPhone software (5.0) is the current version." Click **OK** to close the window. You are done with the update process.

7. If you don't have the latest version of **iTunes**, a window will tell you a new version is available and ask if you would like to update. Click **Yes** or **Update** to do so.

8. **iTunes** will take you through a few screens that describe the update and ask you to agree to the software license. If you agree, click **Next** and **Agree** to download the latest iOS software from Apple. This will take about five to ten minutes.

> **TIP:** We show you all the screens you might see in this update process in the "Reinstalling the iPhone Operating System" section of Chapter 26: "Troubleshooting."

9. Next, **iTunes** will back up your iPhone, a process that might take ten minutes or more if your iPhone is filled with data.

10. Now the new iOS will be installed, and your iPhone will be erased.

11. Finally, you'll be shown a screen asking you to do one of the following:

    a. **Set up as a new iPhone:** Choose this if you want to erase all your data after the update process.

    b. **Restore from the backup of:** Choose this to make sure you select the correct backup file (usually the most recent one).

    At this point, your iPhone will be restored or set up as selected.

12. If you have locked your SIM card, then you will need to enter the four-digit PIN code required to unlock it.

> **CAUTION:** If you have locked your SIM card, then you will need to enter the four-digit unlock code after the update is installed. If you've forgotten the SIM unlock code, then you can use the PUK code to unlock the SIM (you need to get that from your wireless carrier). See the "Setting Security on Your SIM Card" section in Chapter 9: "Using the Phone" for more information.

13. Your iPhone OS update Is complete.

Other Sync Methods

You can navigate to the **Mail**, **Contacts**, **Calendar** app in your **Settings** app on your iPhone to set up and use Exchange. The next section will explain how to do so.

Setting Up Your Google or Exchange Account on Your Device

Use the following steps to set up the wireless sync for either your Exchange account or your Google contacts and calendar:

1. Touch the **Settings** icon.

2. Touch **Mail, Contacts, Calendar**.

3. You'll see a list of your email accounts and, below that, the **Add Account** option.

   If you have no accounts set up, you will see only **Add Account**. In either case, tap **Add Account.**

4. On the next screen, choose **Microsoft Exchange**.

> **NOTE:** You should choose **Microsoft Exchange** if you want to have the wireless sync with your Google Contacts and Calendar. If you select **Gmail**, you will not be able to sync wirelessly with your Google Contacts.

5. Type your email address.

> **TIP:** To type the .com (or .net, .edu, .org, etc.) in the email address, press and hold the **Period** (.) key until you see the **.com** key appear above it. Slide over and press **.com**.
>
>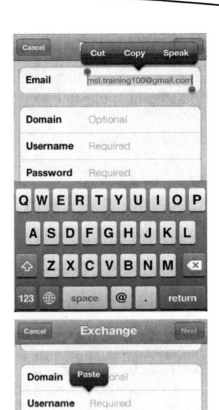

> **TIP:** Since your email address is also usually your username, save yourself some time by copying and pasting it.

6. Copy and paste your email address into the **Username** field (This works well when your username is the same as your email or if it is the same as the first part of your email address before the @ sign):

    a. Touch and hold the **Email** field, then lift your finger to see the black pop-up appear above it.

    b. Tap **Select All**.

    c. Tap **Copy**.

    d. Touch and hold the **Username** field, then lift your fingerto see the pop-up appear. Tap **Paste**.

7. Leave the **Domain** blank. Type your **Password.** If you want, you can adjust the **Description** of the account, which defaults to your email address.

8. Tap the **Next** button in the upper-right corner.

9. You may see an **Unable to Verify Certificate** dialog. If you do see it, click **Accept** to continue.

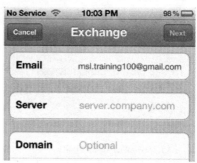

10. In the **Server** field, type **m.google.com** to sync to Google. Otherwise, if you are setting up your Exchange Server account, enter that server address.

11. Click **Next** in the upper-right corner.

12. On this screen you have the option to set the wireless sync for **Mail, Contacts,** and **Calendars** to **ON** or **OFF**. For each sync you'd like to turn on, tap the switch to change it to **ON**.

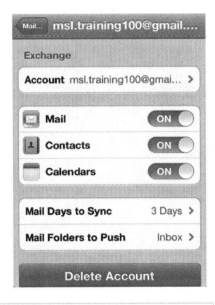

NOTE: If you already have contacts or calendar items on your iPhone, you may see some warnings appear. Your choices are to **Keep on My iPhone** or **Delete**. If you choose **Cancel**, your iPhone stops setting up your Exchange account. Select **Keep on My iPhone** to keep all existing contacts and calendar events on your iPhone. These items will not end up on your Exchange account—they will stay on your iPhone.

Chapter 4

Connect to the Network

We live in a connected world. Wireless Internet (Wi-Fi) access has become the rule, not the exception—and chances are you're already using Wi-Fi at your home or office. You can use it to connect your iPhone to the Internet. And, since your iPhone also has a 3G cellular radio, you can also connect to the Internet anywhere you have cellular data coverage—a much wider area than Wi-Fi networks.

In this chapter, we'll talk about the differences between the two types of connections for your iPhone: Wi-Fi (wireless local area network) and 3G (cellular service—the wide area data network used by your mobile phone). We'll show you all the ways to get connected or disconnected from these two types of networks. For example, there will be times you will want to disable or turn off your 3G connection and only use Wi-Fi to save money in data connection charges.

We will also show you how to get ready for traveling internationally with your iPhone— what you need to do before, during, and after your trip so you don't get surprised with a very large phone bill when you return home.

We will also show you how to use *Internet Tethering*, the ability to make your iPhone become an Internet hub for your laptop, whether it's a PC or Mac. This is a great feature to use when you don't have any other way to connect your laptop to the Internet.

Finally, if you work at an organization with a VPN (*Virtual Private Network*), we will show you how to get connected to that network.

What Can I Do When I'm Connected to a Wi-Fi or 3G Network?

Here are some of the things you can do when connected to a Wi-Fi or 3G network:

- Access and download apps (programs) from the App Store.
- Access and download music, videos, podcasts, and more from the **iTunes** app on your iPhone.
- Browse the web using **Safari**.

- Send and receive email messages.

- Use social networking sites that require an Internet connection like Facebook, Twitter, and so on.

- Play games that use a live Internet connection.

- Do anything else that requires an Internet connection.

Wi-Fi Connections

Every iPhone comes with Wi-Fi capability built in, so let's take a look at getting connected to the Wi-Fi network. Things to consider about Wi-Fi connections include the following:

- There is no additional cost for network access and data downloads (if you are using your iPhone in your home, office, or a free Wi-Fi hotspot).

- Wi-Fi tends to be faster than a cellular data 3G connection.

- More and more places, including some airplanes, provide Wi-Fi access, but you may have to pay a one-time or monthly service fee.

> **NOTE**: iPhone has support for the faster, longer range 802.11n standard. However, it only supports 802.11n on the more crowded 2.4 MHz band, not the less crowded 5 MHz band. If you want to use iPhone with your 802.11n Wi-Fi router, make sure it's either a dual-band router or set the router to 2.4 MHz.

Connecting to a Wi-Fi Network

To set up your Wi-Fi connection, follow these steps:

1. Tap the **Settings** icon.

2. Tap **Wi-Fi** near the top.

3. Make sure the **Wi-Fi** switch is set to **ON**. If it is currently **OFF**, then tap it to turn it **ON**.

4. Once Wi-Fi is **ON**, the iPhone will automatically start looking for wireless networks.

5. The list of accessible networks is shown below the **Choose a Network...** option. This screenshot shows that we have one network available.

6. To connect to any network listed, just touch the network name. If the network is unsecure (does not have a **Lock** icon), you will be connected automatically.

Connecting at a Public Wi-Fi Hotspot with Web Login

In some locations where they offer free Wi-Fi networks, such as coffee shops, hotels, or restaurants; you will see a pop-up window appear as soon as your iPhone comes into contact with the network. In these cases, simply tap the network name. You may be brought to a **Safari** browser screen to complete your login to the network:

1. If you see a pop-up window similar to the one shown, tap the network name you wish to join. In the case to the right, we tap the **Panera** network.

2. In some cases, you may see a **Safari** window pop up, which can be quite confusing because it is so small on your iPhone's screen. You need to use the double-tap or pinch-open gesture (see the Quick Start Guide for help) to zoom in on the Web page. You are looking for a button that says **Login**, **Agree**, or something similar. Tap that button to complete the connection.

NOTE: Some places, like coffee shops, use a web-based login instead of a username/password screen. In those cases, when you click the network (or try to use **Safari**), your iPhone will open a browser screen, and you'll see the web page along with your login options.

Secure Wi-Fi Networks—Entering a Password

Some Wi-Fi networks require a password to connect. This is set when the network administrator creates the wireless network. You will have to know the exact password, including whether it is case-sensitive.

If the network does require a password, then you will be taken to the **Enter Password** screen. Type the password exactly as given to you and press the **Enter** key on the on-screen keyboard (which is now labeled **Join**).

On the **Network** screen, you'll see a **Checkmark** icon showing that you are connected to the network.

> **TIP:** You can paste into the password dialog; so for longer, random passwords, you can transfer
> them to your iPhone (in an email message) and just copy and paste them. Just remember to
> delete the email immediately afterwards, so you can keep things secure. Tap and hold the
> password in the mail message, select it, and then tap **Copy**. In the Wi-Fi network **Password**
> field, tap and then select **Paste**.

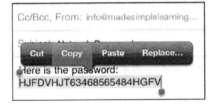 

Switching to a Different Wi-Fi Network

At times you may want to change your active Wi-Fi network. This might occur if you are
in a hotel, apartment, or other place where the network selected by the iPhone is not the
strongest network, or you want to use a secure network instead of an unsecure one.

To switch from the currently selected Wi-Fi network, tap the **Settings** icon, touch **Wi-Fi**,
and then touch the name of the Wi-Fi network you want to join. If that network requires a
password, you'll need to enter it to join.

Once you type the correct password (or if you touched an open network), your iPhone
will join that network.

Verifying Your Wi-Fi Connection

It is easy to see if you are connected to a network (and which one) by looking next to the **Wi-Fi** setting in your main **Settings** screen. Follow these steps to check your Wi-Fi connection status:

1. Tap your **Settings** icon.

2. Look next to the **Wi-Fi** option at the top:

    ■   If you see **Not Connected**, you do not have an active Wi-Fi connection.

    ■   If you see some other name, such as **Panera**, then you are connected to that Wi-Fi network.

Advanced Wi-Fi Options (Hidden or Undiscoverable Networks)

Sometimes you may not be able to see the network you want to join because the name has been hidden (the SSID is not being broadcast) by the network administrator. Next, you will learn how to join such networks on your iPhone. Once you have joined such a network, you will join that network automatically the next time you come into contact with it—with no prompt from your iPhone. You can also tell your iPhone to ask every time it joins a network; we will show you how to do that, as well. Sometimes you may want to erase or forget a network. For example, perhaps you were at a one-time convention and want to get rid of the associated network—you'll learn how to do that, too.

Why Can't I See the Wi-Fi Network I Want to Join?

Sometimes, for security reasons, people don't make their networks discoverable (they hide the network name, called the SSID), and you have to manually enter the name and security options to connect to it.

As you can see, your list of available networks includes Other.

1. Tap the **Other** button, and you can manually enter the name of a network you would like to join.

2. Type in the Wi-Fi network **Name**.

3. Tap the **Security** tab.

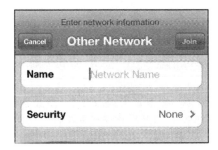

4. Choose which type of security is being used on that network. If you are unsure, you'll need to find out from the network administrator.

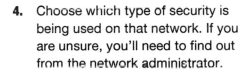

When you have the information you need, enter it along with the proper password, and this new network will be saved to your network list for future access.

Reconnecting to Previously Joined Wi-Fi Networks

The nice thing about the iPhone is that, when you return to an area with a Wi-Fi network you previously joined (whether it was an open or a secure, password-protected, network), your iPhone will automatically join the network again without asking you first. However, you can turn off this automatic-joining feature, as described in the next section.

The Ask to Join Networks Main Switch

There is a main **Ask to Join Networks** switch, which is set to **ON** by default. Known networks are joined automatically, but this only takes effect if no known networks are available. With this switch set to **ON**, you will be asked to join visible Wi-Fi networks. If networks are available that are not known to you, you will be asked before being connected.

If the switch is set to **OFF**, you will have to manually join unknown networks.

Why might you want to turn off this feature?

Doing so could be a good security measure if, for example, you don't want your kids to be able to join a wireless network on the iPhone without your knowledge.

It can also be annoying if your iPhone is continuously popping up the **Join Network** connector screen in areas where you don't want to join Wi-Fi, such as when traveling through a place with many hotspots.

Ask to Join and Ask to Login Switch on Each Network

Sometimes, you may find that a particular Wi-Fi network has additional switches that override the main **Ask to Join Networks** switch. Tap the little blue **Arrow** icon  next to the network name to see details about this Wi-Fi network. **Auto-Join** and **Auto-Login** are set to **ON** by default.

To disable **Auto-Join** or **Auto-Login**, tap each switch to set it to **OFF**.

Forget (or Erase) a Network

If you find that you no longer want to connect to a network on your list, you can **Forget it**—i.e., take it off your list of networks. Follow these steps to do so:

1. Tap the **Settings** icon.

2. Tap **Wi-Fi** to see your list of networks.

3. Tap the small blue **Arrow** 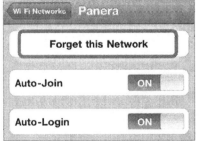 next to the network you want to forget in order to see the screen shown here.

4. Tap **Forget this Network** at the top of the screen.

5. You will be prompted with a warning. Just touch **Forget** and the network will no longer show up on your list.

Cellular Data Connection

Your iPhone can also connect to the cellular data network—the same network you connect to with other mobile phones. Here are things to consider about cellular data connections:

- They provide wider availability than a Wi-Fi connection—you can connect to 3G in a car or away from a city, whereas Wi-Fi is not typically available in these locations.

- There are extra monthly service fees for access to the cellular data network.

NOTE: Check with your local wireless carrier for iPhone data plan pricing in your country.

Select and Monitor Your Cellular Data Usage

When you purchased your iPhone, you had to select a cellular data plan from your wireless carrier. For the iPhone in the US, you can currently choose between AT&T, Verizon, and Sprint. If you selected one plan and now wish to try another plan, contact your carrier—you may be allowed to switch data plans.

TIP: Saving Money on Data Charges

You might be able to save yourself some money with cellular data plan charges by doing the following:

- Always use Wi-Fi when possible.

- Start with a lower cost cellular data plan (e.g., US $15 for 200 MB on AT&T – as of publishing time).

- Monitor your cellular data usage throughout the month to make sure you are not going to exceed the lower cost data plan.

You may find that you can live with the lower cost plan if you use Wi-Fi for most of your data needs.

Follow these steps to check your current cellular data usage:

1. Tap the **Settings** icon.

2. Tap **General**.

3. Tap **Usage**.

4. Scroll to the bottom and tap **Cellular Usage**.

5. Your total data usage will be the sum of the **Sent** and **Received** valuesIf you want to clear out the statistics, tap the **Reset Statistics** button at the bottom of the screen.

Usage	Cellular Usage	
Call Time		
Current Period		17 Hours, 16 Min.
Lifetime		17 Hours, 16 Min.
Cellular Network Data		
Sent		283 MB
Received		1.7 GB
Tether Data		
Sent		22.5 MB
Received		199 MB

> **NOTE:** The iPhone will notify you when you have 20%, 10%, and 0% left on your monthly data plan. It will also give you the option of renewing that plan or upgrading to a higher data plan, if available.

International Travel: Things to Do Before You Go

Depending on which country you are visiting and your current iPhone voice and data plan, you may be well prepared for international travel. However, it is quite likely that your basic iPhone data and phone plans will either not work or cause you to spend a lot more money on data and voice roaming charges.

We always recommend that you call your phone service provider well in advance of a trip to see whether there is an international feature you can turn on for your iPhone as you travel.

Avoiding a Shockingly Large Bill

One thing you want to avoid when traveling is returning home to an unusually high voice or data roaming charge phone bill. For example, we have heard of people who returned home after a trip abroad to find a phone bill totaling $1,000 or more in a single month's data and voice roaming charges. In the sections that follow, we will show you how to take steps before, during, and after your trip to help avoid surprise charges.

These simple steps can help you ensure that your iPhone will successfully and economically connect to the local country's network—no matter where you might be in the world.

Step 1: Call Your Phone Company

You should contact the phone company that supplies your iPhone before you leave home. When you call, you should check the following things:

- Learn about any voice and data roaming charges you might incur when traveling. Be specific about each country you plan to visit.

- Check on any temporary international rate plans that you might be able to activate before you leave. Sometimes, these special plans will cost an additional US $10 or $20 up front, but save you hundreds in additional charges.

■ If you use email, SMS Text, MMS or picture messaging, web browsing, and any other data services, then you will also want to specifically ask about whether any of these services are charged separately when traveling abroad. Usually, text and picture messaging are additional charges.

You might be able to find some information on your phone company's web site, but usually you need to call them.

Step 2: Check If You Can Use an International SIM Card

In some cases, your iPhone wireless company won't offer special deals on international data roaming plans—or its rates will be unreasonably high. In these cases, you may want to ask your phone company to unlock your iPhone, so you can insert a SIM card purchased in the country you're visiting.

> **NOTE**: Apple sells an unlocked, SIM-free iPhone in many countries, including the US, Canada, and the UK. If you are a frequent traveler, an officially unlocked iPhone might be something to consider.

Inserting a local SIM card will eliminate or greatly reduce data and voice roaming charges. However, you should carefully check the cost of placing and receiving international calls on that SIM card.

Using an international SIM card might save you hundreds of dollars, but it's best to do some web research or try to talk to someone who has recently traveled to the same country for advice before settling on that approach.

> **TIP:** If you are going to a country without a good rate plan and your carrier will not unlock your iPhone, you might want to consider renting or purchasing a local cell phone. You may be able to rent a phone for about US $30 / week with much lower voice calling rates. Many cell phone rental companies exist, such as Travel Cell, Mobal, and Cellular Abroad. (Do a web search for "International Cell Phone Rental" to find more information.)

You may also want to do a web search for traveling to countries X, Y, and Z with your iPhone.

> **TIP:** Put a paperclip in your luggage—if you lose the SIM removal tool that came with your unlocked iPhone, you will need it to remove and replace the SIM card in your iPhone.

Step 3: Do Any Data Intensive Stuff Prior to Leaving

You should do all your data-intensive activities before you leave your home country, if possible. If you have a lot of apps that need updating, do that before you leave. Also, look for and add any apps that you might need before your trip. You should also download any large files, such as movies, videos, or music before you leave.

Flying on an Airplane: Airplane Mode

Often when you are flying on an airplane, the flight crew will ask you to turn off all portable electronic devices for takeoff and landing. Then, when you get to a certain altitude, the crew will say that "all approved electronic devices" can be turned back on.

If you need to turn off your iPhone completely, press and hold the **Power** button on the top-right edge, and then **Slide to Power Off** with your finger.

In order to enable **Airplane Mode**, follow these steps:

1. Tap the **Settings** icon.

2. Set the switch next to **Airplane Mode** in the top of the left column to **ON.**

3. Notice that the Wi-Fi is automatically turned **OFF** and that your phone will not work.

> **TIP:** Some airlines have in-flight Wi-Fi networks. On those flights, you may want to turn your Wi-Fi back **ON** at the appropriate time.

You can turn your Wi-Fi connection **OFF** or **ON** by following these steps:

1. Tap the **Settings** icon.

2. Tap **Wi-Fi** near the top of the screen.

3. To enable the Wi-Fi connections, set the switch next to **Wi-Fi** in the top of the page to **ON**.

4. To disable Wi-Fi, set the same switch to **OFF**.

5. Select the Wi-Fi network and follow the steps given by the flight attendant to get connected.

International Travel: When You Arrive

Once you've completed the steps described so far to prepare for your trip, you will need to address some additional issues when you get to your destination. The next sections explain the things you need to keep in mind after you arrive at your destination.

Step 1: Make Sure the Time Zone Is Correct

When you arrive, you will need to make sure your iPhone is displaying the correct local time. Usually, your iPhone will auto-update your time zone when you arrive at a new destination. If it doesn't, you can manually adjust the time zone (see the "Setting Your Date and Time" section in Chapter 1: "Getting Started").

Step 2: Buy and Insert Your International SIM Card

NOTE: This step will only work if the carrier in the country you're visiting offers an iPhone, and your iPhone has been unlocked. Currently, the US carrier AT&T will not unlock iPhone devices. Your fallback plan, especially if you need to make a lot of local in-country calls, is to rent or buy an inexpensive pre-paid mobile phone and reserve your iPhone use for Wi-Fi connections only.

If you have determined that you can use an international SIM card, then you should purchase and insert it when you arrive. We show you how to remove the SIM card tray in Chapter 1. You need to use Apple's SIM removal tool or a paperclip to remove this card.

CAUTION: The iPhone uses a MicroSIM, whereas many other phones use a MiniSIM. This means you'll most likely need to find an international carrier that also has the iPhone available on their network.

Step 3: Reset Your Data Usage When You Land

As soon as you land, you should reset your data usage on your iPhone. This will allow you to keep close track of the amount of wireless data you are using overseas. For example, if you purchased a 20 MB plan, you want to make sure you don't go over that amount. A brief test using **Maps** for about 1 minute in the car resulted in almost 1 MB of data usage. So be careful and try not to use extremely data-intensive apps such as **Maps** while roaming.

We explained exactly how to reset your usage earlier in this chapter's "Select and Monitor Your Cellular Data Usage" section.

> **TIP:** Once you reset your usage, you will want to return to this screen from time to time to see your current usage. You have to add the **Sent** and **Received** values together to get your total usage. If your data usage was 417 MB total—that would cost $8,340 at the $20/MB rate in effect without an international data plan!

Step 4: Turn Off Data Roaming If It's Too Expensive

If you were unable to find an international SIM card—or if you were unable to find the cost of data roaming from your local phone company—then you might want to turn off the data roaming altogether.

This won't stop you from using Wi-Fi; however, it will make sure you don't get any nasty surprises from checking email or accidentally launching a data hungry app while you're away.

> **NOTE: Data Roaming** is usually set to **OFF** by default, but it always makes sense to double-check—just in case—before you leave on a trip.

Follow these steps to set **Data Roaming** to **OFF**:

1. Tap the **Settings** icon.

2. Tap **General**.

3. Tap **Network**.

4. Set the switch next to **Data Roaming** to **OFF**.

Setting the **Data Roaming** value to **OFF** should help you avoid any potentially exorbitant data roaming charges. (You still need to worry about voice roaming charges, but at least you can control those by watching how much you talk on your phone.)

The nice part about setting the **Cellular Data** to **ON** and **Data Roaming** to **OFF** is that you can still enjoy all your data services until the time you leave your home country and immediately when you return—without making any other changes. Of course, you can also use your Wi-Fi network connection any time.

Step 5: Use Wi-Fi When Possible

One good way to save money on cellular data plans is to use local Wi-Fi networks whenever possible, especially when you are going to browse the Web or download large amounts of email or large apps.

> **TIP:** You may be able to find free Wi-Fi networks at Internet cafés, regular coffee shops, public libraries, some hotel lobbies, and Apple retail stores.

International Travel: Returning Home

As you did when you arrived at your travel destination, you will need to make a few changes to your iPhone's settings once you arrive back home before your device will work as expected.

Step 1: Make Sure the Time Zone Is Correct

When you return to your home country, you will need to verify your iPhone is displaying the correct local time. Usually, your iPhone will auto-update your time zone when you arrive back home. However, if it doesn't, you can manually adjust the time zone (see the "Setting Your Date and Time" section in Chapter 1: "Getting Started").

Step 2: Turn Off Your Special International Rate Plan

The final step is optional. If you have activated some sort of special international roaming rate plan with your iPhone wireless company, and you do not need it anymore, then contact the company to turn it off to save yourself some money.

Using all the steps we describe before, during, and after your trip should help you be able to use your iPhone successfully and economically as you travel internationally.

Personal Hotspot

One of the nice features on your iPhone is that you can use it to connect your laptop—PC or Mac—to the Internet. This feature is called *Personal Hotspot*, and it's very useful if you happen to be traveling away from a Wi-Fi network, but are still within wireless cellular data coverage with your iPhone. This greatly expands the places that you can use your laptop to connect to the Internet.

Personal Hotspot vs. Tethering

Connecting your laptop or other device to the Internet over your iPhone's data plan used to be called *tethering*, and it only worked via Bluetooth or by plugging in the USB Dock cable.

Personal Hotspot is similar to tethering; but instead of using Bluetooth or USB, it turns your iPhone into a small, portable Wi-Fi router that can connect multiple devices to the Internet. For example, you might connect your laptop, your friend's laptop, and your iPad. (The exact number of devices that can connect over Personal Hotspot will depend on your carrier, but it's typically four or five.)

> **TIP:** Old-style tethering over Bluetooth and the USB Dock cable are still available options if, for some reason, you don't want to use the Personal Hotspot feature.

Step 1: Contact Your Phone Company

Internet tethering may require a separate plan to be purchased and activated from your phone company. Call your phone company or check on its web site to turn on the Mobile Hotspot or Tethering plan.

> **TIP:** You may be able to save yourself some money by turning off the Personal Hotspot or Tethering plan when you no longer need it. Check with your phone company to find out if there are any penalties or hidden charges for turning off the Tethering plan at a later date.

Step 2: Enable Personal Hotspot on Your iPhone

After you have purchased or activated the Personal Hotspot or Mobile Hotspot from your phone company, you are ready to set it up on your iPhone:

1. Tap the **Settings** icon.

2. Tap **General**.

3. Tap **Network**.

4. Scroll down and tap **Set Up Personal Hotspot**. (If you have already set this up, or if it was set up for you, then you will see **Personal Hotspot** instead.)

5. If you have not yet set up the plan—or the plan you purchased has not yet been activated on your iPhone—you will see a pop-up message similar to this one. If you did purchase the plan, then you may need to wait a little while for the plan to be activated.

6. If your plan has been activated, you should see the **Personal Hotspot** option right on the main **Settings** screen. Tap it.

7. Tap the switch next to **Personal Hotspot** to set it to **ON**.

8. Your iPhone will automatically generate a **Wi-Fi Password** for you. If you're okay with this password, skip ahead to the next section.

9. If you want to change the password, tap **Wi-Fi Password**.

10. Enter your new **Password**. Make sure it contains at least eight characters. A mixture of numbers, uppercase and lowercase letters, and punctuation is best.

Step 3: Connect to Your iPhone Personal Hotspot

Your iPhone is now a small, mobile Wi-Fi router; and you can connect your Mac or Windows PC, your iPad, or any other Wi-Fi enabled device to your iPhone exactly as you connect to your home, business, or school Wi-Fi network. Follow these steps to do so:

1. Check for available Wi-Fi networks on your device.

2. Click the name of your iPhone.

3. Enter the Wi-Fi Password.

If everything works properly, you'll see a blue bar appear on the top of your iPhone, along with the number of devices connected.

Step 4: Set Up Networking on Your Computer

After you have connected your iPhone to your computer, your Windows or Mac computer should recognize your iPhone as a new Internet connection and help you set it up automatically. If your computer does not recognize the iPhone immediately, then go into your **Network** settings on your computer and look for the iPhone as an available connection type.

VPN: Virtual Private Network

Your organization may have what is called a VPN, or *Virtual Private Network*. A VPN allows you to securely connect your iPhone, laptop, or other device to the corporate network.

Getting Connected

In order to get connected, you need to determine the type of VPN and specific login instructions from your organization's help desk or network administrator. Then, you will type these login details into the **VPN** area in the **Settings** app on your iPhone.

> **TIP:** You can probably save yourself a call to the help desk and skip Step 1 if you have already set up your computer to connect to the VPN. This is because your iPhone will most likely use the same VPN login credentials as your computer.
>
> Also, some carriers may require a business account in order to use a VPN over their 3G network. If all your settings look correct and the VPN is still not working, check with your carrier.

Step 1: Contact Your Organization's Help Desk

You need to ask your help desk or VPN administrator for the details about how to log into the VPN. Your iPhone can currently connect with the following types of VPNs: **L2TP**, **PPTP**, and **IPSec** (Cisco). You also need to know if your VPN uses a **Proxy** and whether the configuration is manual or automatic.

Step 2: Set Up the VPN Connection on Your iPhone

Armed with the login instructions and type of VPN connection, you are ready to connect with your iPhone:

1. Tap the **Settings** icon.

2. Tap **General**.

3. Tap **Network**.

4. Scroll down to the bottom of the screen and tap **VPN**.

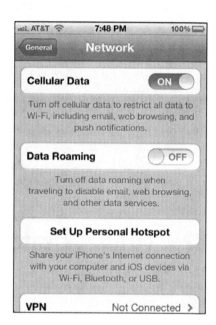

5. On the **VPN** screen, tap the switch next to the **VPN** option to set it to **ON**. You should then be taken to the **Add Configuration** screen. If not, then tap **Add VPN Configuration** at the bottom to set up a new VPN connection.

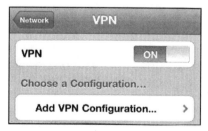

6. The **Add Configuration** screen is where you set up your VPN login details, using the information from your help desk or VPN administrator.

7. If your VPN is an **L2TP** type, then you would use the screen shown here. Scroll to the bottom and enter the **Proxy** information as required.

8. If your VPN is a **PPTP** type, then you would tap **PPTP** at the top and use the screen shown here. Scroll to the bottom and enter the **Proxy** Information as required.

9. If your VPN is an **IPSec** (Cisco) type, then you would tap **IPSec** and use the screen shown here. Scroll to the bottom and enter the **Proxy** information as required.

10. When you are done with your setup, tap the **Save** button in the upper-right corner.

11. If you have trouble logging in, make sure you are in a strong wireless coverage area and verify you have typed all your login credentials correctly. It can be difficult when passwords disappear as you type them. You may want to try re-typing passwords and server information before calling the help desk.

Knowing When You Are Connected to a VPN Network

You will see a small **VPN** icon  just to the right of your network connection status display. You will know that you are securely connected to the VPN network *only* when you see this icon.

Switching VPN Networks

You may have several VPN networks to which you need to connect. You can select between different VPN configurations on your iPhone by following these steps:

1. Tap the **Settings** icon.

2. Tap **General**.

3. Tap **Network**.

4. Scroll down to the bottom of the screen and tap **VPN**.

5. On the VPN screen, tap a different **VPN configuration** to connect to it. Don't tap the blue **Circle** icon with the > symbol, unless you want to change the login settings for that network.

Chapter 5

AirPlay and Bluetooth

In this chapter, we will show you how to connect your iPhone with any AirPlay– or Bluetooth–compatible device, whether it's an Apple TV, stereo speakers, or a wireless headset.

Understanding AirPlay

AirPlay is Apple's proprietary video and audio streaming protocol. AirPlay works over your local home, school, or office Wi-Fi network. Before you can use AirPlay with the iPhone, you have to make sure all your devices are connected to the same Wi-Fi network.

AirPlay Devices That Work with the iPhone

At the time of writing, only the 2010 model Apple TV supports AirPlay video streaming. With it, you can stream content right from your IPhone to your big screen TV to share with business colleagues, friends, and family alike.

Apple's AirPort Express Wi-Fi router has an audio out jack that can be connected to speakers for AirPlay audio. Various third-party accessory makers are also introducing AirPlay–compatible speakers. With AirPlay, you can remotely control the playback and volume right from your iPhone.

Setting Up and Using AirPlay

AirPlay is built right into the iPhone. As long as all your devices are connected to the same Wi-Fi network, no additional setup is needed.

Several of the built-in iPhone apps support AirPlay, including **Videos**, **Music**, and **YouTube**. Several App Store apps that use Apple's default media player (e.g., **Air Video**) also support AirPlay. Follow these steps to use AirPlay from an app that supports the feature:

1. Tap the blue **AirPlay** icon at the lower-right corner of the screen.

2. Choose from the list of available devices for streaming your music.

3. To switch the video or music back to your iPhone, just tap the **AirPlay** icon again and choose **iPhone** from the list.

NOTE: The **AirPlay** icon will bring up a list of both Bluetooth and Wi-Fi connected devices. See the next section for more on Bluetooth.

You can select **Apple TV** by tapping it. Now your music or video will now start to play from the selected AirPlay device. You can verify this by touching the **AirPlay** icon on the screen once more. You should see a **Checkmark** icon next to the new AirPlay Stereo Bluetooth device, and you should hear your music coming from that sound source, as well.

TIP: To save battery life on your iPhone, turn off the screen by pressing the **Sleep** button while streaming AirPlay content to another device. Your music or video will continue to play, but you won't be wasting battery life by keeping your screen lit.

AirPlay Mirroring

The current iPhone does more than let you stream video or music from your iPhone to an Apple TV; it also lets you share the screen of any app—from a business presentation at work, to a board game with the family, to a video call with distant relatives. Being able to take **Keynote** or **Infinity Blade** or **FaceTime** from the small iPhone screen to a giant television set really transforms what was an intimate personal experience into a fun social activity.

Follow these steps to use the AirPlay Mirroring feature:

1. Tap the app you want to mirror. For this example, we're using **Infinity Blade.**

2. Once the app has launched, double-click the Home button to bring up the Fast App Switcher.

3. Swipe from left to right to get to the audio/video controls. (They're all the way at the end, so keep swiping until you can't swipe any more.)

4. Tap the **AirPlay button** to bring up the list of AirPlay–enabled devices on your Wi-Fi network.

5. Select **Apple TV**.

6. Toggle the **Airplay Mirroring** switch to **ON**.

7. Click the **Home** button again to return to your app.

8. You should now see **Infinity Blade** on the big screen. Let 'em have it!

To stop AirPlay Mirroring, repeat the same procedure and choose iPhone from the device list.

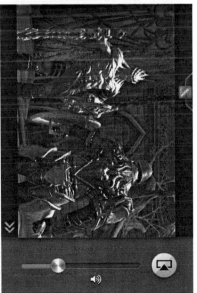

Understanding Bluetooth

Apple's latest iPhone supports Bluetooth 4.0, which includes traditional Bluetooth functionality, along with more advanced high speed and low power capabilities. This means you can talk or listen to music with better quality for longer than ever before.

With many states passing laws that require motorists to use a hands-free method for talking on their phones, using Bluetooth is now more of a necessity than ever. Thanks to the technology known as A2DP, you can also stream your music to a Bluetooth–capable stereo device, including many newer automotive stereos and car kits.

> **NOTE:** You must have a third-party Bluetooth–capable adapter or Bluetooth–capable stereo to stream your music via Bluetooth technology.

Understanding Bluetooth

Bluetooth allows your iPhone to communicate with things wirelessly. Bluetooth is a small radio that transmits from each device. Before you can use a peripheral with the iPhone, you have to pair that device with your iPhone. Many Bluetooth devices can be used up to 30 feet away from the iPhone.

Bluetooth Devices that Work with the iPhone

Among other things, the iPhone works with Bluetooth headphones, Bluetooth stereo systems and adapters, Bluetooth keyboards, Bluetooth car stereo systems, Bluetooth headsets, and hands-free devices. The iPhone supports A2DP, which is known as Stereo Bluetooth; and AVRCP, which allows you to remotely control playback and volume.

Pairing with a Bluetooth Device

Your primary uses for Bluetooth might be with Bluetooth headphones, Bluetooth stereo adapters, or a Bluetooth headset. Any Bluetooth headphones should work well with your iPhone. To start using any Bluetooth device, you need to first pair (connect) it with your iPhone.

Turning On Bluetooth

The first step to using Bluetooth is to turn the Bluetooth radio on. Follow these steps to do so:

1. Tap your **Settings** app.

2. Then, tap **General.**

3. Tap **Bluetooth.** By default, Bluetooth **is initi**ally set to **Off** on the iPhone. Tap **the** switch to move it to the **On** position.

> **TIP:** Bluetooth is an added drain on your battery. If you don't plan on using Bluetooth for a period of time, think about setting the switch back to **Off**.

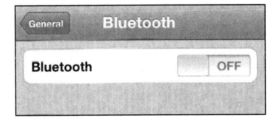

Pairing with a Headset or Any Bluetooth Device

As soon as you turn Bluetooth on, the iPhone will begin to search for any nearby Bluetooth devices, such as a Bluetooth headset or stereo adapter (see Figure 5–1). For the iPhone to find your Bluetooth headset, you need to put that device into *pairing mode*. Read the instructions that came with your headset carefully—usually there is a combination of buttons to push to achieve this.

> **TIP:** Some headsets require you to press and hold a button for five seconds until you see a series of flashing blue or red/blue lights. Some accessories, such as the Apple wireless Bluetooth keyboard, automatically start up in pairing mode.

Once the iPhone detects the Bluetooth device, it will attempt to automatically pair with it. If pairing takes place automatically, there is nothing more for you to do.

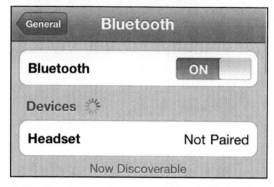

Figure 5–1. *Bluetooth device discovered, but not yet paired*

NOTE: Some Bluetooth devices (e.g., a headset) may ask you to enter a series of numbers (a *passkey*) on the keyboard itself (see Figure 5–2).

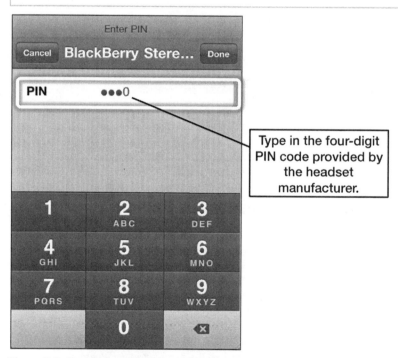

Type in the four-digit PIN code provided by the headset manufacturer.

Figure 5–2. *Type in the four-digit passkey when prompted during the pairing process.*

Newer headsets—like the Aliph Jawbone ICON used here—will automatically pair with your iPhone. Simply put the headset into pairing mode and set your iPhone's **Bluetooth** option to **ON**—that's all you have to do!

Pairing will be automatic and you should never have to re-pair the headset again.

Using the Bluetooth Headset

If your headset is properly paired and on, all incoming calls should be routed to your headset. Usually, you can just press the main button on the headset to answer the call or use the Slide to Answer function on the iPhone.

If you move the phone away from your face (while the iPhone is dialing), you should see an indicator showing that the Bluetooth headset is in use. In the image to the right, you can see the **Speaker** icon next to the **Jawbone ICON** Bluetooth headset.

You will also see options to send the call to your iPhone handset or to the speakerphone (**Speaker**). You can change this at any point while you are on the call.

Touch **Hide Sources** and you will see the iPhone's normal call screen.

Options When on a Call

Once the call is made and you are speaking with your contact, you can still reroute the call to either the iPhone or the speakerphone.

Move the call away from your face (if it is near your face) and you will see

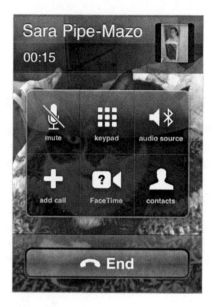

Audio Source as one of the options for you to touch. Touch that icon and you will see all the options for rerouting the call, as shown previously.

Just choose to send the call to any of the options shown and you will see the small **Speaker** icon move to the current source being used for the call (see Figure 5–3).

Figure 5–3. *Changing from Bluetooth headset back to the iPhone while on a call*

Bluetooth Stereo (A2DP)

 One of the great features of today's advanced Bluetooth technology is the ability to stream your music without wires via Bluetooth. The fancy name for this technology is A2DP, but it is more simply known as *Stereo Bluetooth*.

Connecting to a Stereo Bluetooth Device

The first step to using Stereo Bluetooth is to connect to a Stereo Bluetooth–capable device. This can be a car stereo with this technology built in, a pair of Bluetooth headphones or speakers, or even newer headsets like the Jawbone Jambox.

Begin by putting the Bluetooth device into pairing mode per the manufacturer's instructions, and then go to the Bluetooth setting page from the **Settings** icon, as shown earlier in the chapter.

Once connected, you will see the new Stereo Bluetooth device listed under your Bluetooth devices. Sometimes you will see the name or part of the name; other times you will simply see "Headset." Tap the **Arrow** icon to the right of the device and you will see the actual name of the device next to the **Bluetooth** tab in the next screen, as shown here.

Next, tap your **Music** app and start any song, playlist, podcast, or video music library.

Follow these steps to choose your audio output device:

1. Tap the blue **AirPlay** icon in the lower-right corner of the screen.

2. Choose from the list of available devices for streaming your music.

3. To switch the music back to your iPhone, just tap the **AirPlay** icon again and choose **iPhone** from the list.

NOTE: The **AirPlay** icon will bring up a list of both Bluetooth and Wi-Fi connected audio devices, such as Apple TV or AirPort Express connected speakers. You can choose from either one.

We selected the Jawbone JAMBOX by tapping it. Now, your music will now start to play from the selected Bluetooth device. You can verify this by touching the **AirPlay** icon on the screen once more. You should see a **Checkmark** icon next to the new Stereo Bluetooth device, and you should hear your music coming from that sound source, as well.

Disconnecting or Forgetting a Bluetooth Device

Sometimes, you might want to disconnect a Bluetooth device from your iPhone. This is easy to do. Enter the Bluetooth settings, as you did earlier in this chapter. Next, touch the device you want to disconnect to bring up the next screen, tap the **Forget this Device** button, and then confirm your choice.

This will delete the Bluetooth profile from the iPhone (see Figure 5–5).

NOTE: Bluetooth has a range of only about 30 feet. If you are not near a Bluetooth device, then you should turn off Bluetooth. You can always turn it back on when you are actually ready to use it.

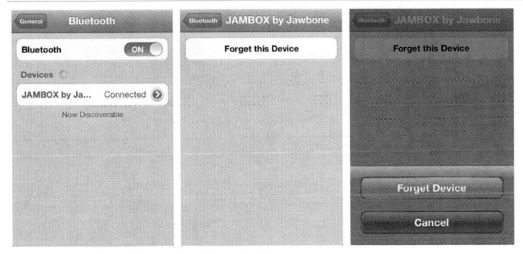

Figure 5–5. *Forgetting or disconnecting a Bluetooth device*

Chapter 6

Icons and Folders

Your new iPhone is very customizable. In this chapter, we will show you how to move icons around and put your favorite icons just where you want them. You've got up to 11 pages of icons to work with, and you can adjust the look and feel of those pages so they reflect your tastes.

Like a Mac computer or an iPad, the iPhone has a *Bottom Dock* where you can put the icons for your favorite apps. iPhones come with four standard icons in the Bottom Dock. You can replace the default icons with the icons for your favorite apps, so they are always available at the bottom of your screen. You can even move an entire folder of apps to the Bottom Dock.

> **TIP:** You can also move or delete icons using the **iTunes** app on your computer. Check out Chapter 22: "iTunes on Your Device" for more information.

Moving Icons to the Bottom Dock

When you turn your iPhone on, you'll notice four icons locked to the Bottom Dock.

Suppose you decide you want to exchange one or more of these icons for apps you use more often. Fortunately, moving icons to and from the Bottom Dock is easy.

Starting the Move

Press the **Home** button to get to your **Home** screen. Now touch and hold any icon on the **Home** screen for a couple of seconds. You'll notice that all the icons start to shake.

Just try moving a couple of icons around at first. You'll see that when you move an icon down, the other icons in the row move to make space for it.

Once you have a feel for how the icons move, you are ready to replace one of the Bottom Dock icons. While the icons are shaking, take the icon you wish to replace from the Bottom Dock and move it up to an area covered by other icons. (If you move it to an empty area, it will simply jump back to the Bottom Dock).

> **NOTE:** You can have up to four icons in the Bottom Dock; so if you already have four icons there, you will have to remove one to replace it with a new one.

For example, suppose you want to replace the **App Store** icon in our example with the **Skype** icon because you like to have **Skype** handy to talk with your children away at college. The first thing to do is to make space in the Bottom Dock by removing the **App Store** icon from the Bottom Dock, as shown in Figure 6–1.

Figure 6–1. *Swapping icons in the Bottom Dock*

Next, locate your **Skype** icon and move it down to the Bottom Dock. As you'll see, the icon becomes semi-transparent until you actually set it into place.

When you are sure that you have the icons just where you want them, simply press the **Home** button once and the icons will lock into place. At this point, you have the **Skype** icon in the Bottom Dock, where you can easily start video calls to your children in college.

Moving Icons to a Different Icon Page

iPhones can hold 16 icons on a page (not including the dock). You can navigate through these pages by swiping (right to left) on your **Home** screen. With all the cool apps available, it is not uncommon to have five, six, or even more pages of icons. You can have up to 11 pages filled with icons, if you feel adventurous!

> **NOTE:** You can also navigate to new pages by swiping from left to right on any screen except the **Home** screen. On the **Home** screen, swiping left to right takes you to **Spotlight Search**; see Chapter 2: "Typing, Copy, and Search" for more information.

You may have an icon that you rarely use on your first page, so you want to move it way off to the last page. Or you may want to move an icon you often use from the last of the pages to the first page. Both tasks are very easy to do; indeed, it's very much like moving icons to the Bottom Dock:

1. Touch and hold any icon to initiate the moving process.

2. Touch and hold the icon you wish to move. For example, let's assume you want to move the **iBooks** icon to the first page (see Figure 6–2).

Figure 6–2. *Moving icons from one page to another*

3. Now drag and drop the icon onto another page. To do this, touch and hold the **iBooks** icon and drag it to the left. You will see all of your pages of icons move by. When you get to the first page, just release the icon, and it is now placed at the very beginning.

4. Press the **Home** key to complete the move and stop the icons from shaking.

Deleting Icons

Be careful—it is as easy to delete an icon as it is to move it. And when you delete an icon on the iPhone, you are actually deleting the program it represents. This means you won't be able to use the program again without reinstalling or redownloading it.

Depending on your Application Sync settings in the **iTunes** app, the program may still reside in your Applications folder in iTunes. In that case, you would be able to reinstall the deleted app simply by checking that application in the list of apps to sync in iTunes.

As Figure 6–3 shows, the process to delete an icon is similar to the process for moving it. Touch and hold any icon to initiate the deletion process. Just as before, touching and holding makes the icons shake and allows you to move or delete them.

> **NOTE:** You may delete only programs you have downloaded to your iPhone; the preinstalled icons and their associated programs can't be deleted. You can tell which programs can be deleted because the icons for apps that can be deleted contain a small black **x** in the upper-left corner.

Just tap the **x** on the icon you'd like to delete. You will be prompted to either **Delete** the icon or **Cancel** the delete request. If you touch **Delete**, the icon and its related app will be removed from your iPhone.

> **NOTE:** If you delete an icon such as a game where your progress has been tracked and saved, your progress will be erased when you delete that game.

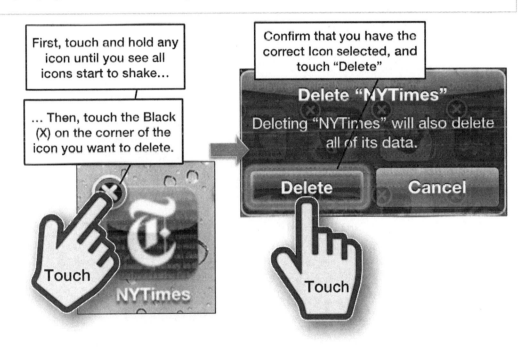

Figure 6–3. *Deleting an icon and its associated program*

Resetting All Your Icon Locations (Factory Defaults)

Occasionally, you might want to go back to the original, factory default icon settings. This might be the case when you've moved too many new icons to your first page and want to see all the basic icons again.

To do this, touch the **Settings** icon. Next, touch **General**, finally, scroll all the way to the bottom to touch **Reset**.

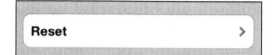

> **NOTE:** Built-in apps will be restored to the same order they were in when Apple shipped the iPhone.

On the **Reset** screen, touch **Reset Home Screen Layout** near the bottom. Now all your icons will be returned to their original settings.

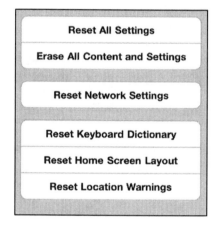

> **CAUTION:** Be careful you don't touch one of the other **Reset** options, as you can inadvertently erase your entire iPhone if you touch the wrong button. If you do, you'll have to restore data from your iTunes backup.

Working with Folders

Your iPhone lets you organize your apps into folders. When you download new apps, they take up a spot on your **Home** page. Once you download many apps, it can become hard to find apps and keep them organized.

Using folders will allow you to keep your games, your productivity apps, and other like-functioning apps together in folders. Each folder can hold up to 12 apps—which can really help you organize your iPhone!

Creating the Folder

Creating folders is intuitive and fun:

1. Hold down an app until all the apps start shaking (as you did before in the "Moving Icons" section).

2. Drag an app onto another like-functioning app. For example, drag one productivity app onto another similar app. The iPhone will initially create a name for the folder.

3. In this example, we dragged all three of the Apple productivity apps (Numbers, Keynote and Pages) on top of one another, and the iPhone created a folder called "Productivity."

4. You can edit the folder name by touching the **Name** field and typing a new name. (see Figure 6–4).

5. Press the **Home** button to set the new folder name.

6. Press the **Home** button again to return to the **Home** screen. At this point, you will see the new folder with its new name.

> **NOTE:** You can place up to 12 app icons in a given folder. If you try to put more than that in a folder, you will see the new icon continually being "pushed" out of the folder. This animation indicates that the folder is full.

Figure 6–4. *Moving icons to create a folder and renaming it.*

Moving Folders

Just like apps, folders can also be moved from one **Home** page to another:

1. Press and hold a folder until the folder and icons on the **Home** screen start to shake.

2. Touch and hold the folder and drag it to your preferred spot on the screen (or to another **Home** screen), and then let go.

3. When you have the folder in the spot you desire, just press the **Home** button to complete the move.

> **TIP:** You can even move a folder down to the Bottom Dock if you like. This is a very handy way of having lots of apps right at your fingertips (see Figure 6–5).

Figure 6–5. *Moving a folder to the Bottom Dock*

Chapter 7

Multitasking and Siri

In this chapter, we will describe how to multitask and jump between apps on your iPhone. Multitasking means you can leave one app running in the background while you do something else, such as stream Internet radio, listen to turn-by-turn directions, or take Skype calls.

We'll also introduce you to Apple's revolutionary Siri service, an artificially intelligent "assistant" that will listen to your voice commands and then send your messages, book your appointments, and search for the information you need—when you need it.

Fast App Switching

The *Fast App Switcher* enables you to leave many of your apps running in the background. It also lets you switch from the current app to another without stopping the app you're currently using.

You might wonder when it might make sense to use the Fast App Switcher. Here are a few scenarios when you might want to consider using multitasking on your iPhone:

- Copy and paste from one app (**Mail**) to another (**Calendar**).

- Answer a phone call or reply to an **SMS** message while playing a game, and then jump back into that game without missing a beat.

- Continue listening to Internet radio (such as **Pandora** or **Slacker**) while checking your email or browsing the Web.

- Forego waiting for photos to upload to Facebook or Flikr; your photos can be running in the background while you go and do other things on your iPhone.

- Use **Skype** to call people—now you can leave it running in the background to receive incoming calls (this was not possible before).

Jumping Between Apps

In order to multitask, you need to bring up the Fast
App Switcher bar at the bottom of the screen.

1. From any app or even the Home
   screen, double-click the Home
   button to bring up the Fast App
   Switcher bar at the bottom of your
   screen.

2. All open apps will be shown on the Fast App
   Switcher bar.

3. Swipe right or left to find the app
   you want and tap it.

4. If you don't see the app you want on
   the Fast App Switcher bar, then
   press the Home button and start it
   from the Home screen.

5. Double-click the **Home** button again
   and tap the app you just left to jump
   back to it.

Killing Apps from the Fast App Switcher Bar

Your iPhone will automatically manage its memory, leaving apps open that are doing
useful things like streaming music, and putting apps that aren't doing anything to
"sleep," so they don't waste memory or processor cycles. Sometimes, however, a *rogue
process* can cause an app not to close properly; at other times, you might want to make
certain a GPS or VoIP app closes early to save battery power. In those cases, you can
use the Fast App Switcher to manually kill apps.

Built-in apps like **Mail** and **Phone** will immediately restart, so you don't miss any
important messages. Apps and games from the App Store will stay closed until the next
time you tap their icons to launch them. Follow these steps to kill an app from the **Fast
App Switcher** bar:

1. Double-click the **Home** button to bring up the **Fast App Switcher** bar.

2. Press and hold any icon in the **Fast App Switcher** bar until they all shake. You will notice that a red **Circle** icon with a minus sign appears in the upper-left corner of each app icon.

3. Tap a red **Circle** icon 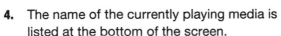 to completely close the app.

4. Keep tapping the red **Circle** icons to close as many apps as you want.

Media Controls and the Screen Portrait Orientation Lock

Swiping from left to right on the **Fast App Switcher** bar will bring up the media controls and the **Portrait Orientation Lock** icon. Follow these steps to access these controls and use the Portrait Orientation Lock feature:

1. From any app or even the **Home** screen, double-tap the **Home** button to bring up the **Fast App Switcher** bar at the bottom of your screen.

2. Swipe left to right to see the media controls and the **Portrait Orientation Lock** icon.

3. Tap the **Portrait Orientation Lock** icon to lock the screen in Portrait (i.e., vertical) orientation. Your iPhone will maintain this orientation even if you turn it on its side. You know the phone is locked when you see a **Lock** icon inside the button and another

    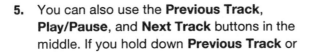

    Lock icon in the top status bar.

4. The name of the currently playing media is listed at the bottom of the screen.

5. You can also use the **Previous Track**, **Play/Pause**, and **Next Track** buttons in the middle. If you hold down **Previous Track** or

Next Track button, it becomes the **Rewind** or **Fast Forward** button, respectively.

6. Or, you can tap the **App** icon to jump to the last app that was playing music on your iPhone.

Volume Controls and AirPlay

If you keep swiping as far left as possible on **Fast App Switcher** bar, you'll find the volume controls and the **AirPlay** button. Follow these steps to manipulate these controls:

1. From any app or even the **Home** screen, double-tap the **Home** button to bring up the **Fast App Switcher** at the bottom of your screen.

2. Swipe left to right, past the media controls, until you get to the volume controls and the **AirPlay** button.

3. Tap the **AirPlay** button to beam your iPhone audio to **AirPlay** compatible speakers, your video to Apple TV, or to mirror your apps on the Apple TV.

4. Slide the **Volume** control left to reduce the volume; slide it to the right to increase it.

Siri: Your Virtual Assistant

Siri is an artificially intelligent virtual personal assistant that is context and relationship aware. This means that you can ask Siri questions, and it will not only answer you, but do things for you like tell you wife you're running late, wake you up from a nap in 15 minutes, recommend you bring a raincoat if you're going outside, find you a place to get a cup of coffee, or tell you who starred in your favorite movie. Siri is neither magic nor science fiction, but Apple has given it a personality, so it often feels like a little bit of both.

NOTE: At the time of writing, Siri is still in beta release. Apple is only providing support for English (U.S., U.K., and Australian), French, and German. You can turn it on in other places, but your results may vary. Also, things like location services (the ability to search maps and find places) were not yet working outside the US.

Finally, Siri has different voices for different areas. For example, in the US, Siri has a female voice. In the U.K., Siri has a male voice.

Enabling and Configuring Siri

Before you can start using Siri, you need to turn the service on. Follow these steps to do so:

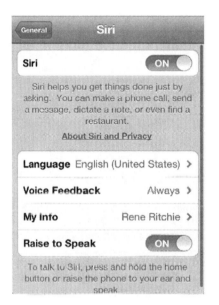

1. Launch the **Settings** app.

2. Scroll down and tap **General**.

3. Tap **Siri**.

4. Toggle the **Siri** switch to **ON**.

To change the language, tap Language and choose a language from the list.

As of publishing time, only English in Australia, U.K. and U.S.; French; and German are supported.

You can choose whether Siri talks back to you **Always** or only when **Hands Free**. If you don't like the idea of your phone speaking out loud, set this option to **Hands Free** only. If you want to experience Siri in a more interactive way, leave it set to **Always.**

To let Siri know who you are, so Siri can call you by name, set **My Info** to your own contact card.

Setting the **Raise to Speak** option to **ON** causes Siri to activate and ask what you'd like any time you wake your iPhone from sleep (by pressing the **Sleep/Wake** button on the top or the **Home** button on the front) and bring it up to your ear.

Using Siri

To use Siri, press and hold the **Home** button. (Or, if your iPhone is on and you enabled the **Raise to Speak** option in the **Settings** app as described in the previous section, then you can simply bring your phone to your ear.)

Your **Home** screen will slide up to reveal a silver **Microphone** icon. Wait for Siri to beep before you begin to speak; and then speak in a clear voice, at a moderate speed, just as you'd speak to another person. When you're done speaking, wait for Siri to beep again. It is at this point that all the fun begins.

What You Can Ask Siri

Apple recommends that you talk to Siri the same way you'd talk to another person. Don't try to remember a set list of commands or queries—there are far too many types and variations to remember them all. Instead, just ask Siri for what you want. Here are some examples of what Siri can do for you:

- Set up reminders, calendar appointments, and clock alarms and timers.

- Send texts, messages, and emails.

- Play music.

- Search for location-based information like restaurant and business listings. You can also search for directions to locations.

- Search Yelp (in the U.S.), Wolfram Alpha, and Google for information.

- Ask about the weather and stocks.

- Read your SMS/iMessage messages.

- Take dictation in any app.

- Ask silly questions—Apple has actually programmed in funny responses to many of these.

More impressively, Siri can combine many of these functions to accomplish complex interactions. For example, Siri can read a message requesting a dinner date, search for a restaurant, get directions, send back a confirmation message, and then add an appointment for the dinner—all as part of an interactive confirmation.

Here are just some of the things you can ask, and some of the ways you can ask them:

- "Siri, remind me to call my mom at work when I leave home."

  This will cause Siri to create a reminder, set the departure location as your home address, and pop up an alert with your mom's work number that's ready to dial when you leave.

- "Siri, tell my boss I'll be there soon."

  Siri will get the contact that's defined as your boss, take the mobile phone number, and send her an SMS/iMessage with the following content: "I'll be there soon."

- "Siri, read my messages."

  Siri will read any new SMS or iMessages that have come in.

- "Siri, wake me up in 30 minutes."

  Siri will set a clock timer that will go off in 30 minutes (hopefully, when your nap is over).

- " Siri, do I need a raincoat today?"

  Siri will check the weather, see if it's likely to rain, and let you know if you need to worry about getting wet.

- "Siri, tell me a joke."

  Siri might just start the one about the two iPhones that walked into a bar...

- "Siri, where can I get Italian for lunch?"

  Siri will search for nearby restaurants and show them to you on a map. In the U.S. it can also order them by Yelp ranking.

- "Siri, who starred in the movie, *Serenity*?"

  Siri will search Wolfram Alpha and give you a cast list from the movie.

- "Siri, what's your favorite color?"

  Siri will give you one of several replies, perhaps saying that your language lacks the dimensions to properly describe the right shade of green.

The results that Siri returns will sometimes be in the form of widgets that you can adjust or disable if you made a mistake. For example, you can quickly turn off an **Alarm** widget, check off a **Reminder** widget as done, tap an email address into a **Contact** widget, and so on.

Note that Siri isn't perfect, yet. For example, sometimes it will misunderstand you. At other times, the servers will be overly busy. So, Siri will make mistakes and do the wrong thing on occasion. But over time, it will get better as it learns more about you, and you learn more about how to phrase your questions and instructions.

It's best just to play with it at first. Experiment with it as much as you can to get a sense of what gives you the best results.

Changing Names and Setting up Relationships

You might have noticed in the preceding examples that we used words like *mom* and *boss*, and Siri understood who we were talking about. Before Siri can do that, however, you need to set these people up. Here's how:

1. Hold down the Home button to launch Siri.

2. Tell Siri whom you want to set up the relationship for, and what the relationship is. For example, you might say: "Jane Smith is my mother."

3. Siri will ask whether you want it to remember "Jane Smith" as your mother.

4. After the beep, say "yes." (Or, just tap the Yes button.)

5. Siri will confirm with this statement: "OK, I've added this relationship." Next, you will see your updated contacts card.

NOTE: Siri can't remove relationships once they're created. If you make a mistake or want to change a relationship later, then you'll have to go to the **Contacts** app, tap **Edit**, and manually **Delete** the relationship yourself.

If you want Siri to call you by a nickname—say, *Bob* instead of *Robert* or even something silly like *Master*—you can easily make the change:

1. Hold down the Home button to launch Siri.

2. Tell Siri the new name you want to be called by saying something like, "Call me Bob."

3. Siri will ask if you want it to remember *Bob* as your new name.

4. After the beep, say "yes." (Or, you can just tap the Yes button.)

5. Siri will confirm the action with a statement like this: "OK, I've added this name." You will then see your updated nickname on a contacts card.

Taking Dictation

The keyboard of the iPhone 4S introduces a new feature: a small Microphone button immediately to the left of the Space bar.

Tap it and your screen will slide up to reveal a glowing, purple microphone. Speak to it as you would to Siri; when you're finished, tap the **Done** button. Everything you say will be transcribed and entered as text.

No text-to-speech engine is perfect, but Siri does a pretty good job transcribing what you said. If it makes any mistakes, you can edit the text just as you would text that you type with the keyboard.

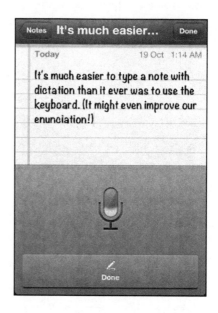

In addition to basic words and names, Siri can understand a wide range of symbols and punctuation. For example, you can say "period," "exclamation point," or even "open parenthesis" or "close square bracket." You can also say, "new line" or "new paragraph." Indeed, you can use Siri to enter almost any character that you know the proper name of.

What Siri Can't Do

Siri can do so many things right out of the box that it can be hard to remember what it can't do. That said, Siri is an online service, and Apple can and will continue to add new functionality over time. Just because Siri can't do something today doesn't mean it won't be able to do that same task tomorrow. At the time of writing, here are some things that Siri can't do:

- Siri can't toggle settings. You can't tell it to turn Wi-Fi on or off, or go into Airplane mode.

- Siri can't launch apps. You can't tell it to launch **Facebook** or your favorite game.

Siri can't read emails or Twitter replies or anything beyond messages. You'll have to get a third-party app like **Tweet Speaker** if you need that functionality.

Chapter 8

Personalize and Secure

In this chapter, you will learn several easy ways to personalize your iPhone. You will also learn how to protect your iPhone with passcode security. We'll show you where you can download free wallpaper to change the look of your **Lock** and **Home** screens. We'll also show you how to personalize the sounds your iPhone makes by adjusting when and what sound you hear for various activities. Many aspects of the iPhone can be fine-tuned to meet your needs and tastes, so you can give your iPhone a more personal look and feel.

Changing Your Lock Screen and Home Screen Wallpapers

There are actually two screens you can personalize on your iPhone by changing the wallpaper.

The **Lock** screen appears when you first turn on your iPhone or wake it up. The wallpaper for this screen image is shown behind the **Slide to Unlock** slider bar.

The **Home** screen features all of your icons. You can see the wallpaper behind the icons. You can use the wallpaper pictures that come with the iPhone, or you can use your own images.

> **TIP:** You may want the wallpaper for your **Lock** screen to be less personal than your **Home** screen wallpaper. For example, you might choose to put a generic landscape image on your **Lock** screen and a picture of a loved one on your **Home** screen. Also, you might want to choose a **Home** screen wallpaper that is less busy, so it does not clash with the icons.

Changing Wallpaper from Your Settings App

There are a couple of ways to change the wallpaper on your iPhone. The first way is very straightforward: simply adjust your wallpaper from your **Settings** app:

1. Tap the **Settings** icon.

2. Tap **Wallpaper**.

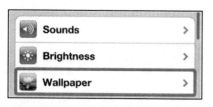

3. Tap the image of your currently selected wallpapers. The **Lock** screen is shown on the left, and the **Home** screen is on the right.

4. Choose an album:

   - Tap **Wallpaper** to select a preloaded wallpaper.

   - Tap **Camera Roll** (or **Photo Stream** if you have it enabled in iCloud) to select from pictures you've taken with your iPhone, images you've saved from the Web; from screenshots (which you take by pressing and hold the **Home** button and **Power/Sleep** key); or even from wallpaper apps.

   - Tap any of the other albums to view pictures you have synced.

5. Once you tap an album, you will see all the images within that album. Swipe up or down to view all images. The images you have most recently added will be at the very bottom of the list.

6. Tap any image to select it and view it full screen.

7. Now you can move and scale the image:

    ■ Move the image by touching and dragging your finger.

    ■ Zoom in or out by pinching your fingers open or closed.

    ■ Tap the **Cancel** button to return to the album if you don't like the image.

8. Tap the **Set** button to set the image as your wallpaper.

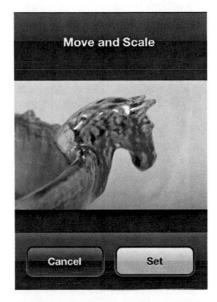

9. Select where you want this wallpaper to be used:

    ■ Tap the **Set Lock Screen** button to set the image only for your **Lock** screen.

    ■ Tap the **Set Home Screen** button to set the image only for your **Home** screen.

    ■ Tap the **Set Both** button to set the image for both your **Lock** and **Home** screens.

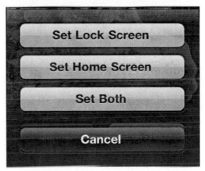

10. Tap the **Home** button to exit the **Settings** app and check out your new wallpapers, as shown in Figure 8–1.

 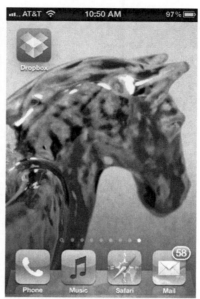

Figure 8–1. *Viewing your **Lock** screen and **Home** screen wallpapers*

Using Any Photo As Wallpaper

The second way to change your wallpaper is to view any picture in your **Photos** collection and select it as your wallpaper. Follow these steps to do so:

1. Tap the **Photos** icon to get started. To learn more about working with photos, check out Chapter 20: "Working with Photos."

2. Touch the photo album you want to look through to find your wallpaper.

3. When you find a photo you want to use, touch it and it will open on your screen.

4. The thumbnail you tap will fill the screen. If this is the image you want to use, tap the **Set as** icon on the lower-left corner of the screen.

5. Tap **Use As Wallpaper**.

6. To move, scale, and set an image as your **Home** or **Lock** screen wallpaper, follow Steps 7-9 from the previous section. If you decide you'd rather use a different picture, choose **Cancel** and pick a different one.

Downloading Great Wallpaper from Free Apps

Go to the App Store and do a search for "backgrounds" or "wallpapers" (see Chapter 23: "The Amazing App Store" for more information on this). You'll find a number of free and low-cost apps designed specifically for your iPhone. In this section, we will highlight one app of many in this genre called **Pimp Your Screen** from Apalon. This app has hundreds of beautiful background images you can download for your iPhone and was currently just $0.99 as of publishing time.

> **NOTE:** With Pimp Your Screen, as with most wallpaper apps, you will need a live Internet connection—either Wi-Fi or 3G. Because image files tend to be quite large, you should probably stick with Wi-Fi unless you have an unlimited monthly data plan for your 3G cellular data network.

Using the Wallpaper App

After you install **Pimp Your Screen**, you're ready to get started:

1. Tap the **Pimp Your Screen** icon to start the app.

2. The app's home screen has a number of categories to choose from: **App Shelves** (shelves to hold your apps - sort of like iBooks or Newsstand), **Neon Combos** (neon backgrounds), **Home Screens** (nice looking home screens), **Icon Skins** (create backgrounds to highlight your icons). Then you can create your own personalized Lock and Home screen using the bottom two options; **Lock Screen Maker** and **Home Screen Maker** as shown in Figure 8–2.

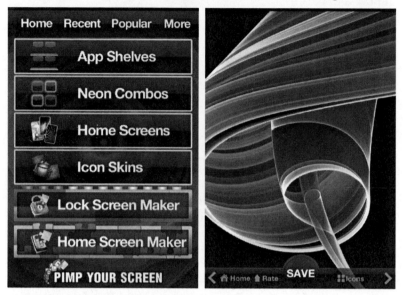

Figure 8–2. *Using the Pimp Your Screen app.*

3. After touching any category, you can swipe left or right to view more wallpaper image options. To save the wallpaper in your **Camera Roll** album, the **Save** button in the middle of the bottom of the image.

4. If you don't like the image, click the **Home** button in the lower-left corner to get back to the Home screen menu.

Using Your Newly Saved Wallpaper

Once you've chosen a wallpaper image and saved it to your iPhone, you need to select it using the steps described in the "Changing Wallpaper from Your Settings App" section earlier in this chapter.

Remember that the downloaded wallpaper will be in the **Camera Roll** album. After you tap **Camera Roll** to open it, you'll need to flick all the way to the bottom to see your recent entries.

Adjusting Sounds on Your iPhone

You can fine-tune your iPhone so that it does or does not make sounds when certain events happen, such as an incoming phone call, a new email, or a calendar alert. You can also customize what happens when you send mail or type on the keyboard.

Follow these steps to adjust the sounds played on your iPhone:

1. Tap your **Settings** icon.

2. Tap **Sounds**.

3. You can adjust whether you want your iPhone to vibrate in both the **Silent** and **Ring** modes. Set the switches to **ON** or **OFF** next to **Vibrate**.

4. To adjust the volume of the ringtone and other alerts, move the slider bar just above **Ringtone**.

5. To change your phone's ringtone or text tone; the sound played when you receive a new mail, tweet, calendar alert, or reminder alert; or the sound played when a sent mail completes—tap the item you wish to change.

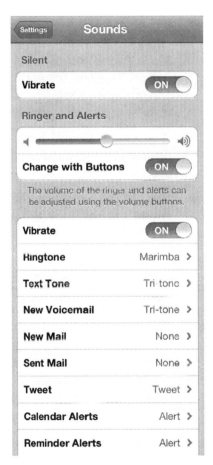

6. This screen lets you select a new ringtone. Tap any ringtone to play it and select it. (You can tell whether a ringtone is selected by the checkmark next to its name. **Bell Tower** is selected in the image to the right.)

7. If none of the tones available appeal to you, you can click **Buy More Tones** and be taken to the iTunes Ringtone Store, where you can purchase some of your favorite songs as tones.

8. When you are done, tap the **Sounds** button in the upper-left corner.

9. Use the same steps to change the sound you hear for a text tone, new mail, tweet, and so on.

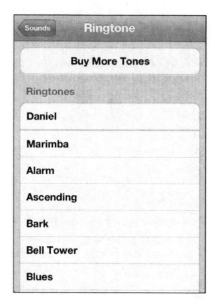

> **TIP:** See Chapter 9: "Using your Phone" to learn about custom ringtones.

10. In all sound categories except **Ringtone**, you can turn off the sound played by selecting the **None** entry at the top of the list.

11. Lock Sounds and **Keyboard Clicks** can be adjusted by tapping the switches to set them to **ON** or **OFF**. When done, press the **Home** button to exit.

> **TIP:** On a related note, you can lock the maximum volume playable from the **Music** app. Do so by going into **Settings ➤ Music ➤ Volume Limit ➤ Lock Volume Limit**. We show you how to do this in Chapter 12: "Playing Music."

Keyboard Options

You can fine-tune your keyboard by selecting various languages and changing settings like **Auto-Correction** and **Auto-Capitalization**. You can even have your iPhone speak the auto-correction suggestions to you as you type. See Chapter 2: "Typing, Copy and Search" for a description of the various keyboard options and how to use them.

Securing Your iPhone with a Passcode

Your iPhone can hold a great deal of valuable information. This is especially true if you use it to save information like the Social Security numbers and birth dates of your family members. It's a good idea to make sure that anyone who picks up your iPhone can't access all that information. Also, if your children are like ours, they'll probably pick up your cool iPhone and start surfing the Web or playing a game. You might want to enable some security restrictions to keep them safe.

Setting a Simple Four-Digit Passcode

On your iPhone, you have the option of setting a four-digit passcode that prevents unauthorized access to your iPhone and your information. If the wrong passcode is entered, however, even you won't be able to access your information, so it is a good idea to use a code you'll remember easily.

Follow these steps to set a passcode to lock your iPhone:

1. Tap the **Settings** icon.

2. Tap **General.**

3. Scroll down and tap **Passcode Lock.**

4. Tap **Turn Passcode On** to set a passcode.

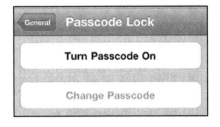

5. The default passcode is a simple four-digit passcode. Use the keyboard to enter a four-digit code. You will then be prompted to enter your code once more.

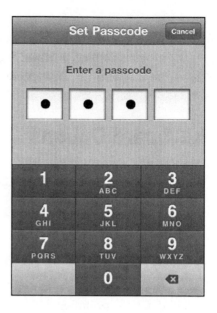

Setting a More Complex Password

If you prefer to have a password that is more complicated than just four digits, you can do so by setting the **Simple Passcode** option on the **Passcode Lock** screen to **OFF**.

You will then be able to enter a new passcode with letters, numbers, and even symbols.

> **CAUTION:** Be careful! If you forget your passcode, you cannot unlock your iPhone.

Adjusting Your Passcode Options

Once you have set your passcode, you will be presented with a few options:

- **Turn Passcode Off**

- **Change Passcode**

- **Require Passcode (Immediately, After 1 Minute, After 5 Minutes, After 15 Minutes, After 1 Hour)**

- **Simple Passcode** (**ON** = four digits; **OFF** = any letters, numbers, or symbols)

- **Siri** (**ON** = allow Siri without entering your passcode; **OFF** = prevent Siri until your passcode is entered)

- **Erase Data** (**ON** = erase all data after ten incorrect password attempts; **OFF** = do not erase data)

> **CAUTION:** You may want to set **Erase Data** to **OFF** if you have young children who like to bang away at the security to unlock the keyboard when it comes out of **Sleep** mode. Otherwise, you may end up with your iPhone being erased frequently.

> **NOTE:** Setting a shorter time for **Require Passcode** is more secure. Setting the time as **Immediately**— the default—is most secure. However, using the setting of **1 Minute** may save you the headache of retyping your passcode if you accidentally lock your iPhone.

Setting Restrictions

You might decide you don't want your kids listening to explicit lyrics in the music on your iPhone. You may also want to block them from visiting YouTube or any other web site. Setting such restrictions is quite easy on your iPhone.

Restricting Apps

Follow these steps to restrict access to content on your iPhone:

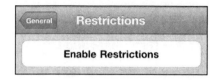

1. Tap **General** in your **Settings** app.

2. Scroll down the page and tap **Restrictions**.

3. Tap the **Enable Restrictions** button.

4. You will now be prompted to enter a Restrictions Passcode—just pick a four-digit code you will remember.

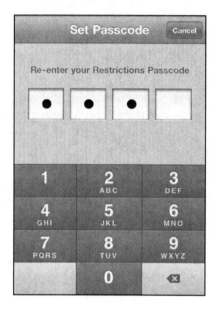

> **NOTE:** This Restrictions Passcode is a separate passcode from your main iPhone passcode. You can certainly set it to be the same, which will make it easier to remember. However, this could be problematic if you let your family know the main passcode, but do not want them adjusting the restrictions. You will need to enter this Restrictions Passcode to turn off restrictions later.

Notice that you can adjust whether to allow certain apps or actions to function. For example, the screen shot to the right lets you adjust restrictions for the following apps: **Safari**, **YouTube**, **Camera**, **FaceTime**, **iTunes**, and **Ping**. This screen also lets you restrict access to **Installing Apps** or **Deleting Apps and Siri and Explicit Language in Siri.** Finally, you can restrict the ability to make changes to **Location** and **Accounts**.

In all cases, **OFF** = restricted.

You might think that **ON** means something is restricted, but it is the opposite. In order to disable or restrict something, you need to touch the slider next to it and change it to **OFF**. If you notice the word **Allow** above all the options, then it makes sense.

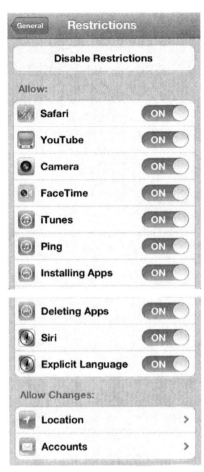

> **NOTE:** The icons for any apps you restrict will disappear. So if you were to restrict access to **YouTube**, the **App Store**, and the **FaceTime** apps; then the **YouTube** and **App Store** icons would disappear from the **Home** screen, and your iPhone's **FaceTime** icon would also be removed.

Allowing Changes

Sometimes you don't want to turn off access to an app completely, but simply stop anyone from making unintended changes. For example, the **Location** option comes with a lot of privacy concerns, so you may want to exercise more granular control over which apps and functions have access to it. Follow these steps to adjust restrictions for the **Location** option:

1. Go to the **Restrictions** screen, as described in the previous section.

2. Scroll down to the bottom to see all of the **Allow Changes** settings.

3. Tap **Location.**

4. Tap **Allow Changes** to make changes to **Location Settings**.

5. Toggle **Location Services** to **OFF** to completely prevent your iPhone from using your location. (Note that this may greatly reduce the convenience of apps like **Google Maps** and prevent turn-by-turn navigation apps from working at all.)

6. Toggle to **OFF** any individual apps that you don't want tracking your location. (For example, set **Location Services** for your **Camera** app to **OFF** to prevent GPS coordinates from being included on pictures you intend to share publicly on the Internet.)

7. Tap **System Services** to change the **Location** permissions for built-in processes.

8. If there are any system services that you don't want to use location data, then toggle them to **OFF**. Options include **Cell Network Search**, **Compass Calibration**, **Diagnostics & Usage**, **Location-Based iAds**, **Setting Time Zone**, and **Traffic**.

9. Tap **Location** at the top left to go back when you're done.

10. If you want to prevent any future changes to **Location Services**, tap **Don't Allow Changes**.

11. Tap **Restrictions** to go back when you're done.

12. Tap **Accounts** and tap **Don't Allow Changes** to prevent any future changes to your **Mail**, **Calendar**, and **Contact** accounts.

13. Tap **Restrictions** to go back when you're done.

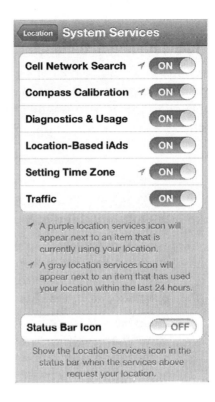

Restricting Content

In addition to setting restrictions for apps, you can set restrictions for content that can be downloaded and viewed on your iPhone. Follow these steps if you might give your iPhone to a child, and you don't want her to have the ability to download music with explicit lyrics or watch movies with adult content:

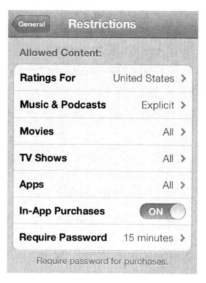

1. Go to the **Restrictions** screen, as described in the previous section.

2. Scroll down to the bottom to see all of the **Allowed Content** settings.

3. To restrict content purchased while inside an app, set **In-App Purchases** to **OFF**. This will include music and videos purchased from the **iTunes** app.

4. If you have small children and worry about them making expensive in-app purchases after you download a new app (e.g., you don't want them to buy **Smurfberries** in the **Smurfs** app), then tap **Require Password** and change that setting to **Immediately**.

5. Tap **Ratings For** to adjust the ratings based on the country where you live. An extensive list of countries are currently supported, including Australia, Austria, Canada, France, Germany, Ireland, Japan, New Zealand, the United Kingdom, and the United States.

6. Tap **Music & Podcasts** to restrict access to lyrics with explicit content. Make sure you set the **Explicit** option to **OFF**, as shown in the figure to the right.

7. Tap the **Restrictions** button in the upper-left corner to return to the list of options.

8. You can also set the ratings cutoff for **Movies**, **TV Shows,** and **Apps** by tapping each item.

9. When you tap an item such as **Movies**, you see a list of allowed ratings. Tap the highest rating level you want to allow. In this image, we tapped **PG-13.** All movies rated above this (**R** and **NC-17)** are not allowed. The red text and lack of checkmarks offer visual clues as to which selections are blocked.

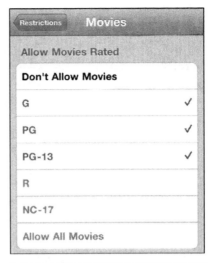

10. Tap **TV Shows** to set those restrictions. Again, tap the highest rating you want to allow. The checkmarks show allowed ratings; the red text shows which ratings are not allowed. In this example, **TV-Y**, **TV-Y7**, and **TV-G** are allowed, but higher ratings are not allowed (i.e., **TV-PG**, **TV-14**, and **TV-MA**).

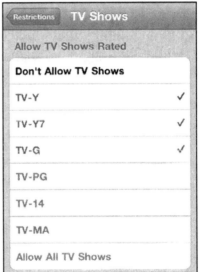

11. Tap **Apps** to set restrictions for various apps.

12. In this screen, we are allowing apps with ratings of **4+**, **9+**, and **12+** to be played. Apps with ratings of **17+** cannot be played or downloaded.

13. Tap the **Restrictions** button in the upper-left corner to return to the list of options.

14. Finally, tap the **Home** button to save your settings.

Restricting Game Center

Game Center is a great way to enjoy social gaming, including match making, challenges, leaderboads, and more. However, if you're a parent with young children, you may not be comfortable with them playing multiplayer games or accepting friend requests without your supervision. Follow these steps to restrict access to Game Center:

1. Go to the **Restrictions** screen, as described in the previous section.

2. Scroll down to **Game Center**.

3. Toggle to **OFF** the **Multiplayer Games** and/or **Adding Friends** options.

Chapter 9

Using Your Phone

The iPhone is capable of so many cool things that it's easy to forget that it's also a very powerful phone. In this chapter, we will cover the many features you would expect to find on a high-end smartphone. We'll begin with the basics, showing you how to dial by name, save time by using your recent call logs, dial by voice, and use voicemail.

Next, we'll explore the more advanced capabilities of the iPhone's Phone features. For example, we'll show you how to handle multiple callers and set up conference calls. And finally, we'll show you how to create new custom ringtones from your music library and set separate ringtones for individual callers.

Getting Started with the Phone Features

The iPhone initially places the **Phone** icon on your Bottom Dock. You can move it around or off your dock by using the steps described in Chapter 6: " Icons and Folders."

Finding Your Phone Number

Maybe you just received your new iPhone and you don't yet know your phone number. Don't worry; you can find your number in the **Settings** app. Tap the **Settings** icon, and then scroll down and tap **Phone**. Your number is listed at the top.

Using the iPhone Headset

If you are in one of the many states or provinces where you cannot legally hold your iPhone while driving a car, you will want to use the headphones or a Bluetooth car stereo connection to talk hands-free.

The headset you received with your iPhone works well for phone calls. There is a microphone built into the wire of the headset, along with volume controls and a **Center** button that allows you to answer or hang up a phone call. When you have your headset on, the phone will ring in the headset. Click the **Center** button on the headset once to answer, and then click it again to hang up.

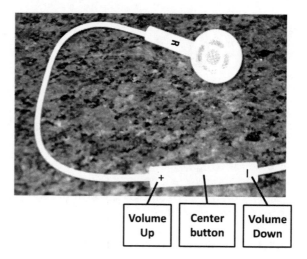

| Volume Up | Center button | Volume Down |

Connecting to a Bluetooth Headset or Car Stereo

You can also connect to a Bluetooth headset or Bluetooth car stereo system to place and receive phone calls. We show you the detailed steps in Chapter 5: "AirPlay and Bluetooth."

Dialing a Number from the Keypad

The simplest way to use your phone is to dial using the keypad. The numbers on the screen are large, so it's easy to dial. Follow these steps to dial a number:

1. Tap the **Phone** icon (see Figure 9–1).

2. If you do not see the keypad to dial, tap the **Keypad** icon at the bottom.

3. Now you can simply start dialing by tapping number keys.

4. If you make a mistake, press the **Backspace** key .

5. If you need to type a **Plus Sign** (+) for an international number, press and hold the **Zero** (0) key.

6. When you are done dialing, press the **Call** key .

TIP: Dialing Pauses in a Phone Number

Sometimes you have to insert a pause in a phone number, and then enter another number such as an extension or a password. You can dial a pause by pressing and holding the **Asterisk** key (*) until you see a comma appear next to the phone number. This causes a two-second pause.

Figure 9–1. *Dialing phone numbers with your iPhone keypad*

Different Phone Views

We have just used the **Keypad** soft key. You can see several icons along the bottom of your **Phone** screen for **Favorites**, **Recents**, **Contacts**, **Keypad**, and **Voicemail** as shown in Figure 9–2.

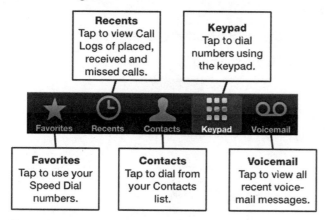

Figure 9–2. *Use soft keys to see different **Phone** screens*

Using Favorites (Speed Dials)

Your **Favorites** are people you call frequently. You can think of **Favorites** as your speed dial list.

> **NOTE:** You can also add **FaceTime** contacts to **Favorites**.

Adding New Favorites

It is easy to add new favorites to your list from your **Contacts** list. Follow these steps to do so:

> **TIP:** You can also add a **Favorite** from your **Recents** call logs. In **Recents**, tap the blue **Arrow** icon 🔵 and, on the next screen, scroll to the bottom of the **Info** page and tap **Add to Favorites**.

1. If you are not in the **Phone** screen, tap the **Phone** icon to start it up.

2. Touch the **Favorites** icon in the bottom row of soft keys.

3. The first time you start your **Favorites**, you will see a blank screen.

4. Tap the **Plus** button  in the upper-right corner to add a new entry. Your contact directory will open.

5. Swipe up or down to locate a contact. Tap any contact to select it.

> **TIP:** To search for your contacts by name, tap the very top of the screen just under the time. This will bring up the **Search** window, where you can type a few letters to find people. Remember that you can view different contact groups by tapping the **Groups** button in the upper-left corner.

6. If an entry has more than one phone number, you will need to select one of them as your favorite entry.

7. After tapping a number, you will be asked if you want to set the number as a **Voice Call** or one of your **Favorites** in **FaceTime**.

8. You are returned to your list of **Favorites**, where you'll see the new person you just added. **Favorites** in **FaceTime** are shown with a little **Video** icon to the right of the person's name.

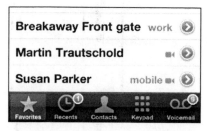

9. Repeat Steps 4–7 to add more people to your **Favorites**. Each new entry is listed below the previous ones at the bottom of the list.

Organizing Your Favorites

As with other lists on your iPhone, you can re-order your **Favorites** list and remove entries:

1. View your **Favorites** list as you did previously.

2. Tap the **Edit** button in the upper-left corner.

3. To re-order the entries, touch and drag the right edge with the three gray bars up or down the list.

4. To delete an entry, tap the red **Circle** icon to the left of the entry to make it turn vertical.

5. Tap the **Delete** button.

6. When you are done re-ordering and deleting entries, tap the **Done** button in the upper-left corner.

Calling a Favorite

To call any person in your **Favorites** list, just touch the name of the individual. There is no prompt or confirmation. As soon as you touch his name, the phone will dial his number (see Figure 9–3).

Figure 9–3. *Dialing one of your **Favorites** by tapping him*

Using Recents (Call Logs)

Using your **Recents** is similar to looking at your call log on other smartphones.

When you touch the **Recents** icon, a list of all your recent calls will be displayed. You can touch the **All** or **Missed** button at the top to narrow down the list (see Figure 9–4).

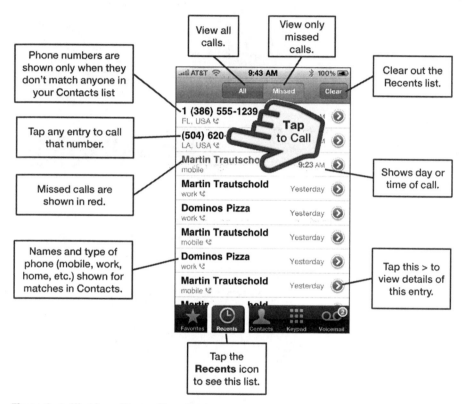

Figure 9–4. *Working with your Recents screen*

Placing a Call from Recents

It's easy to place a call from your **Recents** screen; simply touch the desired name or phone number, and your iPhone will immediately initiate a phone call to the individual.

Clearing All Recents

To clear or erase all your recent call log entries, press the **Clear** button in the upper-right corner.

Details of a Call or Contact Information

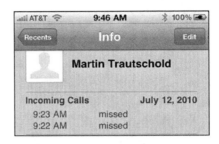

Touch the blue **Arrow** icon next to the name in the **Recents** list, and you will see either the information on the phone number or full contact information for that particular contact if he is in your **Contacts** list. If there are several calls, you will see the history of each call.

Scroll down to the bottom of the contact's **Info** screen to see more options. You can send a **Text Message**, start a **FaceTime** video call, or **Share Contact** by sending the contact information via e-mail or MMS.

Tap **Add to Favorites** to add this person to your **Favorites** list.

Adding a Phone Number to Contacts from Recents

If the **Recents** entry is a phone number not yet connected to someone who is in your **Contacts** list, then you will see two different buttons on the **Info** screen: **Create New Contact** and **Add to Existing Contact**.

Tap **Create New Contact** to create a new contact from this phone number.

Tap **Add to Existing Contact** to add this phone number to one of your existing contacts.

Placing Calls from Contacts

One of the great things about having all your contact information in your phone is that it's very easy to place calls from your **Contacts** list. Follow these steps to do so:

1. If you are not in your **Phone** screen, tap the **Phone** icon to start it up (see Figure 9–5).

2. Touch the **Contacts** icon in the bottom row of soft keys.

3. Locate a contact to call using one of the following methods:

    a. Swipe up or down through the list.

    b. Put your finger on the letters along the right side of the screen and scroll up or down.

    c. Tap the status bar on top where it says the time to jump to the top. Tap in the **Search** window and type a few letters of the contact's first, last, or company name to search for him.

4. When you find the contact entry you want, tap his name.

5. Touch the phone number you wish to call.

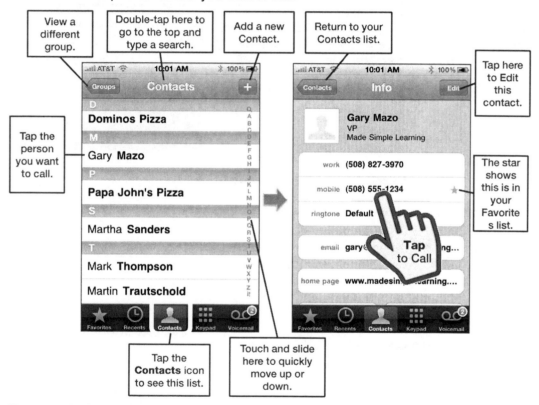

Figure 9–5. *Placing calls from your **Contacts** list*

Calling Any Underlined Phone Number

You will notice that the iPhone underlines almost every phone number it recognizes on the screen.

This happens in e-mail messages (e-mail signatures), SMS and iMessages, notes, web sites, and more.

To call to any of these underlined phone numbers, tap it, and then tap the **Call** button as shown.

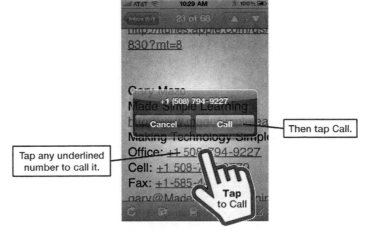

Tap any underlined number to call it.

Then tap Call.

TIP: As with underlined phone numbers, your iPhone also recognizes other information on the screen and allows you to act on it by tapping it. This feature is known as a *Data Detector*. You will see underlined addresses (tap to show the address in **Maps**), underlined dates such as **tomorrow at 9am** (tap to schedule a new **Calendar** event), and shipping numbers such as a FedEx or UPS tracking number (tap to show the tracking information in **Safari)**.

Creating a New Contact from an Underlined Phone Number

If you press and hold any underlined phone number for a few seconds, you will see a list of buttons appear from the bottom of the screen. Tap **Create New Contact** to create a new contact from the number or tap **Add to Existing Contact** if you want to add this number to a person already in your **Contacts** list.

Voice Dialing using Siri

You can use your voice to dial contacts using Siri. You can find all the steps for doing this in the "Siri" section of Chapter 7: "Multitasking and Siri."

Functions While on a Call

You can do a number of things while your iPhone is dialing and even after you connect to the person you are calling.

All the phone functions available to you are clearly shown with the icons and buttons on the **Phone** screen.

You can do all of the following:

- **Mute** yourself.

- Dial additional numbers with the **Keypad**.

- Turn on your phone's speakerphone by tapping **Speaker**.

- Create a conference call by tapping **Add Call**.

- Start a video call with **FaceTime** (assuming the other caller also has a **FaceTime**–enabled iPhone, iPod touch, iPad, or Mac).

- View your **Contacts** list.

NOTE: Why does the screen go blank when you hold the phone to you ear? When you are talking into the iPhone (holding the phone next to your face), the screen senses this and goes blank so you can't accidentally press a button with your face. As soon as you move the iPhone away from your face, you will see the available options.

Using the Keypad

Perhaps the number you're calling requires you to dial an extension. Or maybe you are calling an automated answering service that requires you to input numbers for choices.

In these situations, just touch the **Keypad** icon and the keypad will be displayed. You can then input numbers as prompted.

Finally, press the **Hide Keypad** button at the bottom when you're finished.

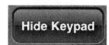

Muting the Call

As the number is dialing, you will see the option in the top-left row to mute the call. Just tap the **Mute** button to mute yourself. Tap it again to turn off mute.

> **TIP:** When you have **FaceTime** enabled, you don't see the **Hold** button. Use the **Mute** icon to put the call on hold.

Using the Speakerphone

If you would prefer to use your iPhone's built-in speakerphone, tap the **Speaker** icon.

Tap that same icon again to turn off the speakerphone.

Putting a Caller on Hold

It's a simple matter to put a caller on hold. Simply tap the **Hold** icon to put the caller on hold.

> **NOTE:** You will only see the **Hold** icon if your **FaceTime** app is disabled (go to **Settings ➤ Phone**, and then set **FaceTime** to **OFF**). As noted earlier, if you don't see a **Hold** icon, just tap the **Mute** icon instead—it will accomplish the same result.

It's just as easy to take someone off hold—tap the **Hold** button again to remove the hold.

> **NOTE:** At the time of writing, Verizon's CDMA network did not officially support placing a call on hold.

Browsing Your Contacts

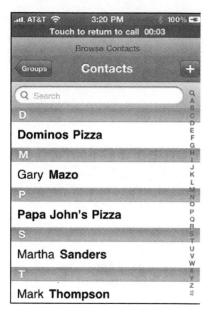

Let's say you need to browse through your **Contacts** list while on a call. For example, you might need to look up someone's e-mail, phone number, or address, so you can share it with your caller. Tap the **Contacts** button and scroll through or search for a contact.

To return to the call, tap the green bar at the top where it says **Touch to return to call**.

NOTE: It's a good idea to use the speakerphone or a Bluetooth headset while doing this (see Chapter 5: "AirPlay and Bluetooth"); this will enable you to continue talking on the phone as you search for the contact.

FaceTime Video Call

If you are chatting with someone who also has a recent iPhone, iPod touch, iPad, or Mac, and this person is on Wi-Fi; then you can tap the **FaceTime** icon to start a video call. (You may be able to use **FaceTime** on a 3G cellular connection in the future; for now, however, this feature requires a Wi-Fi connection.) You will see your picture in the top-left portion of the window and your caller's picture in the main window. You will also notice three buttons at the bottom: **Mute**, **End** call, and **Switch Camera** to swap between your front-facing and rear-facing cameras.

See Chapter 11: "Video Messaging and Skype" for more on using **FaceTime**.

> **NOTE:** You will only see this **FaceTime** icon if your **FaceTime** app Is enabled (you can enable it by going to **Settings ➤ Phone**, and then setting **FaceTime** to **ON**).

Setting up and Using Voicemail

Your iPhone comes with an enhanced voicemail system called *Visual Voicemail*. This feature allows you to quickly see all voicemails and play them in any order. To listen to any message, just tap it. In the image to the right, the number **3** in the red **Circle** icon shows that there are three unheard voicemail messages.

> **NOTE:** If you live outside the US, your carrier may not have implemented Visual Voicemail service. If not, then you will need to dial in to retrieve your messages by pressing the **Voicemail** soft key, just as you would with any other mobile phone.

Setting Up Voicemail

If you've never set up voicemail before, setting it up on your new iPhone is straightforward; simply follow these steps:

1. Tap the **Phone** icon.

2. Tap the **Voicemail** icon  in the bottom row of soft keys.

3. Tap the **Set Up Now** button shown in Figure 9–7.

4. Pick a four-digit password and then re-enter the password.

Figure 9–7. *Setting up your voicemail*

5. Next, you can choose a **Default** or **Custom** greeting. The **Default** greeting will say your phone number in a computer-like voice; it will also indicate that you are not available.

6. If you choose a **Custom** greeting, you will need to record it by tapping the **Record** button. When done, tap the **Stop** button, which is in the same place as the **Record** button.

7. Once recorded, you can tap the **Play** button to see if you like your **Custom** greeting.

> **TIP:** If you hold the iPhone too close to your mouth, your voice may sound a little distorted—be sure to hold the iPhone at a normal distance.

Changing Your Voicemail Password

You may want to change your password. Follow these steps to do so:

1. Navigate to the **Settings** Icon and tap it.

2. Scroll down and tap **Phone.**

3. Scroll down and tap **Change Voicemail Password**.

4. Enter your current password, and then type your new password twice.

Playing Your Voicemail

The beauty of the Visual Voicemail system is that you never have to call in to check your voicemail. All voicemail messages will reside on your phone. You can save them, scroll through them, or delete them.

You will know how many unheard voicemail messages you have by the little number in the red **Circle** icon in the top right of the **Voicemail** icon.

Unheard items, like unread e-mail in your inbox, are marked with a little blue dot.

The **Voicemail** icon will show the number of voicemails in your mailbox. Tap the **Play** button next to the message and the message will play through your handset.

> **TIP:** If you cannot look at the screen, you can still dial in to listen to your voicemail hands-free by pressing and holding the **1** key on your keypad.

Listening to Voicemail Through Your Speaker

If you would like to hear your voicemail through the iPhone's speaker (as opposed to listening through the handset), just touch the **Speaker** button in the upper-right corner.

Adjusting Your Greeting

Tap the **Greeting** button to adjust your voicemail greeting. You can listen to your greeting again, record a new **Custom** greeting, or change the greeting back to **Default**.

Calling Back a Person Who Left Voice Mail

If someone leaves you a voicemail message, you can call her back by touching the **Call Back** button; this will immediately return her call.

Deleting a Voicemail Message

Your iPhone will store all your voicemails if you want to listen to them at a later date. Sometimes voicemails can get a bit hard to manage if you have too many of them. Highlighting a message and touching the red **Delete** button will remove a given message from your iPhone (see Figure 9–7).

> **NOTE:** You have the option to save a "deleted" message. Your **Voicemail** screen will show your deleted messages in their own **Deleted** tab. If you touch a message in this tab, you can tap the **Undelete** button to restore it.

Figure 9–7. *Working with deleted voicemail items*

If you would like to permanently delete all your voicemails, tap **Clear All.**

Conference Calling

In today's busy world, working with several callers at once has become something that we demand from our phones. Fortunately, conference calling is very intuitive on the iPhone.

NOTE: While the AT&T/GSM iPhone can handle up to five-person conference calls, the technical limitations of Verizon's CDMA network limit Verizon iPhones to only three-person conference calls.

Initiating the First Call

As we showed you the earlier in this chapter, you can make a call to any number in **Recents**, to a new number, to a contact, to someone in your **Favorites** list, and so on.

You don't even have to start a call to create a conference call. For example, you can receive a call from the first caller instead of placing one to her. At that point, you can conference in the second person.

Tap Add Call to call another person.

Move the iPhone away from your face to see the phone functions available to you. Most of these were covered earlier in this chapter.

Adding a Second Caller

Touch the **Add Call** button to begin adding a second caller. This will immediately put the first caller on hold.

Touching the **Add Call** button brings you to your **Contacts** list. Simply scroll or double-tap the top to search for the contact you want to add to this call.

You can also add a new caller by choosing her from your **Favorites** or **Recents,** or just by dialing her phone number after pressing the **Keypad** soft key on the bottom.

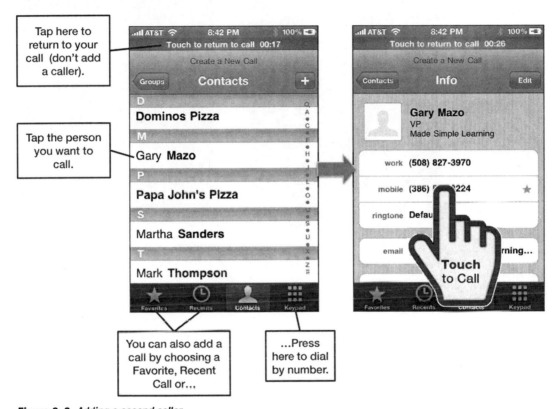

Figure 9–8. *Adding a second caller*

If the contact has more than one phone entry, tap the one you would like to call and the call will be initiated.

Merging Calls

Once the call to the second caller has been initiated, you will notice that the **Add Call** button has now been replaced with a **Merge Calls** button. Tap this button to merge both calls into a three-way conference call (see Figure 9–9).

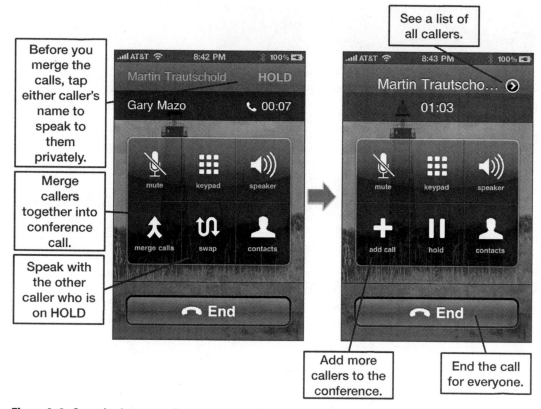

Figure 9–9. *Swapping between callers and merging them into a conference call*

The top of the screen will now scroll a list of all the callers on the conference call.

Talking Privately with or Disconnecting from Individuals

In order to speak to one caller individually or privately from a conference call, perform these steps:

1. Tap the small black **Arrow** icon next to the name at the top of the **Phone** screen (see Figure 9–10).

2. Now you will see a list of all callers. Tap the **Private** button next to a person's name to talk privately with that person. Everyone else is put on hold.

3. To hang up from any caller, tap the red **Phone** icon to the left of his name.

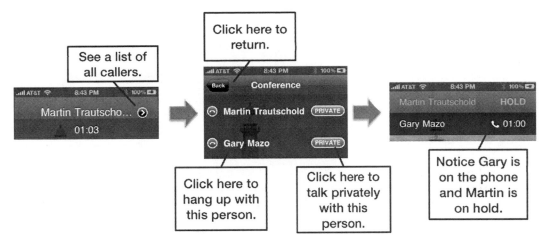

Figure 9–10. *Talking privately with individual callers or hanging up on them*

Phone Options and Settings

You can customize many things In your phone by going into the **Settings** app:

1. Tap the **Settings** icon.

2. Scroll down and tap **Phone**.

The sections that follow describe all the phone settings found here.

Call Forwarding

There may be times when you need to forward your calls to another number. For example, you may be traveling to the house of a friend who lives out in the boondocks, where there is very poor cell reception. In this case, you could forward calls to that person's land line. Follow these steps to do so:

1. In the **Phone** settings screen, tap **Call Forwarding.**

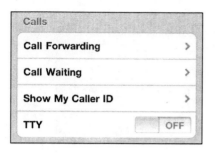

2. Set the **Call Forwarding** switch to **ON.**

3. Tap the **Forward to** row to enter the forwarding number.

4. Once entered, the number will be stored for future reference. All calls will be forwarded from your regular iPhone number to this number until you set **Call Forwarding** to **OFF**.

> **CAUTION:** Call forwarding is not always free. Call your phone company to see if you will be charged for enabling call forwarding.

Call Waiting

Another **Phone** setting is **Call Waiting**. This option alerts you to the fact that another call is coming in while you are on the phone.

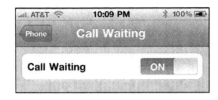

You then have the option to take the new call, hang up on the first call, or set up a conference call, as described previously.

Enabling call waiting is as simple as making sure the **Call Waiting** switch is set to the **ON** position, which is the default setting.

Show or Block (Hide) Your Caller ID

There may be certain situations where you would prefer that your phone number not show up on the caller's phone.

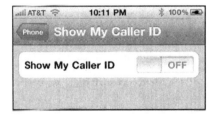

Fortunately, your iPhone gives you the option to block your Caller ID phone number. To do so, set the **Show My Caller ID** switch to **OFF**.

Setting up Security on Your SIM Card

As an added measure of security, you can enable a PIN code to access information stored on your SIM card. If your iPhone is ever lost or stolen, this will prevent anyone from accessing the names and numbers stored on your SIM card.

CAUTION: Setting this SIM PIN may lock your phone so that it is unusable until you enter a PUK (*personal unlocking key*). You can get this eight-digit PUK from your wireless carrier. For AT&T, log into AT&T's web site, click **My Services** at the top of the page, and then click **My Phone/Device** in the middle. Next, select your iPhone and click the Unblock SIM Card link. If you do not have AT&T, then check your carrier's web site or call your carrier's help desk.

Follow these steps to do so:

1. Go to the **Phone** settings menu, as described previously.

2. Scroll down and tap **SIM PIN**.

3. This will take you to the **SIM PIN** screen. If you try to set the **SIM PIN** option to **ON** here, and you see an error message similar to the one shown to the right, then your iPhone has been locked. You can only unlock it by entering the PUK. See the preceding Caution for more details.

4. If you don't see an error message after setting the switch next to **SIM PIN** to **ON**, then you can tap **Change PIN** to enter your new PIN.

> **NOTE:** Verizon's CDMA network doesn't use SIM cases, so the Verizon iPhone doesn't offer SIM PIN locking.

TTY for Deaf People

TTY stands for *Text Telephone Device*. Such devices let deaf people type messages that are sent over phone lines. Your iPhone can communicate with another phone that is equipped with a TTY device—simply set the **TTY** switch to **ON** to do so.

Switching Between Wireless Carriers

In some countries, especially where unlocked iPhones are more popular, you may see a **Carriers** tab in your **Settings** app.

Tap **Carrier** to see the screen where you can switch between carriers for your iPhone.

Leave it set to **Automatic** to have your iPhone select the best network.

If you want to force your iPhone onto a specific network, such as **ROGERS**, then tap that network name

Carrier Services

Pressing the **Carrier Services** button will list the name of your wireless carrier or phone company.

For example, if your carrier is AT&T in the US, tap **AT&T Services** at the bottom of the **Phone** settings screen to see special numbers related to AT&T. If you use a different carrier, this screen will show the special access numbers for your carrier.

> **NOTE:** Not all carriers support this function; if you don't see these options, visit your carrier's web site for account information.

Tap any of the entries on this screen to perform the stated request. For example, if you tap **View My Minutes**, you'll receive a text message response showing details of your minutes remaining in your current billing cycle.

Tap the **View** button to see more details.

Ring Tones, Sounds, and Vibration

Your iPhone can use unique sounds or vibrations to alert you to incoming calls, voice mails received, and other events. These can easily be adjusted using the **Settings** app.

The "Adjusting Sounds on your iPhone" section in Chapter 8: "Personalize and Secure" shows you how to change a ringtone, add vibration to both **Silent** and **Ring** modes, and turn on or off the tone for voicemail messages.

Assigning Unique Ringtones to Contacts

Sometimes, it is both fun and useful to give a unique ringtone to a certain contacts in your address book. This way, you can know who is calling without looking at your phone.

You can use ringtones that are already on your iPhone, or you can acquire new ringtones by doing one of the following:

- Purchase ringtones using the **iTunes** app on your iPhone.
- Create and purchase ringtones using your music from iTunes on your computer.
- Create free ringtones using your music from iTunes on your computer.

For example, one of the authors (Gary) sets the ring tone for his son Daniel to Elton John's "Daniel." Later in this chapter, we will show you how to make a ringtone from your iTunes music.

Giving a Contact a Unique Ringtone

You need to edit a person's information in **Contacts** to change his ringtone. Follow these steps to give a contact a unique ringtone:

1. Tap the **Contacts** icon.
2. Tap the contact you wish to change (in this case, **Daniel**).
3. Tap **Edit**.
4. Tap the **Ringtone** button to see the **Ringtones** screen.
5. Tap any ringtone from the list. In this case, we chose the new custom ringtone, **Daniel**.

Purchasing a Tone from the iTunes App

In this section, we'll show you how to purchase a ringtone (most are US $1.29). You can then follow these steps to immediately attach it to a contact or set is as your **Default Ringtone** right from the **iTunes** app on your iPhone:

1. Start up the **iTunes** app your iPhone.

2. If you see the **Tones** soft key at the bottom, tap it. Otherwise, tap **More** then **Tones**. Next, scroll through the ringtones. Or, you can search for a ringtone by tapping the **Search** soft key at the bottom.

3. You can also browse ringtones by using the buttons at the top: **Featured**, **Top Tens,** and **Genres**.

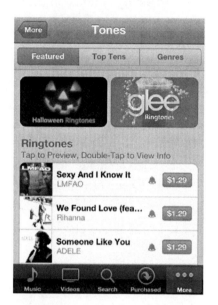

4. We selected **Top Tens** and then **Alternative** to see the image to the right.

5. Tap any name or album cover to preview the ringtone. If you like it, tap the price to buy it, and then tap **Buy Now**.

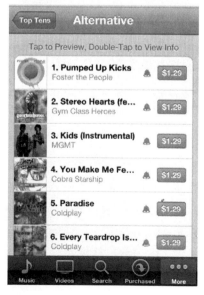

6. Once you select the ringtone to purchase, the **iTunes** app will prompt you to either **Set as Default Ringtone** (your main phone ringtone) or **Assign to a Contact**.

7. If you choose **Assign to a Contact**, your **Contacts** list will launch. Next, scroll through or search for the contact. You will hear the new ringtone each time that contact calls.

Creating Custom Ringtones

Your iTunes library is filled with all your favorite songs. Wouldn't it be great if you could turn your own songs into ringtones for your iPhone? The good news is that you can turn most of your music into a ringtone. There are two ways to do this: an easy way that costs about US $1 per ringtone and a more challenging way that is free. We will show you both ways.

The Free, But More Challenging Way to Create Ring Tones

Let's begin by examining the free but more difficult approach. This method will work on any music in iTunes that is not protected with DRM (Digital Rights Management) copy protection. Older iTunes purchases might contain DRM. Any music you've loaded into iTunes from a CD or other non-DRM music (including newer non-DRM music from iTunes) will work.

Locating a Song

Follow these steps to highlight and select a song in iTunes to use as a basis for your custom ringtone:

1. In the **iTunes** menu, select **File ➤ Get Info**. You can also right-click the song with your mouse and choose **Get Info**.

2. Click the **Options** tab and put a checkmark in the **Start Time:** and **Stop Time:** boxes.

CAUTION: Make sure the total duration is less than 40 seconds; otherwise, the ringtone will be too large.

3. Click **OK** to close the **Get Info** dialog box.

4. In **iTunes**, click the **Advanced** menu and select **Create AAC Version**.

5. You should now see a new version of the song that is only a few seconds long appear in your iTunes list. For example, the new version of **Daniel** is only 30 seconds long.

6. Once you have your new 30-second version, make sure you go back into the original song and uncheck the **Start Time:** and **Stop Time:** boxes via the **Get Info ➤ Options** tab.

7. Once the new, shorter ringtone ACC version of the song is created, just drag it from **iTunes** to your desktop or copy and paste it onto the desktop.

8. You need to change the extension of the file from m4a to m4r, so it will be recognized as a ringtone. You can do so by clicking the file to highlight its name and changing it; or you can right-click the file, choose **Get Info**, and then change the extension.

9. You will see a warning message that the file may be unusable; just accept the change.

10. You must now delete the 30-second version that is still in iTunes.

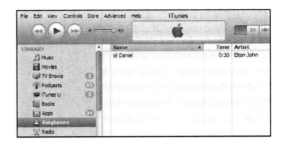

11. Drag the new file with the new m4r extension back into your iTunes library and drop it there.

12. If everything went well, you should now see your ringtone listed when you click **Ringtones** in the left column.

Syncing the Ringtone to Your iPhone

See the "Sync Ringtones" section of Chapter 3: "Sync with iCloud, iTunes and More" to learn how to get the new ringtone onto your iPhone.

Using Your New Custom Ringtone

If you want to tie your ringtone to a particular person in your **Contacts** list, you will need to edit that contact. Follow the steps in the "Giving a Contact a Unique Ringtone" section in this chapter to do so. If you want to use your new ringtone for your main phone ringtone, follow the steps in the "Sounds" section of Chapter 8: "Personalize and Secure."

Chapter **10**

SMS, MMS,
and iMessage

SMS stands for *short messaging service*, but it is commonly referred to as *text messaging*. Text messages are a great way to quickly touch base with people without interrupting them with a voice call. Sometimes you can text people and receive a text reply when it would be impossible or difficult to do a voice call.

MMS is short for *multimedia messaging service*, which provides a quick, standard way to send pictures, video, voice memos, map locations, and contact cards.

iMessage is Apple's new service that does exactly the same thing as SMS and MMS, but works over your data plan and only with other iOS 5 devices.

All of these services can be found in your iPhone's **Messages** app. In this chapter, you will learn how to use these services to send a text message from your **Contacts** app and a picture message from your **Photos** app.

SMS/MMS vs. iMessage

With iOS 5, Apple has built the iMessage service right into same **Messages** app that has always handled SMS and MMS messages.

The advantage to iMessage is that it works over your existing data plan, so it doesn't require an additional, potentially expensive text messaging plan. Nor does iMessage open you up to costly per-message charges if you don't have a plan or you are travelling without a roaming plan.

The disadvantage to iMessage is that it only works with other iOS 5 devices, so you can't use it with your friends or family who have non-Apple smartphones like BlackBerrys or regular feature phones.

SMS, MMS, and iMessage are all built into the same **Messages** app, so you don't have to worry about which one you must use once you set it up. Your iPhone will automatically use iMessage whenever possible, but revert to SMS and MMS when iMessage isn't available (e.g., when you're texting someone who is not on an iOS 5 device).

Does iMessage Count As Text or Data?

iMessages are sent over your carrier's data network, not its SMS channel, so these messages don't count against your SMS/MMS plan (if you have a limited plan). Instead, they count against your data plan cap (if you have limited data).

If you're sending the message to someone who's not using an iPhone, iPod touch, or iPad on iOS 5, then your message is sent via SMS/MMS, and it counts against your texting plan.

How Will Messages Send?

You might have limited text messages and want to make sure you're using the iMessage service as much as possible. Or, you might have limited data and want to make sure you're sticking to SMS/MMS whenever you can. In either case, Apple makes it easy to tell which system you'll be using:

- If iMessage is available, everything from the background of the contact name to the word bubbles containing the messages will be **blue**, and the text entry box will say "iMessage."

- If iMessage is off or unavailable, everything from the background of the contact name to the word bubbles containing the messages will be **green**, and the text entry box will say "Text Message."

Enabling iMessage and Adjusting Settings

Setting up the iMessage service is similar to setting up **FaceTime**:

1. **Launch Settings.**

2. **Tap Messages.**

3. **Toggle iMessages to ON**

4. Then you may be asked for your iMessage password -- this is simply your Apple iTunes password.

> **TIP:** If you get stuck in the **Waiting for activation** message as shown here, then try re-booting your device as shown in Chapter 26: Troubleshooting.

Once you've enabled the iMessages option, your iPhone phone number **and email address** will be registered with the iMessage service, and anything sent to your phone from another iOS 5 device will be sent via iMessage.

If you tap the **Receive At** near the bottom of the iMessage settings screen, you will see a screen similar to this one.

On this screen, you can adjust which email address is associated with your iMessage, add new email addresses and change what is shown on the Caller ID for iMessage.

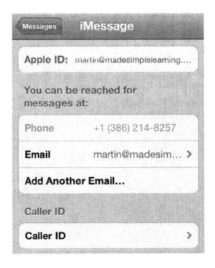

Text Messaging on your iPhone

Text messaging has become one of the most popular services on cell phones today. While it is still used more extensively in Europe and Asia, it is growing in popularity in North America.

The concept is very simple: instead of placing a phone call, you send a short message to someone's handset. Sending a text message is much less disruptive than making a phone call; however, you may have friends, colleagues, or co-workers who do not own an iPhone, so e-mail may not be an option.

One of this book's authors uses text messaging with his children all the time—this is how his generation communicates. "R u coming home 4 dinner?" "Yup." There you have it—meaningful dialogue with an eighteen-year-old—short, instant, and easy.

Composing Text Messages

Composing a message is much like sending an e-mail. The beauty of a text message is that it arrives on virtually any handset, and it is quite simple to reply to.

Composing a Text Message from the Messages App

There are a couple of ways to start your **Messages** app. The easiest is to just tap the **Messages** icon on the **Home** screen.

When you first start the **Messages** app, you most likely won't have any messages, so the screen will be blank. Once you get started with SMS messaging, you will have a list of messages and current "open" discussions with your contacts. Follow these steps to send a text message:

1. Touch the **Compose** icon in the top-right corner of the screen.

2. The cursor will immediately go to the **To:** line. You can start typing the name of your contact, or you can just touch the **Plus (+)** button and search or scroll through your contacts.

3. If you want to just type someone's mobile phone number, then press the **123** button and dial the number.

4. When you find the contact you wish to use, touch the person's name and it will appear in the **To:** line

5. When you are ready to type the SMS message, touch anywhere in the box in the middle of the screen (next to the **Send** button).

6. The keyboard will be displayed. Just type in your message and touch **Send** when you are done.

> **NOTE**: A character counter will appear if you have enabled it in **Settings** > **Messages**.

> **TIP**: If you prefer, you can use the larger landscape keyboard for sending text messages. It can be easier to type with the larger keys, especially when your fingers are a little larger or it is hard to see the smaller keys.

Options After Sending a Text

Once you send the text, the window changes to a *threaded* discussion window between you and your contact. If you're using SMS, the text that you sent is shown in a green bubble on the right side of the screen. If you're using iMessage, the text that you sent appears in a blue bubble. When your contact replies, his message will appear on the opposite side of the screen in a gray bubble.

To leave the **Compose** screen, tap **Messages** in the upper-left corner or click the **Home** button to go back to your **Home** screen.

NOTE: If the message fails to send, you'll see an exclamation mark beside it. You'll also see a **Red Exclamation Point** icon in the upper-right corner of the icon for the **Messages** app.

If this happens, you can send another text, just as you did before. Or you can call the contact or view his contact info.

To initiate a call to the contact with whom you are texting, touch the **Call** button. To look at his contact info, touch the **Contact Info** button.

TIP: While SMS messages are technically limited to 160 characters, many GSM carriers (including AT&T) will break longer texts into several messages and then reassemble them back into one message when they're received. CDMA networks like Verizon sometimes have a problem reassembling texts that are longer than 160 characters; other times, they can deliver them out of order. If you experience this problem, try breaking your texts up on your own and sending several shorter messages rather than one long one.

Composing a Text Message from Contacts

You also have the ability to start the **SMS** app and compose an SMS message to any contact in your iPhone. Follow these steps to do so:

1. Find the contact you wish to text by searching or scrolling through **Contacts**.

2. At the very bottom of the contact info, you will see a box that says **Text Message**. Just touch that box and you will be prompted to choose which number to use (if you have more than one number listed for the contact).

3. Choose the preferred number and follow the steps listed previously.

NOTE: Remember that you can only send SMS messages to a mobile number.

Replying to a Text Message

When a text message is received, your iPhone will play an indicator tone, vibrate, or both—depending on your settings. Also, an indicator will appear in **Notification Center** at the top of the screen, giving you the option of replying right away.

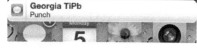

When you see and/or hear the indicator, just tap the notification to go to the **Messages** app and type your response, as shown previously.

If you miss the notification or want to reply later, just pull down the **Notification Center** list from the top, and then tap the message you want to reply to.

NOTE: If your screen is locked, you will see the message as either a popup or as part of the **Lock** screen list. Just slide the **Messages** icon to unlock and you'll be taken to the message.

Viewing Stored Messages

Once you begin a few threaded messages, they will be stored in the **Messages** app. Touch the **Messages** icon and you can scroll through your message threads.

To continue a conversation with someone, just touch the desired thread and it will open up, showing you the back and forth of all past messages. Touch the text box, type in your message, and then touch the **Send** button to continue the conversation.

Text Tone and Sound Options

Your iPhone lets you dictate how it will react when a message comes in. Follow these steps to choose your preferred reaction:

1. Start your **Settings** app, scroll to **Sounds**, and tap the **Sounds** tab.

2. If you have the **Vibrate** feature set to **ON** in the **Sounds** menu when the phone rings (see Chapter 10: "Your iPhone as a Phone"), you will also receive a vibration when an SMS message comes in.

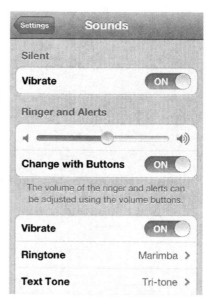

3. Scroll down a bit further and you will see a tab that says **Text Tone**. Tap this and you can choose the tone for the SMS message. You are limited to the choices offered (usually six), or you can choose **None**.

4. Choose your preferred sound for an SMS message

   notification and then touch the **Sounds** 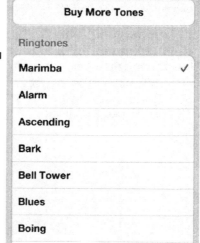 button in the top-left corner to set your selection.

MMS—Multimedia Messaging Service

The **Messages** app gives iPhone users the tools required to send and receive MMS messages—including picture messages and video messages, as well as multimedia iMessages. MMS messages appear right in the messaging window, just like your text messages.

> **NOTE**: You can send image, video, location (from maps), audio (from the **Voice Memo** app), and vCard (from the **Contacts** app) files from the **Messages** app.

Sending a Picture or Video with Messages

To send an MMS message or multimedia iMessage, you use the same **Messages** app we discussed when sending text messages. Follow these steps do so:

1. Tap the **Messages** icon to start messaging–just as you did with SMS.

2. You will notice that next to the text input
    bubble is a small **Camera** icon. Tap this
    icon and you will be prompted to **Take a
    Photo or Video** or **Choose Existing.**

3. To take a photo, follow the instructions
    in Chapter 20: "Working with Photos." If
    you select the **Choose Existing** option,
    just navigate through your
    pictures/videos and find the item you
    would like to add to your message

4. Touch the blue **Choose** button in the lower-right corner
    and you will see the picture load into the small window.

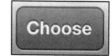

5. Select a recipient (as shown earlier) and type in a short note if you like. Next, touch the blue **Send** button.

If you already have a threaded discussion with that particular contact, then his picture will show up in the midst of that threaded discussion.

NOTE: You can continue to exchange images and text in the midst of a threaded discussion. And you can always scroll through to see the entire discussion—pictures and all!

Choosing a Picture from Photos to Send via Messages

The second way to send a picture or video message is to just go straight to your **Photos** app and choose a picture. Follow these steps to do so:

1. Start your **Photos** app and navigate through your pictures as described in Chapter 21: "Working with Photos."

2. To send just one picture, touch the picture you wish to send and then touch the **Send** icon in the lower-left corner.

3. You will now see **Message** as the second option. Choose **Message** and the photo will load into the bubble, just as it did previously in the **Messages** app.

Sending Multiple Pictures

Follow these steps to send multiple pictures:

1. Start the Photos app, as you did in the previous section.

2. Instead of tapping one picture, tap the Action button in the lower-left corner.

3. Now, just tap up to pictures. You will see them lighten in color, and a Red Checkmark icon will appear in the box.

4. Once you have chosen a maximum number of pictures (this could be 5 or 9, or some other number and will depend on your wireless carrier), tap the Share button in the lower-left corner.

5. Choose Message and the pictures will appear in the message bubble.

Chapter 11

Video Messaging and Skype

Your iPhone brings many new capabilities to your life, some of which seemed like science fiction just a few years ago. For example, video calling is now not only possible, but extremely easy to use with the new **FaceTime** feature. As long as you and your caller are on an iPhone and you're both on a Wi-Fi network, you can have unlimited video calls. In this chapter, we will show you how to enable and use **FaceTime**, as well as how to start having fun with this great new feature.

Making calls over Wi-Fi and even 3G is also possible with **Skype**, the popular video calling and chat program that many of us use on our computers. We will also show you how to use the **Skype** app.

Speaking of video, your iPhone is a very capable video recorder. You can record and export HD video up to 1080p up to 30 frames per second. You can then publish that video straight to YouTube or iCloud, or even send it to an email recipient. We will also show you how to shoot and quickly "trim" your videos, as well as upload them.

Video Calling

For many years, we have watched TV episodes and movies debut future technology like this. For example, many of these episodes and movies show people talking on small, portable phones and having video conversations. Even *The Jetsons* cartoon in the 1970s had this as a future concept.

The iPhone makes that future thinking a reality today. There are a few apps that enable you to make video calls on your iPhone using the front-facing camera. At this time, only one app allows you to use both the front-facing camera and the rear camera: **FaceTime**.

Video Calling with FaceTime

FaceTime is the proprietary app highlighted in many Apple commercials for the iPhone. Essentially, **FaceTime** is free-over-Wi-Fi calling that allows you to see the caller on the other end of the conversation through the phone's front-facing camera.

> **NOTE:** For now **FaceTime** is only available for video calls between recent iOS devices like the iPhone 4, iPhone 4S, iPad 2, and iPod touch 4 as well as Mac computers. Also, it's only available over a Wi-Fi network. Apple says it is exploring expanding this service, so it will also work over standard 3G networks in the near future. The carrier would also have to buy in before you would see this feature on a given network.

Enabling FaceTime Calling on Your iPhone

When you first use your device, **FaceTime** may not yet be enabled. To enable the iPhone to receive and make **FaceTime** calls, follow these steps:

1. Start your **Settings** app.

2. Tap **FaceTime**.

3. Toggle the **FaceTime** switch to the **ON** position.

You may be asked to sign in with your Apple ID.

> **TIP:** You can also scroll to the bottom and tap Caller ID to adjust if your phone number or email address is shown as your FaceTime Caller ID.

Using FaceTime

Once **FaceTime** is enabled, you will see it as an option with every call you place from the iPhone. The **FaceTime** icon will be part of the option display on all phone calls. However, **FaceTime** will only work if the other caller is on an iPhone **FaceTime**–enabled iOS device or Mac.

To initiate a **FaceTime** call, follow these steps:

1. Make a call just as you normally would on your IPhone.

2. Tap the **FaceTime** button (where the **Hold** button usually is), and the app will ask the caller on the other end to **Accept** the **FaceTime** call.

3. Or, you can simply **Accept** the **FaceTime** call from the other caller (see Figure 11–1).

Martin Trautschold
would like FaceTime...

Decline   Accept

Drag the Small
Window
Anywhere on
the Screen.

End

Touch to Accept a
FaceTime Call

Touch to End Call.

Tap this corner to
change views

Figure 11–1. *Accepting a FaceTime call*

Once a **FaceTime** call is initiated, follow these steps to conduct a video conference:

1. Hold the phone away from you a bit.

2. Make sure you are *framed* properly in the window.

3. You can move the small image of yourself around the screen to a convenient spot.

4. Touch the **Switch Camera** button to show the **FaceTime** caller you are looking at. The **Switch Camera** button will now use the standard camera on the back of the iPhone. In Figure 11–2, I get to see the beautiful vistas of Colorado from Martin's vacation, and he gets to see my dog on the couch!

5. Touch the **End** button to end the **FaceTime** call.

6. Touch the **Mute** button to temporarily mute the call.

Touch "Switch Camera" Button to Show What you See using the Main Camera

Figure 11–2. *Switching camera views on a **FaceTime** call*

Making Phone Calls and More with Skype

Social networking is all about keeping in touch with our friends, colleagues, and family. Passive communication through sites such as www.facebook.com and Google+ is nice, but sometimes there is just no substitute for hearing someone's voice.

Amazingly, you can make phone and video calls using the **Skype** app from any iPhone. Calls to other Skype users anywhere in the world are free. A nice thing about the Skype service is that it works on computers and many mobile devices, including the iPhone 4S, older iPhones, iPads and iPod touches, some BlackBerry smartphones, and other mobile devices. You will be charged for calls to mobile phones and land lines, but the rates are reasonable.

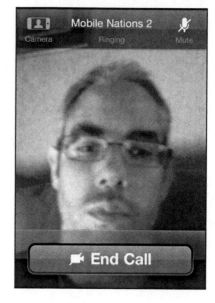

> **NOTE**: Unlike **FaceTime**, the **Skype** app can place video calls over 3G networks. It can also run in the background, so you can answer incoming Skype calls at any time (note that this usually leads to faster battery drain).

Downloading Skype to Your iPhone

You can download the free **Skype** app from the App Store by searching for "Skype" and installing it. If you need help getting this done, please check out Chapter 23: "The Amazing App Store."

Creating Your Skype Account

If you need to set up your Skype account and have not already done so from your computer (see the "Using Skype on Your Computer" section later in this chapter). .

Log into the Skype App

After you create your account, you're ready to log into **Skype** on your iPhone. To do so, follow these steps:

1. If you are not already in **Skype**, tap the **Skype** icon from your **Home** screen.

2. Type your Skype Name and Password.

3. Tap the **Sign In** button in the upper-right corner.

4. You should not have to enter this login information again; it is saved in **Skype**. The next time you tap **Skype**, it will automatically log you in.

Finding and Adding Skype Contacts

Once you have logged into the **Skype** app, you will want to start communicating with people. To do so, you will have to find them and add them to your **Skype** contacts list:

1. If you are not already in the **Skype** app, tap the **Skype** icon from your **Home** screen and log in, if asked.

2. Tap the **Contacts** soft key at the bottom.

3. Tap the **Search** window at the top, and then type someone's first and last name or **Skype** name. Tap **Search** to locate that person.

4. Once you see the person you want to add, tap their name.

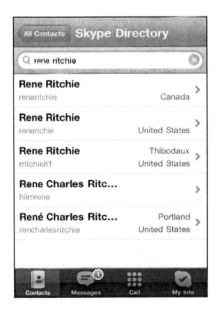

5. If you are not sure whether this is the correct person, tap the **View Full Profile** button.

6. Tap **Add Contact** at the bottom.

7. Adjust the invitation message appropriately.

8. Tap the **Send** button to send this person an invitation to become one of your **Skype** contacts.

9. Repeat the procedure to add more contacts.

10. When you are done, tap the **Contacts** soft key at the bottom.

11. Tap **All Contacts** from the **Groups** screen to see all new contacts you have added.

12. Once this person accepts you as a contact, you will see him listed as a contact in your **All Contacts** screen.

TIP: Sometimes you want to get rid of a Skype contact. You can remove or block a contact by tapping her name from the contact list. Tap the **Settings** icon (upper-right corner) and select either **Remove from Contacts** or **Block**.

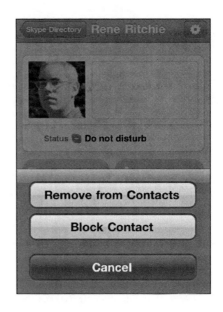

Making Calls with Skype on Your iPhone

So far you have created your account and added your contacts. Now you are ready to finally make that first call with **Skype** on your iPhone:

1. Tap the **Contacts** soft key at the bottom.

2. Tap **All Contacts** to see your contacts.

3. Tap the contact name you wish to call.

4. Tap the **Call** button to make a voice call or the **Video Call** button to make a video call.

5. You may see a Skype button and a Mobile or other phone button. Press the Skype button to make the free call. Making any other call requires that you pay for it with Skype Credits.

> **NOTE:** You can call toll free numbers for free using **Skype Out** on your iPhone. The following notice comes from the Skype web site at www.skype.com:
>
> "The following countries and number ranges are supported and are free of charge to all users. We're working on the rest of the world. France: +33 800, +33 805, +33 809 Poland: +48 800 UK: +44 500, +44 800, +44 808 USA: +1 800, +1 866, +1 877, +1 888 Taiwan: +886 80"

Receiving Calls with Skype on Your iPhone

The iPhone innately supports background VoIP calls. With the new version of **Skype**, you can have **Skype** running in the background and still be able to receive a **Skype** call when it comes in. You can even, in theory, be on a voice call and then answer your **Skype** call!

> **TIP:** If you don't want to leave **Skype** running in the background, but still want to call someone whom you know uses **Skype** on her iPhone, just send her a quick email or give her a quick call to alert her to the fact you would like to talk to her using the **Skype** app.

Buying Skype Credits or a Monthly Subscription

Skype-to-Skype calls are free. However, if you want to call people on their land lines or mobile phones from the **Skype** app, then you will need to purchase Skype Credits or purchase a monthly subscription plan. If you try to purchase the credits or subscription from within the **Skype** app, it will take you to the Skype web site. For this reason, we recommend using **Safari** on your iPhone or using your computer's web browser to purchase these credits.

> **TIP:** You may want to start with a limited amount of Skype Credits to try out the service before you sign up for a subscription plan. Subscription plans are the way to go if you plan on using Skype a lot for non-Skype callers (e.g., regular landlines and mobile phones).

Follow these steps to use **Safari** to buy Skype Credits:

1. Tap the **Safari** icon.
2. Type www.skype.com in the top address bar and tap **Go**.
3. Tap the **Sign In** link at the top of the page.
4. Enter your Skype Name and Password, and then tap **Sign me in**.

5. If you are not already on your **Account** screen, tap the **Account** tab in the right end of the Top Nav Bar.

6. At this point, you can choose to buy credits or a subscription:

   a. Tap the **Buy pre-pay credit** button to purchase a fixed amount of credits.

   b. Tap the **Get a subscription** button to buy a monthly subscription account.

7. Finally, complete the payment instructions for either type of purchase.

Chatting with Skype

In addition to making phone calls, you can also chat via text with other **Skype** users from your iPhone. Starting a chat is very similar to starting a call; follow these steps to do so:

1. If you are not already in **Skype**, tap the **Skype** icon.

2. Tap the **Contacts** soft key at the bottom.

3. Tap **All Contacts** to see all your contacts.

4. Tap the name of the contact you wish to chat with.

5. Tap the **Chat** button.

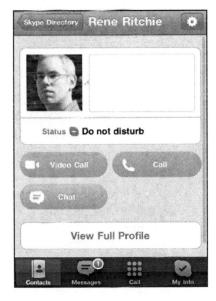

6. Type your chat text and press the **Send** button. Your chat will appear in the top of the screen.

Adding Skype to Your Computer

You can use the **Skype** app on your computer, as well. We will show you how this works next. You can also use **Skype** to make video calls on your computer if you also have a web cam hooked up.

> **NOTE:** When you call from your computer to an iPhone, you will not be able to do a video call.

To create a Skype account and download **Skype** software for your computer, follow these steps:

1. Open a web browser on your computer.

2. Go to: www.skype.com.

3. Click the **Join** link at the top of the page.

4. Create your account by completing all required information and clicking the **Continue** button. Notice that you only have to enter information in the required fields, which are denoted with an asterisk. For example, you do not need to enter your gender, birthdate, or mobile phone number.

5. You are now done with the account setup process. Next, you are presented with the option of buying Skype Credits; however, this is not required for the free Skype-to-Skype phone calls, video calls, or chats.

> **TIP:** You only need to pay for **Skype** if you want to call someone who is not using **Skype**. For example, calls to phones on land lines or mobile phones (not using **Skype**) will cost you. At the time of writing, pay-as-you-go rates were about US 2.1 cents; monthly subscriptions ranged from about US $3 - $14 for various calling plans.

6. Next, click the Get Skype link in the Top Nav Bar of the site to download **Skype** to your computer.

7. Click the **Get Skype for Windows** button or the **Get Skype for Mac** button.

8. Follow the instructions to install the software.

9. Once the software is installed, launch it and log in using your Skype account.

10. You are ready to initiate (or receive) phone calls, video calls, and chats to anyone else using **Skype**, including all your friends with **Skype** on their iPhones.

Video Recording

In addition to letting you make video calls and chat, the iPhone lets you make full-featured videos using the built-in video recorder. You can use your iPhone to shoot HD video in 1080p and then upload this video to Facebook, YouTube, or iCloud. You can also send your videos via MMS or email.

> **NOTE:** When you share a video, it will be compressed, so the quality will no longer be 1080pp.

Next, we will show you how to record video and trim your video right on your iPhone. You will also learn how to produce a high quality, high definition video right on your iPhone.

Starting the Video Recorder

The software for the video recorder is actually part of the **Camera** app (see Figure 11–3). Follow these steps to use the built-in video recorder:

1. Start up the **Camera** app Move the slider in the lower-right corner from the **Camera** icon to the **Video Recorder** icon.

2. Tap the **Camera Switch** button at the top right to alternate between the rear-facing and front-facing cameras.

3. Try to keep the iPhone steady as you record your scene.

4. Tap the **Stop** button when you are done recording.

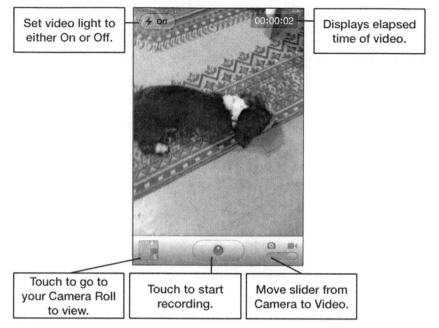

Set video light to
either On or Off.

Displays elapsed
time of video.

Touch to go to
your Camera Roll
to view.

Touch to start
recording.

Move slider from
Camera to Video.

Figure 11–3. *The layout and controls of the video recorder*

Focusing the Video

The iPhone can adjust the focus of the video based on the subject. Follow these steps
to take advantage of this feature:

1. To focus on something in the foreground of the video, tap the screen in the
    foreground. This brings up a small box to show the area of focus.

2. To switch the focus to a subject in the background, tap another part of the
    screen. The box will temporarily display the new area of focus.

Trimming the Video

The iPhone allows you to perform edits on your video right on the phone. Once the
video has been recorded and you press the **Stop** button, the video immediately goes
into your **Camera Roll**.

Tap the small image of the video in the lower-left corner to bring up the video. At the top
of the screen, you will see a timeline with all the frames of your video at the top of the
screen (see Figure 11–4). Follow these steps to edit your just-recorded video:

1. Drag either end of the timeline and you will see that the video goes into Trim
    mode.

2. Drag the ends of the video on either end until it is the length you desire.

3. When the video is the correct length, tap the **Trim** button in the upper-right corner.

4. Next, select either **Trim Original** or **Save as New Clip**. The latter option saves another version of the newly trimmed video.

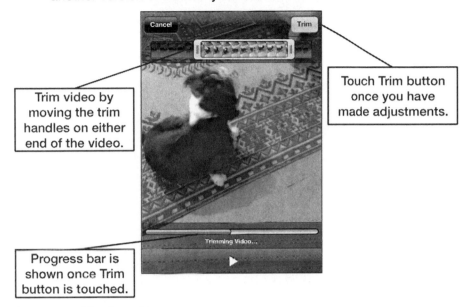

Trim video by moving the trim handles on either end of the video.

Touch Trim button once you have made adjustments.

Progress bar is shown once Trim button is touched.

Figure 11–4. *Trimming a video*

Sending the Video

As with photos, you have several options for using your iPhone to send recorded video to others. Follow these steps to send a video from your iPhone:

1. Touch the **Send** icon ![send icon] in the lower-left corner.

2. Choose your preferred option for sending the video: **Email**, **Message**, or **Send to YouTube**.

3. The next screen you see will depend on the choice you made in Step 2. If you selected **Email**, your **Email** app will launch. If you selected **Message**, your **Messaging** app will launch. And so on.

> **NOTE:** To upload a video to YouTube, you need to have an account with the site.

Chapter 12

Playing Music

In this chapter we show you how to turn your iPhone into a terrific music player. Since the iPhone comes from Apple—which popularized the now famous iPod electronic music player—you'd expect it to have some great capabilities, and it does. We'll show you how to play and organize the music you buy from iTunes or sync from your computer, how to view playlists in a variety of ways, and how to quickly find songs. You'll learn how to use the Genius feature to have the iPhone locate and group similar songs in your library—sort of like a radio station that plays only music you like.

> **TIP:** Learn how to buy music and use Ping (social networking for music lovers) right on your iPhone in Chapter 22: "iTunes on Your Device."

And you'll see how to stream music using an app called Pandora. With Pandora, you can select from a number of Internet radio stations, or create your own by typing in your favorite artist's name, and it's all free.

Your iPhone as a Music Player

Your iPhone is probably one of the best music players on the market today. The touch screen makes it easy to interact with and manage your music, playlists, cover art, and the organization of your music library. You can even connect your iPhone to your home or car stereo via Bluetooth, so you can listen to beautiful stereo sound from your iPhone!

> **TIP:** Check out Chapter 5: "AirPlay and Bluetooth" to learn how to hook up your iPhone to your Bluetooth stereo speakers or car stereo.

Whether you use the built-in **Music** app or an Internet radio app like **Pandora**, you'll find you have unprecedented control over your music on the iPhone.

The Music App

Most music is handled through the **Music** app—the icon is on the **Home** screen, usually in the bottom dock of icons, the last one on the right.

> **NOTE:** For all you readers familiar with the iPhone before iOS 5, yes, the music playing app was called the **iPod** app. Now is is simply the **Music** app.

Touch the **Music** icon and, as Figure 12–1 shows, you'll see five soft keys across the bottom:

- **Playlists** lets you see synced playlists from your computer, as well as playlists created on the iPhone.

- **Artists** lets you see an alphabetical list of artists (searchable like your Address Book).

- **Songs** lets you see an alphabetical list of songs (also searchable).

- **Albums** lets you browse your music by album titles.

- **More** lets you see audiobooks, compilations, composers, genres, iTunes U, and podcasts.

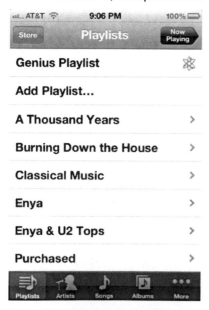

Figure 12–1. *Music app with soft keys at bottom*

Editing the Soft Keys

One very cool feature on the iPhone is that you can edit the soft keys at the bottom of the **Music** app and really customize it to fit your needs and tastes. To do so, first touch the **More** button.

Then touch the **Edit** button at the top left of the screen.

The screen changes to show the various icons that can be dragged down to the bottom dock.

Figure 12-2. *Change the soft keys in the **Music** app.*

Let's say you want to replace the **Albums** icon with the one for **Audiobooks**. Just touch and hold the **Audiobooks** icon and drag it to where the **Albums** icon is on the bottom dock. When you get there, release the icon and the **Audiobooks** icon will now reside where the **Album** icon used to be. You can do this with any of the icons on this **Configure** screen. When you are finished, touch the **Done** button at the top right of the screen.

> **TIP**: You can also reorder the icons across the bottom by dragging and dropping them back and forth along the soft key row.

Playlists View

> **NOTE**: A playlist is a list of songs you create and can include any genre, artist, year of recording, or collection of songs that interest you.

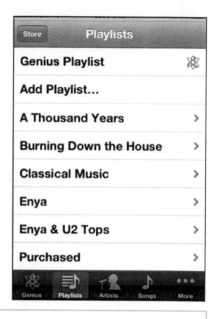

Many people group together music of a particular genre, like classical or rock. Others may create playlists with fast beat music and call it workout or running music. You can use playlists to organize your music just about any way you want.

You can create playlists in iTunes on your computer and then sync to your iPhone (see the iTunes Guide), or you can create a playlist right on your iPhone as we describe in the next section.

Once you've synced a playlist to your iPhone or created one on your iPhone, it shows up on the left-hand side of the **Music** screen, under **Library**.

> **NOTE:** You can edit the contents of some of your playlists on your iPhone. However, you can't edit Genius playlists on the iPhone itself.

If you have several playlists listed along the left side, just touch the name of the one you want to listen to.

Creating Playlists on the iPhone

The iPhone lets you create unique playlists that can be edited and synced with your computer. Let's say you want to add a new selection of music to your iPhone playlist. Just create the playlist as we show below and add songs. You can change the playlist whenever you want, removing old songs and adding new ones—it couldn't be easier!

To create a new playlist on the iPhone, touch the **Add Playlist** tab under **Genius Playlist**.

Add Playlist...

Give your playlist a unique name (we'll call this one "Bike-riding music"), then touch **Save**.

Now you'll see the **Songs** screen. Touch the name of any song you want to add to the new playlist.

You know a song is selected and will be added to the playlist when it turns gray.

> **NOTE:** Don't get frustrated trying to remove or deselect a song you tapped by mistake. You can't remove or deselect songs on this screen; you have to click **Done**, then remove them on the next screen, as we describe.

Select **Done** at the top right and the playlist contents will be displayed.

Searching for Music

Almost every view from your **Music** app (**Playlists, Artists, Songs**, etc.) has a search window at the top of the screen.

If you don't see the search window, tap the time at the top to instantly make it visible.

Tap once in the search window and type a few letters of the name of an artist, album, playlist, or song to instantly see a list of all matching items. This is the best way to quickly find something to listen to or watch on your iPhone.

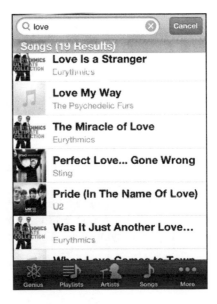

Changing the View in the Music app

The **Music** app is very flexible when it comes to ways of displaying and categorizing your music. Sometimes, you might want to look at your songs listed by the artist. At other times, you might prefer seeing a particular album or song. The iPhone lets you easily change the view to help manage and play just the music you want at a given moment.

In your **Music** app, you have the following views:

- Artists View - shows you a listing of all your music arranged by artist.
- Songs View - shows all your music listed by name of each song.
- Albums View - shows all music arranged by album name.
- Genres View - shows all music arranged by type or genre.
- Composers View - shows music arranged by composer name.
- Audiobooks - shows all your audiobooks.
- Compilations - shows all compilations.
- ITunes U - shows all iTunes U content.
- Podcasts - shows all your podcasts.

Viewing Songs in an Album

When you're in **Albums** view, just touch an album cover or name and the screen will slide, showing you the songs on that album (see Figure 12–3).

> **TIP**: When you start playing an album, the album cover may expand to fill the screen. Tap the screen once to bring up (or hide) the controls at the top and bottom. You can use these controls to manage the song and screen as we describe below.

To see the songs on an album that is playing, tap the **List** button and the album cover and the cover will turn over, revealing all the songs on that album. The song that is playing will have a small blue arrow next to it.

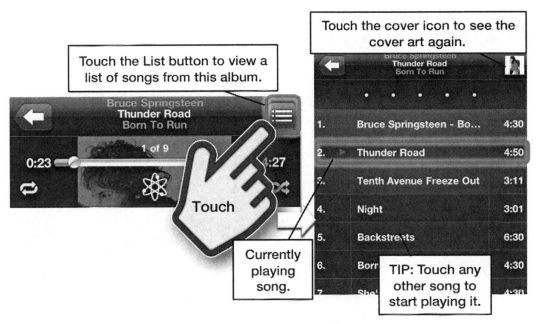

Touch the List button to view a list of songs from this album.

Touch

Currently playing song.

TIP: Touch any other song to start playing it.

Figure 12–3. *Touch the **List** button to see the songs on a particular album.*

Tap the title bar above the list of songs to return to the album cover view.

Navigating with Cover Flow

Cover Flow is a proprietary and very cool way of looking at your music by album covers. If you're playing a song in the **Music** music app and turn your iPhone horizontal — into landscape mode — your iPhone will automatically change to **Cover Flow** view.

Touch the cover and flick left or right to go to another album.

Touch & Flick Left/Right

Touch here to play or pause the song.

Touch here view a list of songs from this album.

Viewing Songs in Cover Flow

Just touch an album cover and the cover will flip, showing you all the songs on that album.

To see the song that is playing now (in Cover Flow view), tap the album cover and it will turn over, revealing the songs on that album (Figure 12–4). The song that is currently playing will have a small blue arrow next to it.

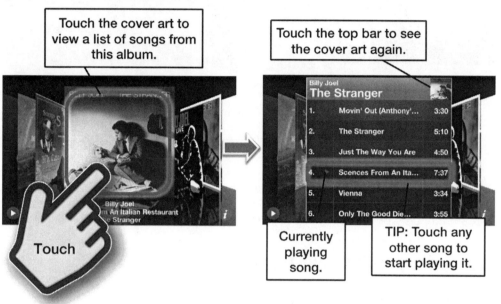

Figure 12–4. *You can look at an album's contents using* **Cover Flow.**

Tap the title bar (above the list of songs) and the album cover will be displayed once more. You can then keep swiping through your music until you find what you are searching for.

NOTE: You can also touch the small "*i*" in the lower right corner and the album cover will flip, showing you the songs, just as if you touched the cover.

Playing Your Music

Now that you know how to find your music, it's time to play it! Find a song or browse to a playlist using any of the methods mentioned above. Simply tap the song name and it will begin to play.

This screen shows a picture of the album that the song I chose comes from, with the name of the song at the top.

Along the bottom of the screen you'll find the **Volume** slider bar, and the **Previous Song**, **Play/Pause**, and **Next Song** buttons.

To see other songs on the album, just double-tap the album cover and the screen will flip, showing all of the other songs.

You can also touch the **List** button in the upper right corner to view a list of songs on the album.

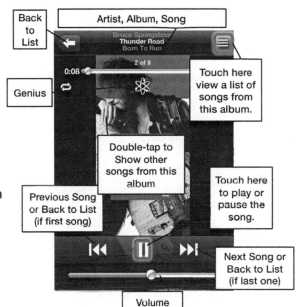

Back to List

Artist, Album, Song

Bruce Springsteen
Thunder Road
Born To Run

Genius

Touch here view a list of songs from this album.

Double-tap to Show other songs from this album

Previous Song or Back to List (if first song)

Touch here to play or pause the song.

Next Song or Back to List (if last one)

Volume

Pausing and Playing

Tap the pause symbol (if your song is playing) or the play arrow (if the music is paused) to stop or resume your song.

To Play the Previous or Next Song

If you are in a playlist, touching the **Next Song** arrow (to the right of the **Play/Pause** button) advances you to the next song in the list. If you are searching through your music by album, touching **Next** moves you to the next song on the album. Touching the **Previous Song** button does the reverse.

> **NOTE:** If you're at the beginning of a song, **Previous** takes you to the preceding song. If the song is already playing, **Previous** goes to the beginning of the current song (and a second tap would take you to the previous song).

Adjusting the Volume

There are two ways to adjust the volume on your iPhone: using the external **Volume** buttons or using the **Volume Slider** control on the screen.

The external **Volume** buttons are on the upper left side of the device. Press the **Volume Up** key (the top button) or the **Volume Down** key to raise or lower the volume. You'll see the **Volume Slider** control move as you adjust the volume. You can also just touch and hold the **Volume Slider** key to adjust the volume.

> **TIP:** To quickly mute the sound, press and hold the **Volume Down** key and the volume eventually reduces to zero.

Volume Slider

Double-Click the Home Button for Media Controls

You can play your music while you are doing other things on your iPhone, like reading and responding to e-mail, browsing the Web, or playing a game. With the iPhone's new multitasking function, a quick double-tap to the **Home** button on the bottom, followed by a swipe to the right, will bring up the "now playing" media controls in the multitasking window. The controls allow you to skip to the previous song, pause or play the current song, skip to the next song, or go directly to the app playing the song.

> **NOTE:** The widgets show whatever app last played audio or video, so if **Pandora** was last, you'll see that instead of **Music,** and the widgets will control **Pandora** instead, same with **Videos**, **YouTube**, etc.

> **TIP**: If you hold down the **Previous Song** control, the song will rewind; if you hold down the **Next Song** control, it will fast forward.

Repeating, Shuffling, Moving around in a Song

In play mode, you can activate additional controls by tapping the screen anywhere on the album cover. You'll then see an additional slider (the scrubber bar) at the top, along with the symbols for **Repeat**, **Shuffle,** and **Genius**.

Moving to Another Part of a Song

Slide the scrubber bar to the right and you'll see the elapsed time of the song (displayed to the far right) change accordingly. If you are looking for a specific section of the song, drag the slider, then let go and listen to see if you're in the right place.

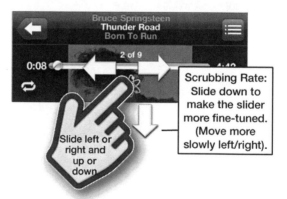

Repeat One Song or All Songs

To repeat the song you're listening to, touch the **Repeat** symbol at the left of the top controls twice until you see it turn blue and display a 1.

To repeat all songs in the playlist, song list, or album, touch the **Repeat** icon until it turns blue (and does not display a 1).

To turn off the **Repeat** feature, press the icon until it turns white again.

Shuffle

If you are listening to a playlist or album or any other category or list of music, you might decide you don't want to listen to the songs in order. You can touch the **Shuffle** symbol so the music will play in random order. You know **Shuffle** is turned on when the icon is blue, and off when it is white.

Shake to Shuffle

The **Shake to Shuffle** feature was introduced in the last iPhone. So, to turn on **Shuffle** mode, all you have to do to change songs is simply give your iPhone a shake, then shake it again. Every time you shake your iPhone, you'll skip to the next randomly selected song in the list.

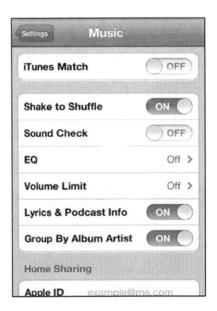

> **TIP**: If you plan on dancing while holding your iPhone, turn off **Shake to Shuffle**!

You can turn on **Shake to Shuffle** in your **Settings** menu.

1. Tap the **Settings** icon.

2. Scroll down and touch the **Music** icon.

3. Move the **Shake to Shuffle** switch to **ON** or **OFF**.

Now Playing

Sometimes you're having so much fun exploring your options for playlists or albums that you get deeply buried in a menu—then find yourself just wanting to get back to the song you're listening to. Fortunately, this is always very easy to do—you can just touch the **Now Playing** icon at the top right of most of the music screens.

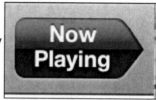

Viewing Other Songs on the Album

You may decide you want to listen to another song from the same album rather than going to the next song in the playlist or genre list.

In the upper-right corner of the **Now Playing** screen, you'll see a small button with three lines on it.

Tap that button and the view switches to a small image of the album cover. The screen now displays all the songs on that album.

Touch another song on the list and that song will begin to play.

> **NOTE:** If you were in the middle of a playlist or a **Genius Playlist** and you jump to another song from an album, you won't be taken back to that playlist. To return to that playlist, you'll need to either go back to your playlist library or tap **Genius** to make a new **Genius Playlist**.

Adjusting Music Settings

There are several settings you can adjust to tweak music-playing on your iPhone. You'll find these in the **Settings** menu. Just tap the **Settings** Icon on your **Home** screen.

In the middle of the **Settings** screen, touch the **Music** tab to go to the settings screen for **Music**. You'll find six settings you can adjust on this screen: **Shake to Shuffle, Sound Check, EQ, Volume Limit, Lyrics & Podcast Info** and **Groupe By Album Artist**.

You'll also find the login area for **Home Sharing**, which lets you stream music from iTunes on your Windows or Mac PC.

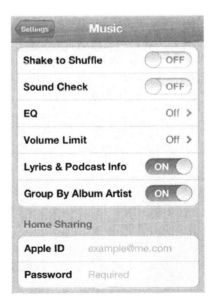

Using Sound Check (Auto Volume Adjust)

Because songs are recorded at different volumes, sometimes during playback a particular song may sound quite loud compared to another. **Sound Check** can eliminate this. If **Sound Check** is set to **ON**, all your songs will play at roughly the same volume.

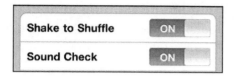

EQ (Sound Equalizer Setting)

Sound equalization is very personal and subjective. Some people like to hear more bass in their music, some like more treble, and some like more of an exaggerated mid-range. Whatever your music tastes, there is an **EQ** setting for you.

> **NOTE:** Using the **EQ** setting can diminish battery capacity somewhat.

Just touch the **EQ** tab and then select either the type of music you most often listen to or a specific option to boost treble or bass. Experiment, have fun, and find the setting that's perfect for you.

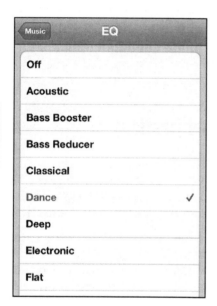

Volume Limit (Safely Listen to Music at a Reasonable Level)

This is a great way for parents to control the volume on their kids' iPhones. It is also a good way to make sure you don't listen too loudly through headphones so you don't damage your ears. You just move the slider to a volume limit and then lock that limit.

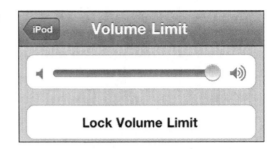

To lock the volume limit, touch the **Lock Volume Limit** button and enter a 4-digit passcode. You will be prompted to enter your passcode once more and the volume limit will then be locked.

Using Home Sharing

If you're like us, you probably have far more music on your big computer hard drive than you can fit on your iPhone. With iPhone and Home Sharing, that's not a problem.

As long as you're on the same Wi-Fi network as your computer, you can stream anything from your desktop iTunes library straight to your iPhone.

To enable Home Sharing, make sure your computer Is logged into Home Sharing with your iTunes email address and password, then log into Home Sharing on your iPhone with the same account.

Once you're logged in, you'll be able to choose between your local (iPhone) and remote (desktop iTunes) libraries. Here's how:

1. Launch the **Music** app

2. Tap the **More** tab at the bottom right

3. Tap the **Shared** tab at the bottom of the list. (If you don't see a **Shared** tab, double check to make sure both your iPhone and computer are both logged into Home Sharing using the same iTunes account)

4. Choose the name of your desktop machine from the **Shared** list, in this example that's **MacPro**. (You can share more than one iTunes library so you may have several to choose from.)

Your iPhone library will disappear and you'll see your desktop iTunes library instead. It will look exactly the same as your iPhone library, only the content will be different.

To switch back to your iPhone library, just repeat the same process but choose **iPhone** from the **Shared** list instead.

Showing Media Controls When Your iPhone is Locked

You may want to get to your media controls even if your iPhone is locked. Here's how: Just double-click the **Home** button and the controls for adjusting the audio show up on the top of the locked screen. There's no reason to unlock the screen and then go to the Music program to find the controls.

In the image to the right, notice that the screen is still locked—yet the music controls are now visible along the top. You can pause, skip, go to a previous song, or adjust the volume without actually unlocking the iPhone.

> **NOTE**: You'll only see these controls if there is audio playing.

Listening to Free Internet Radio (Pandora)

While your iPhone gives you unprecedented control over your personal music library, there may be times when you want to just "mix it up" and listen to some other music.

> **TIP:** A basic **Pandora** account is free and can save you considerable money compared with buying lots of new songs from iTunes.

Pandora grew out of the Music Genome Project. This was a huge undertaking. A large team of musical analysts looked at just about every song ever recorded and then developed a complex algorithm of attributes to associate with each song.

> **NOTE:** There are an ever-increasing amount of "internet radio" or subscription music style apps now available including the popular **Slacker Personal Radio**, **Spotify**, **Rdio, Last.fm**, and others. Please also note that Pandora is a US-only application and Slacker available is only in the US and Canada. Spotfly is available in the US and Europe, and many others vary by region as well. Hopefully, more options will begin to pop up for international users.

Getting Started with Pandora

With Pandora you can design your own unique radio stations built around artists you like. Best of all, it is completely free!

Start by downloading the **Pandora** app from the App Store. Just go to the App Store and search for Pandora.

Now just touch the Pandora icon to start.

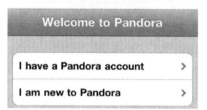

The first time you start Pandora, you'll be asked to either create an account or to sign in if you already have an account. Just fill in the appropriate information—an email address and a password are required—and you can start designing your own music listening experience.

Pandora is also available for your Windows or Mac computer and for most smartphone platforms. If you already have a Pandora account, all you have to do is sign in.

> **TIP:** Remember that you can move apps into folders. As you can see in Figure 12–7, we've put three Music apps, including **Pandora**, into one folder named Music. See more about using folders in Chapter 6: "Icons and Folders."

Figure 12–7. *Put like Music apps, such as Pandora, into one folder for easy retrieval.*

Pandora's Main Screen

Your stations are listed down the screen with the **QuickMix** at the top. Tap any station and it will begin to play. Usually, the first song will be from the actual artist chosen and the next songs will be from similar artists.

Once you select a station, the music begins to play. You'll see the current song displayed, along with album art—very much like when you play a song using the **Music app**.

You'll also see a small **Now Playing** icon in the upper right corner—very much like the **Now Playing** icon in the **Music** app.

Touch the **Detail** view  icon in the upper right corner, just like the one you find in the
Music app, and you'll see a nice bio of the artist, which changes with each new song.
(See Figure 12–8).

Figure 12–8. *Pandora's Album cover view and the Detail view.*

Thumbs Up or Thumbs Down in Pandora

If you like a particular song, touch the
thumbs-up icon and you'll hear more from
that artist.

Conversely, if you don't like an artist on
this station, touch the thumbs-down icon
and you won't hear that artist again.

If you like, you can pause a song and
come back later, or skip to the next
selection in your station.

NOTE: With a free Pandora account, you
are limited in the number of skips per
hour you can make. Also, you'll
occasionally hear advertising. To get rid of
these annoyances, you can upgrade to a
paid "Pandora One" account as we show
you below.

Pandora's Menu

Between the two thumbs is a **Menu** button which looks like a triangle . Touch this and you can bookmark the artist or song, go to iTunes to buy music from this artist, or email the station to someone in your **Contacts**.

Creating a New Station in Pandora

Creating a new station couldn't be easier.

If you are listening to a station, press the **back arrow** in the upper left corner to return to the Pandora main screen. Then tap the **New Station** button along the bottom row. Type in the name of an artist, song, or composer.

When you find what you are looking for, touch the selection and Pandora will immediately start to build a station around your choice.

You can also touch **Genre** and build a station around a particular genre of music.

You'll then see the new station listed with your other stations.

You can build up to 100 stations in Pandora.

> **TIP:** You can organize your stations by pressing the **By Date** or **ABC** buttons at the top of the screen.

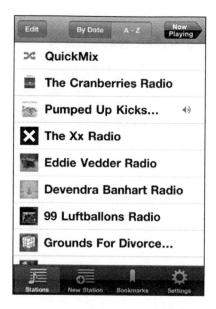

Adjusting Pandora's Settings—Your Account, Upgrading, and More

You can sign out of your Pandora account, adjust the audio quality, and even upgrade to Pandora One (which removes advertising) by tapping the settings icon in the lower right corner of the screen. (See Figure 12–9.)

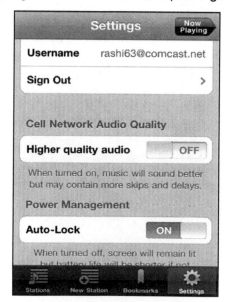

Figure 12–9. *Setting options in Pandora*

To sign out, tap the **Sign Out** button.

To adjust the sound quality, move the switch under **Cell Network Audio Quality** either **ON** or **OFF**. When you are on a cellular network, setting this off is probably better, otherwise you may hear more skips and pauses in the playback.

When you are on a strong Wi-Fi connection, you can set this to **ON** for better quality. See our Chapter 4: "Connect to the Network" chapter to learn more about the various connections.

To save your battery life, you should set the **Auto-Lock** to **ON,** which is the default. If you want the force the screen to stay lit, then switch this to **OFF**.

To remove all advertising, tap the **Upgrade to Pandora One** button. A web browser window will open and you'll be take to Pandora's web site to enter your credit card information. As of publishing time, the annual account cost is $36.00, but that may be different by the time you read this book.

iBooks and E-Books

In this chapter, we will show you how to use your iPhone for a good book-reading experience if you're OK with a slightly smaller screen. For example, we will cover iBooks, including how to buy and download them, as well as how to find some great free classic books. We will also show you other e-book reading options that use the third-party **Kindle** and **Kobo** (formerly **Shortcovers**) readers on your iPhone.

The iPhone can use Apple's proprietary e-book reader, **iBooks**. In this chapter, we will show you how to download the **iBooks** app, how to shop for books in the iBooks Store, and how to read both PDF files (Adobe PDF format) and iBooks as well as take advantage of all the **iBooks** features.

With **iBooks**, you can interact with books and PDF files like never before. Pages turn like a real book; and you can adjust font sizes, look up words in the built-in dictionary, and search through your text.

In the App Store, you can also find apps for Amazon's **Kindle** reader, a **Barnes and Noble** reader, the **Stanza** reader, and the **Kobo** reader. Both the **Kindle** and **Kobo** readers offer a great reading experience on the iPhone.

Downloading iBooks

Search the App Store for "iBooks" or "Apple." You will find the **iBooks** app among the selections listed.

> **NOTE**: On a brand new iPhone, you should get a notice asking: "Do you want to download iBooks now?"
>
> If you don't see this notice right away, tap the **App Store** app and the notice should pop up.

Select the **iBooks** app and touch the **Free** button to download.

Select **Install** and **iBooks** will be downloaded and installed on the iPhone.

The iBooks Store

Before you can start enjoying your reading experience, you need to load up your iBooks library with titles. Fortunately, many books can be found for free in the iBooks store, including the near complete Gutenberg Collection of classics and public domain titles.

> **NOTE**: Paid iBooks content is not available in all countries. However, free content is available everywhere, including the Project Guttenberg collection of classic, public domain literature.

Just touch the **Store** button in the upper-right corner of your bookshelf, and you will be taken to the iBooks Store.

The iBooks Store is arranged much like the App Store. There is a **Categories** button in the top left, opposite the **Library** button. Touch this to see all the available categories from which you can choose your books.

Featured books are highlighted on the front page of the store, with **New** and **Notable** titles displayed for browsing.

At the bottom of the store are five soft keys: **Featured**, **Charts**, **Browse**, **Search**, and **Purchases**.

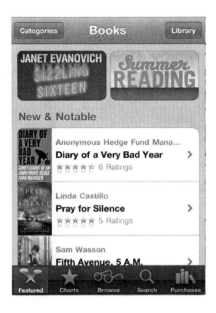

Touch the **Charts** button 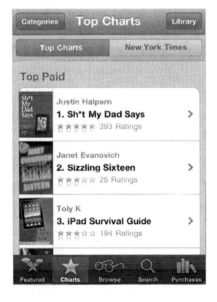 to see all the top charts and New York Times bestselling books. Touch the **Purchases** button to see all the books you have purchased or downloaded for your library.

Purchasing a book is much like purchasing an app. Touch a book title that interests you and browse the description and customer reviews. When you are ready to purchase the title, touch the **Price** button.

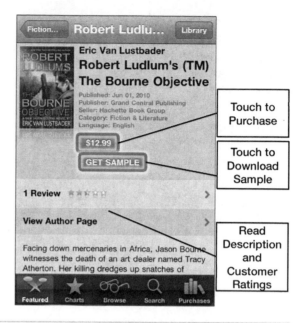

Touch to Purchase

Touch to Download Sample

Read Description and Customer Ratings

NOTE: Many titles have a sample download. It is a great idea to check this sample out if you are not sure that you want to purchase the book. If you download a sample, and you can always purchase the full book from within that sample.

Once you decide to download a sample or purchase a title, **iBooks** switches to the **Bookshelf** view, and you can see the book being deposited onto your bookshelf. Your book is now available for reading.

Using the Search Button

Just like iTunes and the App Store, the iBooks Store gives you a **Search** window in which you can type virtually any phrase. You can search for an author, title, or series. Just touch **Search** at the bottom of the screen, and the on-screen keyboard pops up. Type in an author, title, series, or genre of book, and then press the **Search** button.

You will see suggestions pop up that match your search; just touch the appropriate suggestion to go to that title.

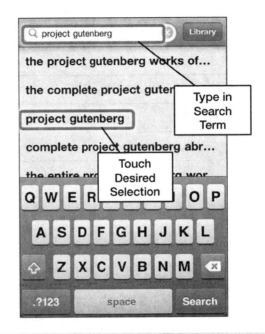

TIP: Do a search for "Project Gutenberg" to see thousands of free, public domain titles.

Switching Collections (Books, PDFs, More)

Your iBooks app has multiple collections of books or PDF files (Adobe PDF format reader).

You can easily switch collections between these two and add new collections by tapping the Collections button at the middle of the top of the library.

This button will show you the currently visible collection. In this image, **Books** is the currently collection. Tap the Books button to see the available collections.

From this screen, you can tap any
collection to view it.

Notice that you can also create **New**
collections and **Edit** collections you have
created by using the buttons at the
bottom.

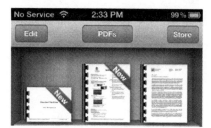

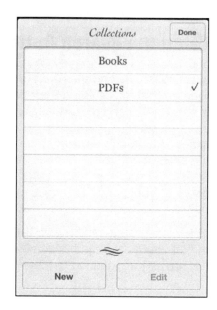

Reading PDFs

Switch collections to view your PDFs
collection as shown above.

Tap any book to open it up and start
reading. All the same navigation features
work as described in the "Reading iBooks"
section.

One difference is that you will see
thumbnail images of the pages of the PDF
file at the bottom of the page. Tap any
thumbnail to jump to that page. Drag your
finger back and forth along the thumbnail
Images to jump to a specific page.

Reading iBooks

Touch any title in your library to open it for
reading. The book will open to the very
first page, which is often the title page or
other *front matter* in the book.

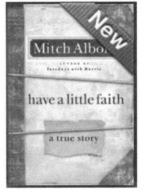

In the upper-left corner, next to the **Library**
button, you can see a **Table of Contents**
button. To jump to the table of contents,
either touch the **Table of Contents** button
or simply turn the pages to advance to the
table of contents.

You can turn pages in one of three ways.
First, you can touch the right-hand side of
the page to turn to the next page. Second,
you can slowly touch and hold the screen
on the right edge of the page; and, while
continuing to touch the screen, gently and
slowly move your finger to the left.

> **TIP:** If you move your finger very slowly you can actually see the words on the back of the page
> as you "turn" it—a very cool visual effect.

Customizing Your Reading Experience: Brightness, Fonts, and Font Sizes

In the upper center of the book, there are three icons available: **Brightness**, **Size**, and
Search. These options help to make your reading experience much more immersive.

Touch the **Brightness** icon and you can adjust the brightness of the book.

If you are reading in bed in a very dark room, you might want to dim the tablet by sliding the **Brightness** slider all the way to the left. If you are out in the sunlight, you may need to slide it all the way to the right. However, you should keep in mind that high screen brightness consumes more battery power than most other features, so turn this feature back down when you don't need your screen to be so bright anymore.

> **NOTE:** The preceding tip adjusts the brightness only within **iBooks**. To adjust the global brightness of the iPhone, use the **Settings** app (go to the **Settings** icon > **Brightness & Wallpaper**).

The **Font Size and Type** icon lets you adjust font values to suit your preferences.

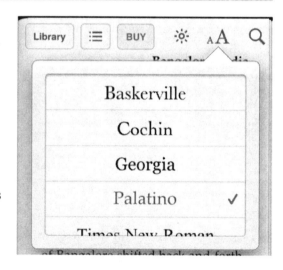

Do this to **Increase the Font Size:**

Tap the large **A** icon multiple times.

Do this to **Decrease the Font Size:**

Tap the small **a** icon multiple times.

At the time of writing, there are six available font styles—but there may well be more fonts available when you read this book.

Have fun and try out some of the various fonts. The default selection is the Palatino font, but all of the fonts look great, and a larger font size can make a difference for some. The goal is to adjust the font size so the text is as comfortable and easy to read as possible.

Grow Your Vocabulary Using the Built-In Dictionary

iBooks contains a very powerful built-in dictionary, which can be quite helpful when you run across a word that is new or unfamiliar.

NOTE: The first time you attempt to use the dictionary, your iPhone will need to download it. Follow the on-screen prompts to download the dictionary.

Accessing the dictionary could not be easier. Just touch and hold any word in the book. A pop-up will appear with various options that let you highlight a word, create a note, or search for other occurrences of this particular word.

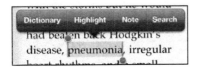

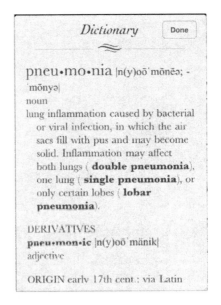

Touch **Dictionary** and a pronunciation and definition of the word will be displayed. Touch **Done** to leave the dictionary and go back to your book.

Setting an In-Page Bookmark

There may be times when you wish to set an in-text bookmark for future reference.

The upper-right corner displays a **Bookmark** icon. Touch the **Bookmark** icon and it will change to a red bookmark on the page.

To view your bookmarks, just touch the **Table of Contents** icon at the top left of the screen (next to the **Library** icon), and then touch **Bookmarks**. Touch the bookmark highlighted and you will jump to that section in the book.

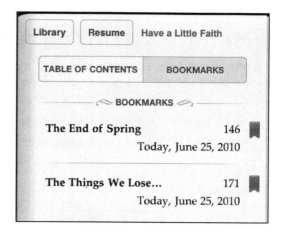

> **TIP:** You do not need to set a bookmark every time you leave **iBooks**. The app will automatically remember where you stop reading in a book. This holds true no matter how many books you open and read, so can always return to exactly where you stopped reading in a given book. The **iBooks** app will also sync with the version of **iBooks** on your iPad, so you can move back and forth between devices and keep your place in a given book.

Using Highlighting and Notes

There are some very nice "added touches" to the **iBooks** app. For example, there may be times that you want to highlight a particular word to come back to at another time. And there may be other times you want to leave yourself a note in the margin.

Both of these things are very easy to do in **iBooks**.

Highlighting Text

Follow these steps to highlight text in the iBooks app:

1. Touch and hold any word to bring up the menu options.

2. Choose **Highlight** from the menu options.

3. To remove the highlight, tap the word and then select **Remove Highlight**.

Changing the color of a highlight is as simple as following these steps:

1. Tap the highlighted word.

2. Choose **Colors** from the menu.

3. Choose a new color.

Jobs quickly became bored with college. He liked being at Reed, jus[Yellow][Green][Blue][Pink][Purple] surprised when he found out that, for all of its hippie aura, there were strict course requirements. When Wozniak came to visit, Jobs waved his schedule at him and complained,

Adding Notes

It's also easy to add a note in the margin in **iBooks**:

1. Touch and hold any word, as you did previously.

2. Choose **Note** from the menu.

3. Type in your note and then touch **Done**. The note now appears on the side of the page in the margin (see Figure 13–1).

> **TIP:** Your notes will also appear under your bookmarks on the title page. Just touch the **Title Page** button and then touch **Bookmarks**. You can find the notes you write at the bottom of the page.
>
> You can change the color of notes the same way you change the color of highlights!

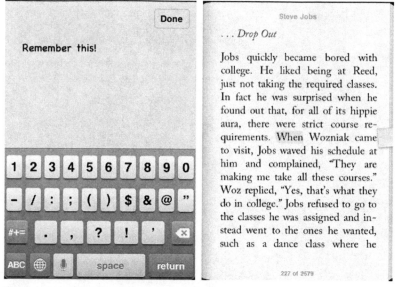

Figure 13–1. *Using the Notes feature in* ***iBooks***

Using Search

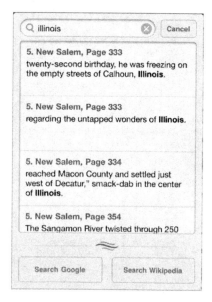

iBooks contains a powerful search feature built right in. Just touch the **Search** icon, and (as in other programs on the iPhone) the built-in keyboard will pop up. Type in the word or phrase you are searching for and you will see a list of chapters where that word occurs.

Just touch the selection desired and you will jump to that section in the book. You also have the option of jumping right to Google or Wikipedia by touching the appropriate buttons at the bottom of the **Search** window.

> **NOTE:** Using the Wikipedia or Google search will take you out of **iBooks** and launch **Safari**.

Moving and Deleting Books

Deleting books from your iBooks library is very similar to deleting applications from the iPhone. You can delete or move iBooks by tapping the **Edit** button in the **Library** view.

top-left corner.

Once you touch the **Edit** button, you will notice a small black "**x**" in the upper-left corner of each book.

Just touch the "**x**" and you will be prompted to delete the book. Once you touch **Delete**, the book will disappear from the shelf.

Other E-Book Readers: Kindle and Kobo

As we have noted, the **iBooks** app offers an unparalleled e-book reading experience. However, there are other e book reader apps available for the iPhone that are worth checking out.

Many users already have a Kindle and have invested in a Kindle library. Others use the **Kobo** e-reader software (formerly called **Shortcovers**) and have invested in a library of books for that platform.

Fortunately, both e-book platforms have apps in the iPhone App Store. When either program is downloaded and installed, you can sign in and read your complete library for its respective platform on your iPhone.

> **NOTE:** No matter which of these other e-readers you choose, you can always just "sign in," see your complete library, and pick up just where you left off in your last book—even if you started reading on a different device.

Download E-Reader Apps

It's a trivial matter to download alternative e-reader apps. Simply go to the App Store, touch **Categories,** and then touch **Books**. In this section, you will find the **Kindle** and **Kobo** apps. Both are free apps, so just touch the **Free** button to begin downloading one of them.

> **TIP:** It is usually faster to search by the name of the app if you know which one you are looking for.

Once your desired e-reader software is installed, touch the app's icon to start it.

The Kindle Reader

Amazon's Kindle reader is the world's most popular e-reader. Millions of people have Kindle books, and the **Kindle** app allows you to read your Kindle books on your iPhone.

The iPhone and iPad versions of the **Kindle** app have just been updated to support audio and video, making these versions even more advanced than the one found on the Kindle hardware itself.

> **TIP:** If you use a Kindle device, don't worry about signing in from your iPhone. You can have several devices tied to a single account. You will be able to enjoy all the books you've purchased for your Kindle right on the **Kindle** app on the iPhone.

To use the **Kindle** app on your iPhone, just
touch its icon and either sign in to your
Kindle account or create a new account
with a user name and password.

Once you sign in, you will see your Kindle
books on the **Home** page. You can touch
a book to start reading it.

NOTE: In order to buy or download new books, you need to go to www.amazon.com in the **Safari**
web browser. Once you've bought or downloaded a new book to your account, it will appear in the
Kindle app.

To read a Kindle book, touch its cover and it will open.

To see the options for reading, just touch the screen and they will be shown along the bottom row of icons.

You can add a bookmark by touching the **Plus** (**+**) button. Once the bookmark is set, the **Plus** (**+**) button turns into to a **Minus** (**-**) button.

You can go to the cover, table of contents, or beginning of the book (or specify any other location in the book) by touching the **Book** button.

The font, as well as the color of the page, can be adjusted. One very interesting feature is the ability to change the page to **Black**—which is great when reading at night.

To advance pages, either swipe from right to left or touch the right side of the page. To go back a page, just swipe from left to right or touch the left side of the page.

Tap the screen and a slider appears at the bottom; you can move this to advance to any page in the book.

To return to your list of books, just touch the **Home** button.

The Kobo Reader

Like the **Kindle** reader, the **Kobo** reader begins by asking you to sign into your existing Kobo Books account. All of your existing Kobo Books will then be available for reading.

Kobo's **Shelf** view uses a bookshelf metaphor, similar to the one used by **iBooks**. Tap the book cover for whichever book you wish to open.

Or, you can touch the **List** tab to see your books organized in a **List** view.

Open any book, and you will see two buttons along the top of the Kobo reader: **I'm Reading** and **Settings**.

Touching the **I'm Reading** button places a bookmark where you left off in the book and returns the screen to your **Shelf** view.

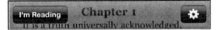

Touching the **Settings** button will display a series of buttons along the bottom of the screen for viewing bookmarks, seeing information about the book, and adjusting the page transition style and font. Under those buttons are four icons: **Font**, **Brightness**, **Screen Lock**, and **Nighttime Reading**. Touch any of these buttons to make adjustments to your viewing experience.

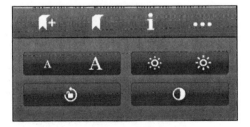

To advance pages in the **Kobo** reader, touch the right side of the page. To go back a page, just touch the left side of the page. You can also use the slider at the bottom to advance through the pages.

Chapter 14

Newsstand and More

In the last chapter, we spoke about how the iPhone has revolutionized the world of reading with iBooks. Not only is the iPhone unparalleled for reading e-books, it's Newsstand folder is unequaled in dealing with new media such as online newspapers and magazines. Plus, the App Store makes it easy to find comic books readers, PDF readers, and more. The iPhone is even set to revitalize the comic book industry with comic books that look beautiful and are amazingly interactive.

In this chapter, we'll explore how to enjoy new media using the iPhone's vivid screen and terrific touch interface.

Newsstand

The Newsstand is a special folder on your iPhone's Home screen that looks like a bookshelf and collects and organizes all your magazine and newspaper apps. This folder does not behave like a regular iPhone folder. If a magazine or newspaper app supports Newsstand, then it will show you the latest cover art or front page for that periodical sitting on the shelf, rather than the Newsstand Folder icon (you will also see this cover or front page in the Fast App Switcher).

If the magazine or newspaper app offers subscriptions and you're a subscriber, then Newsstand apps can also automatically download the latest issues overnight, so you have something new to read when you open it in the morning.

The Newsstand folder also has a **Store** button that takes you to a special section of the App Store. This section lists all the magazine and newspaper apps that currently support Newsstand.

Other than the special presentation and ability to download new issues automatically, a Newsstand app otherwise functions just like any other app.

> **NOTE:** It's up to each magazine and newspaper app to add Newsstand support. At the time of writing, many but not all magazine apps have added Newsstand support. If an app doesn't support Newsstand, it will download to the **Home** screen and behave just like any regular, non-Newsstand app.
>
> Also, magazine and newspaper selection can vary greatly by country. Use the **Store** button in Newsstand to see the latest selection in your area.

Buying and Subscribing to Periodicals

The newspaper and magazine apps in **Newsstand** are typically free; however, they also typically come with very little or even no content built in. To get the content, you need to either buy individual issues or subscribe to a number of issues.

Buying issues is handled like any other in-app purchase. Typically, you'll be shown a list of recent issues with the cover art on the left and a content blurb on the right, along with the price of the issue. Tap the price and you'll be asked for your iTunes password to confirm the purchase. Once you confirm a purchase, your issue will begin to download.

Subscribing to newspapers and magazines is handled like a special in-app purchase that lasts for a specified period of time. For example, you can often purchase a year's worth of newspapers for a set price. Some newspapers and magazines offer different subscription length options, such as three years, six months, and so on. Some also offer bundles that include both the print and digital editions. Make sure you read your options carefully and figure out which one provides you with the greatest value.

You might wonder what you do if you've bought a subscription or an individual issue, and you need to re-install the app that displays the content. If that happens, you can simply re-install the app and then restore your subscription or re-download any individual issues you've previously purchased. In other words, the process of restoring content in Newsstand apps is identical to that of restoring content for any other in-app purchase.

Newspapers

Remember the days when newspapers were delivered to the house? Invariably, if there was one puddle in the sidewalk, that was where the newspaper landed! You took it out of that plastic bag, shook it off, and tried to make out what was in the section that got soaked.

Well, those days may be gone forever. You now have the opportunity to interact with the news and even get your paper delivered every day—but to your iPhone instead of your driveway.

Many newspapers and news sites are developing apps for the iPhone, with new apps seeming to appear every day. Some of these apps provide a level of free content, but require you to create an account or subscribe to get more. Others apps provide content only with a subscription.

> **NOTE:** If you already subscribe to the print edition of your local newspaper, it might provide you with discounted or even free access to its iPhone app. Be sure to read any registration or subscription offers carefully to see if you qualify.
>
> Many newspapers also have dedicated web sites. Some are optimized for the iPhone and **Safari**, while others offer a full web experience. Some require registration or a paid subscription to view the paper's full content.

Let's take a quick look at *The New York Times*, one of largest newspapers in the U.S., and see how that paper has revolutionized reading the news on the iPhone.

The New York Times app

The New York Times provides various apps, both free and paid, to bring you the news on the iPhone.

The New York Times offers a slimmed-down version of the paper in its free iPhone app.

There are four soft keys at the bottom of the page: **Top News, Most E-Mailed, Favorites and Sections.** Each section carries a sampling of stories from those sections in the current day's paper.

Touching **Sections** shows you tabs for all sections of the *New York Times*.

Navigating **The New York Times** app is as simple as touching an article and scrolling through the story. While reading a story, just touch the center of the screen and the soft keys on the top and bottom will appear.

To go back to the **Home** page, touch the **Latest News** button in the upper left-hand corner.

NOTE: If you were in another section—say *Technology*—the button in the upper-left corner would

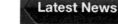

say **Technology**.

To email an article, just touch the **Share** icon in the lower-left corner. This button is only available when you are inside an article, not on the **Home** page.

Touch the icon and you can send the article via email, copy the link, or Twitter.

Moving Through and Enjoying Content

After you play for a while with different newspaper apps, you'll begin to realize that there is no real standard for navigating newspaper content. This means you'll need to become familiar with each app's own way of navigating articles, as well as how to return to the main screen. Here's a short guide for generally navigating these types of apps:

- **Showing or Hiding Control buttons or Captions:** Tapping the screen once usually shows hidden controls or picture captions. You can tap the screen again to re-hide these elements.

- **Getting to the Details of an Article:** Usually, you scroll through the articles, just as you would on a web page.

- **Viewing a Video:** Typically, you just tap a video to start playing it. See Chapter 15: "Viewing Videos" to learn how to navigate videos on the iPhone.

- **Expanding a Video or Image Size:** You can try pinching open in the video or image and then double-tapping it. You can also look for an **Expand** button or try rotating to Landscape mode.

- **Reducing a Video or Image Size:** You can try pinching closed inside the video or image to reduce the size of a video. You can also look for a **Close** or **Minimize** button or try rotating back to Portrait mode.

- **Sharing an Article:** Sending an article link via email—or sharing it over a social network like Twitter, Facebook, or LinkedIn—is a common feature. Look for an **Action** or **Share** button.

- **Adjusting Font Sizes**: Many newspaper apps have a button or settings option for increasing or decreasing the default font size to make the content easier to read.

Magazines

It is no secret that both newspapers and magazines have suffered declines in readership over the last few years. The iPhone offers a totally new way of reading magazines that might just give the industry the boost it needs.

Pictures are incredibly clear and brilliant in magazines on the iPhone. Navigation is usually easy, and stories seem to come to life, much more so than in their print counterparts. Add video and sound integration right into the magazine, and you can see how the iPhone truly enhances the magazine reading experience.

Some magazines, such as *TIME Magazine*, include links to live or frequently updated content. These links might be called *Newsfeeds*, *Live Editions*, or *Updates*. Check for them in any magazine you purchase—these links will help you access the most up-to-date information.

> **TIP:** Make sure to check the user ratings for a magazine or other app before you purchase it. Doing so may save you some money or grief!

The App Store has a couple different kinds of magazine apps. First, you can find apps that let you purchase individual magazines or view limited content from a given magazine for free. Second, you can find magazine readers that provide samples of many magazines; these allow you to subscribe to weekly or monthly delivery of a given magazine.

If you browse in the **App Store** by **Categories** > **Newsstand**, then tap Top Free a the top, you can check out all the free magazines and newspapers.

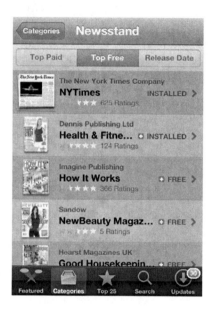

The Zinio Magazine App—A Sampler

The **Zinio** app takes a unique approach. This app is free in the App Store, and it gives you the ability to subscribe to hundreds of magazine titles. Reading magainzes in **Zinio** requires a few simple steps:

1. Log into the **Zinio** app (You can create a free account).

2. View and download free samples in the **My Library** section or click the **Shop** button at the bottom to purchase magazines.

3. Some magazines may be giving away full, free issues. Just look in the **My Library** section to see what is available.

There are many popular magazines you can choose from. The categories cover everything from art to sports and more. Prices vary, but often you can buy either a single issue or a yearly subscription.

For example, the latest issue of *Popular Mechanics* was US $1.99 on **Zinio**, and a yearly subscription was US $7.99.

Some of the subscriptions make great sense. A single issue of *Bike Magazine* was US $4.99 at the time of writing, while a yearly subscription was only US $9.00.

A closer look revealed that there were more than 16 cycling magazines you could subscribe to at the time of writing.

Comic Books

One genre of "new media" poised for a comeback with the advent of the iPhone is the comic book. The iPhone, with its high-definition screen and powerful processor, makes the pages of comic books come alive.

There are already a few comic book apps available, including one from the famous Marvel Comics. DC Comics has just launched its app, as well. This app was created by the same people who make the Marvel app.

To locate the **Marvel Comics** app in the App Store, go to **Categories** and then **Books**. The app is free, and you can purchase comic books from inside the app.

At the bottom of the **Home** screen, you'll see five buttons: **My Comics**, **Featured**, **Free**, **Top 25,** and **Browse**. Purchases you make will be under the **My Comics** heading.

The App Store gives you the opportunity to download both free comics and individual issues for sale. Most sell for $1.99 per issue.

Each tab takes you to a new list of comics to browse, much like the iTunes store.

Touch the **Browse** button to browse by **Series, Creator, Genre, Rating, Storylines/Arcs, or Release Date**. Or you can type in a search to find a particular comic.

You can read a comic book in one of two ways. First, you can swipe through the pages and read one page after another. Second, you can double-tap a frame to **Zoom** in, and then tap the screen to advance to the next frame in the comic strip. From there, you can just swipe from right to left to advance a frame; or, if you want to go back, swipe from left to right.

To return to the **Home** screen or to see the onscreen options, just tap the center of the screen. You'll see a **Settings** button in the top-left corner. Touch this and you can **Jump to the First Page**, **Browse to a Page,** or go to the **Settings** menu.

NOTE: The makers of this app, **ComiXology**, also make the app that contains the Marvel comics, as well as a bunch of others, including DC, Archie, Image, and Top Cow.

The iPhone as a PDF Reader

There are several programs available that turn the iPhone into a very capable PDF viewing program. For example, you can also read PDF files in the **iBooks** app. However, another great PDF reader is called **GoodReader for iPhone.**

> **NOTE:** Chapter 17: "Communicate with Email" showed you how to open attachments, including PDF files. One great benefit of the **GoodReader** app is that it lets you use Wi-Fi to transfer large PDF files.

You can find the **GoodReader for iPhone** app in the **Productivity** section of the App Store. At the time of writing, this app costs US $4.99.

> **NOTE: iBooks** can also read PDF files that are emailed as attachments. If **iBooks** is installed, just choose **Open in iBooks** when opening a PDF.

Transferring Files to your iPhone

One of the great things about the **GoodReader for iPhone** app is that you can use it to wirelessly transfer large files from your Mac or PC to the iPhone for viewing in the **GoodReader** app. You can also use **GoodReader** for document sharing in iTunes, as discussed in Chapter 3: "Sync with iCloud, iTunes, and More. " Follow these steps to transfer a file with **GoodReader**:

1. Touch the small **Wi-Fi** icon at the bottom left of the screen,

   and the **Wi-Fi Transfer Utility** pops up. You are prompted either to type in an IP address into your browser or a Bonjour address if you use the **Bonjour** service.

2. Type the address shown in the window from **GoodReader** into a web browser on your computer. Now you can make your computer act as a server. You'll see that your computer and iPhone are now connected. You might bookmark this page on your browser, however, beware because it can change if you re-start your wireless network router and your iPhone gets a different wireless network address.

3. Click the **Choose File** button in the web browser on your computer to locate a file to upload to your iPhone.

4. Once you've selected the file, click **Upload Selected File** and the file will be automatically transferred to your iPhone.

How is this useful? Well, for one of the authors (Gary), the iPhone has become a repository for more than 100 pieces of piano sheet music. This means no more downloading PDF files, printing them out, putting them into binders, and then trying to remember which song is in which binder. Now, all his music is catalogued on the iPhone. All he has to do is put the iPhone on the piano, and he has access to all his music in one place.

> **NOTE:** Good Reader can even unzip files you receive as email attachments.

Navigating the **GoodReader** PDF viewer is quite easy. This app is more sensitive than others, so tap the center of the screen quickly to bring up the onscreen controls. You can then go to your library or touch the **Turn Page** icon to turn the page.

The easiest way to move through pages is to touch the lower-right side of the screen to advance a page, or touch the upper-left side of the screen to go back a page. This becomes quite natural after a while.

You can also flick up or down to turn pages.

To go to another PDF file or another piece of sheet music, just touch the center of the iPhone quickly and touch the **My Documents** button in the upper-left corner.

Connecting to Google Docs and other Servers with GoodReader

You can also connect to **Google Docs** and other servers with **GoodReader**. Follow these steps to do so:

1. In the **Web Downloads** tab, choose **Connect to Servers**.

2. Select **Google Docs.** (You can select a number of different servers: mail servers, MobileMe iDisk, Public iDisk, Dropbox, box.net, FilesAnywhere.com, MyDisk.se, WebDAV Server, and FTP Servers.)

3. Enter your **Google Docs** username and password to log in.

4. Once you've made the connection, a new **Google Docs Server** icon will appear under the **Connect to Server** tab on the right side of the page.

5. Tap the new **Google** tab to connect to the server (an Internet connection is required).

6. Now you'll see a list of all the documents you have stored on **Google Docs**. Tap any document and select the file type to download it. Usually, PDF works well for this. (Google docs can do a **Save As...**, and PDF files are easier to work with.)

Once the file is downloaded, it will appear on the left side of **GoodReader**; you can simply touch it to open it.

Chapter 15

Viewing Videos

The iPhone gives you an amazing platform to enjoy videos, TV shows and movies. Nowhere is this more apparent than in the various video-viewing applications available.

In this chapter, we will show you how you can watch movies, TV shows, podcasts, and music videos on your iPhone.

You can buy or download many videos for free from the iTunes store or iTunes University. You can also link your iPhone to your Netflix account (and most likely other video rental services soon), allowing you to watch streaming TV shows and movies.

With your iPhone, you can also watch YouTube videos and videos from the Web on your **Safari** browser and through various apps from the App Store.

> **NOTE:** At the time of publishing, the **Netflix** app was only available in the U.S. and Canada. We hope similar apps will make their way to the broader international market.

Your iPhone as a Video Player

The iPhone is more than a capable music player; it is also a fantastic portable video-playing system. Its widescreen, fast processor, incredible pixel density, and great operating system make watching anything from music videos to TV shows and full-length motion pictures a real joy. The size of the iPhone is perfect for sitting back in a chair or watching on an airplane. It is also great for the kids in the back seat of long car trips. The near 10-hour battery life means you can even go on a coast-to-coast flight and not run out of power! You can also buy a "power inverter" for your car to keep the iPhone charged even longer (see the "Charging Your iPhone and Battery Tips" section in Chapter 1: "Getting Started").

Loading Videos onto Your iPhone

You can load videos on your iPhone just like your music by using the **iTunes** app on your computer or right from the **iTunes** app on your iPhone.

If you purchase or rent videos from **iTunes** on your computer, then you will manually or automatically sync these videos to your iPhone.

Watching Videos on the iPhone

To watch videos, simply tap your **Videos** app.

> **NOTE:** You can also watch videos from the **YouTube** app, the **Safari** app, and other video-related apps you load from the App Store.

Video Categories

Each section of the **Videos** app under the **Video** tab in the **iPod** app is separated by horizontal bars with one of several possible category names inside the bar: **Movies, TV Shows, Podcasts,** and **Music Videos**. The first category is the **Movies** section; these will be visible if you have movies loaded on the iPhone.

You may see more or fewer categories depending on the types of videos you have loaded on your iPhone. If you have only **Movies** and **iTunes U** videos, then you will see only those two category buttons. Just scroll up or down to show the corresponding videos in that category.

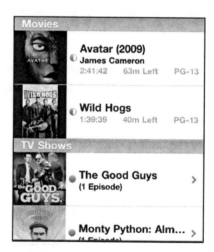

Searching for Videos

If you have a lot of videos, and other content loaded on your iPhone and want to find a particular video, you can do it by following these steps:

1. Tap the time at the very top of your screen to jump to the search box.

2. Type a few letters or a word or two of the title of the video.

3. In this example we typed "email" to find any videos related to using email on our iPhone. Up popped a video tutorial showing how to work with email attachments from one of the author's web sites: www.MadeSimpleLearining.com.

4. Tap any video that appears in the search results to start playing it.

Playing a Movie

Just tap the movie you wish to watch and it will begin to play. Most videos take advantage of the relatively large screen real estate of the iPhone by playing in Widescreen (i.e., Landscape) mode. Just turn your iPhone on its side to watch them.

A video will begin playing automatically. When it first starts, there are no menus, controls, or anything else on the screen, except for the video.

You can tap anywhere on the screen to make the control bars and other options become visible. Most options in the **Videos** app are very similar to those in the **Music** app Tap the **Play/Pause** button and the video will pause. Tap the **Play/Pause** button again and the video will resume playing.

Fast-Forward or Rewind the Video

On either side of the **Play/Pause** button are the usual **Fast-Forward** and **Rewind** buttons. To jump to the next chapter-specific part of the video, just touch and hold the **Fast-Forward** button (to the right of **Play/Pause**). When you get to the desired spot, release the button and the video will begin playing normally.

After pressing **Pause** to stop the video, you can press and hold the **Fast-Forward** or **Rewind** buttons to do slow motion forward or backward. The fun thing is that you can hear the audio slowed down as well.

To rewind to the beginning of the video, tap the **Rewind** button. To rewind to a specific part or location, touch and hold as you did while you were fast forwarding the video.

> **NOTE:** If this is a full-length movie with several chapters, tapping either **Reverse** or **Fast-Forward** will move either back or ahead one chapter.

Using the Time Scrubber Bar

At the top of the video screen is a slider that lets you *scrub* through the elapsed time of the video. If you know exactly (or approximately) which point in the video you wish to watch, just hold the slider bar and then drag it to that location. Some people find this to be a little more exact than holding down the **Fast-Forward** or **Rewind** buttons.

> **TIP:** Drag your finger down to move the slider control more slowly.

Changing the Size of the Video (Widescreen vs. Full Screen)

Most of your videos will play in widescreen format. However, if you have a video that was not converted for your iPhone or is not optimized for your screen resolution, you can touch the **Expand** button, which is to the right of the upper Status bar.

You will notice that there are two arrows on the button. If you are in Full Screen mode, the arrows point in, toward each other. If you are in Widescreen mode, the arrows point outward.

If a widescreen movie is not taking up the full screen of the iPhone, touching this button will zoom in a bit. Touching it again will zoom back out.

> **NOTE:** You can also simply double-tap the screen to zoom in and fill the screen. Be aware that, just like on your widescreen TV, trying to force a non-widescreen video into Widescreen mode can sometimes cause you to lose part of the picture.

Using AirPlay

Apple's AirPlay mirroring feature lets you beam your video to an Apple TV, so you can enjoy it on your big screen TV. Just tap the AirPlay button on the bottom right and select Apple TV as your output destination. After a few moments, your iPhone screen will go dark and your video will start to play on your big screen TV, right where you left off.

To return the video to your iPhone, tap AirPlay again and choose iPhone as the destination.

> **TIP:** If you don't have or want an Apple TV, you have a couple other ways to watch your movies. For example, you can purchase a VGA or HDMI adapter to plug your iPhone into a VGA computer monitor or HDTV.
>
> VGA supports video only, requires that the app support this feature, and it isn't usually compatible with DRM. HDMI supports video and audio, and it also requires that the app support that feature. However, it's also HDCP-compliant, so it will work with DRM content like iTunes videos.
>
> Apple also makes component video cables that are DRM-compliant and work with most TVs.
>
> See the "Accessories" section of the Quick Start Guide for more information.

Using the Chapters Feature

Most full-length movies purchased from the iTunes store—and some that are converted for the iPhone—will give you a Chapters feature. Watching one of these on your iPhone is very much like watching a DVD on your home TV.

Just bring up the controls for the video by tapping the screen, and then select **Chapters**.

This will bring you back to the main page for the movie.

Tap the **Chapters** button in the upper-right corner, and then scroll through to find and then touch the chapter you wish to watch.

Viewing the Chapters

You can scroll through or flick through quickly to locate the scene or chapter that you wish to watch.

You will also notice that, to the far right of each chapter, is the exact time (relative to the start of the movie) that the chapter begins.

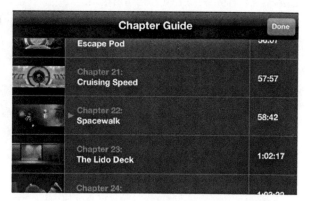

In addition to the chapter menu mentioned previously, you can also quickly advance to the previous or next chapter in a movie by tapping the **Rewind** or **Fast-Forward** button. One tap moves you one chapter in either direction.

> **NOTE:** The Chapters feature usually works only with movies that are purchased from the iTunes store. Movies that are converted and loaded onto your iPhone usually will not have chapters.

Watching a TV Show

The iPhone is great for watching your favorite TV shows. You can purchase TV shows from the iTunes store, and you can download sample shows from some iPhone apps, such as the **Hulu Plus** app.

Just scroll down to the **TV Shows** category separator to see the shows you have downloaded on your iPhone. Scroll through your available shows and touch **Play**. The video controls work just like the controls for watching a movie.

> **NOTE:** At the time of writing, iTunes in the Cloud allows users in the U.S. to re-download previously purchased TV shows directly onto their iPhone (see Chapter 22: "iTunes on Your Device" for more information).

Watching Podcasts

We normally think of podcasts as being audio-only broadcasts that you can download using iTunes. Video podcasts are now quite prevalent and can be found on any number of sites, including many public broadcasting web sites. They can also be found in the **iTunes U** section of iTunes; this section lists university podcasts and other, related information.

Here's an interesting iTunes U story from Gary Mazo:

> *"Recently, I was browsing the **iTunes U** section inside the **iTunes** app on the iPhone with my son, who was just accepted to CalTech. We were wondering about the housing situation and, lo and behold, we found a video podcast showing a tour of the CalTech dorms. We downloaded it, and the podcast went right into the **podcast** directory for future viewing. We were able to do a complete virtual tour of the housing without flying out there from the East Coast."*

Watching Music Videos

Music videos are available for your iPhone from a number of sources. Often, if you buy a "Deluxe" album from iTunes, it will include a music video or two. You can also purchase music videos from the iTunes store, and many record companies and recording artists make them available for free on their web sites.

Music videos will automatically get sorted into the **Music Videos** section of your **Videos** app.

The **Music Videos** are usually located right under **TV Shows** in the **Videos** list. The controls work just as they do in all other video applications.

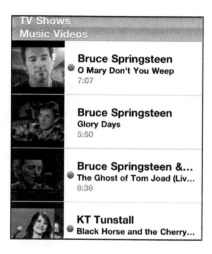

Video Options

As in your music player, there are a few options that you can adjust for the video player. These options are accessed through the **Settings** icon from your **Home** screen.

Tap the **Settings** icon, scroll down to tap **Video** to see the available options.

Here you can also set your Home Sharing settings to be able to watch videos that are stored on your computer's iTunes library right from your iPhone.

The Start Playing Option

Sometimes, you will have to stop watching a particular video. This option lets you decide what to do the next time you want to watch that video. Your options are either to watch the video from the beginning or to watch from where you left off. Just select the option that you prefer and that will be the action your iPhone takes from now on.

Closed Captioning

If your video has closed captioning capabilities, setting the **Closed Captioning** switch to **ON** will let you see closed captioning on your screen.

Deleting Videos

To delete a video (to save space on your iPhone), just scroll up or down and select the video to delete..

> **NOTE:** If you're syncing videos from iTunes, make sure to uncheck the video you're deleting from there as well; otherwise, iTunes just might sync it right back to your iPhone on the next sync!

Just touch and swipe to the right on a video you wish to delete. As when deleting an email, a red **Delete** button will appear in the top-left corner. Touch the **Delete** button and you will be prompted to delete the video.

Finally, touch the **Delete** button and the video will be deleted from your system.

> **NOTE:** This process deletes the video only from your iPhone—a copy will still remain in your video library in iTunes, assuming that you have synced with your computer after purchasing the video. You can load it back onto your iPhone at a later time, if you so desire. However, if you delete a rented movie from the iPhone, it will be deleted permanently!

YouTube on your iPhone

Watching YouTube videos is certainly one of the most popular things for people to do on their computers these days. Now YouTube is as close to you as your iPhone.

You can see the YouTube icon on your Home screen. Just touch this icon to be taken to the YouTube app.

Searching for YouTube Videos

When you first start **YouTube**, you usually see the **Featured** videos on YouTube that day.

Just scroll through the video choices as you do in other apps.

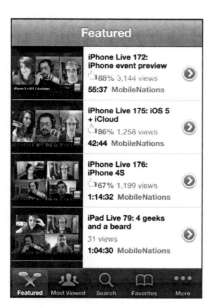

Using the Bottom Icons

Along the bottom of the **YouTube** app are five icons: **Featured, Most Viewed, Search, Favorites,** and **More**. Each option is fairly self-explanatory.

To see the videos that YouTube is featuring that day, touch the **Featured** icon. To see those videos that are most-viewed online, touch the **Most Viewed** icon.

After you watch a particular video, you will have the option to set it as a favorite on **YouTube** for easy retrieval later. If you have set bookmarks, they will appear when you tap the **Favorites** icon.

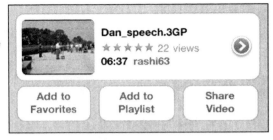

You can also search the huge library of YouTube videos. Tap the **Search** box (as in other apps discussed previously), and the keyboard will pop up. Type in a phrase, topic, or even the name of a video.

In this example, I am looking for the newest Made Simple Learning video tutorial—so I just type in "Made Simple Learning" to see a list of such videos.

When I find a video I want to watch, I can touch it to see more information. I can even rate the video by touching it during playback and selecting a rating.

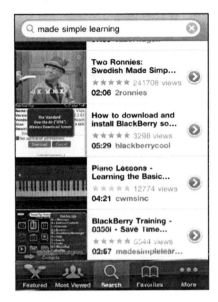

Playing Videos

Once you have made your choice, tap the video you want to watch. Your iPhone will begin playing the YouTube video in Portrait or Landscape mode. To force Portrait mode, just turn the iPhone so that the screen orientation is vertical.

Video Controls

Once the video begins to play, the on-screen controls disappear, so you see only the video. To stop, pause, or activate any other options while the video is playing, just tap the screen.

The on-screen options are very similar to what you see when watching any other video.

To fast-forward through the video (in Landscape mode), touch and hold the **Fast-Forward** arrow. To quickly move in reverse, touch and hold the **Reverse** arrow. To advance to the next video in the YouTube list, tap the **Fast-Forward/Next** arrow. To watch the previous video in the list, tap the **Reverse/Back** arrow.

To set a video as a favorite, tap the leftmost icon: **Favorites**.  To beam the video to your Apple TV, tap the **AirPlay** button.

To Add to Favorites, Email or Tweet the video, tap the **Share** icon and you can do any of these options.

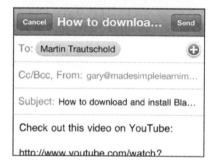

Checking and Clearing your History

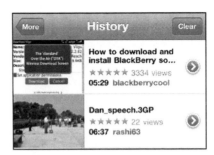

Touch **More** and then **History**, and your recently viewed videos will appear.

If you want to clear your history, just touch the **Clear** button in the upper-right corner and confirm with the button at the bottom.

To watch a video from your history, just touch it and it will start to play.

CAUTION: The **Netflix** app uses a great deal of data, so make sure you have a strong Wi-Fi signal if you are streaming videos over Wi-Fi. If you are using the app over a 3G cellular network, make sure you have an adequate data plan.

Chapter **16**

Safari Web Browser

Now, we'll take you through one of the most fun things to do on your iPhone: surfing the Web. You may have heard that web surfing on the iPhone is a more intimate experience than ever before—and we agree! We'll show you how to touch, zoom around, and interact with the Web like never before with **Safari** on your iPhone. You'll learn how to set and use bookmarks, quickly find things with the search engine, open and switch between multiple browser windows, and even easily copy text and graphics from web pages.

Web Browsing on the iPhone

You can browse the Web to your heart's content via Wi-Fi or with your iPhone's 3G connection. Like its larger cousin, the iPad, your iPhone has what many feel is the most capable mobile browsing experience available today. Web pages look very much like web pages on your computer. With the iPhone's ability to zoom in, you don't even have to worry about the smaller screen size inhibiting your web browsing experience. In short, web browsing is a much more satisfying experience on the iPhone.

You can choose to browse in Portrait or Landscape mode, depending on your preference. Quickly zoom in on a video by double-tapping it or pinching open on it—the same motions you use to zoom in on text and graphics.

Why Do Some Videos and Sites Not Appear? (Flash Player Required)

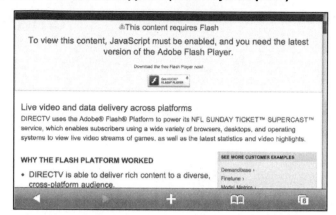

Apple does not support Flash on iOS and Adobe has recently decided to discontinue development of Flash Player Mobile . If you tap a video and the video does not play—or you see something like "Flash Plugin Required," "Download the Latest Flash Plugin to view this video," or "Adobe Flash Required to view this site"—then you will not be able to view the video or web page. Fortunately, an increasing number of sites are starting to use HTML5 video instead of **Flash**, including YouTube, Vimeo, TED, the *New York Times*, and *Time* magazine, all of which will play on your iPhone.

One way around this limitation: Some alternative browsers on the App Store (e.g., **Skyfire**) render **Flash** videos on their own servers and send HTML5 video to the iPhone instead.

An Internet Connection Is Required

You do need a live Internet connection on your iPhone—either Wi-Fi or 3G—to browse the Web (check out Chapter 4: "Connect to the Network" to learn more).

Launching the Web Browser

You should find the **Safari** (web browser) app on your **Home** screen. Usually, the **Safari** icon is in the Bottom Dock.

Touch the **Safari** icon and you will be taken to the browser's **Home** page. Most likely, this will be Apple's iPhone page.

Just turn your iPhone on its side to see the same page in the wider Landscape mode. As you find web sites you like, you can set bookmarks to easily jump to these sites. We will show you how to do this later in this chapter.

Layout of the Safari Web Browser Screen

As you look at your screen, notice that the Address bar is in the upper left of the screen. This bar displays the current web address.

If you are viewing a web page with suitable text content, you will notice the Reader button appear in the address bar. Tap **Reader** to see the web content in an easy-to-read format. Check out more on this in the "Safari Reader" section in this chapter.

The **Search** window is to the right of the Address bar. By default, this is set to Google search, but you can change it to another search engine if you want.

At the bottom of the screen are five icons: Back, Forward, Action, Bookmarks, and Pages view.

Typing a Web Address

The first thing you'll want to learn is how to get to your favorite web pages. Just like on your computer, you type in the web address (URL) into the browser. Follow these steps to enter a web address in **Safari**:

1. To start, tap the **Address** bar at the top of the browser. You see the keyboard appear and the window for the **Address** bar expand.

2. If there is already an address in the window and you want to erase it,

   press the ⊗ at the right end of the bar.

3. Start typing your web address (you don't need the "www.").

4. When you start typing, you may see suggestions appear below the **Address** bar; just tap any of those suggestions to go to that page. The suggestions are very complete because they are pulled from your browsing history, bookmarks, the web address (URL), and web page titles.

5. Remember the **.com** key at the bottom of the page. If you press and hold it, you will see **.edu**, **.org**, and other common domain types.

6. When you are finished typing, tap the **Go** key to go to that page.

> **TIP:** Don't type the "www." because it's not necessary. Remember to use the **colon, forward slash**, **underscore**, **dot**, and **.com** keys at the bottom to save time.

> **TIP:** Press and hold the **.com** key to see all the options: **.org, .edu, .net, .de**, and so on.

Moving Backward or Forward Through Open Web Pages

Now that you know how to enter web addresses, you'll probably be jumping to various

web sites. The **Forward** and **Back** arrows ◀ ▶ at the bottom of the screen make it very easy to go to recently visited pages in either direction. If the **Back** arrow is grayed out, this chapter's "Using the Open Pages Button" section can help you figure out why.

Let's say you were looking at the news on the *New York Times* web site, and you jumped to ESPN to check sports scores. To go back to the *New York Times* page, just tap the **Back** arrow. To return to the ESPN site again, touch the **Forward** arrow.

Using the Open Pages Button

Sometimes, when you click a link, the web page you were viewing moves to the background and a new window pops up with new content (e.g., another web page or a video). You will see the page you were on move to the background and a new page being opened. In such cases, the **Back** arrow in the new browser window will not work.

Instead, you have to tap the **Open**

Pages icon in the lower-right corner to see a list of open web pages, and then tap the one you want. In the example shown here, we touched a link that opened a new browser window. The only way to get back to the old one was to tap the Open Pages icon and select the desired page.

Zooming In and Out in Web Pages

Zooming in and out of web pages is very easy on the iPhone. There are two primary ways of zooming—double-tapping and pinching.

Double-tapping

If you tap twice on a column in a web page, the page will zoom in on that particular column. This lets you home in on exactly the right place on the web page, which is very helpful for pages that aren't formatted for a mobile screen.

To zoom out, just double-tap once more (you can see how this looks in the "Quick Start Guide" at the beginning of this book).

Pinching

This technique lets you zoom in on a particular section of a page. It takes a little bit of practice, but it will soon become second nature. Check out the "Quick Start Guide" to see how this looks.

Place your thumb and forefinger close together at the section of the web page you wish to zoom in on. Slowly pinch out, separating your fingers. You will see the web page zoom in. It takes a couple of seconds for the web page to focus, but it will zoom in and be very clear in a short while.

To zoom out to where you were before, just start with your fingers apart and move them slowly together; the page will zoom out to its original size.

Activating Links from Web Pages

When you're surfing the Web, often you'll come across a link that will take you to another web site. Because **Safari** is a full-function browser, you simply touch the link to jump to a new page.

Working with Safari Bookmarks

As soon as you start browsing a bit on your iPhone, you will want to quickly access your favorite web sites. One good way to do this is to add bookmarks for one-tap access to web sites.

> **TIP:** You can sync your bookmarks from your computer's web browser (**Safari** or **Internet Explorer** only) using iCloud over the air or the **iTunes** app on your computer. Check out Chapter 3: "Sync with iCloud, iTunes and More" for more details.

Adding a New Bookmark

Adding new bookmarks on your iPhone takes just a few taps:

1. To add a new bookmark for the web page you are currently viewing, tap

   the **Action** button ![Action button] at the bottom of the screen.

2. Choose **Add Bookmark**.

   ![Add Bookmark button]

3. We recommend that you edit the bookmark name to something short and recognizable.

4. Tap **Bookmarks** if you want to change the folder where your bookmark is stored.

5. When you're finished, tap the **Save** button.

Using Bookmarks and History

Once you have set a few bookmarks, it is easy to view and work with them. In the same area, you can also see and use your web browsing history. A very useful tool on your iPhone is the ability to browse the web from your **History**, just as you would on a computer. Follow these steps to do so:

1. Tap the **Bookmarks** icon at the bottom of the page.

2. Swipe up or down to view all your bookmarks.

3. Tap any bookmark to jump to that web page.

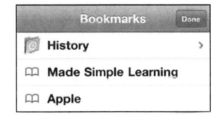

4. Tap the **History** folder to view your recent history of visited web pages.

5. Notice that, at the bottom of the list, you see additional folders for **Earlier Today** and previous days.

6. Tap any history item to go to that web page.

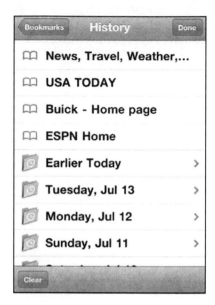

> **TIP:** To clear your history, tap the **Clear** button in the lower-left corner. You can also clear your history, cookies, and cache in the **Settings** app. Tap **Settings**; tap **Safari**; scroll to the bottom; and then tap **Clear History, Clear Cookies,** or **Clear Cache**.

Managing Your Bookmarks

It is very easy to accumulate quite a collection of bookmarks because setting them up is so easy. However, you may find you no longer need a particular bookmark, or you may want to organize them by adding new folders.

If you have organized your **Phone Favorites** list, you already know how to organize your bookmarks; you use the same steps.

As with other lists on your iPhone, you can reorder your **Bookmarks** list and remove entries. Follow these steps to do so:

1. View your **Bookmarks** list as you did previously.

2. Tap the **Edit** button in the lower-left corner.

3. To reorder the entries, touch and drag the right edge with the three gray bars up or down the list. In this case, we are dragging the bookmark to the **iPad Made Simple** book page on Amazon.com up to the top.

4. To create a new folder for bookmarks, tap the **New Folder** button in the lower-right corner.

5. To delete a bookmark, tap the red **Circle** icon to the left of the entry to make it turn vertical.

6. Tap the **Delete** button.

7. When you are finished reordering and deleting entries, tap the **Done** button in the upper-left corner.

8. To edit a bookmark name, folder, or web address, tap the bookmark name itself.

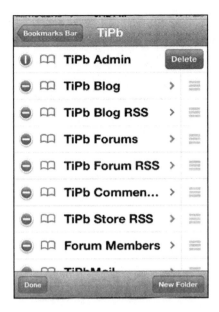

9. Now you can make any adjustments to the name, web address, or folder.

10. To change the folder where the bookmark is stored, tap the button below the web address. In this image, it says **Bookmarks**; but on your iPhone, it may be different. This bookmark points to the iPad Made Simple page on Amazon.com.

11. Tap **Done** when you're finished.

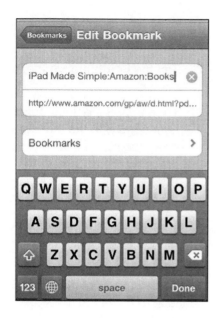

Reading List

Reading List is a special type of bookmark that lets you quickly save a web article, so you can read it later at your leisure. The Reading List feature can sync via iCloud, so it's a great way to quickly mark articles on **Safari** on your home or work Mac or Windows PC to read on your iPhone or iPad while traveling. You can also use this feature to save a bookmark on your iPhone to read more comfortably when you get back to your iPad or PC.

Follow these steps to use the Reading List feature:

1. Go to the article you want to save in **Safari.**

2. Tap the **Action** button at the bottom middle of the page.

3. Tap **Add to Reading List**.

Follow these steps to view a Reading List article later:

1. Tap the **Bookmark** button at the bottom right of the page.

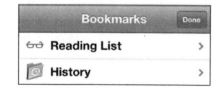

2. Tap the **Glasses** icon for the **Reading List** option. (If you don't see the **Glasses** icon, you might be inside a Bookmarks folder. Just tap the **Arrow** icon at the top left to back out of the folder or folders you're in until the Arrow disappears, and you can see the Glasses icon.)

1. To see everything in your Reading List, tap the **All** tab at the top left. To see only the articles you haven't read yet, tap the **Unread** tab at the top right.

2. Tap the article you want to read.

Finally, follow these steps to delete an article from Reading List:

1. Swipe from left to right across the article you'd like to remove from Reading List.

2. Tap the red **Delete** button.

Safari Reader

Safari's Reader feature allows you to enjoy an article on the web as a clean, clear page of nicely sized text, without the distraction of busy layouts or ads.

> **NOTE:** While Safari does an excellent job detecting most web page articles because of the white variety of content and formatting, it might occasionally miss one. If you don't see the Reader button, it means Safari couldn't detect the article.

1. Follow these steps to activate this feature:

2. Go to the article you want to read.

3. Tap the Reader button on the right side of the URL field, see Figure 16–1.

4. Tap the Font Size button to make the type bigger or smaller.

Figure 16–1. *The same web page in standard view (left) and Reader View (right).*

TIP: If you find yourself wishing you could get the functionality of both Reading List and Reader—along with other features like browser access, social sharing, and more—then check out App Store apps like **Instapaper**.

Safari Browsing Tips and Tricks

Now that you know the basics of how to get around, we will cover a few useful tips and tricks for making web browsing more enjoyable and faster on your iPhone.

Jumping to the Top of the Web Page

Sometimes, web pages can be quite long, which can make scrolling back to the top of the page a bit laborious. One easy trick is to tap the gray title bar of the web page; you'll automatically jump to the top of the page.

Emailing or Tweeting a Web Page

Sometimes while browsing, you find a page so compelling you just have to share it with a friend or colleague. Tap the **Action** button in the middle of the bottom bar, and then select **Mail Link to this Page** to create an email message with a link that you can send. Select **Tweet** to create a new Twitter message with a link you can share, as shown in Figure 16–2.

Figure 16–2. *Using the Action button to do various functions with a Safari web page.*

Printing a Web Page

With the iPhone, you can easily print any web page you come across to any **AirPrint** compatible printer over your local Wi-Fi network. Tap the **Action** button and then select **Print**.

Watching Videos in Safari

You will often see videos on web sites. And you will be able to play many—but not all— of these videos. For example, videos formatted with **Adobe Flash** will not be playable on your iPhone (see our note at the beginning of this chapter).

When you tap the **Play** button, you will be taken out of **Safari** into the **iPod** video player.

You can then turn your iPhone on its side to view the video in Landscape, or wide-screen, mode.

Tap the screen to bring up the player controls if they have disappeared.

When you are finished watching the video and want to return to the web page, tap the **Done** button in the upper-left corner.

> **TIP:** Check out the video player tips and tricks in Chapter 15: "Viewing Videos."

Saving or Copying Text and Graphics

From time to time, you may see text or a graphic you want to copy from a web site. We tell you briefly how to do this in this section; however, to see how to get this done in more depth, including how to use the Cut and Paste functions, please see the "Copy and Paste" section in Chapter 2: "Typing, Copy and Search." Here's a quick synopsis of how to copy text or a graphic from a web page:

- To copy a single word, touch and hold the word until you see it highlighted and the **Copy** button appears. Next, tap **Copy.**

- To copy a few words or entire paragraph, touch and hold a word until it is highlighted. Next, drag the blue dots left or right to select more text. You can flick up or down to select an entire paragraph. Finally, tap **Copy**.

> **TIP:** Selecting a single word puts the copy feature in word-selection mode, where you can drag to increase or decrease the number of words selected. If you go past a single paragraph, it will typically switch to element-selection mode where, instead of corners, you get edges that you can drag out to select multiple paragraphs, images, and so on.

- To save or copy a graphic, touch and hold the picture or image until you see the pop-up asking if you would like to save or copy the image.

Saving Time with AutoFill

The AutoFill feature gives you a great way to save time typing your personal information, including usernames and passwords on web sites. The AutoFill tool can remember and fill in information required in web forms. You will save a lot of time by enabling AutoFill.

Check out the steps we show you later in this chapter in the "Enabling AutoFill" section to set up AutoFill to work on your iPhone.

Once you enable the **AutoFill** option, just go to any web page that has a field to fill out. As soon as you touch the field, the keyboard will come up at the bottom of the screen. At the top of the keyboard, you will see a small button that says **AutoFill**. Touch it and the web form should be filled out automatically.

> **CAUTION:** Having your name and password entered automatically means that anyone who picks up your iPhone will be able to access your personal sites and information. You may want to enable passcode security, as explained in Chapter 8: "Personalize and Secure."

Entering Usernames and Passwords

The first time you go to a web site where you have to enter a username and password, type them in and press **Submit** or **Enter**. At that time, AutoFill will ask if you want your iPhone to remember them.

Tap **Yes** if you want them to be remembered and automatically entered the next time you visit the site.

The next time you visit this login page, your username and password will be automatically filled in.

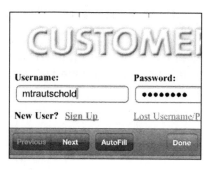

For Personal Information

There are many times on the Web where you have to enter your name, email address, home address, and more. With AutoFill set up and tied to your contact record on the iPhone, filling in these forms just takes a single tap of your finger.

You will go to many sites with web forms that need to be completed. For example, check out this example of a web form on www.madesimplelearning.com for free iPhone tips. It would take a while to manually type your email address, first name, and last name.

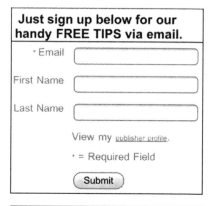

As soon as you tap the first field—**Email**, in this case—you see the **AutoFill** bar appear just above your keyboard.

Tap the **AutoFill** button, and your email address and name are immediately filled in from your contact record.

Adding a Web Page Icon to Your Home Screen

If you love a web site or page, it's very easy to add it as an icon to your **Home** screen. That way, you can instantly access the web page without going through **Safari**'s bookmark selection process. You'll save lots of steps by putting the icon on your **Home** screen. This is especially good for quickly launching web apps (e.g., Gmail from Google or web-based games).

Follow these steps to add a web app's icon:

1. Tap the **Action** button ![action icon] at the bottom of the browser.

2. Tap **Add to Home Screen**.

3. Adjust the name to shorten it to ten or fewer characters; you should do this because there's not much room for the icon's name on your Home screen.

4. Tap the **Add** button in the upper-right corner.

Adjusting the Safari Browser Settings

As with other settings we've adjusted so far, the settings for **Safari** are found in the **Settings** app.

1. To access settings for **Safari**, tap the **Settings** icon.

2. Tap **Safari**.

Changing the Search Engine

By default, the search engine for the **Safari** browser is **Google**. To change this to **Yahoo** or **Bing**, touch the **Search Engine** button and then choose the new search engine.

> **TIP:** If you don't want to change your default search engine, you can use Siri as a way to occasionally search Yahoo! or Bing. Just activate Siri and say "Search Yahoo! for…" or "Search Bing for…" and Siri will get you the results.

Enabling AutoFill

As we showed you earlier in this chapter, AutoFill is a convenient way to have **Safari** automatically fill out web page forms that ask for your name, address, phone number, or even username and password. It can save you a tremendous amount of time typing and retyping your name and other information.

To enable the **AutoFill** option, follow these steps:

1. From the **Safari** menu in the **Settings** app, tap **AutoFill**.

2. Set the switch next to **Names & Passwords** to **ON**.

3. Set the switch next to **Use Contact Info** to **ON**.

4. After setting **Use Contact Info** to **ON**, you will be brought to your **Contacts** list to select a contact to use.

5. Swipe up and down to find someone or double-tap the top bar that says **Contacts** to bring up the **Search** window.

6. Once you find the contact you want to use, tap it to be returned to **Safari**'s **Settings** screen.

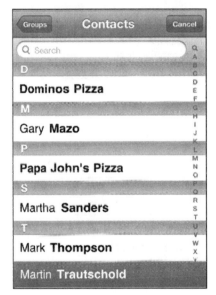

Adjusting Privacy Options

Turning on the **Private Browsing** option means that no information, history, or cookies will be stored when you visit web sites. If you're concerned about other people knowing which web sites you visit or about the web sites you visit tracking you, then you should toggle **Private Browing** to the **ON** position.

You can also **Clear History** and **Clear Cookies and Data** options.

> **TIP:** If you notice your web browsing get slow or sluggish—or if Safari is crashing on you frequently—then try clearing both your **History** and **Cookies and Data** by tapping them and confirming your choices.

Adjusting Security Options

Under the **Security** heading, the **Fraud Warning**, **JavaScript**, and **Block Pop-ups** options should be set to **ON** by default. You can modify any of these settings by sliding a given switch to **OFF**.

> **NOTE:** Many popular sites like Facebook require JavaScript to be **ON**.

Tap the **Accept Cookies** button to adjust your browser's ability to accept cookies to **Always**, **Never**, or **From visited**. We recommend keeping it as **From visited**. If you make it **Never**, some web sites will not work properly.

Chapter 17

Communicate with Email

In this chapter, we will explore the world of email in the **Mail** app on your iPhone. You will learn how to set up multiple email accounts, check out all the various reading options, open attachments, and clean up your inbox.

And for cases when your email is not working quite right, you will learn some good troubleshooting tips to help you get back up and running.

Getting Started with Mail

Setting up email on your iPhone is fairly simple. Probably the fastest way to get your email up and running is to set up your accounts directly on the phone. We show you how using the **Mail, Contacts and Calendar** account setup screens in this section. You could also copy these account settings using a screen in the **iTunes** app on your computer. You do need a network connection to get email up and running.

A Network Connection Is Required

Mobile email is certainly all the rage today. You can view, read, and compose replies to emails already synced to your iPhone without a network connection; however, you will need to have network connectivity (either Wi-Fi or 3G/cellular) to send and/or receive email from your iPhone. Check out Chapter 4: "Connect to the Network" to learn more. Also, check out the "Reading the Top Connectivity Status Icons" section in the Quick Start Guide in Part 1.

> **TIP:** If you are taking a trip, simply download all your email before you get on the airplane; this lets you read, reply, and compose your messages while offline. All emails will be sent after you land and re-establish your connection to the Internet.

Setting up Email on the iPhone

As mentioned a moment ago, you have two options for setting up your email accounts on the iPhone:

1. Set up your email accounts directly on the iPhone.

2. Use iTunes to sync email account settings.

The first option, setting up your email accounts directly on the iPhone, works best if you want a special setup on your iPhone, such as Gmail over Exchange. This is also a good approach if you don't use an email program on your Windows or Mac PC.

If you have a lot of POP3 or IMAP accounts already set up on your Windows or Mac computer, you can also choose to sync them over your USB dock cable via iTunes.

Entering Passwords for Email Accounts

In Chapter 3, we showed you how to sync your email account settings to your iPhone. After this sync completes, you should be able to view all of the email accounts on your iPhone by opening the **Settings** app. All you will need to do is enter the password for each account.

To enter your password for each synced email account, follow these steps:

1. Tap the **Settings** icon.

2. Tap the **Mail, Contacts, and Calendars** option.

3. Under **Accounts**, you should see all your synced email accounts listed.

4. Tap any listed email account, type its password, and click **Done**.

5. If all the information is entered correctly, checkmarks will appear and you're account will be enabled.

6. Repeat for all listed email accounts.

Adding a New Email Account on the iPhone

To add a new email account on your iPhone, follow these steps:

1. Tap the **Settings** icon.

2. Tap the **Mail, Contacts, and Calendars** option.

3. Tap **Add Account** below your email accounts.

    If you have no accounts set up, you will only see the **Add Account** option.

> **TIP:** To edit any email account, just touch that account.

4. Choose which type of email account to add on this screen:

    ▪ Choose **iCloud** if you use this service.

    ▪ Choose **Microsoft Exchange** if you use a Microsoft Exchange email server.

    ▪ You should also choose **Microsoft Exchange** if you use Google Calendar and Google Contacts to store your personal information, and you want to wirelessly sync them to your iPhone.

> **NOTE:** We show you how to set up both Google/Microsoft Exchange and iCloud in Chapter 3: "Sync with iCloud, iTunes and More."

    ▪ Choose **Gmail** if you use Google for your email, but you do *not* (or do *not* want to) wirelessly sync email with your **Google Contacts**.

- Choose **Yahoo!, AOL, or WindowsLive Hotmail** if you use those services.

- Choose **Other** if none of the above apply, and you want to sync a standard POP or IMAP email account. Finally, choose **Add Mail Account** from the next screen.

5. Type your name as you would like others to see it when they receive mail from you into the **Name** field.

6. Next, add the appropriate information into the **Address**, **Password**, and **Description** fields.

7. Tap the **Next** button in the upper-right corner.

Specifying Incoming and Outgoing Servers

Sometimes, the iPhone will not be able to automatically set up your email account. In these cases, you will need to type in a few more settings manually to enable your email account.

> **TIP:** You may be able to find the settings for your email provider by doing a web search for your email provider's name and email settings.

If the iPhone is unable to log into your server with only your email address and password, then you will see a screen similar to this one.

Under **Incoming Mail Server**, type the appropriate information into the **Host Name**, **User Name**, and **Password** fields. Usually, your incoming mail server is something like **mail.**name_of_your_isp**.com**.

To adjust the name of your outgoing server, tap **Outgoing Mail Server.** You can adjust the outgoing mail server on the following screen. These server names usually look like either **smtp.**name_of_your_isp**.com** or **mail.**name_of_your_isp**.com**.

You can try to leave the **Server Name** and **Password** fields blank. If that doesn't work, you can always go back and change them.

You may be asked if you want to use SSL (secure socket layer), a type of outgoing mail security that may be required by your email provider. If you don't know whether you need SSL, just check the mail settings with your email provider.

> **TIP:** The authors recommend that you use SSL security whenever possible. If you do not use SSL, then your login credentials, messages, and any private information are sent in plain text (unencrypted), leaving them open to snoopers.

Verifying that Your Account Is Set Up

Once all the information is entered, the iPhone will attempt to configure your email account. You may get an error message; if that happens, you need to review the information you input.

If you are taken to the screen that shows all your email accounts, look for the new account name.

If you see it, your account was set up correctly.

Fixing the Cannot Get Mail Error

You will need to enter your password if you tap **Mail** icon and you receive an error that says "Cannot Get Mail—No password provided for *(your account)*."

Review this chapter's "Enter Passwords for E-Mail Accounts Synced from iTunes" section for help with this issue.

The Mailboxes Screen—Inboxes and Accounts

The top-level screen is your **Mailboxes** screen. You can always get to it by tapping the button in the upper-left corner. Keep tapping this upper-left button until you see no more buttons. When that happens, you are in the **Mailboxes** screen.

From the **Mailboxes** screen, you can access the following items:

- **The unified inbox:** Access this by tapping **All inboxes**.

- **The inbox for each individual account:** Access this by tapping that email account name in the **Inboxes** section.

- **The folders for each email account in the Accounts section**: Access these by tapping the account name to see all folders.

Adding or Editing Email Folders or Mailboxes

With iOS 5, you can now add or edit email folders right on your iPhone if you are using an iCloud-synced mail account or your mail server supports this feature. Say, you wanted to change a mail folder name or add a new mail folder to better organize your messages inbox. One example might be to create a new folder called "Requires Attention" and put all those emails that you cannot get to right now, but need to make sure you address later when you back at your desk. To add or edit a mailbox on your device, follow these steps:

1. From the **Mailboxes** screen scroll to the bottom and tap any of your email accounts listed under Accounts.

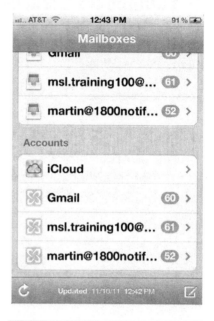

2. In this example, we will edit the iCloud account mailboxes. On this screen tap **Edit** in the upper right.

3. Then, you can do the following:

- Tap the **New Mailbox** at the bottom to create a new mailbox.

- Tap any mailbox folder to edit the name or delete it.

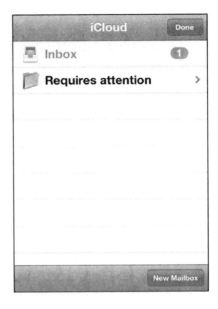

Inbox, Flagged (Marked) and Threaded Messages

You will notice that any unread messages are marked with a

blue dot  to the left of the message.

You will also notice that some messages show a number and a right-facing arrow (>) to the right

of the message, like this: . This shows that there are **three** related messages (replies and forwards) to the message shown.

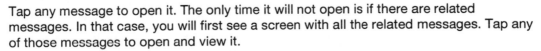

Messages that are marked have a little flag to the left of them like this:

Tap any message to open it. The only time it will not open is if there are related messages. In that case, you will first see a screen with all the related messages. Tap any of those messages to open and view it.

To leave the **Inbox** view, tap the button in the upper-left corner.

You can tell which email account you are viewing by looking at the button in the upper-left corner:

- If the button says **Mailboxes**, you know you are looking at all your inboxes together.

- If the button says an account name, such as **iCloud** or **Exchange**, then you know you are only looking at the inbox for that account.

Move, Delete, or Mark (Flag) Multiple Messages

If you want to move or delete several messages at once, you can do so from the Inbox screen. Follow these steps to delete multiple messages at once:

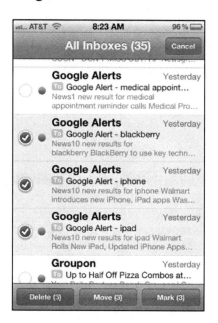

1. Tap the **Edit** button in the upper-right corner while you are viewing an Inbox screen.

2. Tap to select the desired messages; a red **Checkmark** icon next to a message indicates it is selected.

3. To delete the messages, tap the **Delete** button at the bottom.

4. To move the messages to another folder, tap the **Move** button and select the folder.

5. To Mark a message with a Flag or as Unread, tap the **Mark** button. Unread will put the blue dot back next to the message. If you flag a message you will see a little

flag appear next to it like this:

Viewing an Individual Message

When you tap a message from the **Inbox** screen, you see the **Main** message view. You can look at messages in both portrait and landscape modes, see Figure 17–1. Portrait mode will typically display more text. Landscape mode will typically let you enjoy bigger text and images.

Figure 17–1. *Viewing email messages in portrait and landscape modes.*

TIP: If you are setting your iPhone down on a desk or holding it in your lap, then you may want to use the **Portrait Lock** icon to lock your view in Portrait (vertical) mode. This will prevent the image from flipping around unnecessarily. To lock the view, follow these steps:

1. Double-tap the **Home** button and swipe left to right.
2. Tap the **Portrait Lock** button to lock the screen in Portrait mode.

Composing and Sending Emails

To launch the email program, tap the **Mail** icon on your **Home** screen.

TIP: If you left the **Mail** app while viewing a particular email, list of folders, or an account, then you will be returned directly to that same location when you return to the **Mail** app.

If you are going into your email for the first time, you may see an empty inbox. Hit the **Refresh** button in the lower-left corner of the window to retrieve the latest email. The iPhone will begin to check for new mail and then display the number of new messages for each account.

Composing a New Email Message

When you start the **Mail** program, your first screen should be your **Accounts** screen. At the bottom-right corner of the screen, you will see the **Compose** icon. Touch the **Compose** icon to start creating a new message.

Addressing Your Message—Choose the Recipients

You have a few options for selecting recipients, depending on whether the person is in your **Contacts** list on your iPhone:

Option 1: Type a few letters of someone's first name; hit the **Space** key, and then type a few letters of that person's last name. The person's name should appear in the list; tap that person's name to select that contact.

Option 2: Type an email address. Notice the **@** and **Period** (**.**) keys on the bottom, which help your typing.

> **TIP:** Press and hold the **period** key to see **.com**, **.edu**, **.org**, and other email domain name suffixes.

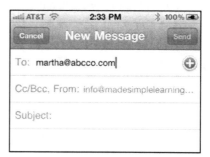

Option 3: Hit the **Plus Sign (+)** 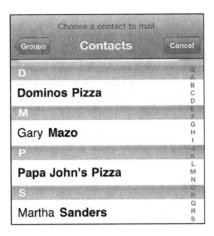 to view your entire **Contacts** list and search or select a name from it.

If you want to use a different contact group, tap the **Groups** button in the upper-left corner.

Double-tap **Contacts** at the top of the screen to see the **Search** window. Next, type a few letters to search for your contact.

Deleting a Recipient

If you need to delete a name from the recipient list (**To:**, **Cc:**, or **Bcc:**), tap the name to select it *To: martha@abcco.com* and hit the **Backspace** key.

> **TIP:** If you want to delete the last recipient you typed (and the cursor is sitting next to that name), hit the **Delete** key once to highlight the name and hit it a second time to delete it.

Adding a CC or BCC Recipient

To add a carbon copy (**Cc:**) or blind carbon copy (**Bcc:**) recipient, you need to tap the **Cc:** or **Bcc:** field just under the **To:** field at the top of the email message. Doing so opens up the tapped field.

Moving Recipients

If you originally add a recipient as the **To**: field, but change your mind and decide you'd rather add her to a **Cc**: or **Bcc**: field (or vice versa), then simply tap and hold the recipient's name and drag it to the preferred field.

Changing the Email Account to Send From

If you have more than one email account set up, the iPhone will use whichever account is set as the default account. (This is set in **Settings > Mail, Contacts, Calendars > Default Account** at the bottom of the **Mail** section.)

Follow these steps to change the email account you send from:

1. Tap an email's **From:** field to highlight it.

2. Tap the **From:** field again to see a list of your accounts in a scroll wheel at the bottom of the screen.

3. Scroll up or down, and then tap a new email account to select it.

4. Tap the **Subject** field to finish changing the email address you send from.

Typing Your Subject

Now you need to enter a subject for your email.
Follow these steps to do so:

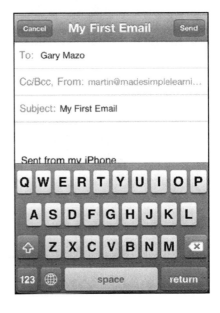

1. Touch the **Subject:** line and enter text
    for the **Subject:** field of the email.

2. Press the **Return** key or tap the **Body**
    section of the email to move the cursor
    to the **Body** section.

Typing Your Message

Now that the cursor is in the **Body** section of the email (under the subject line), you can
start typing your email message.

> **CAUTION:** There is only one email signature on your iPhone, which gets automatically applied to
> each message you send from your iPhone—even if you have multiple email accounts set up. So,
> be careful if you are running two different businesses or don't want your personal email
> signature to go to all your business contacts. It's probably best to make your email signature
> fairly generic.

Formatting Text, Defining Words, Quoting Text and More

You can tap any text to highlight it, use the blue handles to expand the selection. Then using the popup menu above the selection, you can do any of the following:

- Tap **Cut**, **Copy** or **Paste** to perform those functions.

- Tap **Suggest** if the word is underlined and you want to correct the spelling.

- Tap the triangle at the right edge to see more options.

- Tap B / U to adjust formatting to **Bold**, **Italics** or **Underline**.

- Tap **Define** to look the selected word up in the dictionary.

- Tap **Speak** to have the word spoken to you.

- Tap **Quote Level** to increase or decrease the quote level of the selected text.

Email Signatures

The default email signature is shown in the image to the right: **Sent from my iPhone**.

TIP: You can change this signature to be anything you want; see the "Changing Your E-Mail Signature" section later in this chapter to learn how to change your e-mail signature.

Keyboard Options

While you are typing, remember you have two keyboard options: the smaller **Portrait** (vertical) keyboard and the larger **Landscape** (horizontal) keyboard, see Figure 17–2.

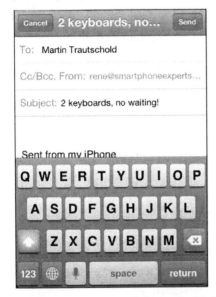

Figure 17–2. *Turn your device on its side to get the larger landscape keyboard.*

> **TIP:** If you have larger hands, it might be easier to type when the keyboard is larger. Once you get the hang of typing on the larger keyboard with two hands, you will find that it is much faster than typing with one finger. See Chapter 2: "Typing, Copy and Search" for more typing tips.

Auto-Correction and Auto-Capitalization

As you type, you will notice that some words will be auto-capitalized and automatically corrected. Red underlined words are flagged as misspelled by the spelling checker. See Chapter 2: "Typing, Copy and Search" to learn how these all functions work; this chapter also provides some additional typing tips.

Send Your Email

Once you have typed your message, tap the blue **Send** button in the top-right corner.

Your email will be sent, and you should hear the iPhone's sent mail sound, which confirms that your email was sent. You can learn how to enable or disable this sound in the "Adjusting Sounds on your iPhone" section of Chapter 9: "Personalize and Secure."

Save As Draft to Send Later

If you are not ready to send your message, but want to save it as a draft message to send later, follow these steps:

1. Compose your message, as described earlier.

2. Press the **Cancel** button in the upper-left corner.

3. Select the **Save Draft** button at the bottom of the screen.

Later, when you want to locate and send your draft message, follow these steps:

1. Open the **Drafts** folder in the email account from which you composed this message. See the "Moving Around in Mail Folders" section earlier in this chapter for help getting into the **Drafts** folder.

2. Tap the email message in the **Drafts** folder to open it.

3. Tap anywhere in the message to edit it.

4. Tap the **Send** button.

Checking Sent Messages

Follow these steps to confirm that the email was sent correctly:

1. Tap the **Email account name** button in the upper-left corner to see the mail folders for the account you just used to send your message.

2. Tap the **Sent** folder.

3. Verify that that the top email you see in the list is the one you just composed and sent.

NOTE: You will only see the **Sent** and **Trash** folders if you have actually sent or deleted email from that account on the iPhone. If your email account is an IMAP account, you may see many folders other than those described in this chapter.

Reading and Replying to Mail

Follow these steps to read your email:

1. Navigate to the inbox of the email account you want to view using the steps described earlier in this chapter.

2. To read any message, just touch it from your inbox.

3. New, unread messages are shown with a small blue dot to the left of the message.

4. Flick your finger up or down in the inbox to scroll through your messages.

5. When you are reading a message, swipe up or down to scroll through it.

Marking Messages as Unread or Flagged

If you read a message but want to make sure you can quickly find it again later, you can choose to click either **Mark** as **Unread** or **Flag**, so it gets your attention later.

Follow these steps to **Mark** a message:

1. Tap the word **Mark** located to the right of the time and date.

2. Choose **Flag** or **Mark** as **Unread** from the slide up menu.

A message you **Flag** will have a small red **Flag** icon to the left of the **Mark** text. A message you **Mark** as **Unread** will have a small blue dot to the right of the **Mark** text.

To **Unmark** a message:

1. Tap the word **Mark** located to the right of the time and date

2. Choose **Unflag** or **Mark as Read** from the slide up menu.

Zooming In or Out

As when browsing the Web, you can zoom in to see your email in larger text. You can also double-tap, just as you do on the Web; and you can also **Pinch** to zoom in or out (see the "Zooming" section in the Quick Start Guide in Part 1 of this book for more information on these features).

Email Attachments

Some email attachments are opened automatically by the iPhone, so you don't even notice that they were attachments. Examples of these include Adobe's portable document format (PDF) files (used by **Adobe Acrobat** and **Adobe Reader,** among other apps) and some types of image, video, and audio files. You may also receive documents as attachments, such as Apple's **Pages, Numbers,** and **Keynote** files; or Microsoft's **Word, Excel,** and **PowerPoint** files. You will need to open these manually.

Knowing When You Have an Attachment

Any email with an attachment will have a little **Paperclip** icon next to the sender's name, as shown to the right. When you see that icon, you know you have an attachment.

Receiving an Auto-Open Attachment

Some types of email attachments, like images, Quicktime movies, and single-page PDF files are usually opened and displayed and displayed for you inline in the mail message.

(If you're on a 3G data connection, however, you'll have to tap on them to download and display them.)

> **TIP:** If you want to save or copy an auto-opened attachment, simply press and hold it until you see the pop-up window. At this point, you can select **Copy** or **Save Image**. When you save an image, it will be placed in your **Photos** app in the **Camera Roll** album.

Opening Email Attachments

Instead of immediately opening in the body of the email as we just described, other types of attachments—such as spreadsheets, word processing documents, and presentation files—will need to be opened manually.

Tap for Quick Look Mode

Follow these steps to open attachments in Quick Look mode:

1. Open the message with an attachment, as shown in Figure 17–3.

2. Quickly tap the attachment to instantly open it in Quick Look mode.

3. You can navigate around the document. Remember you can zoom in or out and swipe up or down.

4. If you open a spreadsheet with multiple tabs or spreadsheets, you will see tabs across the top. Touch another tab to open that spreadsheet.

5. When you are done looking at the attachment, tap the document once to bring up the controls, and then tap **Done** in the upper-left corner.

6. If you have apps installed that can open the type of attachment you are viewing (in this case, a spreadsheet), then you will see an **Open In** button in the upper-right corner. Tap the **Open In** button to open this file in another app.

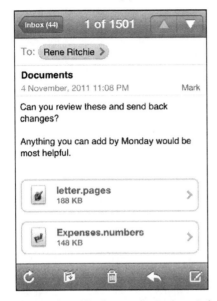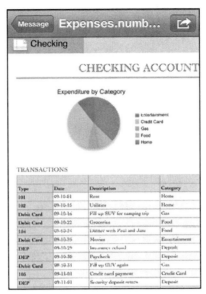

Figure 17–3. *Viewing email attachments in Quick Look mode.*

Opening Docs in Other Apps

You may want to open an attachment in another application. For example, you might want to open a spreadsheet in **Numbers**, a PDF file in **iBooks, Stanza,** or **GoodReader.** Follow these steps to do so:

1. Open the email message.

2. Press and hold the attachment until you see the pop-up window.

3. Select the **Open In...** or **Open in "Numbers"** option. You may see specific apps listed after Open In as Numbers is shown here when the format of the attachment matches apps on your device.

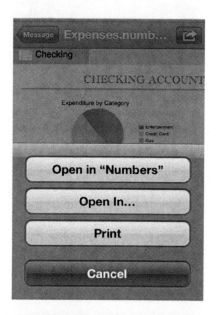

4. Select the application you would like to use from the list.

5. Finally, you can edit the document, save it, and email it back to the sender.

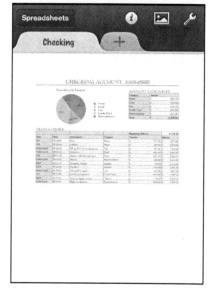

Viewing a Video Attachment

You may receive a video as an attachment to an email. Certain types of videos can be viewed on your iPhone (see the "Supported E-Mail Attachment Types" section later in this chapter for a list of supported video formats). Follow these steps to open a video attachment:

1. Tap the video attachment to open it and view it in the video player.

2. When you are done viewing the video, tap the screen to bring up the player controls.

3. Tap the **Done** button in the upper-left corner to return to the email message.

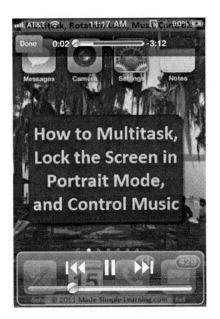

> **NOTE:** This is an image from a video tutorial by Martin Trautschold (one of this book's authors) that shows you how to use your iPhone. Check out some free sample tutorials at www.madesimplelearning.com, Martin's web site.

Opening and Viewing Compressed .zip Files

Your iPhone will not be able to open and view a compressed file in .zip format unless you install an app such as **GoodReader**. At the time of publishing, **GoodReader** was still a free app and well worth installing.

> **TIP:** Learn how to install and use **GoodReader** it in Chapter 14: "Newsstand and More."

Follow these steps to open a .zip file in the program:

1. Install the free **GoodReader** app from the App Store.

2. Open up the email message with the .zip file attachment.

3. Touch and hold the .zip attachment until you see a pop-up at the bottom with a button that says: **Open in "GoodReader."** Tap that button to open the .zip file in **GoodReader**.

4. **GoodReader** should now open, and your .zip file should be at the top of the list of files. To open or decompress the .zip file, tap it and select the **Unzip** button.

5. Now you should see the uncompressed file—in this case, an Adobe .pdf file in the list of files above the .zip file.

6. Tap that uncompressed file to view it.

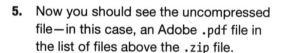

7. When you are done reading the attachment, double-click your **Home** button and tap the **Mail** icon to return to your reading your email.

Supported Email Attachment Types

Your iPhone supports the following file types as attachments:

- .doc and .docx (**Microsoft Word** documents)
- .htm and .html (web pages)
- .key (a **Keynote** presentation document)
- .numbers (an **Apple Numbers** spreadsheet document)
- .pages (an **Apple Pages** document)

- .pdf (Adobe's portable document format, used by programs such as **Adobe Acrobat** and **Adobe Reader**)

- .ppt and .pptx (**Microsoft PowerPoint** presentation documents)

- .txt (a text file)

- .vcf (a contact file)

- .xls and .xlsx (**Microsoft Excel** spreadsheet documents)

- .mp3 and .mov (audio and video formats)

- .zip (compressed files): These are only readable if you have an app installed that can read them, such as **GoodReader**—see the "Opening and Viewing Compressed .zip Files" section earlier in this chapter.

Replying, Forwarding, or Deleting a Message

At the bottom of your email reading pane is a toolbar.

From this toolbar, you can move the message to a different mailbox or folder; delete it; or reply, reply all, or forward it.

Touch the small **Arrow** Icon  to see these option buttons appear: **Reply**, **Reply All**, and **Forward**.

> **NOTE:** The **Reply All** button appears only if there was more than one recipient for the email message.

Replying to an Email

You will probably use the **Reply** command most frequently. Follow these steps to respond to an email on your iPhone:

1. Touch the **Reply** button.

   You will see that the original sender is now listed as the recipient in the **To:** line of the email. The subject will automatically state: "Re: *(Original subject line)*."

2. Type your response.

3. When you are done, just touch the blue **Send** button at the top-right corner of the screen.

Using Reply All

Using the **Reply All** option is just like using the **Reply** function, except that all of the original recipients of the email and the original sender are placed in the address lines. The original sender will be in the **To:** line, while all other recipients of the original email will be listed on the **Cc:** line. You will only see the **Reply All** option if more than one person received the original email.

> **CAUTION:** Be careful when you use **Reply All**. This can be dangerous if some of the recipients are not shown on the original email because they stretch off the edge of the screen. If you do use **Reply All**, then make sure you check the **To:** and **Cc:** lists to make sure everyone should be receiving your reply.

Using the Forward Button

Sometimes, you get an email that you want to send to someone else. The **Forward** command will let you do that (see the "E-Mail Attachments" section in this chapter for more about working with attachments).

NOTE: You need to forward attachments to send them to others. If you want to send someone an attachment from an email you receive, you must choose the **Forward** option. (Note that choosing the **Reply** and **Reply All** options will not include the original email attachment(s) in your outgoing message.)

When you touch the **Forward** button, you may be prompted to address whether you want to **Include or Don't Include** the attachments from the original message.

At this point, you follow the same steps described previously to type your message, add addressees, and send it.

Cleaning up and Organizing Your Inbox

As you get more comfortable with your iPhone as an email device, you will increasingly find yourself using the **Mail** program. It will eventually become necessary to occasionally do some email housecleaning. You can delete or move email messages easily on your iPhone.

Deleting a Single Message

To delete a single message from your inbox, follow these steps:

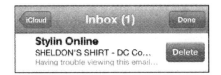

1. Swipe right or left on a message in the inbox to bring up the **Delete** button.

2. Tap **Delete** to remove the message.

Deleting, Moving or Marking Several Messages

We showed you earlier in this chapter how to get this done in the "Move, Delete, or Mark (Flag) Multiple Messages" section.

Deleting from the Message Viewing Screen

The **Message** viewing screen includes another way to delete messages. Open any message to read it and tap the **Trash Can** icon ⬛ in the middle of the bottom of the screen. You will see the email shrink and fly into the **Trash Can**, so it can be deleted.

> **TIP:** You can use the **Settings** app to make your iPhone ask you before deleting email. To do so, tap **Mail, Contacts, Calendars** and set the switch next to **Ask Before Deleting** to **Yes**.

You can organize your mail by moving it into other folders. Email messages can be moved out of your inbox for storage or for reading at another time.

> **NOTE:** If you are using iCloud or another supported email server, you can create, rename or delete mail folders right on your device, see section "Adding or Editing Email Folders or Mailboxes" earlier in this chapter. If this does not work for you, then, you need to set them up in your main email account and sync them to your iPhone. We will show you how to do this in this chapter's "Fine Tune Your E-Mail Settings" section.

Moving an Email to a Folder While Viewing It

Sometimes, you may want to organize your email for easy retrieval later. For example, you might receive an email about an upcoming trip and want to move it to the Travel folder. Sometimes you receive emails that require attention later, in which case you can move them to the Requires Attention folder. This can help you remember to work on such emails later.

Follow these steps to move an email message:

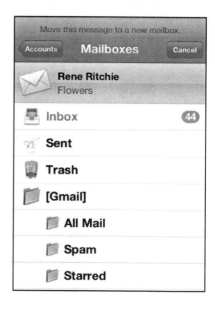

1. Open the email message.

2. Tap the **Move** icon in the upper-right corner.

3. Choose a new folder, and the message will be moved out of the current inbox.

Copy and Paste from an Email

Here are a few tips to select text or pictures and copy them from an email message:

- Double-tap text to select a word, then drag the blue handles up or down to adjust the selection. Next, select **Copy**.

- Press and hold text, and then choose **Select** or **Select All**.

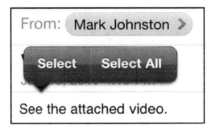

- Press and hold an image, and then select **Save Image** or **Copy**.

For a more complete description, please check out the "Copy and Paste" section in Chapter 2: "Typing, Copy and Search."

Searching for Email Messages

The iPhone has some good built-in search functionality to help you find your emails. You can search your inbox by the **From:**, **To:**, **Subject**, or **All** fields. This helps you filter your inbox, so you can find exactly what you are searching for.

Activating Email Search

It's easy to initiate an email search. Begin by navigating to the **inbox** of the account you wish to search. If you scroll up to the top, you will now see the familiar **Search** bar at the top of your **inbox.**

If your email account supports the feature, you can also search the server for email messages. At the time of writing, a few of the supported types of searchable email accounts include **Exchange**, iCloud (formerly called **MobileMe**), and **Gmail IMAP**. Follow these steps to search through your email on a server:

1. **Tap** the **Search** bar to see a new menu of soft keys under the **Search** bar.

2. Type the text you wish to search for.

3. **Tap one of the tabs** under the Search window:

   a. **From**: Searches only the sender's email addresses.

   b. **To**: Searches only the recipients' email addresses.

   c. **Subject**: Searches only message **Subject** fields.

   d. **All**: Searches every part of the message.

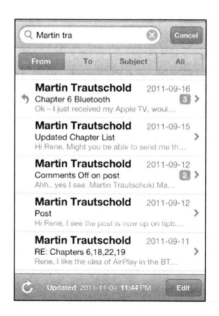

For example, assume that we want to search an inbox for an email from "Martin." We would type Martin's name into the **Search** box and then touch **From**. The inbox would then be filtered to show only the emails from Martin.

Fine Tuning Your Email Settings

You can fine-tune the email accounts on your iPhone with the myriad options available in the **Settings** app. Follow these steps to change these settings: tap the **Settings** icon, then tap **Mail, Contacts, Calendars.** The sections that follow explain the adjustments you can make.

Automatically Retrieve Email (Fetch New Data)

In addition to the options under **Advanced**, you can use the **Email** settings to configure how often your email is fetched or pulled to your iPhone. By default, your iPhone automatically receives mail or other contact or calendar updates when they are "pushed" from the server.

You can adjust this setting by taking the following steps:

1. Tap the **Settings** app.

2. Tap **Mail, Contacts, Calendars**.

3. Tap **Fetch New Data** under the email accounts listed.

4. Set **Push** to **ON** (default) to automatically have the server push data. Set it to **OFF** to conserve your battery life.

5. Adjust the timing schedule to pull data from the server. This is how frequently applications should pull new data from the server.

> **NOTE:** If you set this option to **Every 15 Minutes**, you will receive more frequent updates; however, this option sacrifices battery life compared to a setting of **Hourly** or **Manually**.

Having automatic retrieval is very handy if you just want to turn on your iPhone and see that you have messages; otherwise, you need to remember to check.

Advanced Push Options

At the bottom of the **Fetch New Data** screen, below the **Hourly** and **Manually** settings, you can touch the **Advanced** button to see a new screen with all your email accounts listed.

Tap any email account to adjust its settings.

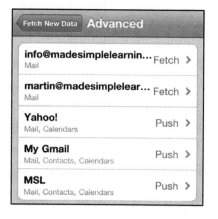

Most accounts can be **Fetched** on the schedule you set or set to **Manual**. The **Manual** option requires that you retrieve data using the **Update** button. This screen gives you the ability to adjust **Fetch**, **Manual**, or even **Push** settings for each account you have set up.

Adjusting Your Mail Settings

Under the **Accounts** section, you can see all the email settings listed under **Mail**. The **Default** settings may work well for you; but if you need to adjust any of these, you can follow these steps:

Show: This sets how many emails are pulled from the server. You can specify anywhere from 50 to 1,000 messages (the default is 50 recent messages).

Preview: This option lets you set how many lines of text in addition to the **Subject** are shown in the inbox **Preview**. You can adjust this value from **None** to **5 Lines** (the default is **2 Lines**).

Minimum Font Size: This is the default font size shown when opening an email the first time. It is also smallest font size that you are allowed to zoom out to when viewing an email. Your options are **Small**, **Medium**, **Large**, **Extra Large**, and **Giant** (the default is **Medium**).

TIP: You can expand the font size further in the Accessibility area of settings. Check out Chapter 2: "Typing, Copy and Search" for more details.

Show To/Cc Label: With this option **ON**, you will see a small **To** or **Cc** label in your inbox before the subject. This label shows which field your address was placed in (the default state of this option is **OFF**).

Ask Before Deleting: Turn this option **ON** to be asked every time you try to delete a message (the default is **OFF**).

Load Remote Images: This option allows your iPhone to load all the graphics (remote images) that are placed in some email messages (the default value for this option is **ON**).

Organize by Thread: This option groups related emails together. It shows only one message, with a number next to it. That number indicates how many related emails exist. This feature gives you a good way to keep all discussions together in one place (the default value of this option is **ON**).

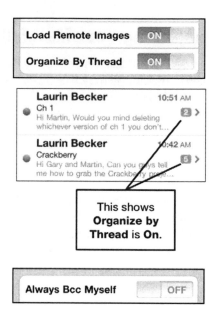

This shows **Organize by Thread** is **On**.

Always Bcc Myself: This option sends a blind carbon copy (**Bcc:**) of every email you send from your iPhone to your email account (the default value of this option is **OFF**).

Changing Your Email Signature

By default, emails you send will say "Sent from my iPhone." Follow these steps to change the **Signature** line of the email:

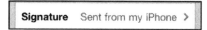

1. Tap the **Signature** tab and type in the new email signature you want at the bottom of emails sent from your iPhone.

2. When you are done editing the **Signature** field, tap the **Mail, Contacts...** button in the upper-left corner. This will return you to the **Mail** settings screen.

Changing Your Default Mail Account (Sent From)

If you have multiple email accounts set up on your iPhone, you should set one of them—usually, the one you use most—as your **Default Account**. When you select **Compose** from the **Email** screen, the default account is always chosen. Follow these steps to change the email account you send from by default:

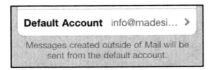

1. Tap the **Default Account** option, and you will see a list of all your email accounts.

2. Tap the email account you wish to use as your **Default Account** choice.

3. When you are done, touch the **Mail, Contacts...** button to return to the **Mail** settings menu.

Toggling Sounds for Receiving and Sending Email

You may notice a little sound effect every time you send or receive email. What you hear is the default setting on your iPhone.

If you want to disable this or change it, you do so in the **Settings** program:

1. Tap your **Settings** icon.

2. Tap **Sounds**.

3. You will see various switches to turn sound effects on or off. Tap **New Mail** and **Sent Mail** to select your mail tone options.

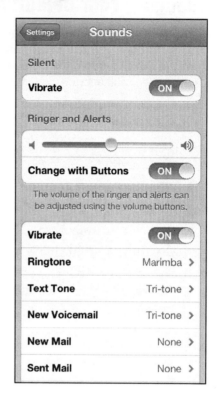

Advanced Email Options

> **NOTE:** Email accounts set up as Exchange, IMAP, or iCloud will not have this **Advanced** email settings screen. This only applies to POP3 email accounts.

To get to the **Advanced** options for each email account, follow these steps:

1. Touch the **Settings** icon.

2. Touch **Mail, Contacts, Calendars**.

3. Touch an email address listed under **Accounts**.

4. At the bottom of the mail settings pop-up window, tap the **Advanced** button to bring up the **Advanced** dialog.

Removing Email Messages from Your iPhone After Deletion

You can select how frequently you want email removed completely from your iPhone once it is deleted.

Touch the **Remove** tab and select the option that is best for you; the default setting is **Never**.

Using SSL and Authentication

The SSL and Authentication features were discussed previously; however, this screen gives you another location to access these features for a particular email account.

Deleting from Server

You can configure your iPhone to handle the deletion of messages from your email server. Usually, this setting is left at **Never**, and this function is handled on your main computer. If you use your iPhone as your main email device, however, you might want to handle that feature from the phone itself. Follow these steps to remove deleted emails on the server from your iPhone.

1. Touch the **Delete from Server** tab to select the feature that best suits your needs: **Never**, **Seven Days**, or **When removed from inbox**.

2. The default setting is **Never**. If you want to choose **Seven Days**; that option should give you enough time to check email on your computer, as well as your iPhone, and then decide what to keep and what to get rid of.

Changing the Incoming Server Port

As you did with the **Outgoing Server Port** earlier, you can change the **Incoming Server Port** if you are having trouble receiving email. It is very rare that your troubles will be related to the port you receive mail on; consequently, you will rarely need to change this number. If your email service provider gives you a different number, just touch the numbers and input a new port. The value for an **Incoming Server Port** is usually **995**, **993**, or **110**; however, the port value could also be another number.

Troubleshooting Email Problems

Usually, your email works flawlessly on your iPhone. However, sometimes your email may not work as flawlessly as you would hope. This could be due to a server issue, a network connectivity issue, or an email service provider requirement that isn't being met.

More often than not, there is a simple setting that needs to be adjusted or a password that needs to be re-entered.

If you try out some of the troubleshooting tips that follow and your email is still not working, then your email server may just be down temporarily. Check with your email service provider to make sure your mail server is up and running; you might also check whether your provider has made any recent changes that would affect your settings.

> **TIP:** If the tips that follow do not solve the problem, please check out Chapter 26: "Troubleshooting" for more helpful tips and resources.

E-Mail Isn't Being Received or Sent

If you can't send or receive email, your first step should be to verify that you are connected to the Internet. Check this by looking at your network connectivity symbols in the upper-left corner of your **Home** screen (see Chapter 4: "Connect to the Network" for details).

Sometimes, you need to adjust the outgoing port for email to be sent properly. Do so by following these steps:

1. Tap **Settings**.

2. Touch **Mail, Contacts and Calendars**.

3. Touch your email account that is having trouble sending messages under **Accounts**.

4. Touch **SMTP** and verify that your outgoing mail server is set correctly; also check that it is set to **ON**.

5. Touch **Outgoing Mail Server** at the top and verify all the settings, such as **Host Name**, **User Name**, **Password**, **SSL**, **Authentication**, and **Server Port**. You might also try **587**, **995**, or **110** for the **Server Port** value; sometimes that helps.

6. Click **Done** and the email account name in the upper-left corner to return to the **Email** settings screen for this account.

7. Scroll down to the bottom and touch **Advanced**.

8. You can also try a different port setting for the server port on this screen, such as **587**, **995**, or **110**. If those values don't work, contact your email service provider to get a different port number and verify your settings.

Chapter 18

Contacts and Notes

Your iPhone gives you immediate access to all your important information. Just like your computer, your iPhone can store thousands of contacts for easy retrieval. In this chapter, we'll show you how to add new contact, customize your contacts by adding new fields, organize your contacts with groups, quickly search or scroll through contacts, and even see a contact's location with the iPhone's **Maps** app. We will also show you how to customize the **Contacts** view so it is sorted and displayed just the way you like it. Finally, we will cover a few troubleshooting tips that will save you some time when you run into difficulties.

We will also give you an overview of the **Notes** app, which you can use to write notes, make grocery lists, and make lists of movies you'd like to watch or books you'd like to read. We will show you how to organize and email notes to yourself or others. Ideally, we hope that **Notes** will become so easy on the iPhone that you can eventually get rid of most, if not all, of your paper sticky notes!

What is also great is that you can use iCloud to wirelessly synchronize, share and back up your contacts and notes. So you never have to worry about losing your important information or whether or not you have the latest information on your device or computer.

Loading Your Contacts onto the iPhone

Chapter 3: "Sync with iCloud, iTunes and More" covered how to load your contacts onto the iPhone using the **iTunes** app on your Mac or Windows computer. You can also load contacts onto your phone using the Google Sync or iCloud services.

> **TIP:** You can add new contact entries from email messages you receive. Learn how in Chapter 17: "Communicate with Email."

When Is Your Contact List Most Useful?

The **Contacts** app is most useful when two things are true:

1. You have many names and addresses in it.

2. You can easily find what you need.

Improving Your Contact List

We have a couple of basic rules that can help you make your contact list on your iPhone more useful:

Rule 1: Add anything and everything to your contacts.

> You never know when you might need that obscure restaurant name, plumber's number, and so on.

Rule 2: As you add entries, make sure you think about how to find them in the future (first name, last name, company).

> We have many tips and tricks in this chapter to help you enter names, so you can find them instantly when you need them.

> **TIP:** Here's a good way to find restaurants. Whenever you enter a restaurant into your contacts list, make sure to put the word "restaurant" into the company name field, even if it's not part of the name. When you type the letters "rest," then you should instantly find all your restaurants!

Adding a New Contact on Your iPhone

You can always add your contacts right on your iPhone. This is handy when you're away from your computer—but have your iPhone—and need to add someone to your contacts. It's very easy to do; the next section will show you how.

Start the Contacts App

From your **Home** screen, touch the **Contacts** icon and you'll see the **All Contacts** list. Tap the **Plus Sign** button (**+**) in the upper-right corner to add a new contact, as shown in Figure 18–1.

Figure 18–1. *Entering a new contact name*

Tap each field to enter the new contact's first name, last name and Company name.

> **TIP:** Keep in mind that the contacts search feature uses first, last, and company names. When you add or edit contacts, adding a special word to the company name can help you find a particular contact later. For example, adding the words "Cece friend" to the **Company** field can help you find all of Cece's friends quickly using the search feature.

Under the **First Last** button are fields for **mobile phone, email, ringtone, text tone, home page, add new address** and **add field**. Under that, you can Link contacts together.

Adding a New Phone Number

Tap the **Phone** button and use the **Numbers** keyboard to input the phone number.

> **TIP:** Don't worry about parentheses, dashes, or dots—the iPhone will put the number into the correct format. Just type the digits of the area code and number. If you know the country code, it's a good idea to put that in, as well.

Next, choose which type of phone number this is—mobile, home, work, or other. There are nine fields you can choose from, and there's also a **Custom** field if you find none of the built-in fields apply.

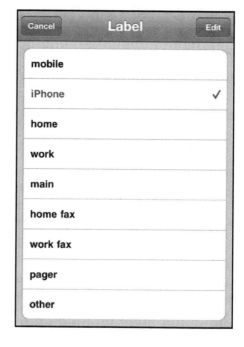

TIP: Sometimes you need to add a pause to a phone number—for example, when the phone number is for someone at an organization where you have to dial the main number and then an extension. This is easy to do on the iPhone. You just tap the **Symbols** button (+*#) and then tap **Pause** or **Wait**. **Pause** will add a comma between the main number and the extension, like this: 386-555-7687, 19323. When you dial this number (e.g., from your iPhone), your phone will dial the main number, pause for two seconds, and then dial the extension. If you need more of a pause, simply add more commas. **Wait** will add a semi-colon between the main number and the extension (or conference call ID, or whatever extra digits you may need to enter). Once the first number is dialed, a second button will appear with the extra numbers. Tapping it will dial them.

Adding Email Addresses

Touch the **Email** tab and enter the email address for your contact. You can also touch the tab to the left of the email address and select whether this is a home, work, or other email address.

After you add one address, you will see another field appear to add more email addresses.

Custom Ringtone or Text Tone

Touch the **ringtone** or **text tone** tabs to select a custom ringtone or text tone when this person calls or sends you a text message.

Entering Web Site Addresses

You will also see a **home page** field in which you can enter the address of your contact's web site or even multiple web sites.

> **NOTE**: If you used iCloud to sync your contacts, iCloud may automatically look for a Facebook home page to integrate into the contact info.

Adding the Street Address

Below the **home** field are the fields for adding the address. Input the **Street**, **City**, **State**, and **Zip Code**. You can also specify the **Country** and whether this is a home or work address.

Adding New Fields

Tap the **Add Field** tab and select any of the suggested fields to add it to that particular contact (see Figure 18–2).

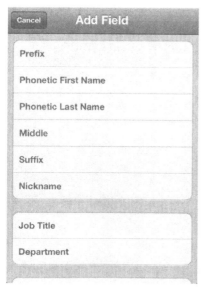
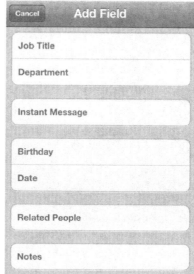

Figure 18–2. *New fields available to add to your Contact entry*

When you touch **Birthday**, you're presented with a wheel. You can turn the wheel to the corresponding date to add the birthday to the contact information.

When you are finished, just touch the **Done** button in the upper-right corner of the **New Contact** form.

> **TIP:** Suppose you meet someone at the bus stop—someone you want to remember. Of course, you should enter your new friend's first and last names (if you know them); however, you should also enter the words "bus stop" in the **Company name** field. Then, when you type the letters "bus" or "stop," you should instantly find everyone you've met at the bus stop, even if you can't remember their names!

Adding a Photo to Contacts

You may want to associate a photo with a contact. From the **New Contact** screen we've been working in, simply touch the **Add Photo** button next to the **First Last** tab.

If you are changing a photo when you are in "edit contact" mode, you'll see **edit** at the bottom of the existing photo.

After you touch the **add photo** button, you'll see that you can do the following:

- ■ Take Photo
- ■ Choose Photo

If there's a photo already in place, you can also do these things:

- ■ Edit Photo
- ■ Delete Photo

To choose an existing photo, select the photo album where the picture is located and touch the corresponding tab. When you see the picture you want to use, just touch it.

You'll notice that the top and bottom of the photo become grayed out and that you can manipulate the picture by moving it, pinching to zoom in or out, and then arranging it in the **Picture** window.

Once the picture is sitting where you want it, just touch the **Choose** button in the lower-right corner and that picture will be set for the contact.

> **TIP:** If you just moved into a new neighborhood, it can be quite daunting to remember everyone's name. Therefore, it's good practice to add the word "neighbor" into the **Company name** field for every neighbor you meet. To instantly call up all your neighbors, simply type the letters "neigh" to find everyone you've met!

Searching Your Contacts

Let's say you need to find a specific phone number or email address. Just touch your **Contacts** icon as you did previously, and you'll see a **Search** box at the top of your **All Contacts** list (see Figure 18–3).

> **TIP:** If you are somewhere in the middle or bottom of your **Contacts** list, you can quickly jump to the top of the **Contacts** screen and see this **Search** window by tapping the time at the very top of your iPhone.

Figure 18–3. *The contacts **Search** box*

To find a contact, enter the first few letters of any of these three searchable fields:

- First Name
- Last Name
- Nickname
- Company Name

The iPhone begins to filter immediately and displays only those contacts that match the letters typed.

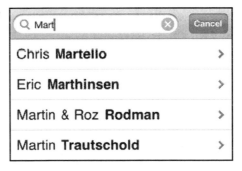

> **TIP:** To further narrow the search, hit the **Space** key and type a few more letters.

When you see the correct name, just touch it and that individual's contact information will appear.

Quickly Jump to a Letter by Tapping and Sliding on the Alphabet

If you hold your finger on the alphabet on the left edge of the screen and drag it up or down, you can jump to that letter.

Search by Flicking

If you don't want to manually input letters, you can just move your finger and flick from the bottom up, and you'll see your contacts move quickly on the screen. Just continue to flick or scroll until you see the name you want. Tap a name and the contact information for that person will appear.

Search Using Groups

If you have your contacts sorted by groups on your PC or Mac and you sync your iPhone with your computer or over the air using iCloud then those groups will be synced to your iPhone. When you start your **Contacts** app, you will see **Groups** at the top. Under the **Groups** heading, you will see **All Contacts**.

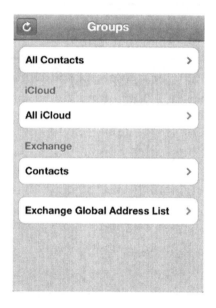

Choose **All Contacts** to search all the available contact information on the iPhone.

If you have multiple accounts synced, you will see a tab for each individual account and one for **All Contacts** at the top.

This example shows two groups—one is from a Microsoft Exchange account (i.e., a company email account), and one is from a group of iCloudontacts.

If you have an Exchange ActiveSync account and your company has enabled it, your Exchange Global Address List shows up here, under Groups, as well. You can search to find anyone in your company there.

NOTE: You can't create groups in the **Contacts** app on the iPhone—they must be created on your computer or synced when you add contact accounts to your iPhone.

Adding Contacts from Email Messages

Often you'll receive an email message and realize that the contact is not in your address book. Adding a new contact from an email message is easy.

Open the email message from the contact you'd like to add to your **Contacts** list. Next, in the email message's **From** field, just touch the name of the sender next to the **From:** tag.

If the sender is not in your address book, you'll be taken to a screen that lets you choose whether to add that email address to an existing contact or to create a new one.

If you select **Create a New Contact**, you'll be taken to the same **New Contact** screen we saw earlier (see Figure 18–1).

But suppose this is someone's personal email address, and you already have an entry for that person with a work email address. In that case, you would select **Add to Existing Contact** and choose the correct person. Next, you'd give this email address a new tag—*personal*, in this case.

Linking a Contact to Another App

You might have contact information for the sender of the email message in another app on the phone. The iPhone makes it easy to link these contacts together.

For example, assume Steve, the sender of the email message, is in a list of your LinkedIn contacts, but not a contact on your iPhone, for some reason. Here is how you can link his contact information in your iPhone to the information you have in the **LinkedIn** app:

1. Add him to your contacts, as shown previously.

2. Start the **LinkedIn** app—see Chapter 25: "Social Networking" for more information on the topic.

3. Find your contact information for Steve to verify that he is in your **LinkedIn** app.

4. Go to the **Connections** icon.

5. Choose **Download All** in the top-right corner.

6. The **LinkedIn** app will inform you that doing this will add the photo, current company and title, email addresses, and web sites associated with this contact (see Figure 18–4).

7. This is exactly what you want in your iPhone contacts, so choose **Download All New Connections**.

8. Steve's picture and updated information are then brought into his contact information on your iPhone.

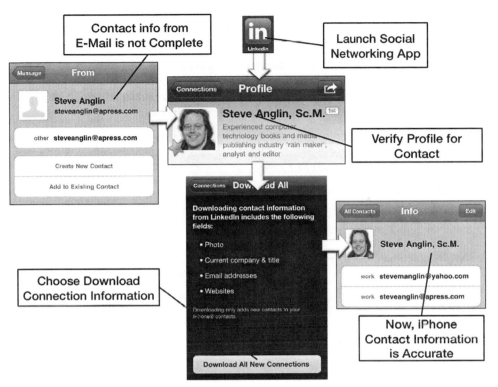

Figure 18–4. *Linking a new contact in an email message to an existing social networking contact*

> **TIP:** Learning the names of the parents of a school-age child's friends can be fairly challenging. In the **First** field, however, you can add, not just the name of your child's friend, but also the names of the child's parents (e.g., **First: Samantha (Mom: Susan, Dad: Ron))**. Next, in the **Company** field, add the name of your child and "school friend" (e.g., **Ccoc school friend**). Now, just typing your child's name in the **Search** box of your **All Contacts** list instantly finds every person you ever met at your child's school. Now you can say, without missing a beat: "Hello, Susan, great to see you again!" *Try your best to covertly look up the name.*

Sending a Picture to a Contact

If you want to send a picture to a contact, then you will need to do that from the **Photos** app (see Chapter 20: "Working with Photos").

Sending an Email Message from Contacts

Many of the core apps (e.g., **Contacts**, **Mail**, and **Messages**) are fully integrated, so one app can easily trigger another. If you want to send an email message to one of your contacts, simply open the contact and tap the email address. The **Mail** app will launch, and you can compose and send an email message to this person.

Start your **Contacts** app by touching the **Contacts** icon. Either search or flick through your contacts until you find the contact you need.

> home **martin@madesimplelearni...**

In the contact information, touch the email address of the contact you'd like to use.

You'll see that the **Mail** program launches automatically with the contact's name in the **To:** field of the email message. Finally, type and send the message.

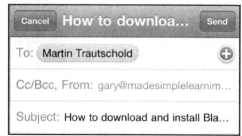

Showing Your Contacts Addresses on the Map

One of the great things about the iPhone is its integration with Google Maps. This is very evident in the **Contacts** app. Let's say you want to map the home or work address of any contact in your address book. In the old days (pre-iPhone), you'd have to use Google, MapQuest, or some other program, and then laboriously retype or copy and paste the address information. This is very time-consuming—but you don't have to do this on the iPhone.

Simply open the contact as you did earlier. This time, touch the address at the bottom of the contact information.

> work **25 Forest View Way**

Your **Maps** app (which is powered by Google Maps) immediately loads and drops a **Push-Pin** icon at the exact location of the contact. The contact's name will appear above the **Push-Pin**.

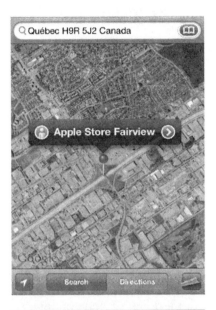

Touch the tab on the top of the **Push-Pin** to get to the **Info** screen.

Now you can select **Directions To Here** or **Directions From Here**.

Next, type the correct start or end address and touch the **Route** button in the lower-right corner. If you decide you don't want the directions, just tap the **Clear** button in the top left.

What if you had just typed the address in your **Maps** app, instead of clicking from your contact list? In that case, you might want to touch **Add to Contacts** to add this address.

TIP: To return to your contact information, tap the **Map** button, exit **Maps**, and then start up **Contacts**. You can also use multi-tasking (see Chapter 7: "Multitasking and Siri") by double-clicking the **Home** button and choosing the **Contacts** app.

Changing Your Contact Sort and Display Order

Like other settings, the **Contact** app's options are accessible via the **Settings** icon.

Touch the **Settings** icon, scroll down to **Mail, Contacts, Calendars**, and then touch the tab.

Next, scroll down until you see **Contacts** and the two options underneath it. To change the sort order, touch the **Sort Order** tab and select whether you want your contacts sorted by first name or last name.

You may want to change how your contacts are displayed. Here's where you get it done; you can choose **First, Last** or **Last, First**. Tap the **Display Order** tab and choose whether you want your contact displayed in first name or last name order. Tap the **Mail, Contacts...** button in the upper-left corner to save your settings changes.

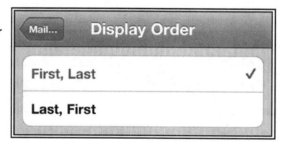

Searching for Global Address List (GAL) Contacts

If you have an Exchange account configured, you should have an option for a Global Address List. This gives you access to your Global Address List if you are connected to your organization's server.

Open your **Contacts** app and look under Exchange for a tab that says **Exchange Global Address List**.

Contacts Troubleshooting

Sometimes, your **Contacts** app might not work the way you expect. (If you don't see all your contacts, review the steps in the Chapter 3: "Sync with iCloud, iTunes and More" for information on how to sync with your address book application.) Make sure you have selected **All Groups** in the settings of the **iTunes** app.

> **TIP:** If you are syncing with another contact application, such as **Contacts** in Gmail, then make sure you select the option closest to **All Contacts**, rather than a subset like a particular group.

When Global Address List Contacts Don't Show Up (For Microsoft Exchange Users)

Sometimes contacts in the Global Address List won't show up on your iPhone. If this occurs, begin by making sure you are connected to a Wi-Fi or 3G cellular data network.

Next, check your Exchange settings and verify you have the correct server and login information. To do so, tap the **Settings** button, and then scroll to and touch **Mail, Contacts and Calendar**. Find your Exchange account on the list and touch it to look at the settings. You may need to contact technical support at your organization to make sure your Exchange settings are correct.

The Notes App

If you are like many people, your desk is filled with little yellow sticky notes—notes to do everything imaginable. Even with our computers, we still tend to leave these little notes as reminders. One of the great things about the iPhone is that you can write your notes on familiar yellow notepaper, and then keep them neatly organized and sorted. You can even email them to yourself or someone else to make sure that the information is not forgotten. You can also backup your notes using iTunes and, if you choose, sync notes to your computer or other web sites such as Google.

> **TIP:** The **Notes** app that comes with the iPhone is pretty basic and utilitarian. If you need a more robust notes application that can sort, categorize, import items (PDF, Word, and so on), have folders, search, and more, you should check out the App Store on your iPhone. Do a search for "notes," and you will find at least a dozen notes-related apps ranging from free to $0.99 and up.

The **Notes** app on the iPhone gives you a convenient place to keep your notes and simple "to-do" lists. You can also keep simple lists, such as a grocery list, or a list for other stores, such as a hardware or pet store. If you have your iPhone with you, you can add items to these lists as soon as they occur to you, and they can be accessed and edited at any time.

Sync Notes

You can sync notes between iOS devices like iPhone and IPad, or with your computer or other web site using the methods we show you in Chapter 3: "Sync with iCloud, iTunes and More." The nice thing about syncing notes is that you can add a note on your computer and have it just "appear" on your iPhone. Then when you are out and about, you can edit that note and have it synced back to your computer. No more re-typing or remembering things. You always have your iPhone with you, so taking notes anywhere, anytime, can be a great way never to forget anything important.

Getting Started with Notes

Like all other apps, simply tap the **Notes** icon to start it After starting the **Notes** app, you see what looks like a typical yellow note pad.

Multiple Notes Accounts

If you happen to be syncing over iCloud, Exchange, or at least one IMAP email account and your computer using iTunes, then you will see that your notes from each of these accounts are kept separate. This is very much like how your contacts are kept in separate groups by email account and how your calendars are kept separate by email account.

In order to see multiple notes accounts, you have to set a switch in the account setup screen.

When you setup your IMAP email account, in **Settings** > **Mail, Contacts, Calendars**, you will see options to turn Notes syncing on or off. In order to see these notes accounts, you have to set the **Notes** switch to **On**, as shown for this Gmail account.

To view the various notes accounts, tap the **Accounts** button in the upper left corner of the **Notes** app.

Then, on the next screen, you can tap selections to view **All Notes,** or your notes for each account. In this image, the Gmail or MobileMe account are options.

Notes you add to an individual account will be kept with that account. For example, If you add notes to Gmail, then those would show up only on your Gmail account.

How Are My Notes Sorted?

You see that all notes are listed in reverse chronological order, with the most recently edited notes at the top and the oldest at the bottom.

The date that is shown is the last time and date that the particular note was edited, not when it was first created. So you will notice the order of your notes moving around on the screen.

This sorting can be a good thing because your most recent (or frequently edited) notes will be right at the top.

> **TIP:** If you want to keep track of your to-do lists, you can use the built in reminders app on your iPhone, If you want something more powerful, check out **Things, Appigo Todo,** or **OmniFocus** in the App Store.

Adding a New Note

To start a new note, tap the plus sign  in the upper right-hand corner.

The notepad is blank, and the keyboard pops up for you to begin typing.

> **TIP:** You can turn your iPhone on its side to see the larger, landscape keyboard.

Adding a Title to the Note

The first few words you type before you hit the **Return** key will become the title of the note. So think about what you want as the title, and type that first. In the image shown, **Grocery list** becomes the title of the note.

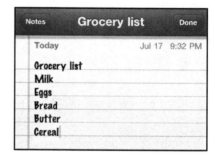

Put a new item on each line, and tap the **Return** key to go to the next line.

When you are done, touch the **Notes** button in the top left-hand corner to return to the main Notes screen.

Viewing or Editing Your Notes

Your notes appear in the list as tabs to touch. Touch the name of the note you wish to view or edit. The contents of the note are then displayed.

You can scroll in Notes as you do in any program. You will notice that the date and time the note was last edited appear in the upper right-hand corner.

When you are done reading the note, just touch the **Notes** button in the top left-hand corner to return to the main Notes screen.

To advance through multiple notes, just touch the arrows at the bottom of the

screen. Touch the **Forward** 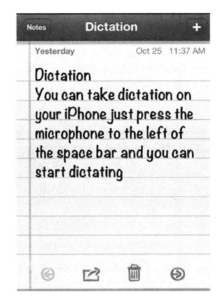 arrow. The page turns, and you can see the next

note. To go back, just hit the **Back** arrow.

Using Voice Dictation for Your Notes

Remember, the iPhone can take dictation for you. When you are editing or starting a new note, tap the microphone button to the left of the space key and start talking.

You know dictation is working when you see the purple microphone appear at the bottom. The amount of purple showing will pulse up and down with the volume of your voice.

When you're done, tap Done and see how well it works!

> **TIP:** You can use dictation to enter punctuation, symbols, and formatting, for example, "period" or "question mark," "open parenthesis" or "close square brackets," "new paragraph," or even "smiley face."

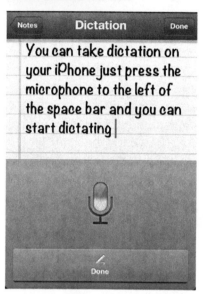

Deleting Notes

To delete a note, swipe your finger on the note from left to right on the list and tap **Delete**.

Or, if you are viewing the note, then tap the **Trash Can** icon ____ at the bottom. The iPhone prompts you to delete the note or cancel.

Emailing or Printing a Note

One of the **Notes** app's convenient features is the ability to email or print a note. Let's say you wrote a grocery note and wanted to email it to your spouse, or you made a list of gift ideas and want to hand them out. To email or print a note, just tap the **Action**

button icon ____ at the bottom of the screen.

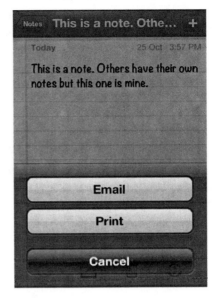

Data Detectors - Cool Things With Underlined Words

If you type in the words "tomorrow morning" in a note and save it. The next time you open that note, you will see that the words have been underlined. If you tap and hold the underlined words, you will see a button asking if you want to Create Event. Tap the button to create a new calendar event for tomorrow morning.

TIP: Whenever date and time words are underlined, the iPhone recognizes them as potential calendar events. This works in notes, email messages and other places on your iPhone. The iPhone also has other "data detectors", for example it can recognize phone numbers, web site addresses, and even tracking numbers for packages.

Chapter 19

Calendar and Reminders

The iPhone makes the old calendar that used to hang on the fridge obsolete. In this chapter, we will show you how to utilize the **Calendar** app of the iPhone to its full potential. For example, we will show you how to schedule appointments, manage multiple calendars, change views on your calendar, and even how to deal with meeting invitations.

In iOS 5, Apple has added the **Reminders** app for easy management of all your tasks and to-do lists, which are based on both time and location!

> **NOTE:** For most of this chapter, we will talk about syncing your iPhone calendar with another calendar because it is nice to have your calendar accessible on your iPhone and in other places. If you choose, you can also use your iPhone in a *standalone* mode, where you do not sync to any other calendar. In the latter case, all the steps we describe for events, viewing, and managing events still apply equally to you. It is critical, however, that you use the iCloud or iTunes automatic backup feature to save a copy of your calendar, just in case something happens to your iPhone.

Calendars, Reminders and Siri

Apple's new, artificially intelligent personal assistant, Siri, can quickly and easily create calendar events and reminder items for you. If it's something relatively simple, Siri can even add it more quickly and easily than you could create them yourself through "old fashioned" button tapping. Here are some examples of what Siri can do with calendars and reminders.

- "Show me my calendar for tomorrow". Siri will show all events for any day or date you request.

- "Schedule an appointment for 9pm tomorrow with my boss." Siri will even alert you if you have conflicts.

- "Move my appointment at 9pm tomorrow." Siri will even tell you if it's a recurring appointment and offer to change the current one only, or all future events.

- "Show me my reminders." Siri will give you a list your reminders and you can quickly check off any you've already completed.

- "Remind me to call my wife when I get to work." Siri will create a location-based reminder.

- "Add cookies to my shopping list." Siri will create a reminder to buy cookies on the list named "Shopping".

Managing Your Busy Life on Your iPhone

The **Calendar** and **Reminders** apps provide powerful, easy-to-use functionality that helps you manage your appointments, keep track of what you have to do, set reminder alarms, and even create and respond to meeting invitations (for Exchange and iCloud users).

Syncing or Sharing Your Calendar and Reminders

If you maintain a calendar or task list on your computer, or a calendar on a web site such as iCloud or Google Calendar, then you can synchronize or share that data with your iPhone either by using the iTunes app and your sync cable or by setting up a wireless synchronization (see Chapter 3: "Sync iCloud, iTunes, and More" for information on syncing).

After you set up the calendar and task syncing, all of your computer calendar appointments and to-do lists will be synced with your iPhone calendar automatically, based on your sync settings (see Figure 19–1).

If you use **iTunes** to sync with your calendar (e.g., **Microsoft Outlook** or Apple's **iCal**), your appointments and tasks will be transferred or synced every time you connect your iPhone to your computer.

If you use another method to sync (e.g., iCloud, Exchange, or similar), this sync is wireless and automatic, and it will most likely happen without you having to do anything after the initial setup process.

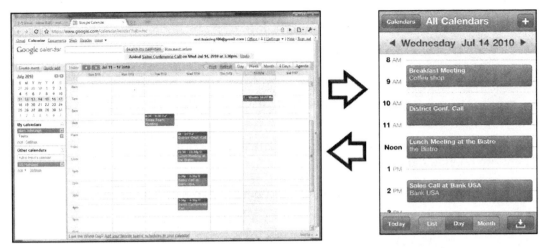

Figure 19–1. *Syncing a PC or Mac calendar to an iPhone*

Today's Day and Date Shown on the Calendar Icon

The **Calendar** icon is usually right on your iPhone's **Home** screen. You will quickly notice that your **Calendar** icon changes to show today's date and the day of the week. The icon to the right shows that it is a Friday, the 16th day of the month.

TIP: If you use your iPhone's **Calendar** app often, you might want to think about pinning or moving it to the Bottom dock; you learned how to do this in the section on docking icons in Chapter 6: "Icons and Folders."

Viewing Your Appointments and Getting Around in Calendar

The default view for the **Calendar** app shows your **Day** view. This view shows you at a glance any upcoming appointments for your day. Appointments are shown in your calendar. If you happen to have multiple calendars set up on your computer, such as **Work** and **Home**, then appointments from the different calendars will display as different colors on your iPhone's calendar.

You can manipulate the calendar in various ways:

- **Move a day at a time**: If you tap the triangles next to today's date at the top, you move forward or backward a day.

> **TIP:** Touch and hold the triangles next to the date to advance quickly through days.

- **Change views**: Tap the **List**, **Day**, and **Month** buttons at the bottom to change the view.

- **Jump to today**: Tap the **Today** button at the bottom-left corner.

The Four Calendar Views

Your **Calendar** app comes with four views. **Day**, **List**, **Week**, and **Month** are all available in Portrait orientation; and you can switch between views by tapping the name of the view at the bottom of the screen. **Week** view is only available in Landscape orientation, and you can switch to it by turning your iPhone sideways. Here's a quick overview of the four views:

- **Day view**: When you start the iPhone's **Calendar** app, the default view is usually the **Day** view. This allows you to quickly see everything you have scheduled for the day. You can find buttons to change the view at the bottom of the **Calendar** app.

  To move from one day to the next, simply swipe from right to left. To move back a day, swipe from left to right.

■ **List** view (also known as **Agenda** view): Tap the **List** button at the bottom, and you can see a list of your appointments.

Depending on how much you have scheduled, you could see the next day or even the next week's worth of scheduled events.

Swipe up or down to see more events.

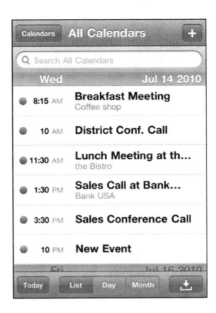

■ **Month view**: Tap the **Month** button at the bottom, and you can see a layout of the full month. Days with appointments have a small dot in them. Dots for the current day will show up highlighted in blue.

> **TIP:** To return to the **Today** view, just touch the **Today** button at the bottom left.
>
>

Go to the next month: Tap the triangle to the right of the month shown at the top.

Go to the previous month: Tap the triangle to the left of the month.

- **Week** view: Turn you iPhone sideways to landscape orientation to access the week view.

- Swipe left or right to see more days.

Working with Several Calendars

The **Calendar** app lets you view and work with more than one calendar. The number of calendars you see depends on how many you are syncing. For example, you may have iCloud or Google Calendar syncing for home and Exchange for work,

To view just one calendar at a time, tap the **Calendars** button at the top and select only the calendar you wish to see.

When you set up your **Sync** settings, you were able to specify which calendars you wanted to sync with your iPhone. You can customize your calendar further by following these instructions:

- **Changing the colors**: If you don't like the color of a calendar on your iPhone, it's easy to change:

a. Tap on the **Calendars** button at the top right

b. Tap on the **Edit** button at the top right.

c. Tap on the calendar you want to change.

d. You'll be presented with a list of color choices. Tap the one you want are your new color will be set.

- **Adding a new calendar**: If you are using iCloud to sync, you will be able to add a new calendar on your iPhone:

    a. Tap **Calendars** at the top-right.

    b. Tap **Edit** at the top-right.

    c. Scroll down and tap **Add Calendar...** in the iCloud section

    d. Enter a name and choose a color for your new calendar, and you're done!

Adding New Calendar Events

You can easily add new events or appointments right on your iPhone. These new events and appointments will be synced (or shared with) your computer the next time a sync takes place.

Adding a New Appointment

Your instinct will most likely be to try to touch the screen at a particular time to set an appointment; and with iOS 5, you can finally do just that!

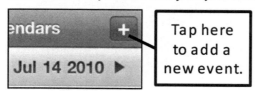

Tap here to add a new event.

To add a new calendar event from any **Calendar** view, follow these steps.

1. Tap and hold your finger on the screen at the place where you want the appointment until a new colored bubble appears. (You can also still tap the + icon at the upper-right corner of the screen to add a new event.

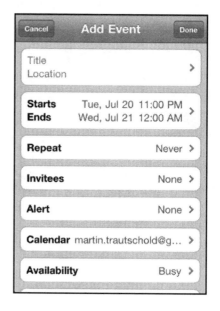

2. On the **Add Event** screen, touch
the box marked **Title & Location**.

Type in a title for the event and the location
(optional). For example, you might type
"Meet with Martin" as the title and input the
location as "Office." Or, you might choose to
type "Lunch with Martin" and then choose a
very expensive restaurant in New York City.

3. Touch the blue **Done** button in the
upper-right corner to return to the
Add Event screen.

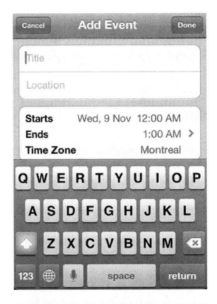

4. Touch the **Starts** or **Ends** tab to
adjust the event timing. To change
the start time, touch the **Starts**
field to highlight it in blue. Next,
move the rotating dials at the
bottom to reflect the correct date
and start time of the appointment.

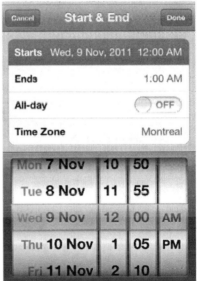

5. Alternatively, you can set an all-
day event by touching the switch
next to **All-day** to set it to **ON**.

NOTE: You will see a tab labeled **Invitees** after the **Repeat** tab only if your event is set up on an Exchange/Google or iCloud calendar.

Recurring Events

Some of your appointments happen every day, week, or month at the same time. Follow these steps if you are scheduling a recurring appointment:

1. Touch the **Repeat** tab and then select the interval of time for the recurring appointment from the list.

2. Touch **Done** to return to the main **Event** screen.

3. If you set a **Repeat** meeting, then you will also have to say when the repeating event ends. Tap the **End Repeat** button to set this.

4. You can select **Repeat Forever** or set a date.

5. Tap **Done** when finished.

Calendar Alerts

You can have your iPhone 4 give you an audible reminder, or *alert*, about an upcoming appointment. Alerts can help you keep from forgetting an important event. Follow these steps to create an alert:

1. Touch the **Alert** tab and then select the option for a reminder alarm. You can have no alarm (**None**) at all or set a reminder that ranges from **At time of event** all the way to **2 days before** the event, depending on what works best for you.

2. Touch **Done** to get back to the main **Event** screen.

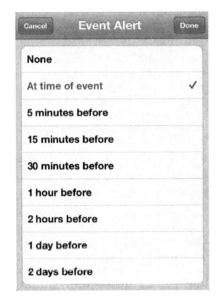

Second Alert

NOTE: You will see a **Second Alert** option if the calendar you are using is synced using iTunes or iCloud. However, you will not see a second alert if your event is tied to a Google Calendar synced using the Exchange setting.

In most cases, you will see a tab for a **Second Alert** option once you set your first **Alert** option. You can set this second alert to another time before or after the first alert. Some people find a second alert very helpful for remembering critical events or appointments.

TIP: Here's a practical example that illustrates when you might want to set up two calendar alerts.

If your child has a doctor or dentist appointment, then you might want to set the first event to go off the night before. This will remind you to write a note to the school and give it to your child.

You can then set the second event for 45 minutes prior to the appointment time. This will leave you enough time to pick up your child from school and get to the appointment.

Choosing a Calendar

If you use more than one calendar , ,tap on the **Calendar** tab to change the calendar to which your new event is assigned.

Touch the **Calendar** button in the upper- left corner to see all your calendars.

Tap the calendar you want to use for this particular event. Usually, the calendar selected by default is the one you selected the last time you used your iPhone to schedule an event.

Availability

You can also let others know about your availability during the scheduled event. You can choose your availability from the following options: **Busy** (default), **Free**, **Tentative**, or **Out of Office**. (Tentative and Out of Office only appear when you sync an account with the Exchange setting.)

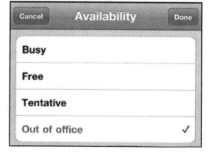

NOTE: You will only see the **Availability** or **Invitees** fields if the calendar you are using for this event is synced with the iCloud, Exchange, or Exchange/Google settings, and each provides slightly different options. If you are synced with iCloud, you will also see a **URL**field where you can add a website address for later reference.

Adding Notes to Calendar Events

Follow these steps if you want to add some notes to a calendar event:

1. Tap **Notes** and type or copy and paste a few notes.

2. Tap **Done** to finish adding notes.

3. Tap **Done** again to save your new calendar event.

TIP: If this is a meeting somewhere new, you might want to type or copy and paste some driving directions.

Using Copy and Paste Between the Email and Calendar Apps

The iPhone software's new Fast App Switcher means you can now easily jump between your **Email** and your **Calendar** programs to copy and paste information. This information could be anything, ranging from critical notes you need at your fingertips for a meeting to driving directions. Follow these steps to copy and paste information between your **Email** and **Calendar** programs:

1. Create a new calendar event or edit one, as explained previously in this chapter.

2. Scroll down to the **Notes** field and tap it to open it.

3. Double-tap the **Home** button to bring up the Fast App Switcher.

4. If you see the **Mail** icon, tap it. If you don't see **Mail** icon, swipe left or right to look for it. Once you find it, tap it to open the **Mail** app.

5. Double-tap a word, then use your fingers to drag the blue handles to select the text you want to copy.

6. Tap the **Copy** button.

7. Double-tap the **Home** button to bring up the Fast App Switcher.

8. Tap the **Calendar** icon. It should be the first icon on the left, since you just jumped out of the app.

9. Now tap and hold in the **Notes** field. When you let go, you should see the **Paste** pop-up field. If you don't see it, then hold your finger down a bit longer until you do see it.

10. Tap **Paste**.

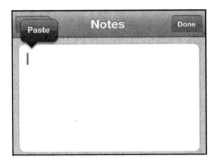

11. Now you should see the text you copied and pasted into the **Notes** field.

12. Tap **Done** to save your changes.

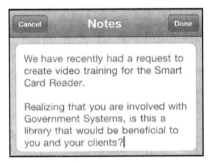

Editing Appointments

Sometimes, the details of an appointment may change and need to be **adjusted**. Fortunately, it's easy to revise an appointment on your iPhone. If all you want to do is change the time, you can simply move it on the screen.

1. Touch and hold your finger down on the appointment you want to change.

2. Drag the appointment to its new time slot.

If you need to change the time more drastically than touch-and-drag allows, or if you need to change other fields, you can also use the **Edit** button.

3. Tap the appointment that you want to change.

4. Tap the **Edit** button in the upper-right corner to see the **Edit** screen that shows the appointment details.

5. Touch the tab in the field you need to adjust, just like you did when creating the event. For example, you can change the time of this appointment by touching the **Starts** or **Ends** tab, and then adjusting the event's starting or ending time.

Editing a Repeating Event

You edit a recurring or repeating event in exactly the same manner as any other event. The only difference is that you will be asked a question after you finish editing the event. You need to answer this question and tap the **Done** button.

Tap **Save for this event only** if you want to make changes to only this instance of the repeating event.

Tap **Save for future events** if you want to make changes to all instances of this repeating event.

Switching an Event to a Different Calendar

If you mistakenly set up an event on the wrong calendar, then go ahead and tap the **Calendar** button to change the calendar. Next, select one of the different calendars you have synced to your iPhone.

> **NOTE:** Different fields may appear or disappear, depending on the calendar you choose to use.
>
> If you change your event from a calendar synced using **iTunes** to one synced with Exchange, then you will see the **Second Alert** field disappear. Also, you will see two new fields appear with an Exchange, Google, or iCloud calendar: **Invitees** and **Availability**.

Deleting an Event

Notice that, at the bottom of the **Edit** screen, you also have the option to delete this event. Simply touch the **Delete Event** button at the bottom of the screen to do so.

Meeting Invitations

For those who use Microsoft Exchange, **Microsoft Outlook**, or iCloud regularly, meeting invitations become a way of life. You receive a meeting invitation in your email, you accept the invitation, and then the appointment gets automatically placed in your calendar.

On your iPhone, you will see that invitations you accept are placed into your calendar immediately.

If you touch the meeting invitation in your calendar, you can see all the details that you need: the dial in number, the meeting ID, and any other details that might be included in the invitation.

Calendar Options

There are only a few options to adjust in your **Calendar** app; you can find these in the **Settings** app. Follow these steps to adjust these options:

1. Tap **Settings** from your **Home** screen.

2. Scroll down to **Mail, Contacts, Calendars** and tap it.

3. Scroll down to **Calendars** (it's at the very bottom!) to see a few options.

4. The first option is a simple switch that notifies you about **New Invitation Alerts**. If you receive any meeting invitations, it is good to keep this option set to the default **ON** position.

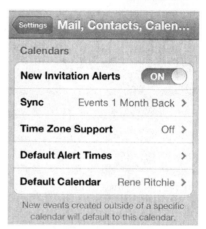

5. Next, you may see the **Sync** option if you sync your **Calendar** program using Exchange or iCloud. You can adjust the setting to sync events to **2 Weeks Back, 1 Month Back, 3 Months Back, 6 Months Back**, or to show all **All Events**.

6. Next, you can choose your time zone. This setting should reflect your **Home** settings from when you set up your iPhone. If you are traveling and want to adjust your appointments for a different time zone, you can change the **Time Zone** value to whatever city you prefer.

7. Default alert times can be set for birthdays, events, and all-day events. Events contain the usual options while birthdays and all-

day events allow for the day of the event, 1 day before, or 2 days before (all at 9am), or 1 week before.

Changing the Default Calendar

We mentioned earlier that you can have multiple calendars displayed on your iPhone. The **Default Calendar** screen allows you to choose which calendar will be your default calendar.

Specifying a calendar as the default means that, when you go to schedule a new appointment, this calendar will be selected by default.

If you wish to use a different calendar—say, your **Work** calendar—then you can change that when you actually set the appointment, as shown earlier in this chapter.

Reminders

Reminders is a new app in iOS 5 that lets you simply and easily keep track of the things you need to get done, the dates and times you need to get them done by, and even the locations where they need doing. You can think of this app as Apple's answer to task or to-do lists.

Reminder Views

Your **Reminders** app has three main views: **List**, **Date,** and **Month.** What follows is a quick overview of these views.

List is the default view for **Reminders** and shows you at a glance all the tasks you need to accomplish.

> **NOTE:** The default **List** view for iCloud accounts is called **Reminders**. The default **List** view for Microsoft Exchange accounts is called **Tasks.**

If you have multiple lists, you can move between them by swiping from right to left, just as when moving between the different app pages on your iPhone's **Home** screen.

Swipe from left to right to see a list of your **Completed** tasks.

Date view lets you see your reminders on the day they're due. You can easily swipe from one day to the next; you can also scroll along the **Date** slider at the bottom. Follow these steps to change the date shown:

- **Go to the next day**: Swipe from right to left.

- **Go to the previous day**: Swipe from left to right.

- **Go to Completed Task list**: Swipe from left to right from the current day.

> **TIP**: To return to the **Today** view, just touch the **Today** button at the top right.

To see the **Month** view, tap the **Month** button  at the top left of the **Date** view. This will show you a layout of the full month. Days with reminders due are colored red.

> **TIP**: To return to the **Today** view, just touch the **Today** button at the top right.
>
> Today

Follow these steps to move back and forth between months:

- **Go to the next month:** Scroll down.

- **Go to the previous month:** Scroll up.

Adding a New Reminder

To add a new task from any **List** view, follow these steps:

1. Tap the first blank line at the end of your current list.

2. Type in a title for your task.

3. When you're finished, tap the black **Done** button on the top right.

> **NOTE:** You can also tap the **Add** button to create a new task.

Adding Reminder Details

To add *details* to a task, tap the task's title. The **Details** screen lets you add the due date or location for **Remind Me**, the **Priority** of the reminder, which **List** you'd like it attached to, and any **Notes** you might want to add.

The **Details** page is also where you can delete a task.

> **NOTE:** If you don't see all the options at first, tap the **Show More** button to reveal them.

Setting Due Dates and Locations

The **Reminders** app includes standard due dates you can set for your reminders. When a task reaches its due date, you'll receive a popup notification to remind you about it.

The **Reminders** app also includes powerful geo-fencing capabilities; that is, it lets you set up location-based alerts for reminders. This means you can set reminders to change the light bulb when you arrive at your mother's house or to pick up milk when you leave the office.

> **NOTE:** Location-based reminders are currently available only if you're using iCloud and you assign the task to an iCloud associated list.

Follow these steps to set a **Remind Me** date or location:

1. Tap Remind Me.

2. To set a due date, toggle the On a Day option to ON. By default, the date will be set to the current day.

3. To change the date, tap it and move the rotating dials at the bottom to reflect the correct date for the task.

4. Tap **Done** to return to the main Details screen.

5. To set a place, toggle **At a Location** to **ON**. By default, the place will be set to your current location.

6. To change your location, tap the field beneath At a Location and then tap **Choose Address**.

7. Select an address from your Contacts list.

8. Tap **Done** to return to the main Details screen.

> **TIP:** Before you can use a location in **Reminders**, the location must be in your **Contacts**. To quickly add locations to your **Contacts**, use the **Maps** app (see Chapter 21: "Maps").

1. If you want to be reminded when you leave a location, tap **When I Leave**.

2. If you want to be reminded when you arrive at a location, tap **When I Arrive**.

3. Tap **Done** to return to the main **Details** screen.

> **NOTE:** If you set both a due date and a location, **Reminders** will send you an alert for whichever occurs first—you arrive at or leave a location or a reminder reaches the set time.

Recurring Reminders

Some of your reminders need to be triggered every day, week, or month at the same time or place. Follow these steps if you are scheduling a repeating or recurring task:

1. Tap the **Repeat** tab and then select the time interval for the repeated event from the list.

2. Tap **Done** to return to the main **Details** screen.

Changing Lists

Each treminder belongs to a list. You can have work lists, home lists, vacation lists, shopping lists—anything you like. The **Details** page will show the name of the list currently associated with your new task. Follow these steps to change your current list:

1. Tap the current list name.

2. Tap the list you want to change to.

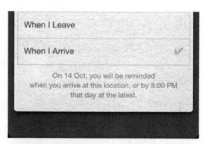

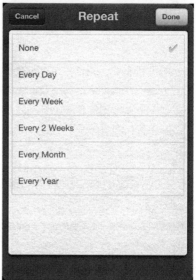

Adding Notes to a Task

Follow these steps if you want to add some notes to a task:

1. Tap **Notes** and type or copy and paste a few notes.

2. Tap **Done** to finish adding notes.

> **TIP:** If this is a shopping list, you might want to include extra information like clothing sizes, food brands, or anything else that could be helpful.

Completing Reminders

It's incredibly easy to mark a reminder as Completed. Simply tap the box immediately to the left of the reminder's title and a Checkmark icon will appear. That will move the reminder from its current list to the special Completed list, so you can go back and refer to it later, if necessary.

If you make a mistake, just tap the box again to remove the Checkmark icon and return the reminder to its previous status. If the task has already been moved to the Completed list, swipe left until you get to the Completed list and then tap the box to uncheck it and move the reminder back to its previous list.

Editing Reminders

Sometimes, the details of a task may change and need to be adjusted. Luckily, changing any reminder is as simple as following these steps:

1. Tap the reminder that you want to change.

2. Tap the tabs on the Details page and adjust the details, just as you do when setting up a new task.

Deleting a Reminder

Notice that, at the bottom of the **Details** screen, you also have the option to delete a task. Simply tap the **Delete** button at the bottom of the screen to do so.

Adding a New List

The **Reminders** app lets you have multiple lists, which is handy for keeping your tasks organized. For example, you can make a new list to help you pack for an upcoming trip or shop for an upcoming birthday.

You can create a new list for either iCloud Reminders or Exchange Tasks accounts, or local lists On my iPhone. Follow these steps to create a new list:

1. Tap the **Lists** button  on the top left of the screen.

2. On the Lists page, tap the **Edit** button at the top right.

3. If you have more than one account syncing with Reminders, choose the one you want to add the new list to.

4. Tap the **Create New List**... tab.

5. Type in the name of your new list.

6. Tap the grey **Done** button at the top right.

Moving and Deleting Lists

From the **Lists** page, you can also move and delete lists.

To move a list, touch and hold the **Gripper** icon to the far right, and then drag it to its new position.

To delete a list, tap the red **Circle** icon to the left of the list's name, and then tap the **Delete** button to confirm your choice.

Reminders Options

There are only two options to adjust in the **Reminders** app; you can find these in the **Settings** app:

1. Tap the **Settings** icon from your **Home** screen.

2. Scroll down to **Mail, Contacts, Calendars** and tap it.

3. Scroll down to **Reminders** (it's at the very bottom!) to see the two options.

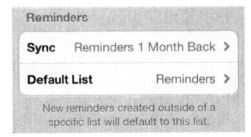

4. The first option is **Sync.** You can adjust this setting to sync **2 Weeks Back, 1 Month Back, 3 Months Back, 6 Months Back**, or to show **All Reminders**.

Changing the Default List

We mentioned earlier that you can have multiple lists displayed on your iPhone. The **Default List** screen allows you to choose which list will be your default list.

Specifying a list as the default means that, when you go to create a new reminder, it will be assigned to the specified list by default.

Chapter 20

Working with Photos

While previous versions of the iPhone have included a camera, the camera on the current iPhone is truly incredible. The iPhone 4S comes with not one, but two cameras: an 8.0-megapixel, *f*/2.4 aperture camera on the back with a LED flash; and a 0.3-megapixel VGA camera on the front for video chats and self-portraits. You can learn more about using the front-facing camera in the **FaceTime** app in Chapter 11: "Video Messaging and Skype."

Viewing and sharing your pictures on the iPhone is truly a joy, due in large part to its beautiful high-resolution screen. In this chapter, we will discuss the many ways to get pictures onto your iPhone. We will also show you how you to use the touch screen to navigate through your pictures, as well as how to zoom in and out and manipulate your photos.

> **TIP:** Did you know you can take a picture of the entire screen of your iPhone by pressing two keys simultaneously? This is great to show someone a cool app or to prove that you got the high score on **Tetris**!
>
> Here's how to get it done: press both the **Home** button and the **On/Off/Sleep** key on the top-right edge (you can press one key, hold it, and then press the other). This is a little tricky and takes some practice. If you have done this correctly, the screen should flash, and you'll hear a camera sound. The screen capture you have taken will be in your Camera Roll album in the **Photos** app.

Taking Photos Quickly

Apple has recently added some great shortcuts to help you take photos more quickly and more conveniently. If your child is in the middle of an especially adorable or memorable moment, if you come across a rare bird in the woods, or if you need to grab a fast photo of something suspicious in your neighborhood, then you can use one of the following techniques to snap a picture quickly:

- Double-click the **Home** button to bring up a **Camera** icon right on the **Lock** screen. Tapping the **Camera** icon will take you right to the **Camera** app, ready to take a photo. This means you no longer need to unlock your phone, swipe to find the **Camera** app, and then wait for it to launch.

- Use the **Volume Up** hardware button to snap your photo. Rather than trying to hit the camera software button on the screen, you can use something more tactile and similar to traditional camera controls.

- Take multiple pictures. Apple claims it has gotten the time it takes to shoot the first photo down to a remarkable 1.1 seconds; however, the second photo—and every photo thereafter—now takes only 0.5 seconds. This is especially handy for sports or any other fast-moving activity. Just keep pressing the volume up key as fast as you can.

- Auto-focus and face detection mean snapshots of your friends and family automatically come out sharper and with better exposure.

Using the Camera App

The **Camera** app should be on your **Home** page— usually on the first screen at the top. If you don't see it, then swipe left or right until you find it.

Touch the **Camera** icon and the shutter of the camera opens with an animation on your screen.

Once the shutter opens, you will find controls along the top to set the **Flash** to **On**, **Off**, or **Auto**; **Options** to set the **Grid** overlay and **HDR** (high dynamic range) to **On** or **Off**; and a toggle to switch between the front-facing and rear-facing cameras. Along the bottom, you'll find a thumbnail to take you to the Camera Roll album, the **Camera** button to take a picture, and a slider to switch between Still Photography and Video Recording modes.

> **TIP:** You can also take a picture or start a video recording by pressing the **Volume Up** hardware button.

Geo-Tagging

Geo-tagging is a feature that puts your GPS (geographic positioning system) coordinates into the picture file. If you upload your pictures to programs like Flickr, the coordinates of your picture can be used by your friends to locate you and locate the site where the picture was taken.

> **NOTE:** For Mac users, **iPhoto** uses geo-tagging to put photos into the **Places** category of **iPhoto**.

If you have **Location Services** set to **ON** when you start the camera (see Chapter 1: "Getting Started"), you will be asked if it is OK to use your current location.

To double-check this setting, do the following:

1. Start your **Settings** app.

2. Go to **General**.

3. Touch **Location Services**. You will see a screen like the one here.

4. Make sure the switch next to **Camera** is toggled to **ON**.

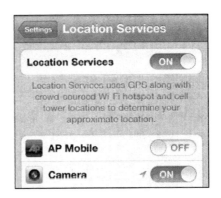

Taking a Picture

Taking a picture is as simple as pointing and shooting, but there are some adjustments that you can make if you choose.

Once your camera is on, center your subject in the screen of your iPhone.

When you are ready to take a picture, just touch the **Camera** button along the bottom or press the **Volume Up** hardware button (the one with the + on it) on the side of your iPhone. You will hear a shutter sound, and the screen will show an animation indicating that the picture is being taken.

Once the picture is taken, it will drop down into the window in the lower-left corner. Touch that small thumbnail, and the Camera Roll album of your **Photos** app will load.

Using the Zoom

The iPhone includes a 5x digital zoom..

> **NOTE:** A digital zoom is never as clear as an analog zoom, so be aware that picture quality is usually degraded slightly when using the zoom.

To use the zoom, just touch the screen with two fingers and pinch to zoom in or out. The further you spread your fingers apart, the further you will zoom out. Once the zoom begins, a Zoom slider will also appear to help you change the zoom level.

Using the Flash

Your iPhone has a built-in LED flash. The default flash setting is **Auto**, but you can also manually turn set it to **On** or **Off**:

1. Touch the **Flash** icon in the upper-left corner.

2. Touch either **On**, **Off**, or **Auto**.

> **TIP:** We recommend keeping the **Flash** setting on **Auto**; however, if you notice that a photo looks over-exposed, just touch the **Flash** icon to set the flash to **Off**.

Camera Options

To help you take better pictures, Apple has built in both **Grid** lines and a version of **HDR** (high dynamic range) photography.

The **Grid** option overlays two horizontal and two vertical lines over the screen. This can help you properly compose your shots. It can also help you make sure faces and eyes look great for portraits, items look great for still life images, and the scenery is balanced for landscapes.

HDR takes not only a regular picture, but an underexposed version and an overexposed version. It then merges them together to give you better detail in both shadowy and lit areas.

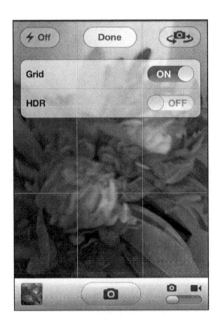

Switching Cameras

As mentioned previously, the iPhone comes with two cameras: an 8.0 megapixel camera on the back for most photography and a VGA camera (640 x 480) on the front for self-portraits or for use in **FaceTime** video calls (see Chapter 11: "Video Messaging and Skype").

To switch between the cameras, do the following:

1. Touch the **Switch Camera** icon from the **Camera** app.

2. Wait for the camera to switch to the front-facing camera and line up the shot.

3. Touch the **Switch Camera** icon again to switch back to the standard camera.

> **TIP:** Because of the placement of the front-facing camera, faces can look somewhat distorted. Try moving your face back a bit and adjusting the camera angle to get a better image.

Viewing Pictures You Have Taken

Your iPhone will store pictures you take on the iPhone in what is called your *Camera Roll*. You can access the Camera Roll from inside both the **Camera** and **Photos** apps. In the **Camera** app, touch the **Pictures** icon in the bottom-left corner of the **Camera** screen.

Once you touch a picture to view, you can swipe through your pictures to see all the pictures in the Camera Roll.

To get back to the Camera Roll, press the **Camera Roll** button in the upper-left corner.

To take another picture, touch the **Done** button in the upper-right corner.

Editing Photos

With iOS 5 you can now do basic photo editing right on your iPhone. You can rotate your photos; enhance their exposure, contrast, and levels; crop them; and even automatically remove red-eye from pictures of your friends and family.

Follow these steps to edit a photo:

1. Browse to the photo you'd like to edit.

2. Tap the **Edit** button at the top right.

Follow these steps to rotate a photo:

1. Tap the **Rotate** arrow button at the bottom left to turn your photo 90 degrees counter-clockwise (to the left).

2. Tap the **Rotate** button again to keep rotating in 90-degree increments.

3. When you've rotated the image to the position you want, tap the yellow **Save** button at the top right.

Similarly, follow these steps to auto-enhance a photo:

1. Tap the **Auto-Enhance** magic wand button.

2. If you like the results, tap the yellow **Save** button at the top right.

3. If you don't like the results, tap **Auto-Enhance** again to set it to **Off**.

4. Tap **Cancel** to exit Auto-Enhance mode.

Follow these steps to remove red-eye from a photo:

1. Tap the **Red-Eye** button to activate red-eye removal.

2. Tap each red eye in your photo to apply reduction (i.e., remove the red color from the eye).

3. If you like the results, tap the **Apply** button at the top left.

4. If you don't like the results, tap each red eye again to remove the reduction.

5. Tap **Cancel** to exit this mode.

Finally, follow these steps to crop a photo:

1. Tap the **Crop** 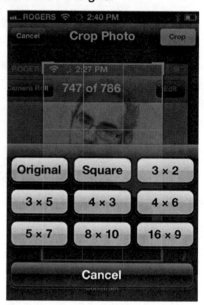 button on the bottom right. A nine section grid will appear over the photo.

2. Touch an edge or corner of the grid and drag to make the crop area taller, shorter, thinner, or wider.

3. Touch inside the grid and drag to move the photo around behind the grid.

4. Pinch and zoom to make the photo bigger or smaller inside the grid.

5. Tap the **Constrain** button to choose from a list of standard aspect ratios, including **Original**; **Square**; traditional photo ratios like **3 x 2**, **4 x 6**, and **8 x10**; TV ratios like **SD 4 x 3** and **HD 16 x 9**; and so on.

6. If you're happy with the crop, tap the yellow **Crop** button at the top right to apply it.

7. If you don't like the crop, tap the **Cancel** button at the top left to return to the **Edit** screen.

Getting Photos onto Your iPhone

You have many options for loading photos onto your device:

*   **Sync using iCloud or iTunes:** Probably the simplest way to load photos onto your iPhone is to use iCloud or iTunes to sync photos from your computer (see Figure 20–1). We describe this in detail in Chapter 3: "Sync with iCloud, iTunes and More."

- **Receive as email attachments:** While this is not useful for large numbers of pictures, it works well for one or even a few photos. Check out Chapter 17: "Communicate with Email" for more details about how to save attachments. (Once saved, these images show up in the Camera Roll album.)

- **Save images from the Web:** Sometimes you'll see a great image on a web site. Press and hold it to see the pop-up menu, and then select **Save Image**. (Like other saved images, these end up in the Camera Roll album.)

- **Download images from within an app:** A good example of this is the wallpaper image shown in Chapter 8: "Personalize and Secure."

- **Sync with iPhoto** (for Mac users)**:** If you use a Mac computer, your iPhone will most likely sync automatically with **iPhoto**. Here are a few steps to get the sync feature in **iPhoto** up and running:

  1. Connect your iPhone and start the **iTunes** app.

  2. Go to the **Photo** tab along the top row of Sync Options.

  3. Choose the **Albums, Events, Faces,** or **Places** you want to keep in sync with the iPhone.

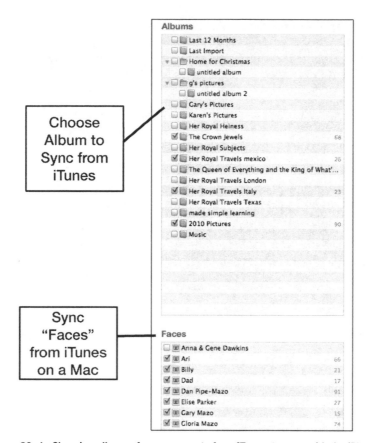

Figure 20–1. *Choosing albums, faces, or events from* **iTunes** *to sync with the iPhone*

- **Drag and drop** (for Windows users): Once you connect your iPhone to your Windows computer, it will appear in **Windows Explorer** as a portable device, as shown in Figure 20–2. Follow these steps to drag and drop photos between your iPhone and computer:

  1. Double-click the **iPhone** image under **Portable Devices** to open it.

  2. Double-click **Internal Storage** to open it.

  3. Double-click **DCIM** to open it.

  4. Next, you may see one or more folders with strange names like: 823WGTMA, 860OKMZO, and 965YOKDJ. Try double-clicking to open each one. One of these will have the photos or videos you seek.

  5. You will see all the images in the Saved Photos album on your iPhone.

6. To copy images from your iPhone, select and then drag and drop images out of this folder onto your computer. You cannot copy images to your iPhone using this drag-and-drop method. Instead, you can use iTunes or iCloud.

Figure 20–2. *Windows Explorer showing the iPhone as a portable device (connected with a USB cable)*

TIP: Selecting Multiple Images in Windows

You have several ways to select images in Windows: you can draw a box around the images, click a single image, or press **Ctrl+A** to select them all. You can also hold down the **Ctrl** key and click individual pictures to select them. Right-click one of the selected pictures and choose **Cut** (to move) or **Copy** (to copy) all of the selected images. To paste the images, press and click any other disk or folder (e.g., **My Documents**), and then navigate to where you want to move or copy the files. Finally, right-click again and select **Paste**.

Viewing Your Photos

Now that your photos are on your iPhone, you have a few very cool ways to look through them and show them to others.

Launching from the Photos Icon

If you like using your **Photos** app, you might want to place its icon in your Bottom Dock for easy access if it's not already there (see Chapter 6: "Icons and Folders").

To get started with photos, touch the **Photos** icon.

The first screen shows your photo albums, which were created when you set up your iPhone and synced with iCloud or iTunes. In Chapter 3: "Sync with iCloud, iTunes and More," we showed you how to choose which photos to sync with your iPhone. As you make changes to the library on your computer, they will be automatically updated on your iPhone.

If you're using iCloud's Photo Stream feature, this is also where you'll find your Photo Stream images.

Choosing a Library

From the **Photo Albums** page, touch one of the library buttons to show the photos in that album. In the image to the right, we touched a photo library, and the screen immediately changed to show us thumbnails of the pictures in this library.

Tap and drag your finger up and down to view all the pictures in a library. You can also flick up or down to quickly move throughout the album.

Managing Libraries

iOS 5 introduces the ability to add new albums, move photos between albums, and delete albums right on your iPhone.

Follow these steps to add a new album:

1. Tap the **Edit** button on the top right.

2. Tap the **Add** button that appears on the top left.

3. Enter a name for your new album.

4. Tap **Done** at the top right.

Follow these steps to delete an album:

1. Tap the **Edit** button on the top right.

2. Tap the red **Circle** icon to the left of the album you want to delete.

3. Tap the red **Delete** button to confirm.

Finally, follow these steps to move photos between albums:

1. Tap the **Action** button at the bottom left.

2. Tap the pictures you want to move.

3. If you tap a picture by accident, just tap it again to deselect it.

4. Tap the **Add To** button on the bottom.

5. Choose **Add to Existing Album** if you already have an album that you want to move the pictures into. Or, you can choose **Add to New Album** if you want to create a new album now.

Working with Individual Pictures

Once you locate the picture you want to view, just tap it. The picture then loads onto the screen.

> **NOTE:** Your pictures will not usually take up the full screen on your iPhone if they were shot in Landscape mode.

> **TIP:** The picture here was shot in Landscape mode; to see it in full screen, simply turn your iPhone on its side or double-tap it.

Moving Between Pictures

The swipe gesture is used to move from one picture to the next. Just swipe your finger left or right across the screen, and you can move through your pictures.

> **TIP:** Drag your finger slowly to move more gradually through the picture library.

When you reach the end of an album, just tap the screen once and you'll see a tab in the upper-left corner that has the name of the photo album. Touch that tab and you'll return to the thumbnail page of that particular album.

To get back to your main photo album page, touch the button that says **Albums** in the top-left corner.

Zooming in and out of Pictures

As described in the "Getting Started" section of the book, there are two ways to zoom in and out of pictures on your iPhone: double-tapping and pinching.

Double-Tapping

As the name implies, double-tapping is a quick double-tap on the screen to zoom in on the picture (see Figure 20–3). You will zoom in on the spot where you double-tap. To zoom out, just double-tap once more.

See Chapter 1: "Getting Started" for more information on double-tapping.

Figure 20–3. *Double-tapping a picture to zoom in on it*

Pinching

Also as described in Chapter 1: "Getting Started," pinching is a much more precise form of zooming in. While double-tapping zooms in or out only to one set level, pinching really allows you to zoom in or out just a little bit or quite a lot.

To pinch, hold your thumb and forefinger close together and then slowly (while touching the screen) separate them, making the picture larger. To zoom out, start with your thumb and forefinger apart and move them together.

> **NOTE:** Once you have activated the zoom using either method, you will not be able to swipe easily through your pictures until you return the picture to its standard size.

Viewing a Slideshow

You can view the pictures in your photo album as a slideshow if you so desire. Just tap the screen once to bring up the on-screen soft keys. In the center, you will see a **Slideshow Play** button—touch it once to start the slideshow. You can start the slideshow from any picture you are viewing.

Selecting **Photos** in the **Settings** app lets you adjust how long each picture remains on the screen and other settings such as **Repeat** and **Shuffle** (see Figure 20–4). To end the slideshow, just tap the screen.

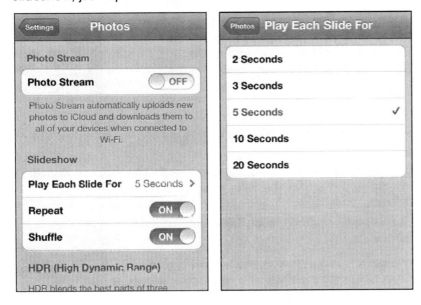

Figure 20–4. *Configuring your slideshow*

Using a Picture As Your iPhone Wallpaper

We show you how to select and use a picture as your iPhone wallpaper (and other wallpaper options) in Chapter 8: "Personalize and Secure."

> **NOTE:** You can have different pictures for your **Home** screen and **Lock** screen, or you can use the same picture for both.

Emailing or Tweeting a Picture

As long as you have an active Internet connection (Wi-Fi or 3G; see Chapter 4: "Connect to the Network"), you can send any picture in your photo collection via email or post it to Twitter. Tap the **Options** button on the thumbnail bar—this is the button furthest to the left on the bottom row of soft keys. If you don't see the icons, tap the screen once.

To mail the picture, choose the **Email Photo** option and the **Mail** app will automatically launch.

Tap the **To** field as you did in Chapter 17: "Communicate with Email," and then select the contact to receive the picture. Tap the blue **Plus Sign** (+) button to add a contact.

Type in a subject and a message, and then touch **Send** in the upper-right corner—that's all there is to it.

To tweet the picture, choose the **Tweet** option and a **Twitter** sheet will automatically appear. Just fill out the message you want to be shown with your picture and hit the **Send** button.

> **NOTE:** The **Tweet** option will only appear if you've entered your Twitter username and password in the **Settings** app.

Share, Copy, Print, or Delete Several Pictures at Once

If you have several pictures you want to email, message, copy, print, or delete at the same time, you can do so from the thumbnail view:

1. **Tap the Action button at the bottom left.**

1. Tap the pictures you want to select.

2. If you tap a picture by accident, just tap it again to deselect it.

3. Choose an action from the bottom of the screen: **Share** (email, message, or print), **Copy**, **Add To** (a different photo album), or **Delete**.

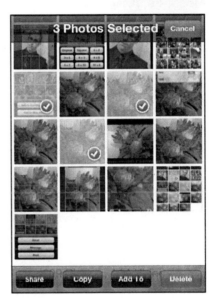

> **NOTE:** The **Copy** function allows you to copy and paste multiple pictures into an email message or other app. **Share** renames the image to *photo*.png, while **copy-and-paste** adds .png to the DCIM folder file name.
>
> At the time of publishing, you could not share more than one video, nor could you share more than five pictures. This may change in future iterations of the software.

Assigning a Picture to a Contact

Chapter 18: "Contacts and Notes" shows you how to add a picture when editing a contact. You can also find a picture you like and assign it to a contact. Begin by finding the photo you want to use.

As you did when setting the wallpaper and emailing a photo, tap the **Action** button—the one furthest to the right of the upper row of soft keys. If you don't see the icons, tap the screen once.

When you touch the **Action** button, you'll see a drop-down list of choices: **Email Photo**, **Message**, **Assign to Contact**, **Use as Wallpaper**, **Tweet**, and **Print**.

Touch the **Assign to Contact** button.

You will see your contacts on the screen. You can either perform a search using the **Search** bar at the top or just scroll through your contacts.

Once you find the contact that you would like to add as a recipient to the picture, touch that name.

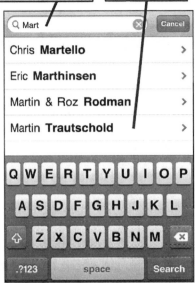

You will then see the **Move and Scale** screen. Tap and drag the picture to move it; use pinch to zoom in or out.

When you have this set just how you want it, touch the **Set Photo** button to assign the picture to that contact.

> **NOTE:** You will return to your Photo Library, not to the contact. If you want to double-check that the picture was set to your contact, then exit the **Photo** app, start the **Contact** app, and search for that contact.

Viewing a Photo on Your Apple TV

Chapter 5: "AirPlay and Bluetooth" shows you how to use Apple's AirPlay feature to stream videos from your iPhone to your Apple TV over your local Wi-Fi network. Apple has built the same functionality into the Photos app, so you can easily beam your pictures to your big screen TV.

Follow these steps to send your photos to your Apple TV:

1. Tap the **AirPlay** button.

2. Choose **Apple TV** from the source list.

To move to the next photo, simply swipe from right to left, just as you would to switch photos on your iPhone. To move to the previous photo, swipe back from left to right.

To go back to viewing photos on your iPhone, tap the AirPlay button again and choose iPhone from the source list.

Deleting a Picture

You might wonder why you can't delete some pictures from your iPhone (the **Trash Can** icon is missing).

For example, you'll notice that the **Trash Can** icon is not visible for any photo that is synced from iTunes. You can delete such pictures only from your computer library. The next time you sync your iPhone, they will be deleted.

Trash Can Icon is **Only** Visible in "Camera Roll."

When you are looking through pictures in your Saved Photos (this folder is not synced with iTunes, but is instead comprised of pictures you save from email messages or download from the Web), then you'll see the **Trash Can** icon in the bottom icon bar. This **Trash Can** icon does not appear when you are viewing pictures from your Photos Library or other synced albums.

If you don't see the bottom row of icons, tap the photo once to activate them, and then tap the **Trash Can** icon. You will be prompted with the option to delete the picture.

Touch **Delete Photo** and the picture will be deleted from your iPhone.

Downloading Pictures from Web Sites

We have shown you how you can transfer pictures from your computer to your iPhone and save them from email messages. You can also download and save pictures right from the Web onto your iPhone.

> **CAUTION:** We strongly encourage you to respect image copyright laws as you download and save images from the Web. Unless the web site indicates an image is free, you should check with the web site owner before downloading and saving any pictures.

Finding a Picture to Download

The iPhone makes it easy to copy and save images from web sites. This can be handy when you are looking for a new image to use as wallpaper on your iPhone.

First, tap the **Safari** web browser icon and type a search for iPhone wallpaper to locate a few sites that might have some interesting possibilities. (See Chapter 16: "Safari Web Browser" for help with this topic.)

Once you find a picture you want to download and save, tap and hold it to bring up a new menu of options that includes **Save Image** (among others), as shown in Figure 21–5. Choose this option to save the picture in your Saved Photos album.

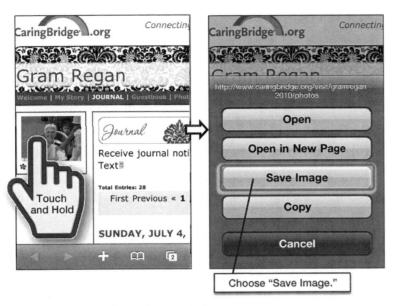

Figure 20–5. *Saving an image from a web site*

Now touch your **Photo** icon and you should see the picture in the Camera Roll album.

The **Saved** Photo is now in your Saved Photos Directory

Chapter 21

Maps

Mapping on your iPhone is very convenient and pretty amazing. As we explore the power of the **Maps** app in this chapter, you'll see how to find your location on a map and get directions to just about anywhere. You'll also learn how to switch between the **Standard**, **Satellite**, and **Hybrid** views. You'll also see how, if you need to find the best route to somewhere, you can check out the traffic using the **Show Traffic** button in **Maps** options. If you want to find the closest pizza restaurant, golf course, or hotel to your destination, that's easy, too. And you can use Google's Street View right from your iPhone to help you get to your destination. It is easy to add an address you have mapped to your contacts. There's also a Digital Compass feature that is fun to play with.

Getting Started with Maps

The beauty of the iPhone is that its apps are designed to work with one another. You've already seen how your contacts are linked to the **Maps** app; just look back at Chapter 18: "Contacts and Notes."

The **Maps** app is powered by Google Maps, the leader in mobile mapping technology. **Maps** lets you locate your position, get directions, search for things nearby, see traffic, and much more.

Simply touch the **Maps** icon to get started.

Determining Your Location (the Blue Dot)

When you start the **Maps** app, you can have it begin at your current location. Follow these steps to use your current location as the default starting location:

1. Tap the small blue **Arrow** icon at the lower-left corner.

2. **Maps** will ask to use your current location—touch **OK** or **Don't Allow**.

   We suggest choosing **OK**, which makes it much easier to find directions from or to your current location.

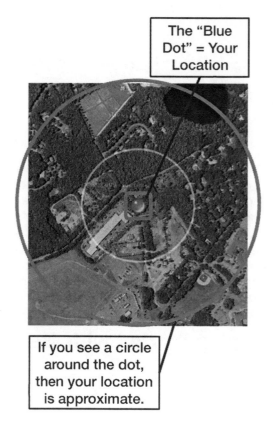

The "Blue Dot" = Your Location

If you see a circle around the dot, then your location is approximate.

Changing Your Map Views

The default view for **Maps** is the **Standard** view, a basic map that shows a generic background overlaid with street names. Maps can also show you a **Satellite** view or a combination of the **Satellite** and **Standard** views called **Hybrid**. Finally, the **List** view is handy if you've searched for something that provided multiple results, like local coffee shops. It is also handy if you've asked for directions to a location. You can switch among all the views by following these steps:

1. Tap the turned-up edge of the map in the lower-right corner.

2. The corner of the map turns up to reveal buttons for views, traffic, pins, and more.

3. Tap the view you'd like to switch to (see Figure 21–1):

   ▪ **Standard** is a regular map with street names.

   ▪ **Satellite** is a satellite picture with no street names.

   ▪ **Hybrid** is a combination of the **Satellite** and **Standard** views; that is, a **Satellite** view with street names.

   ▪ **List** is available only when your search produces multiple results (like "starbucks") or you've asked for directions.

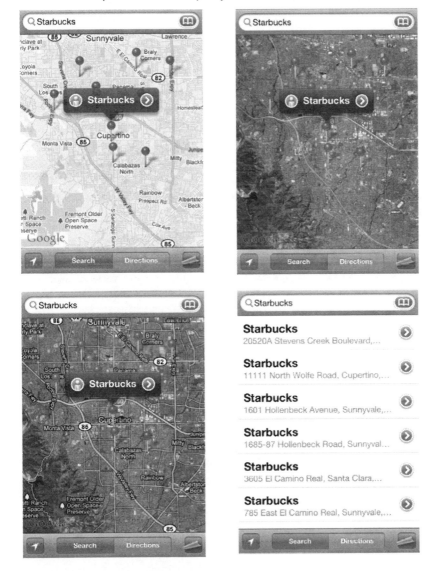

Figure 21–1. *Various views available in the **Maps** app: From upper left: Standard, Satellite, Hybrid and List.*

Checking Traffic

Not only does your **Maps** app tell you how to get somewhere, but it can also check traffic along the way. This feature is supported only in the United States for now. Follow these steps to check the traffic for a given route:

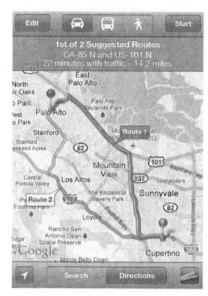

1. Tap the lower-right corner of the map to see the options.

2. Tap **Show Traffic**.

On a highway, if there is a traffic situation, you usually see yellow lights instead of green ones. Sometimes, the yellow lights might be flashing to alert you to traffic delays.

You may even see **Construction Worker** icons to indicate construction zones.

Maps uses color on major streets and highways to indicate the speed that traffic is moving at:

   ▓ Green = 50 MPH or more

   ▓ Yellow = 25–50 MPH

   ▓ Red = Less than 25 MPH

   ▓ Gray (or no color) = No traffic data currently available

Searching for Anything

Because **Maps** is tied to Google Maps, you can search for and find just about anything: a specific address, type of business, city, or other point of interest, as shown in Figure 21–2. Follow these steps to search for a specific location:

1. Touch the **Search** bar in the top-right corner of the screen.

2. Type in the address, point of interest, or town and state you would like to map on your iPhone.

Google Maps Search Tips

You can enter just about anything in the **Search** bar, including the following:

- First name, last name, or company name (to match your Contacts list)

- 123 Main Street, City (some or all of a street address)

- Orlando Airport (to find an airport)

- Plumber, painter, or roofer (any part of a business name or trade)

- Golf courses + city (to find local golf courses)

- Movies + city or ZIP/postal code (to find local movie theaters)

- Pizza 32174 (to search for local pizza restaurants in ZIP code 32174)

- 95014 (the ZIP code for Apple Computer's headquarters in California, United States)

- Apress

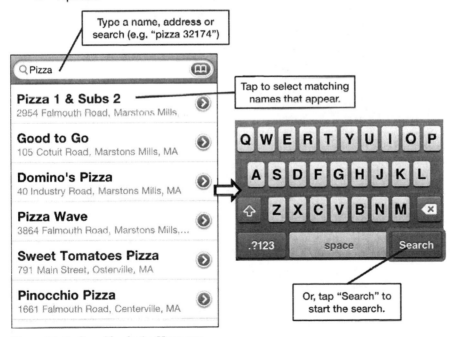

Figure 21-2. *Searching in the Maps app*

To use numbers, tap the **123** key on the keyboard. For letters, tap the **ABC** key to switch back to a letter keyboard.

Mapping Options

Now that your address is on the **Maps** screen, follow these steps to access the available options:

1. Touch the blue **Arrow** icon 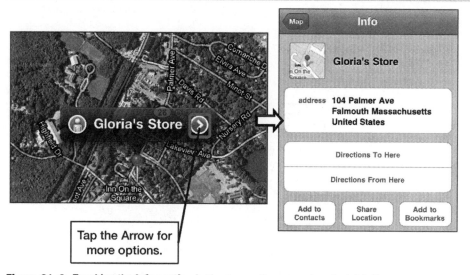 next to the address to see some of these options.

2. If you have mapped one of your contacts, you'll see the contact details, as shown in Figure 21–3. **Maps** will also pull up contact information for specific searches. You can also get directions, share a location, or add a location as a bookmark.

> **NOTE:** You can also tap and hold the address to bring up the **Copy** pop-up menu.

Figure 21–3. *Touching the **Information** button to see the mapped contact details*

Working with Bookmarks

Bookmarks in **Maps** work much as they do in **Safari**. A bookmark simply creates a record of places you've visited or mapped and want to remember in the future. It is always easier to look at a bookmark than to perform a new search.

Adding a New Bookmark

Bookmarking a location is a great way to simplify finding a place again:

1. Map a location, as shown in Figure 21–4.
2. Touch the blue **Information** icon next to the address.
3. Touch **Add to Bookmarks**.

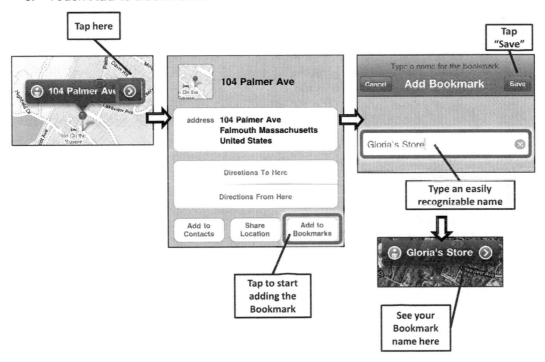

Figure 21–4. *Adding a bookmark*

4. Edit the bookmark name to make is short and recognizable—in this case, we edited the address to simply say **Gloria's Store**.
5. When you are done, just touch **Save** in the top-right corner.

TIP: You can search for bookmark names just as you search for names in **Contacts**.

Accessing and Editing Your Bookmarks

To view your bookmarks, follow these steps:

1. Tap the **Bookmarks** icon next to the **Search** window in the top row.

2. Tap any bookmark to immediately jump to it.

3. Tap the **Edit** button at the top of the bookmarks to edit or delete your bookmarks.

    a. To reorder the bookmarks, touch and drag the right edge of each bookmark up or down.

    b. To edit the name of a bookmark, touch it and retype the name. After editing the name, touch the **Bookmarks** button in the top left to get back to your list of bookmarks.

    c. To delete a bookmark, swipe to the left or right on the bookmark, and then tap the **Delete** button.

4. Tap the **Done** button when you are finished editing your bookmarks.

Adding a Mapped Location to Contacts

It is easy to add a location you mapped to your Contacts list:

1. Map an address.

2. Tap the **Arrow/Information** icon.

3. Tap **Add to Contacts**.

4. Tap either **Create a New Contact** or **Add to Existing Contact**.

5. If you choose **Add to Existing Contact**, you can then scroll through or search your contacts and select a name. The address will automatically be added to that contact.

Searching for Establishments Near You

Follow these steps to search for establishments around your current location:

1. Map a location on the map or use the blue dot for your current location.

2. Tap the **Search** window. Let's say you want to search for the closest pizza restaurants, so you type "pizza." This will map all local pizza restaurants.

3. Notice that each mapped location may have a **Street View** icon on the left and an **Information** icon on the right.

4. You can double-tap to zoom in, or pinch the screen open or closed to zoom in or out.

5. Just as with any mapped location, touching the blue **Information** icon brings up all the details, including the pizza restaurant's phone number, address, and web site as shown in Figure 21–5.

6. If you want directions to the restaurant, just touch **Directions to Here**, and a route is instantly calculated.

Figure 21–5. *Using the Info screen to do more things with mapped locations.*

NOTE: If you touch the **Home Page** link, you will exit **Maps**, and **Safari** will start up. You will need to restart **Maps** when you're done.

Zooming In and Out

You can zoom in and out in the usual way by double-tapping and pinching. To zoom in by double-tapping, just double-tap the screen as you would on a web page or picture.

Dropping a Pin

Let's say you're looking at the map, and you find something you'd like to set either as a bookmark or as a destination.

In this example, we are zooming in and looking around the greater Boston area. We stumble upon Fenway Park and decide it would be great to add it to our bookmarks, so we drop a pin on it. Follow these steps to drop a pin on a map:

1. Map a location or move the map to a location where you'd like to drop the pin.

2. Tap the lower-right corner of the map.

3. Tap **Drop Pin**.

4. Now, drag the pin around the map by touching and holding it. In our example, we moved it right onto Fenway Park.

5. To remove a dropped pin or do other things, tap the blue **Arrow**

   icon  next to the pop-up above the pin. If the pop-up went away, tap the pin to bring It back.

6. From the **Info** screen, you can get **directions**, **Remove Pin**, **Add to Contacts**, **Share Location**, or **Add to Bookmarks**.

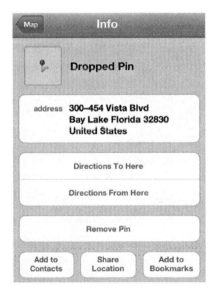

TIP: Finding the Street Address of any Location on the Map

When you drop a pin, Google Maps will show you the actual street address. This is very handy if you find a location by looking at the **Satellite** or **Hybrid** view, but need to get the actual street address.

Dropping a pin is also a great way to keep track of where you parked, which is especially helpful in an unfamiliar location.

Using Street View

Google Street View (see Figure 21–6) is a really fun feature in **Maps** on the iPhone. Google has been hard at work photographing just about every address across the United States and elsewhere. The pictures are then fed into its database, and that's what shows up when you want to see a picture of your destination or waypoint.

NOTE: Google Street View is in a small number of countries now: much of North America, western Europe, Australia, and now South Africa.

If there is a Street View available, you will see a small orange **Person** icon to the left of the address or bookmark on the map.

In this example, we wanted to check the Street View of the store of Gloria, Gary's wife, on Cape Cod:

1. To map the address, we tapped the work address under Gloria's name on our Contacts list. We could have mapped it by typing an address into the **Search** window, by searching for a type of business, or by touching the address in the **Contacts** app.

2. The **Street View** icon is shown to the left of Gloria's name.

3. We tapped the icon to immediately shift to a Street View of the address. What is very cool is that we can navigate around the screen in a 360-degree rotation by swiping left, right, or even up or down, looking at the places next to and across the street from our destination.

4. To return to the map, we just touched the lower-right corner of the screen.

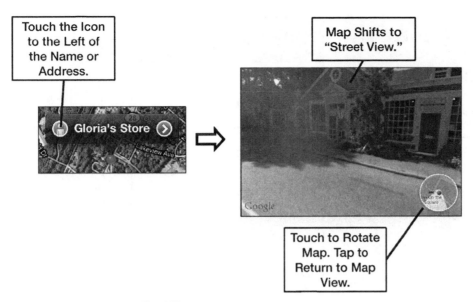

Figure 21–6. *Using Google Street View*

Getting Directions

One of the most useful functions of the **Maps** app is that you can easily find directions to or from any location. Let's say we want to get directions from our current location (Gloria's store) to Fenway Park in Boston.

Tap the Current Location Button First

To find directions to or from your current location, you don't have to waste time typing your current address—the iPhone will assume you want directions from where you are unless you specify otherwise. You may need to tap the **Location** button a few times until you see the blue dot on the screen.

Now you can do one of two things:

- Tap the **Directions** button at the bottom.
- Touch the blue **Arrow** as we did previously, and then select **Directions from Here** (see Figure 21–7).

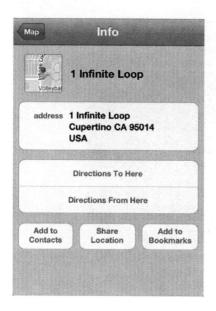
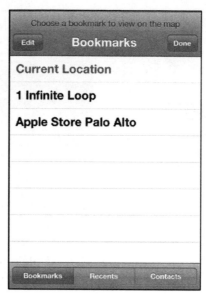

Figure 21–7. *Choosing* ***Directions From Here*** *and then* ***Bookmarks***

Choosing Start or End Location

Follow these steps to select a Start or End location and then choose a suggested route:

1. Touch the blue **Arrow** icon above the pin.

2. Tap **Directions From Here**.

3. Tap the **Bookmarks** button

4. Tap **Bookmarks**, **Recents**, or **Contacts** to find your destination. In this case, we tapped **Bookmarks** and then **Fenway Park**.

> **NOTE:** As soon as you touch the **Directions From Here** button, your recent searches will be automatically displayed (see Figure 21–5). You can also touch the **Destination** box and type in a destination.

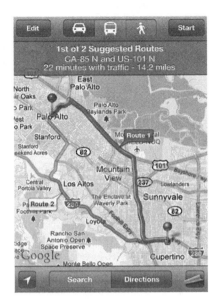

5. After you select your destination, the routing screen takes you to an overview screen. In our case, we see the routing screen to get from Apple's 1 Infinite Loop headquarters to the Palo Alto Apple Store.

6. A green pushpin is dropped at the start location, and a red one is dropped at the end location—Fenway Park, in our example.

7. A bright blue line will connect the two pins, showing you the route. If there is more than one route, others will be indicated in light blue.

8. Tap a gray route to select it. Once it's selected, it will turn bright blue, and any other routes will fade to light blue.

Looking at the Route

Before you start the trip, you will see a **Start** button in the upper-right corner of the screen. Tap the **Start** button, and the routing directions begin. The **Start** button changes to **Arrow** buttons that allow you to move between the steps in the trip.

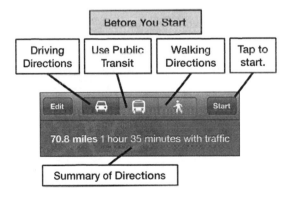

As Figure 21–8 shows, you can look at the route either as a path on the map or as a list.

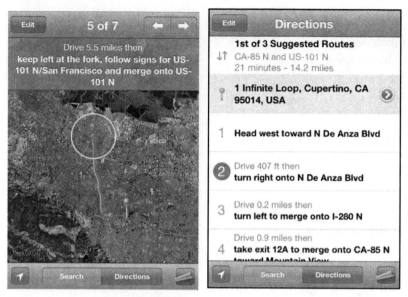

Figure 21–8. *Two ways of viewing directions*

You can move the screen with your finger to look at the route, or just touch the **Arrow** buttons at the bottom to show the route in step-by-step snapshots.

You can also tap the **Page Curl** button on the bottom-right, then the **List** button, which will show detailed step-by-step directions.

Switching Between Routes

As noted in Steps 6 and 7 of the preceding example, if more than one route is available, the **Maps** app will mark its best recommendation with a bright blue line and flag it as **Route 1**. If other routes are also available, Maps will mark them with a light blue line. Tapping a gray line will turn it bright blue and flag it with its corresponding number—**Route 2**, for example.

If you know from recent experience that construction or something else is making Route 1 less than desirable, or you need to stop somewhere on the way that's off the recommended Route 1, then switching to a different route is a great option.

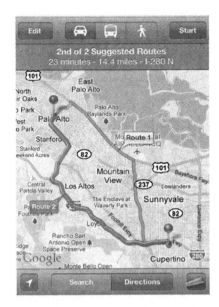

Switching Between Driving, Transit, and Walking Directions

Before you start your directions, you can choose whether you are driving, using public transportation, or walking by tapping the icons on the left side of the blue bar at the top of the directions screen, as shown in Figure 21–9.

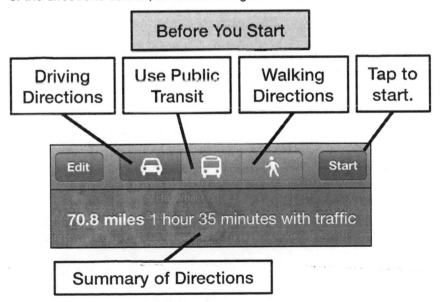

Figure 21–9. *Choosing your mode of transportation*

Reversing the Route

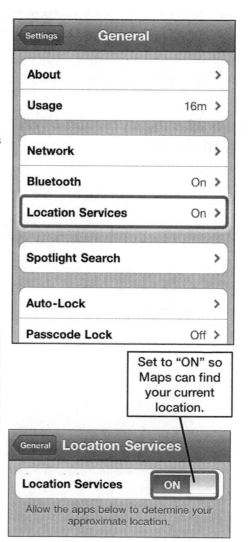

To reverse the route, touch the **Reverse** button, which is at the top, between the **Start** and **End** fields. This can be useful if you're not great about reversing directions on your own or if your route uses lots of one-way streets.

Maps Options

Currently, the only setting that affects your **Maps** app is Location Services, which is critical for determining your current location. Follow these steps to adjust the settings for the **Maps** app:

1. Touch the **Settings** icon.

2. Tap the **General** tab

3. Now find the **Location Services** switch about halfway down. Move this switch to the **ON** position, so that **Maps** can approximate your location.

> **NOTE:** Keeping the **Location Services** switch **ON** will reduce battery life by a small amount. If you never use **Maps** or care about your location, then set it to **OFF** to save your battery life.

Using the Digital Compass

The iPhone has a very cool Digital Compass feature built in. This can be helpful when you need to literally get your bearings and figure out which way is north.

Calibrating and Using the Digital Compass

Before you can use the Digital Compass, you need to calibrate it. You should only need to calibrate the compass the first time you use it. Follow these steps to do so:

1. Start **Maps** as you normally would.

2. Tap the current location button twice—it changes from to .

3. You'll see a **Digital Compass** icon appear on the screen, as shown in Figure 21–10.

4. The first time you use the Digital Compass feature, the **Calibration** symbol appears on the screen.

5. Move your iPhone in a figure-eight pattern, as shown on the screen.

> **NOTE:** The iPhone may ask you to move away from any source of interference while you go through the calibration process.

6. Hold your iPhone level to the ground. If you calibrated it successfully, the compass will rotate and point north.

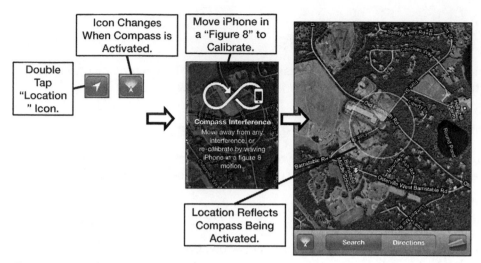

Figure 21–10. *Using the Digital Compass feature*

iTunes on Your Device

In this chapter, you will learn how to locate, buy, and download media using the **iTunes** app right on your iPhone. With **iTunes**, you will be able to download music, movies, TV shows, podcasts, and audiobooks. You will also learn about free educational content from leading universities from the **iTunes U** section on iTunes, as well as how to redeem iTunes gift cards.

Some of us still remember going to the record store when that new single or album came out. It was an exciting feeling to look at all the music we wanted, browsing first through all the vinyl albums, then tapes, and, finally, CDs.

Those days are long gone with the iPhone. Music, movies, TV shows, and more are available right from the iPhone itself.

iTunes is a music, video, TV, podcast, and more store. Virtually every type of media you can consume on your iPhone is available for purchase or rent (and often for free) right from the iTunes store.

Getting Started with iTunes

Earlier in this book, we showed you how to get your music from iTunes on your computer into your iPhone (see Chapter 3: "Sync With iCloud, iTunes, and More"). One of the great things about iTunes is that the store makes it very easy to buy or obtain music, videos, podcasts, and audiobooks, and then use them within minutes right on your iPhone.

The iPhone allows you to access the iTunes site (the mobile version) right on your device. After you purchase or request free items, they will be downloaded to your **Music** or **Videos** app on the iPhone. If you have have iCloud and have turned on automatic downloads, any music you buy will automatically be downloaded to your other iOS devices and iTunes on your PC. Movies will transfer the next time you sync with your desktop iTunes library.

A Network Connection Is Required

You do need an active Internet connection (either Wi-Fi or 3G/cellular) in order to access the iTunes store. Check out Chapter 4: "Network Connectivity" to learn more about this.

Starting iTunes

When you first received your iPhone, **iTunes** was one of the icons on the first **Home** screen page. Touch the **iTunes** icon, and you will be taken to the mobile version of the iTunes Store.

NOTE: The **iTunes** app changes frequently. Since the **iTunes** app is really a web site, it is likely to change somewhat between the time we wrote this book and when you are looking at it on your iPhone. Some of the screen images or buttons may look slightly different than the ones shown in this book.

Also, iTunes content can vary considerably from country to country. Depending on where you live, you might not have access to movies, TV shows, or other media. However, Apple continues to add iTunes content to more and more regions, so be sure to check back occasionally.

Navigating iTunes

The **iTunes** app uses icons similar to other programs on the iPhone, so getting around is quite easy. There are three buttons at the top and five soft keys at the bottom to help you. You can customize these soft keys and we show you how In the next section.. Notice in the image to the right the soft keys at the bottom. Scrolling in **iTunes** is just like scrolling in any other program; move your finger up or down to look at the selections available.

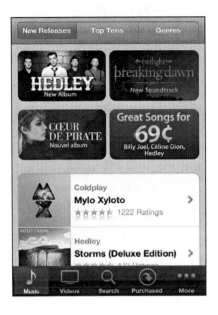

Customizing iTunes Soft Keys

It's simple to customize the soft keys shown at the bottom of the iTunes screen. Tap the **More** soft key in the lower left corner. Then tap **Edit** in the upper right corner.

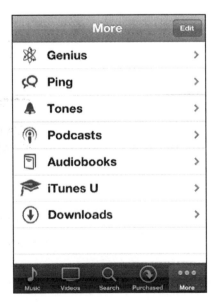

Now, you can change the soft keys by dragging and dropping any of the icons from the top down onto the soft key toolbar at the bottom. Any item you drop will replace the icon that was currently there.

Tap **Done** to complete the changes and return to iTunes.

Finding Music with New Releases, Top Tens, and Genres

Along the top of the screen of the iTunes music store are three buttons: **Featured**, **Top Charts**, and **Genius**. By default, you are shown the **Featured** selections when you start **iTunes**.

Top Tens: The Popular Stuff

If you like to know what is popular in a particular category, you will want to browse the categories under **Top Tens**. Tap **Top Tens** at the top, and then tap a category or genre to see what is popular in that category.

> **CAUTION:** Items in the **Top Tens** categories are selling well, but that doesn't mean that they will necessarily appeal to you. Always preview an item and check out its reviews before you pay for it.

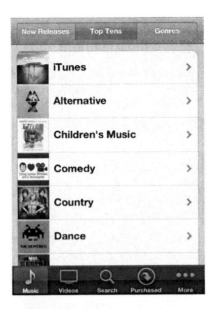

Genres: Types of Music

Touch the **Genres** button to browse music based on a genre. This is particularly helpful if you have a favorite type of music and would like to browse just that category.

There is an extensive list of genres to browse; just scroll down the list as you would in any other iPhone app.

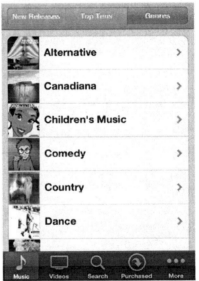

Go ahead and browse through the music until you see something that you would like to preview or buy.

Browsing for Videos (Movies)

Touch the **Movies**, **TV Shows,** or **Movie Videos** buttons on the top to browse all the video-related items.

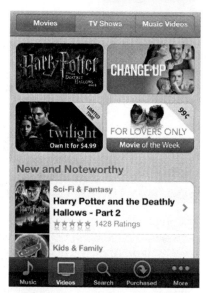

You can also use your finger to scroll all the way to the bottom of the page to check out the links there, including these links in particular:

- **Top Tens**

- **Genres**

> **TIP:** At the very bottom of most pages, you can also Redeem a gift card or log out of your Apple ID and log into another Apple ID account. This is useful if someone (maybe your children) has changed the Apple ID and you want to get back to yours.

Tap any movie or video to see more details or preview the selection. You have the option to rent or buy some movies and TV shows:

- **Rentals**: Some movies are available for rent for a set number of days. Click this button to rent a title.

> **NOTE:** The rental period in the US is 24 hours, and the rental period in Canada is 48 hours. The rental periods for other countries may vary slightly.

- **Buy**: Clicking this button allows you to purchase and own the movie or TV show forever.

Finding TV Shows

When you're done checking out the movies, tap the **TV Shows** button at the top to see what is available from your favorite shows.

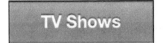

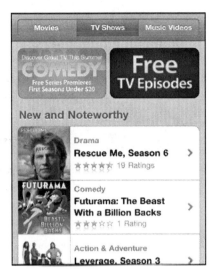

When you tap a TV series, you will see the individual episodes available. Tap any episode to check out the 30-second preview (see Chapter 15: "Viewing Videos" for more on watching videos). When you're finished with the preview, tap the **Done** button.

When you are ready, you can buy an individual episode or the entire TV series. Many, but not all, TV series allow you to purchase individual episodes as shown in Figure 22–1.

For example, you might want to get your fix of *Modern Family* and see the pilot episode that you missed. You can do this quickly and easily on your iPhone.

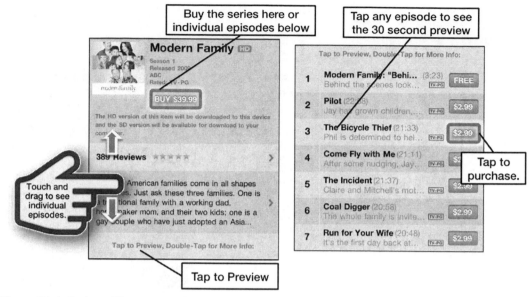

Figure 22–1. *Buying a TV season or episode*

> **NOTE:** There is also a **Free TV Episode** category, where you can get samples and bonus content.

Audiobooks in iTunes

Audiobooks are a great way to enjoy books without having to read them. Some of the narrators are so fun to listen to that it is almost like watching a movie. For example, the narrator of the Harry Potter series can do dozens of truly amazing voices. We recommend that you try out an audiobook on your iPhone; audiobooks are especially great when you are on an airplane and want to escape from the rest of the passengers, but don't want to have the light on.

> **TIP:** If you're a big audiobook listener, getting an Audible.com subscription can get you the same content at cheaper prices.

Audiobooks

If you are an audiobook aficionado, be sure to check out the **Audiobooks** section in iTunes.

You can click the one of the top three buttons to browse the following areas in **Audiobooks**:

- **Featured**
- **Top Tens**
- **Categories**

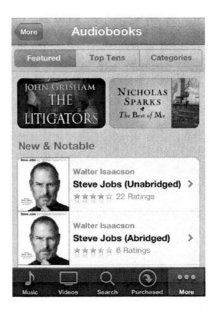

iTunes U: Great Educational Content

If you like educational content, then check out the **iTunes U** section. You will be able to see whether your university, college, or school has its own section.

One good example we discovered in just a few minutes of browsing was a panel discussion with three Nobel Prize–winning economists moderated by Paul Solman (the economic correspondent for the PBS News Hour). You can find the podcast by navigating through the following menus: **iTunes U ➤ Universities & Colleges ➤ Boston University ➤ BUNIVERSE - Business ➤ Audio**. Like much of the content in **iTunes U**, this podcast is free!

If you are in a location with a good wireless signal, you can tap the title of the audio or video item, and then listen to or watch it streaming. If your signal gets interrupted, however, you will lose your place in the video. There are many advantages to actually downloading the file (if possible) for later viewing, not least of which is that you get more control over the video-watching experience.

Download for Offline Viewing

If you know you are going to be out of wireless coverage for a while, such as on an airplane or in the subway, you will want to download the content for later offline viewing or listening. Tap the **Free** button to change it to a **Download** button, and then tap it again. You can then monitor the download progress (some larger videos may take ten minutes or more to complete) by tapping the **Downloads** button at the bottom right of the screen. When the download is complete, the item will show up in the correct area of your **Music** or **Videos** app.

> **NOTE:** Any file larger than 20MB cannot be downloaded over the 3G network; you must use Wi-Fi for larger files.

Searching iTunes

Sometimes you have a good idea of what you want, but you are unsure where it is located or perhaps you don't feel like browsing or navigating all the menus. The **Search** tool is for you.

In the top-right corner of the **iTunes** app (as in virtually every other iPhone app), you have a **Search** window.

Touch **Search**, and the **Search** window and the on-device keyboard will pop up. Once you start typing, the iPhone will begin to match your entry with possibilities.

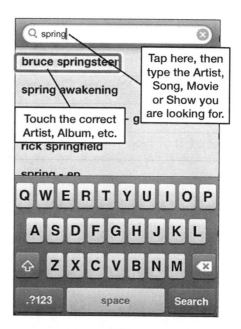

Type in the artist, song name, video name, podcast name, or album you are searching for, and the iPhone will display detailed matches. You can be as general or as specific as you like. If you are just looking to browse all particular songs by an artist, type the artist's name. If you want a specific song or album, enter the full name of the song or album.

When you locate the song or album name, simply touch it and you will be taken to the purchase page.

Purchasing or Renting Music, Videos, Podcasts, and More

Once you locate a song, video, TV show, or album, you can touch the **Buy** or (if you see it) **Rent** button. This will cause your media to start downloading. (If the content is free, then you will see the **Free** button, which turns into a **Download** button when you tap it.)

We suggest you view or listen to the preview, as well as check out the customer reviews first, unless you are absolutely sure you want to purchase the item.

> **NOTE:** You can also purchase *tones* for your phone from the iTunes store. Make sure to check out Chapter 9: "Using the Phone," where we show you how to create your own tones for free!

Previewing Music

Touch either the title of the song or its track number to the left of the song title; this will flip over the album cover and launch the preview window.

You will hear a representative clip of 90 seconds of the song.

Touch the **Stop** button and the track number will again be displayed.

Check Out Customer Reviews

Many items in iTunes offer customer reviews. The reviews range from a low of one star to a high of five stars.

> **CAUTION:** *Be aware that the reviews can have explicit language.* Many of the reviews are clean; however, some do contain explicit language that may not be caught by the iTunes store right away.

Reading the reviews can give you a fairly good idea of whether you would like to buy the item.

Previewing a Video, TV Show, or Music Video

Pretty much everything on iTunes offers a preview. Sometimes you will see a **Preview** button, as with music videos and movies. TV shows are a little different; you tap the episode title in order to see the 30-second preview.

We highly recommend checking out the reviews, as well as trying the preview before purchasing items on iTunes.

Typical movie previews or trailers will be longer than 30 seconds. Some are two and a half minutes or longer.

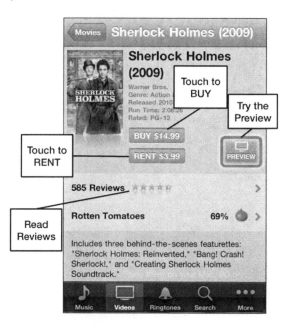

Purchasing a Song, Video, or Other Item

Once you are sure you want to purchase a song, video, or other item, follow these steps to buy it:

1. Touch the **Price** button of the song or the **Buy** button.

2. The button will change and turn into a green **Buy Now**, **Buy Song**, **Buy Single**, or **Buy Album** button.

3. Tap the **Buy** button.

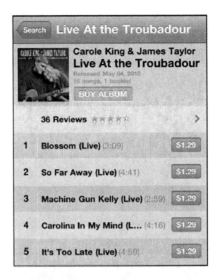

4. You will see an animated icon jump into the shopping cart. Type in your iTunes password and touch **OK** to complete the sale.

Tap the **More** button, then tap Downloads to see the download progress for each song on the album.

The song or album will then become part of your music library, and it will be synced with your computer the next time you connect your iPhone to iTunes on your computer. Note: iCloud will do this sync automaticlly.

After the download is complete, you will see the new song, audiobook, podcast, or iTunes U podcast inside the correct category within your **Music** app.

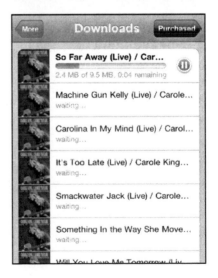

> **NOTE:** Purchased videos and iTunes U videos go into the **Videos** app on your iPhone and podcasts will show up in the **Music** app.

Podcasts in iTunes

Podcasts are usually a series of audio segments; these may be updated frequently (such as hourly news reports from National Public Radio) or not updated at all (such as a recording of a one-time lecture on a particular topic).

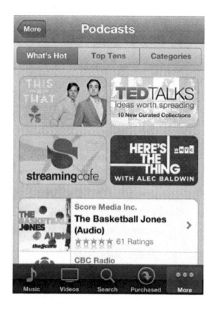

You can click the top three buttons to browse the podcast categories in iTunes:

- ■ **What's Hot**
- ■ **Top Tens**
- ■ **Categories**

Downloading a Podcast

Podcasts are available in video and audio varieties. When you locate a podcast, just touch the title of the podcast (see Figure 22–2). Luckily, most podcasts are free. If it is free, you will see a **Free** button instead of the typical **Buy** button.

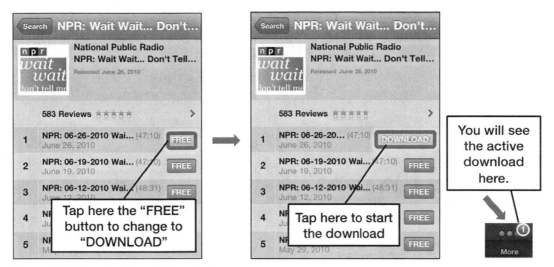

Figure 22–2. *Downloading an NPR podcast*

When you touch the button, it turns into a green **Download** button. Touch **Download** and an animated icon jumps into your **Downloads** icon at the bottom bar of soft keys. A small number displayed in red reflects the number of files downloading.

The Download Icon: Stopping and Deleting Downloads

As you download items, they appear in your **Downloads** screen. This behavior is just like the behavior of the **iTunes** app on your computer.

You can tap the **More** soft key and then tap the **Downloads** tab to see the progress of all your downloads.

Where the Downloads Go

You can see all of your downloads in either your **Music** or **Videos** apps by clicking the **More** icon, which shows your downloads organized by category. In other words, if you download a podcast, you will need to go into your **Music** app, touch **More**, and then the **Podcasts** tab to see the downloaded podcast.

Sometimes, you decide that you do not want the all downloads you selected. If you want to stop a download and delete it, swipe your finger over the download to bring up the **Delete** button, and then tap **Delete** (see Figure 22–3).

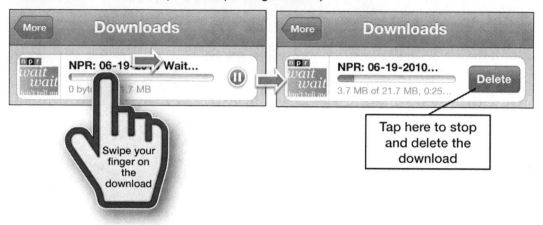

Figure 22–3. *Deleting a file while downloading it*

Redeeming an iTunes Gift Card

One of the cool things about the **iTunes** app on your iPhone is that, just as with the **iTunes** app on your computer, you can redeem a gift card and receive credit in your iTunes account for your purchases.

At the bottom of the **iTunes** screen, you should see the **Redeem** button (see Figure 22–4).

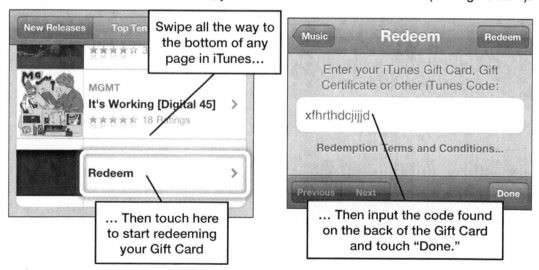

Figure 22–4. *Redeeming an iTunes gift card*

Tap the **Redeem** button to start the process of entering your iTunes gift card number for an iTunes store credit.

Ping

Ping is Apple's social network for music. You can access it by tapping the **Ping** button at the bottom center of the tab bar.

With Ping, you can see what music is being bought and commented on by the artists and people you follow, and your followers can see the music you buy and comment on. Ping also lets you tweet out your purchases.

There are three sections in Ping:

- **Activity:** Shows you all the purchases and comments made by the people you follow. You can view either **All** activity, **Artists** activity only, or **People** (non-artists) only.

- **People:** Gives you a list of all the other Ping users you **Follow**; a list of Ping users that **Follow** you; and lists of **Featured**, **Recommended Artists**, and **Recommended People** that Ping thinks you might like to follow.

- **My Profile:** Shows you all of your own recent activity and gives you access to **My Info**, which displays your profile information and album art from music you like.

NOTE: At the time of this writing, Ping has not gained significant popularity. If you're a huge music fan, and you and your friends buy a lot of music from iTunes, then we certainly recommend you at least try it out. However, you might also find more established (if more generic) social networks like Twitter and Facebook more to your liking.

Chapter 23

The Amazing App Store

You have just seen how easy it is download music, videos, and podcasts from iTunes right to your iPhone. You have also seen how easy it is to download iBooks from the iBooks store.

It is just as easy to download new applications from Apple's amazing App Store. Apps are available for just about any function you can think of: games, productivity tools, social networking, and anything else you can imagine. As the advertising says, *There's an app for that*.

In this chapter, you will learn how to navigate the App Store, as well as how to search for and download apps. You will also learn how to maintain and update your apps once they are downloaded onto your iPhone.

Learning More About Apps and the App Store

In this chapter, we will focus on accessing the App Store directly from your iPhone. However, you should remember that you can also shop at the App Store using the **iTunes** program on your Mac or PC (see Figure 23–1).

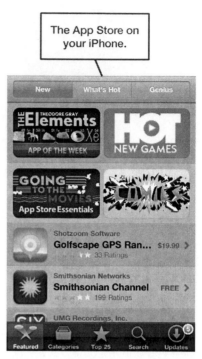

Figure 23–1. *Accessing the App Store from the* **iTunes** *program on your computer or the* **App Store** *icon on your iPhone*

In a very short amount of time, the App Store has exploded in popularity. There are apps for just about anything you can imagine. These apps are available at all price levels; in many cases, the apps are even free!

Where to Find Apps News and Reviews

You can find reviews for many apps in the App Store itself, and we recommend that you check out the App Store reviews. However, sometimes you will probably want more information from expert reviewers. If so, blogs are a great place to find news and reviews for particular apps or content.

Here is a list of Apple iPhone- and iPod-related blogs with reviews of apps:

- The iPhone Blog: www.tipb.com
- Touch Reviews: www.touchreviews.net
- Touch Arcade: www.toucharcade.com
- The Unofficial Apple Weblog: www.tuaw.com
- 148apps: www.148apps.com
- App Advice: www.appadvice.com

App Store Basics

With a little time, you should find the App Store to be quite intuitive to navigate. We'll cover some of the basics for getting the most out of the App Store, so that your experience will be as enjoyable and productive as possible.

> **NOTE:** App availability varies by country. Some apps are only available in some countries, and some countries may not have certain games sections due to local ratings laws.

A Network Connection Is Required

After you set up your App Store (iTunes) account, you still need to have the right network connectivity (either Wi-Fi or 3G) to access the App Store and download apps. Check out Chapter 4: "Connect to the Network" to learn how to tell whether you are connected.

Starting the App Store

The **App Store** icon should be on your first page of icons on the **Home** screen. Tap the icon to launch the **App Store** app.

The App Store Home Page

We'll look at several parts of the App Store's **Home** page: the top bar, middle content, and the bottom soft keys.

We'll look at the top bar first. At the top of the page shown in Figure 23–2, you will see three buttons: **New**, **What's Hot**, and **Genius**. Tap any of these to change the view.

> **TIP: Genius** is a feature that suggests apps you might like based on apps you have already downloaded and installed on your iPhone. It can be quite a nice way to filter through the hundreds of thousands of apps to find the ones that might interest you.

The middle of the page is your main content area. This main content area shows you a list of apps or the details of a specific app that you are viewing. You can swipe up or down to view more apps in a list or details for a specific app. You can also swipe left or right when viewing screen shots. On the **Featured** apps page, you will notice that there are a few large icons at the top. Clicking these icons will show you either types of apps or individual apps. Below the larger icons (you have to swipe down), you will see a number of featured apps.

The bottom of the App Store's **Home** page has five soft key buttons:

- **Featured**: Shows apps that have been highlighted by the App Store or by the app developers.

- **Categories**: Shows a list of categories used to organize the apps, so you can browse by category.

- **Top 25**: Shows top selling or top downloaded apps.

- **Search**: Finds an app using entered search terms.

- **Updates**: Lets you update any apps you have installed, and redownload any apps you've already acquired.

You can tell that Figure 23–2 is showing **Featured** apps because the **Featured** soft key is highlighted on the bottom row of soft keys. Scrolling is handled the same way as in other programs—just move your finger up and down to scroll through the page.

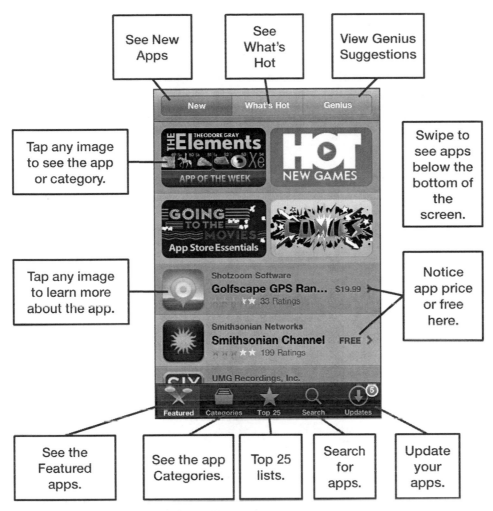

Figure 23-2. *The layout of the App Store's **Home** page*

NOTE: The App Store is essentially a web site, so it changes frequently. Some of the details and nuances of the App Store might look a bit different after this book goes to print.

Viewing App Details

If you see an app in a list that looks interesting, tap it to learn more. The **Details** screen for the app includes its price, a description, screen shots, and reviews (see Figure 23-3). You can use this information to help you determine whether the app will be a good choice for you.

Swipe down to read more details about the app on the **Info** page. Swipe left or right to view more screen shots of the app. Tap the **Rating** button near the bottom to read all the reviews for an app.

You can also see other details about the app, such as its file size, its version number, and developer information near the bottom of the **Info** page.

You can also **Tell a Friend** or **Report a Problem** using the buttons at the bottom of the screen.

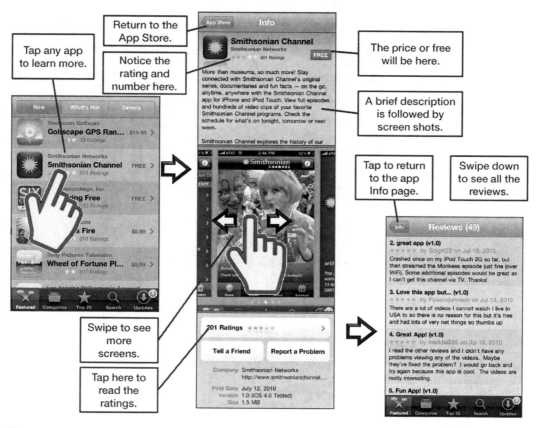

Figure 23–3. *Viewing details about an app*

Finding an App to Download

If you want to search for an app to download, begin by looking around in the default view, which shows the **Featured** apps. Scroll down the page to see all the featured apps.

> **NOTE:** As with the iTunes Store, you can only download apps less than 20MB in size while on 3G. Downloading larger file sizes requires a Wi-Fi connection.

Viewing the New Apps

The default view in the App Store shows new and featured apps. This is the view shown back in Figure 23–2. You can tell that this view shows new featured apps because the

Featured soft key ![Featured] is highlighted at the bottom of the screen, and the **New**

button ![New] at the top of the page is pressed.

Viewing What's Hot

Touch the **What's Hot** button at the top of the screen, and the "hottest" apps in the store will be shown on the screen. Again, just scroll through the hottest apps to see if something catches your eye.

> **NOTE:** The fact that an app is in the "What's Hot" category does not necessarily mean you will also believe it is useful or fun. Check out the app descriptions and reviews carefully before you purchase anything.

Genius

The third button at the top of the **Featured** apps section takes you to the **Genius** feature. This feature works like the identically named feature in the **iTunes** app that plays music on your computer. For example, it displays apps you might like based on apps you already have installed on your iPhone.

> **NOTE:** The first time you use the Genius feature, you will have to accept the terms and conditions presented before the feature will be enabled.

Based On

Notice that there is a **Based on (*app name*)** label above each app. This label shows you that the suggested app was based on a specific app you've installed on your iPhone. For example, the **CBS Radio** suggestion was based on the fact that **Pandora Radio** is installed. We didn't know about CBS Radio, but maybe we'll give it a try based on this recommendation.

Swipe to Remove

If you do not like a Genius suggestion, then you can swipe left or right on it to bring up the **Delete** button, just as you would to remove email or other items from lists on your iPhone. Tap the **Delete** button to remove that app from the list.

Disable Genius Feature

To disable the Genius feature, you need to go into your **App Store** settings (see the "App Store Settings" section later in this chapter to learn how to disable this feature).

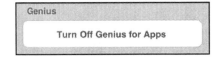

Categories

Sometimes, all the choices presented can be a bit overwhelming. If you have a sense of what type of app you are looking for, touch the **Categories** button along the bottom row of soft keys (see Figure 23–4).

The current categories available are shown in Table 23–1.

Table 23–1. *The App Store Category Listing*

▪ **Games**	▪ **Reference**	▪ **Finance**
▪ **Entertainment**	▪ **Travel**	▪ **Business**
▪ **Utilities**	▪ **Sports**	▪ **Education**
▪ **Social Networking**	▪ **Navigation**	▪ **Weather**
▪ **Music**	▪ **Healthcare & Fitness**	▪ **Books**
▪ **Productivity**	▪ **News**	▪ **Medical**
▪ **Lifestyle**	▪ **Photo & Video**	

NOTE: The categories listed are fluid and change over time, so it is possible that the categories you see will have changed by the time this book finds its way into your hands.

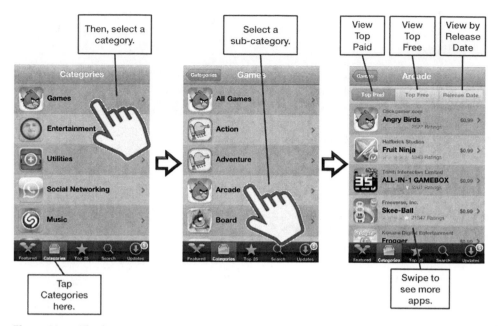

Figure 23–4. *Viewing apps by category—Games, in this example*

Looking at the Top 25 Charts

Touch the **Top Charts** soft key along the bottom row, and the App Store will change the view again. This time, you will see the top 25 paid, free, and top-grossing apps. Just touch one of the **Top Paid, Top Free**, or **Top Grossing** buttons at the top to switch between the views.

> **NOTE:** The **Top Grossing** category refers to the highest money-making apps, which is sales volume times selling price. This view will help more expensive apps get up higher in the charts. For example, a US $4.99 app that sells 10,000 units will rank much higher on the **Top Grossing** chart than a US $0.99 app that sells the same number of units.

Searching for an App

Let's say you have a specific idea of the type of app you want to find. Touch the **Search** soft key and type in either the name of the program or the type of program.

So, if you are looking for an app to help you with rowing, just type in "rowing" to see what comes up.

You may see some suggested search terms appear; tap these to narrow your search.

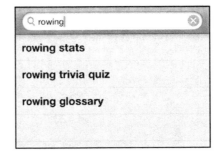

Tapping **Rowing Stats** in the suggested search terms yields only one result.

We want to see all the rowing-related apps, so we tap in the **Search** bar and use the **Backspace** key to erase the word "stats." Next, we tap the **Search** button in the lower-right corner to see a broader list of rowing-related results.

> **TIP:** If you row on the water (instead of only on a rowing machine), you might want to check out **SpeedCoach Mobile**, which sells for $49.99. There is also a free (at the time of writing) alternative called **iRowPro**.

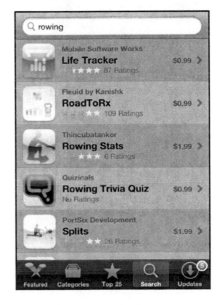

Downloading an App

Once you find the app you are looking for, you can download it right to your iPhone, as shown in Figure 23–5.

After locating the app you want to buy, notice the small button that says either **Free** or **$0.99** (or whatever the price is).

Just touch that button, and it will change to say **Install** if it is a free program or **Buy Now** if it is a paid program.

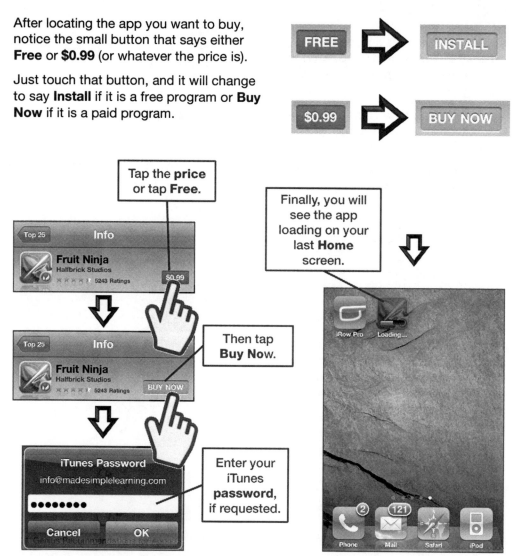

Figure 23–5. *Buying an app or downloading a free app*

Once you have read the reviews and the app description (and perhaps visited the developer support site), go ahead and download or purchase the app. Once you tap the **Download App** button, you will be prompted to input your iTunes password.

Input your password and tap **OK**; the app will be downloaded to your iPhone.

Finding Free or Discounted Apps

After browsing around, you will notice a couple of things about the App Store. First, there are lots of *free* apps. Sometimes, these are great applications. Other times, they are not so useful—but they can still be fun!

Second, you will notice that there will be sales for some of the apps, while other apps will become less expensive over time. If you have a favorite app and it costs $6.99 today, you might see its price decrease if you wait a few weeks or a month before buying it.

Redeeming Gift Cards or iTunes Codes

You can redeem gift cards or iTunes codes by swiping all the way to the bottom of most pages in the **App Store**.

At the bottom, tap the **Redeem** button.

Enter your code on the next screen. (You may have to scratch off something from the back of the gift card to see the code.)

Tap the **Redeem** button.

Maintaining and Updating Your Apps

Often, developers will update their apps for the iPhone. You don't need to use your computer to perform the update—you can do it right on your iPhone.

You can even tell if you have updates, and how many, by looking at the **App Store** icon. The one shown here has five app updates available for you to download.

Once you enter the App Store, tap the right-most icon on the bottom row. This is the **Updates** icon.

If you have apps with updates available, there will be a small number indicated in red. This number corresponds to the number of apps with updates.

When you tap the **Update** button, the iPhone shows you which apps have updates.

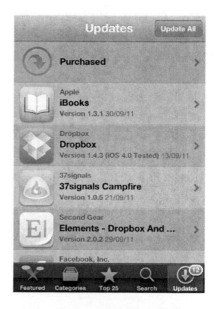

To get your updates, you could touch an individual app. However, it is easier to touch the **Update All** button

in the upper-right corner to have all your apps updated at once. The iPhone will leave the App Store, and you can see the progress of the updates in the little status bars. All apps updating will have icons that look grayed out.

Some status messages will show **Waiting**, while others will show **Loading** or **Installing**. When the update is complete, all your icons will return to their normal colors.

NOTE: You will need to relaunch the **App Store** app to get back in. The update process takes you completely out of the store.

Redownloading Apps

Once you've downloaded an app, whether free or paid, you can download it again as often as you like at no additional charge. For example, assume you buy an app to take with you on vacation. Once you've finished your trip, you can safely delete it and then download it again the next time you travel. This can help keep your **Home** screen clean and help prevent you from running out of storage on your iPhone.

To get a list of apps you've previously bought or downloaded, tap the **Update** button and then tap the **Purchased** tab at the very top of the screen.

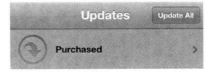

Inside the **Purchased** section, you have a choice of two views. First, you can view a list of all the apps you've ever bought or downloaded. Alternatively, you can view a list of apps that *aren't* currently installed on your iPhone.

> **NOTE:** Are you seeing apps listed that you don't remember buying or downloading? If so, this might be because you downloaded apps on your iPod touch, purchased universal apps on your iPad, or you shared your iTunes account with a spouse or family member who has downloaded apps to his device(s).

Automatic Downloads

The iCloud online service lets you set up your iPhone so it automatically downloads and installs any apps you purchase through iTunes on your Windows or Mac PC—or even on another iOS device, such as your iPad.

Follow these steps to turn on Automatic Downloads:

1. Tap the **Settings** icon.

2. Scroll down and tap **Store**.

3. Toggle **Automatic Downloads** for **Apps** to **ON**.

If you no longer wish to download apps automatically, simply toggle **Automatic Downloads** for **Apps** back to **OFF**.

You can also choose whether to **Use Cellular Data** to download your purchases. If you're on a slow network or have a limited data plan, consider turning this option **OFF**.

Other App Store Settings

Inside the settings for the **App Store** app, you can also check which account is logged into the store, log out, turn off the Genius feature, view your iTunes account, and work with your newsletter subscriptions.

> **TIP:** If you want to prevent someone from buying apps on your iPhone using your iTunes account, you need to sign out of iTunes using the steps described next.

Follow these steps to change the other settings for the **App Store** app:

1. Note that you can see the account you are logged in with at the top of this screen.

2. Tap **Sign Out** if you wish to log out of the iTunes service. For example, you might to give your iPhone to someone you don't using your phone to buy apps with your iTunes account.

3. Tap **View Account** to see the details of your account (you will need to sign in).

4. The figure to the right shows your account information. Tap **Payment Information** to adjust your billing information (e.g., your credit card type and number).

5. Tap **Billing Address** to update your address.

6. Tap **Change Country** to change your country.

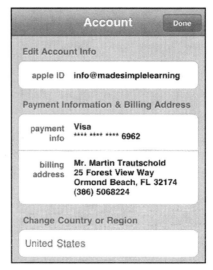

7. Scroll down to see more settings.

8. You can **Turn Off Genius for Apps** (or if it is off, this button will allow you to turn it on). Or, you can **Subscribe** or **Unsubscribe** to the iTunes newsletter from this dialog.

9. Tap **Done** in the upper-right corner when finished.

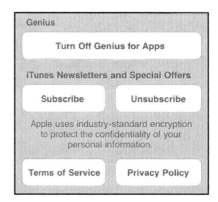

Chapter 24

Games and Fun

Your iPhone excels at many things. It is a multimedia workhorse, and it can keep track of your busy life. Your iPhone particularly excels in two areas: as a gaming device and for displaying apps that take advantage of its beautiful, high-resolution touch screen and powerful graphical processor. You can even find versions of popular games for the device that you might expect to find only on dedicated gaming consoles.

The iPhone brings many advantages to portable gaming: the high definition (HD) screen delivers realistic visuals; the high quality audio provides great sound effects; and the gyroscope and the accelerometer allow you to interact with your games in a way that many PCs and dedicated gaming consoles (outside of the Wii) don't. For example, in racing games, the last feature lets you steer your car by turning the iPhone as you hold it.

With AirPlay Mirroring, you can even beam your game to an Apple TV on the same Wi-Fi network and play on your big screen television.

The iPhone is also great for lots of other fun stuff such as following your local baseball team and even using the iPhone as a musical instrument with great apps like **Ocarina** (which we will show you later in the chapter).

Using the iPhone As a Gaming Device

The iPhone includes a built-in accelerometer and *gyroscope*, which is essentially a device that detects movement (acceleration) and tilt.

Combine the accelerometer with a fantastic screen, lots of memory, and a fast processor, and you have the makings of a great gaming platform. With literally thousands of gaming titles to choose from, you can play virtually any type of game you wish on your iPhone.

With multitasking, you can even take a phone call and come back to the exact place you left off.

NOTE: Some games require that you have an active network connection, either Wi-Fi or 3G, to engage in multiplayer games.

With the iPhone, you can play a driving game and use the iPhone itself to steer. You do this simply by turning the device. You can touch the iPhone to brake or tilt it forward to accelerate.

This game is so realistic that it might make you car sick!

Real Racing also has a nice Party Play feature, where you can race against your friends - give it a try!

Or, you can try a fishing game, where you case and reel in fish from the perspective of being on a boat!

"Flick Fishing"

Wind with your finger to reel in your fish

If music/rhythm games are your thing, then you will find many such programs in the App Store such as **Rock Band**. There are also fantastic fighting games like **Infinity Blade**, which is powered by the Epic Unreal 3 Engine; first-person shooters (FPS) like **Call of Duty: Zombies**; and some of the most popular casual games on the planet, such as **Angry Birds**.

The iPhone also has a very fast processor and a sophisticated graphics chip. Bundling these together with the accelerometer gives you a very capable gaming device.

Acquiring Games and Other Fun Apps

As is the case for all iPhone apps, games can be found at the App Store (see Figure 24–1). You can get them either through the **iTunes** app on your computer or through the device's **App Store** app.

Figure 24–1. *The layout of the App Store's **Games** section*

To get a game, fire up the **App Store** app, as you did in the previous chapter. Next, use the **Categories** icon to go to the **Games** tab. You will also find many games in the **Featured** section of the App store, as well as in the **New and Notable** section. Figure 24–2 shows the app purchase page for a game available for the iPhone.

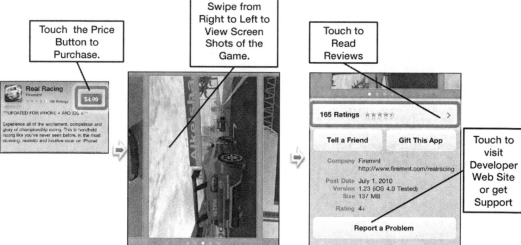

Figure 24–2. *The layout of the* ***App Purchase*** *page*

Reading Reviews Before You Buy

Many of the games have user reviews that are worth perusing. Sometimes, you can get a good sense of the game before you buy it. If you find a game that looks interesting, don't be afraid to do a simple Google search to see whether any mainstream media outlets have performed a full review.

Looking for Free Trials or Lite Versions

Increasingly, game developers are giving users free trials of their games to see if they like them before they buy. You will find many games have both a *Lite* version and a *Full* version in the App Store.

Some "free" games are supported by the inclusion of ads within the game. Other games are free to start, but require in-app purchases for continued play or additional features.

Being Careful When You Play

You might use the iPhone to cast your line in a fishing game, as you would in real life. You can also move around a bit in driving and first-person shooter games. The point: Be mindful of your surroundings as you play! For example, make sure you have a good grip on your device, so it doesn't slip out of your hand; we recommend a good silicone case to help with this.

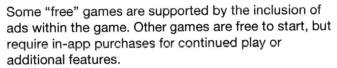

CAUTION: Games such as **Real Racing** can be quite addictive!

Two-Player Games

The iPhone really opens up the possibility for two-player gaming. In this example, we are playing checkers against one another, using the iPhone as a game board.

You can find similar two-person gaming apps for other board games, such as chess, Monopoly, and Uno..

Online and Wireless Games

The iPhone also allows online and wireless, peer-to-peer gaming (if the game supports it). Many new games are incorporating this technology. In **Scrabble**, for example, you can play against multiple players on their own devices. You can even use the iPhone as your game board and up to four individual iPhones as wireless "racks" to hold the letters of all the players. Just flick the letters off the rack, and they go onto the board—very cool!

In this example, I selected **Online** from the **Real Racing** menu. I now have the option to either play against another opponent through Wi-Fi or to join an online league race.

NOTE: If you just want to play against a friend who is nearby, select Wi-Fi mode for multiplayer games. If you just want to play against new people, try going online for a league race or game.

Other Fun Stuff: Baseball

There are many great apps that can provide you with endless hours of entertainment on the iPhone. Since the iPhone was released on opening day of the Major League Baseball season, it is appropriate to highlight an app that was honored as the first "App of the Week" in the iPhone App Store.

At Bat 2010 for iPhone is a US $14.99 application that is well worth the entry fee for any baseball fan. It also highlights the iPhone's capabilities.

The main view of the app changes, based on whether there are baseball games currently being played. When you first register the app, you pick your favorite team. The favorite team on the iPhone in this example is set to the Red Sox. So, if this team is playing, then the view automatically goes to that team's game first. If the team is not playing, then it displays a recap of the team's previous game. Alternatively, it might list the details of the team's next game.

The main view during game time shows a batter at the plate. This batter represents the real batter. Batters will switch sides of the plate, depending on whether the batter currently up hits from the left or right side of the plate. The current pitch count is shown above the plate, and the score is displayed at the top of the screen.

When you see a player at the plate or on base, you can touch the player's image to bring up his baseball card and view his stats.

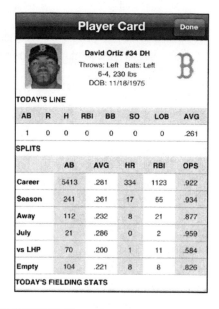

AirPlay Mirroring

The latest iPhone comes with the ability to not only stream video or music from your iPhone to an Apple TV, but also to share the screen of any app, including games. This lets you and your entire family watch and enjoy the game on the big screen while using your iPhone as the controller. It can be especially effective with board games and multiplayer games where the whole family or group can sit around and play together.

Follow these steps to use the AirPlay Mirroring feature:

1. Tap the app you want to mirror. For this example, we're using Infinity Blade.

2. Once the app has launched, double-click the Home button to bring up the Fast App Switcher.

3. Swipe from left to right to get to the audio/video controls. (They're all the way at the end, so keep swiping until you can't swipe any more.)

4. Tap the AirPlay icon to bring up the list of AirPlay–enabled devices on your Wi-Fi network.

5. Select Apple TV.

6. Click the Home button again to return to your app.

7. You should now see Infinity Blade on the big screen. Let 'em have it!

To stop AirPlay Mirroring, repeat the same procedure and choose iPhone from the device list.

> **NOTE**: Some games allow you to do multiplayer AirPlay Mirroring, like **Real Racing 2**'s Party Play feature where up to 4 people can use their iPhones or iPads to race against each other on the same big screen TV.

Chapter 25

Social Networking

Some of the most popular places to "connect" these days are those sites that are often called *social networking sites*—places that allow you to create your own page and connect with friends and family to see what is going in their lives. Some of the biggest web sites for social networking are Facebook, Twitter, and LinkedIn.

In this chapter, we will show you how to access these sites. You will learn how to update your status, *tweet*, and keep track of those who are both important or simply of interest to you.

Facebook

Facebook was founded in February of 2004. Since that time, It has served as the premier site for users to connect, re-connect, and share information with friends, co-workers, and family. Today, over 800 million people use Facebook as their primary source of "catching up" with the people who matter most to them.

> **NOTE:** *You cannot play Facebook games inside the **Facebook** app or via the Facebook.com web site on your iPhone.* This may disappoint you if you are a big Facebook game player; however, you can often get the same games (e.g., **FarmVille**) from the App Store, and then connect them to your Facebook computer version to keep your place.

On your iPhone, you have three primary ways of accessing your Facebook page at the time of publishing:

1. Use **Safari** to go to the standard (full) web site: www.facebook.com.

2. Use **Safari** to go to the mobile site: http://touch.facebook.com.

3. Use the iPhone **Facebook** app.

> **NOTE:** The iPhone version of the **Facebook** app is a bit more limited than the full web site, but it is much easier to navigate.

Different Ways to Connect to Facebook

You can access Facebook by using its iPhone-specific app or using one of the two previously mentioned Facebook web sites in your **Safari** browser. We will focus on the **Facebook** app for the iPhone for the duration of this chapter.

Downloading and Installing the Facebook App

In order to find the app, use the **Search** feature in the App Store and simply type in "Facebook."

You can also go to the **Social Networking** category in the App Store and find the official **Facebook** app, as well as many other Facebook-related apps.

> **NOTE:** Some of the apps may look like "official" Facebook apps, and they do cost money. However, the only "official" app is the iPhone/iPod app shown to the right.

In order to connect to your account on Facebook, you will need to locate the icon you just installed and click it. We use the example of **Facebook** here, but the process is very similar for the rest of the apps.

Once **Facebook** is successfully downloaded, the icon should look something like this.

The Facebook App

To get the **Facebook** app installed on your iPhone, start up the **App Store** and search for "Facebook." Tap the **Install** button from the **Facebook** app listing.

Facebook App Basics

Once **Facebook** is downloaded and installed, the first thing you will see is the **Login** screen. Input your account information—your email address and password.

After you log in the first time, you will see a **Push Notifications** warning message.

Click **OK** if you want to allow these messages, which can be pokes from other Facebook friends, notes, status update notifications, and more.

Once you log in, you will see the **Facebook** screen main screen. Tap the **Facebook** logo to navigate around the app.

Navigating Around Facebook

Toggle between the **Navigation** icons and your current location by tapping the word **Facebook** at the top of the page.

For example, if you are in the **News Feed** and tap **Facebook**, you will see all the icons. Tap **Facebook** again and you will return to the **News Feed**.

From the icons page, you can access your **News Feed, Profile, Friends, Messages, Places, Groups, Events, Photos,** and **Chat.**

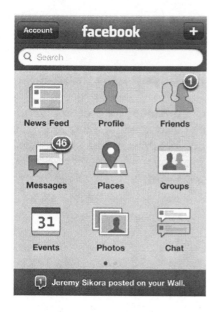

Communicating with Your Friends

Follow these steps to communicate with your friends on Facebook from the **Facebook** app on your iPhone:

1. Tap **Facebook** at the top to see all the icons.

2. Tap the **Friends** icon and your list of friends is displayed.

3. Touch the friend and you will go to his Facebook page, where you can then write on her **Wall** and see her **Info** or **Photos.**

Uploading Pictures with the Facebook App

An easy and fun thing to do with Facebook is to upload pictures. Here, we show you how to upload pictures in the **Facebook** app:

1. From the Facebook main icons, tap **Photos**.

2. Choose an album, such as Mobile Uploads.

3. Tap the **Camera** next to the **What's on your mind?** box.

4. Tap the **Take Photo or Video** button to snap a picture or take a video to upload. Or, tap **Choose From Library** to navigate through the pictures on your iPhone until you find the picture you wish to upload.

5. Next, tap **Write a caption...** to write a caption, if so desired.

6. To finish the upload, tap the blue **Upload** button and the photo will go into your Mobile Uploads folder.

> **NOTE:** When you upload a photo, the image quality won't be the same as it was originally on your iPhone.

Gary Mazo Went to get the mail and a huge hawk was having lunch.

9 minutes ago

Facebook Notifications

Depending on your settings for Facebook push notifications, you can be inundated by updates, wall posts, and invitations. If you don't have too many Facebook friends and you want to know when someone is writing something on your wall or commenting on a post or picture, just set your push notification to **ON**, as shown in the next section.

When a notification comes in, it will appear in Notification Center or as Lock Screen Info if your phone is locked.

To access Facebook from the notification, just slide the **Facebook** icon across the screen or slide the **Arrow** button to unlock and read the message.

Settings to Customize Your Facebook App

Here's how to adjust the settings for the **Facebook** app:

1. Tap the **Settings** app.

2. Tap **Facebook** in the left column.

3. You can now adjust various options:

   ■ **Shake to Reload**: This feature reloads or updates the page when you shake your iPhone.

   ■ **Vibrate:** This feature vibrates to signal you when chat or message alerts are available.

   ■ **Play Sound:** This feature lets you add an audible tone to chat and message alerts.

Follow these steps to adjust push notification settings:

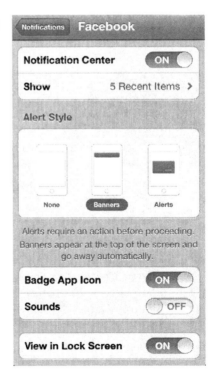

1. Tap the **Settings** app.

2. Tap **Notifications**.

3. Scroll down and tap **Facebook**.

4. Set **Notification Center** to **ON** to receive push notifications.

5. Tap **Show** to choose how many notifications appear in the list.

6. Set the **Alert Style** to **None** for no notifications, **Banners** for new Notification Center–style alerts, or **Alerts** for old style pop-up notifications.

7. Set **Badge App Icon** to **ON** to see the number of new notifications appear on the **Facebook** icon.

8. Set **Sounds** to **ON** to hear an audible tone when you get a notification.

9. Set **View in Lock Screen** to get notification info even when your phone is locked.

> **TIP:** The **Facebook** app will bring in Facebook profile pictures to your **Contacts** list. This can be quite humorous, depending on the pictures. However, it can also upload your own, non-Facebook contacts' information to Facebook's servers, which might raise privacy concerns for you, your family, and friends.

LinkedIn

LinkedIn has core functionality very similar to Facebook, but it tends to be focused on business and career interests. This is in contrast to Facebook, which is focused more on personal friends and games. With LinkedIn, you can connect and re-connect with current and past business associates, send messages, see what people are up to, have discussions, and more.

At the time of publishing, the status of LinkedIn was very similar to Facebook. You can go to the regular LinkedIn site on the **Safari** browser, or you can download the **LinkedIn** app for the iPhone.

Which is better? We liked the **LinkedIn** app for the iPhone slightly better than the full LinkedIn.com site in **Safari**. It was easier to navigate using the **LinkedIn** app with the large buttons, but you could see more on the screen in the **Safari** version. We recommend giving both options a try and seeing which you like better—it is really a matter of personal preference.

Downloading the LinkedIn App

The process for downloading the **LinkedIn** app is similar to the process for downloading the **Facebook** app. Start the **App Store** app on your iPhone, type "LinkedIn" into the **Search** window, and then locate the app. The **LinkedIn** app is free, so tap the **FREE** button to install it.

Logging In to LinkedIn App

Once the app is installed, click the **LinkedIn** icon and enter your login information.

Navigating Around the LinkedIn App

LinkedIn has a zone-based navigation system. Tap any stack to move to that zone, and then tap the LinkedIn logo at the top to return to the Home screen.

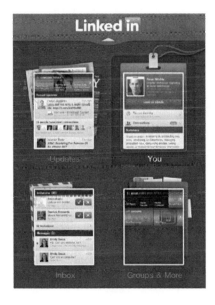

Communicating with LinkedIn Connections

One of the things you will most likely do the most with the **LinkedIn** app is communicate with your connections. The easiest way to do that is to follow these steps:

1. From the **Home** page, tap the **You** stack at the top right.

2. Tap the **Connections** button midway down the screen.

3. Scroll through your connections or tap the **Magnifying Glass** search icon and type in a connection name in the **Search** box.

4. Tap the connection you are looking for.

5. Tap the **Phone** icon to call him (if he has chosen to share a phone number) or the **Mail** icon to send him a message.

Twitter

Twitter was started in 2006. Twitter is essentially an SMS (text message)–based social networking site. It is often referred to as a *micro-blogging site*, and it is a place where the famous and not-so-famous can share what's on their mind. The catch is that you have only 140 characters to get your point across.

With Twitter, you subscribe to *follow* someone who *tweets* messages. You might also find that people will start to follow you. If you want to follow us, we are @garymadesimple on Twitter.

Setting up Twitter

1. With iOS 5, the **Twitter** app is built right into your iPhone. This means that the app lets you share content like pictures and posts from within other apps, like Photos. Follow these steps to set up Twitter:

2. Tap the **Settings** app.

3. Scroll down and tap **Twitter**.

4. If **Twitter** for the iPhone isn't already installed on your iPhone, tap the Install button to the right of the **Twitter** icon. (If **Twitter** for the iPhone is already installed, the Install button will be grayed out.)

5. Tap User Name and enter your Twitter `@username`.

6. Tap **Password** and enter your Twitter password.

7. Tap the **Sign In** button.

8. If you don't have a Twitter account, tap the **Create New Account** button at the bottom of the screen and fill in the form to get one.

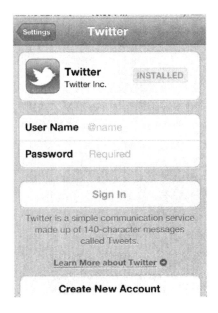

9. Once you're logged in, tap Account to change your options.

10. If you want your friends to be able to find you on Twitter based on your email address, toggle Find me by **Email** to **ON**.

11. If you want your location to be recorded every time you tweet from within an app, toggle **Tweet Location** to **ON**.

NOTE: If you tweet your location, potentially anyone on Twitter could find out where you are—including the fact that you're not at home or work. If privacy is a concern, toggle **Tweet Location** to **OFF**.

Using Twitter

The official **Twitter** app takes a streamlined approach to using Twitter. The **Home** screen shows you the tweets from those you are following, and the full message is nice and large.

Along the bottom are five icons, the first being the main **Twitter** feed. The other icons are **Mentions, Direct Messages, Search,** and the **More** button, which takes you to your **Profile, Favorites, Drafts, Lists,** and **Accounts and| Settings**.

The **Compose Tweet** icon is in the top-left corner (see Figure 25–1).

Compose Tweet.

Touch More to see Profile, Favorites, Drafts and Lists.

Feed, Mentions, Inbox, Search and More.

Figure 25–1. *The layout of the* ***Twitter*** *app's* ***Home*** *page*

Refreshing Your List of Tweets

To refresh your list of tweets, just pull down the main page and you will see the **Pull down to refresh** notification at the top. Once the page is pulled down, you will see a **Release to refresh** note. Release the page and it will refresh the tweets.

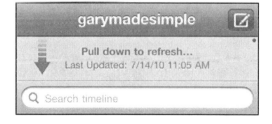

Your Twitter Profile

To display your Twitter profile, touch the **More** button and then touch **My Profile**.

To see your tweets, just touch **Tweets**.

To see those tweets you have labeled as favorites, touch the **Favorites** button.

To see those individuals you are following, touch the **Following** button.

> **NOTE:** The number corresponding to your followers, those you are following, and your tweets is displayed above the title of the button.

Scroll down the page to see your **Retweets**; your **Lists**; and **Services** to which you can subscribe.

The Compose Button

Touch the **Compose** button  and the **New Tweet** screen pops up. The character counter will count down from 140 as you type your message. Here are some things you can do from the **New Tweet** screen:

- Tap the **@** symbol to search for other usernames to mention in your tweet.

- Tap the **#** symbol to search for trending topics to tag in your tweet.

- Tap the **Camera** icon to take a photo or video with your iPhone or choose an existing one from your library to add to your tweet.

- Tap the **Arrow** icon to add your current location to your tweet.

Options within Tweet

From your **Twitter** app's **Home** screen, just touch one of your tweets for the following options:

- Tap the **Back Arrow** at the bottom left of the screen to **Reply** to a tweet.

- Tap the square **Double Arrows** to retweet or quote a tweet.

- Tap the **Star** icon to favorite a tweet.

- Tap the **Paperclip** icon to view an attachment.

- Tap the **Action** button to copy a link to tweet, mail a tweet, or translate a tweet.

NOTE: Unlike with Facebook and LinkedIn, you can find a variety of alternative third-party Twitter apps in the App Store. If you don't like the official **Twitter** for iPhone app, try out **Tweetbot**, **Twitterrific**, or one of the many other apps.

Chapter 26

Troubleshooting

The iPhone is usually highly reliable. Occasionally, as with your computer or any complicated electronic device, you might have to reset the device or troubleshoot a problem. In this chapter, we will give you some useful tools to help get your iPhone back up and running as quickly as possible. We will start with some basic quick troubleshooting and move onto more in-depth problems and resolutions in the "Advanced Troubleshooting" section.

We will also cover some other odds and ends related to your iPhone and give you a list of resources where you can find help for your iPhone.

Basic Troubleshooting

We will begin by covering a few basic tips and tricks to get your iPhone back up and running. when something goes wrong.

What to Do If the iPhone Stops Responding

Sometimes, your iPhone won't respond to your touch—it simply freezes in the middle of a program. If this happens, try these steps to see whether the iPhone will start responding (see Figure 26–1):

1. Click the **Home** button once to see whether that exits the app to the **Home** screen.

2. If a particular app is causing trouble, try double-clicking the **Home** button to open the **App Switcher** bar. Next, press and hold *any* icon in the **App Switcher** bar until they all shake and a red **Circle** icon with a minus sign appears in the upper-left corner of the app icon.

3. Tap the red **Circle** icon to close the app.

4. If the iPhone continues to be unresponsive, try pressing the **Sleep/Power** key until you see **Slide to Power Off**.

5. Press and hold the **Home** button until you return to the **Home** screen—this should quit the program.

6. Make sure your iPhone isn't running out of power. Try plugging it in or attaching it to your computer (if it's plugged in) to see whether it will start to respond.

7. If holding the **Home** button doesn't work, you will need to try to turn off your iPhone by pressing and holding the **Power/Sleep** button for three to four seconds.

8. Next, slide the **Slide to Power Off** slider at the top of the screen. If you cannot power off the iPhone, then you will need to reset the iPhone. Skip ahead to the next section to learn how.

9. After you power off the iPhone, wait a minute or so, and then turn on the iPhone by holding the same **Power** button for a few seconds.

10. You should see the **Apple** logo appear on the screen. Wait until the iPhone starts up, and you should be able to access your programs and data.

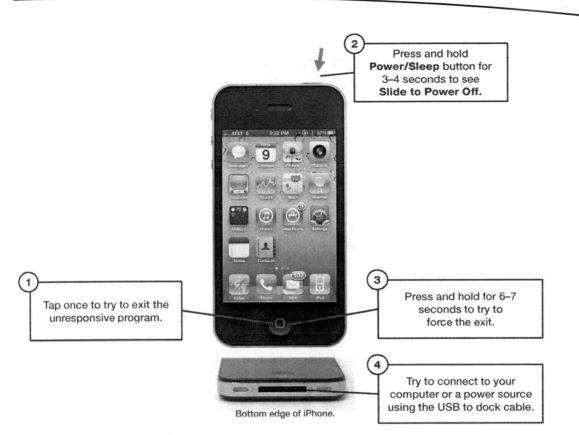

2 Press and hold
Power/Sleep button for
3–4 seconds to see
Slide to Power Off.

1 Tap once to try to exit the
unresponsive program.

3 Press and hold for 6–7
seconds to try to
force the exit.

Bottom edge of iPhone.

4 Try to connect to your
computer or a power source
using the USB to dock cable.

Figure 26–1. *Basic troubleshooting steps*

If these steps don't work, you will need to reset your iPhone.

How to Hard-Reset Your iPhone

Resetting your device is another option for dealing with an unresponsive iPhone. It is perfectly safe to do this, and it usually fixes many problems (see Figure 26–2).

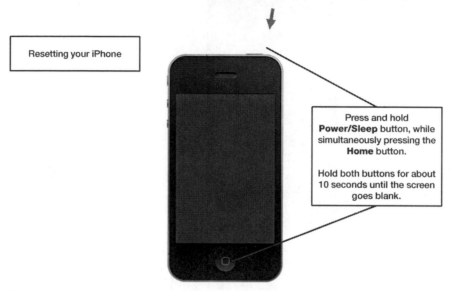

Resetting your iPhone

Press and hold **Power/Sleep** button, while simultaneously pressing the **Home** button.

Hold both buttons for about 10 seconds until the screen goes blank.

Figure 26–2. *Resetting your iPhone*

Follow these steps to hard-reset your iPhone:

1. Using two hands, press and hold the **Home** button and the **Power/Sleep** button at the same time.

2. Keep both buttons held down for about eight to ten seconds. You will see the **Slide to Power Off** slider. Ignore that and keep holding both buttons until the screen goes blank.

3. After a few more seconds, you should see the **Apple** logo appear. When you see the logo, just release the buttons, and your iPhone will be reset.

How to Soft-Reset Your iPhone

There are various things you can reset in the **Settings** app, from the **Home** screen layout to the network settings to all the data on your device:

1. Tap the **Settings** icon.

2. Tap **General**.

3. Swipe up to see the bottom of the page.

4. Tap **Reset**.

5. Tap **Reset All Settings** to reset the network, keyboard, **Home** screen layout, and location warnings. Tap **Reset** to confirm in the pop-up window.

6. Tap **Erase All Content and Settings** to erase everything from your iPhone, and then tap **Erase** to confirm in the pop-up window.

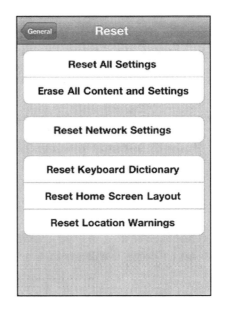

7. Tap **Reset Network Settings** to clear all your Wi-Fi (and 3G) network settings.

8. Tap **Reset Keyboard Dictionary** to reset the spelling dictionary.

9. Tap **Reset Home Screen Layout** to return to the factory layout; this restores your iPhone's **Home** screen to its original layout.

10. Tap **Reset Location Warnings** to reset the warning messages you receive about allowing apps to use your current location.

No Sound in Music, Video, Alerts or Phone Ringer

Few things are more frustrating than missing phone calls, hoping to listen to music or watch a video, only to find that no sound comes out of the iPhone. Usually, there is an easy fix for this problem:

1. If you are not hearing the phone ring or any other alerts, then check to make sure your **Mute** switch on the upper left edge of your device is not turned on. You know the Mute switch is set to on when it's switched toward the back of your device and you see a little orange color next to the switch. Make sure the **Mute** switch is pushed toward the front of your device, which is the off position.

2. Check the volume by using the **Volume Up** key in the upper-left edge of your iPhone. You might have accidentally lowered the volume all the way or muted it.

3. If you are using wired headphones from the headphone jack, unplug your headphones, and then put them back in. Sometimes, the headset jack isn't connected well.

4. Follow these steps if you are using wireless Bluetooth headphones or a Bluetooth stereo setup:

   a. Check the volume setting (if available on the headphones or stereo).

   b. Check to make sure the Bluetooth device is connected. Tap the **Settings** icon, tap **General**, and then tap **Bluetooth**. Make sure you see your device listed and that its status is **Connected**. If it is not connected, then tap it and follow the directions to pair it with the iPhone.

> **NOTE:** Sometimes you may actually be connected to a Bluetooth device and not know it. If you are connected to a Bluetooth Stereo device, no sound will come out of the actual iPhone.

5. Make sure the song or video is not in Pause mode.

6. Open the iPhone music or video controls. Double-clicking the **Home** button should open the **App Switcher** bar. Swipe from left to right to see your media controls.

7. Swipe one more time to the right to see the volume controls. Verify that the song is not paused and that the volume is not turned down all the way.

8. Finally, check the **Settings** icon to see whether you (or someone else) has set the **Volume Limit** on the iPhone:

   a. Tap the **Settings** icon.

   b. Swipe down the page and tap **Music**.

   c. See whether **Volume Limit** is **On**.

   d. Tap **Volume Limit** to check the setting level. If the limit is unlocked, simply slide the volume to a higher level.

   e. If it is locked, you need to unlock it first by tapping the **Unlock Volume Limit** button and entering the four-digit code.

If none of these steps helps, check out the "Additional Troubleshooting and Help Resources" section later in this chapter. If that doesn't help, then try to restore your iPhone from a backup file using the steps in the "Restore Your iPhone from a Backup" section in the chapter. Finally, if that does not help, then contact the store or business that sold you your iPhone for assistance.

If You Can't Make Purchases from iTunes or the App Store

You have this cool new device, so you decide to visit the iTunes Store or the App Store. But what if you receive an error message, or you are not allowed to make a purchase? Try these steps if this happens to you:

1. Both stores require an active Internet connection. Make sure you have either a Wi-Fi connection or a cellular data connection. For assistance, check out Chapter 4: "Connect to the Network."

2. Verify you have an active iTunes account.

Advanced Troubleshooting

Thus far we've covered the basic troubleshooting steps on your iPhone. In the upcoming sections, we will delve into some more advanced troubleshooting steps.

When Your iPhone Does Not Show Up in iTunes

Occasionally, your iPhone may not be recognized by the **iTunes** app when you connect your iPhone to your PC or Mac. Consequently, your iPhone will not appear in the left nav bar.

After you connect your iPhone to your computer, you should see it listed in the left nav bar under **DEVICES**. There are a few steps you can take to try and get the **iTunes** app to recognize your iPhone:

1. Check the battery charge of the iPhone by looking at the battery level in the top right of the **Home** screen. If you have let the battery run too far down, the **iTunes** app won't see it until the level of the battery rises a bit.

2. If the battery is charged, try connecting the iPhone to a different USB port on your computer. Sometimes, if you have always used one USB port for the iPhone and switch it to another port, the computer won't see it.

3. If this still does not fix the problem, try disconnecting the iPhone and restarting the computer.

4. Next, reconnect the iPhone to the USB port.

5. If the iTunes app still doesn't see your iPhone, then download the latest update to **iTunes**, or completely uninstall and reinstall the **iTunes** app on the computer. If you choose this option, make sure that you back up all the information in **iTunes** first.

6. You also might want to try another sync cable, it could be possible that your USB sync cable is defective.

Synchronization Problems

Sometimes, you might encounter errors when synchronizing your iPhone with your computer (PC or Mac). How you address the problem depends on your sync method.

Using iTunes to Sync

If you are using iTunes to sync your personal information, then follow these steps to resolve synchronization problems:

1. First, follow all the steps we outlined in the "iPhone Does Not Show Up in iTunes" section of this chapter.

2. If the iPhone still will not sync, but you can see it in the left nav bar of your **iTunes** app, go back to Chapter 3: "Sync with iCloud, iTunes, and More" and review your sync settings very carefully.

Using Apple's iCloud or Microsoft Exchange to Sync

If you are using the iCloud service or Microsoft Exchange method to sync your email and personal information, then follow these troubleshooting steps to resolve synchronization problems:

1. Both iCloud and Exchange sync require a wireless Internet data connection in order to sync your email and personal information. Verify that you have a live data connection by checking Table 1 in the Quick Start Guide's "Reading the Connectivity Status Icons" section.

2. If you do not have a wireless data signal, then verify your Wi-Fi or 3G connection is set up correctly (see Chapter 4: "Connect to the Network").

3. After you have verified your connection, you need to check that your sync settings are correct on your computer and iPhone (see Chapter 3).

> **TIP:** Sometimes your problem can be as simple as a changed password. If this is the case, then make sure to correct your password on your iPhone for your sync settings. These are found by tapping your **Settings** icon, then tapping **Mail, Contacts and Calendars**. Finally, tap the account name and adjust the password.

Reinstalling the iPhone Operating System (with or Without a Restore)

Sometimes, you might have to do a clean install of your iPhone operating system to get your iPhone back up and running smoothly. If an update is currently available, then this process will also result in upgrading your iPhone software.

> **TIP:** This process is virtually identical to the process of updating your iPhone with a new version of the operating system.

During this process, you will have three choices:

- If you want to return the iPhone to its normal state with all your data, you will have to use the **Restore** function in the **iTunes** app.

- If you plan on getting a clean start and tying the iPhone to an iTunes account, then you will need to use the **Setup a new iPhone** function at the end of this process.

- If you plan on giving away or selling your iPhone, then you will simply need to eject the iPhone from **iTunes** at the end of this process (before doing a restore or new setup).

> **CAUTION:** This restore process will wipe your iPhone totally clean. You will need to resynchronize and reinstall all of your apps and enter your account information, such as your email accounts. This process could take 30 minutes or longer, depending on how much information you have synced to your iPhone.

To reinstall the iPhone operating system software with the option of restoring data to your iPhone from a previous backup, follow these steps:

1. Connect your iPhone to your computer and load the **iTunes** app.

2. Click your **iPhone** in the **DEVICES** category in the left nav bar.

3. Click **Summary** in the top nav bar.

4. You will see the **Summary** screen with all the information about your iPhone. Click the **Restore** button in the middle screen, as shown here (see Figure 26–3).

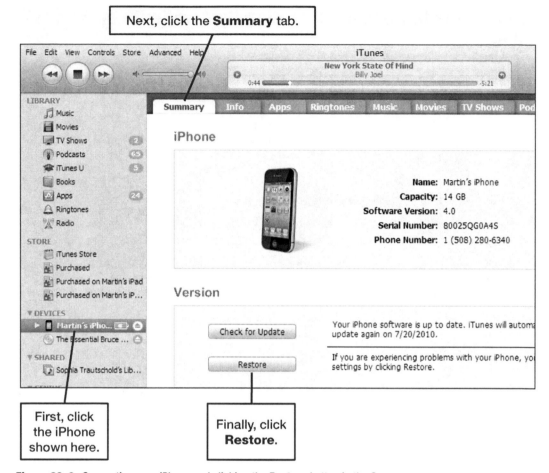

Next, click the **Summary** tab.

First, click the iPhone shown here.

Finally, click **Restore**.

Figure 26–3. *Connecting your iPhone and clicking the **Restore** button in the **Summary** screen*

5. Now you will be asked whether you want to back up your phone. Click **Back Up** just to be safe (see Figure 26–4).

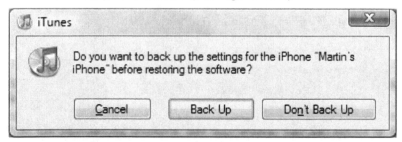

Figure 26–4. *Backing up before you restore in **iTunes***

6. On the next screen, you are warned that all data will be erased. Click
    Restore or **Restore and Update** to continue (see Figure 26–5).

Figure 26–5. *Backing up your iPhone in* **iTunes** *before a restore*

7. You will see an iPhone **Software Update** screen. Click **Next >** to
    continue.

8. Next, you will see the **Software License Agreement** screen. Click
    Agree to continue and start the process.

9. **iTunes** will download the latest iPhone software, back up and sync your
    iPhone, and then reinstall the iPhone software. This process completely
    erases all data and restores your iPhone to its original, "clean" state.
    You will see status messages at the top of **iTunes** similar to the one
    shown in Figure 26–6.

Figure 26–6. *The software update/restore process, with a status window at top of* **iTunes**

10. After the backup and sync, your iPhone screen will go black. Next, the
    Apple logo will appear, and you will see a status bar under the logo.
    Finally, a small pop-up window will appear in **iTunes** to tell you the
    update process is complete. Click **OK** to go to the **Set Up Your iPhone**
    screen. You will have a couple options at this point:

    a. If you want to keep your iPhone clean (i.e., without any of your
        personal data), then select the top option, **Set up as a new
        iPhone**. You might want to use this option if you are setting up this
        iPhone for someone else (you will need her Apple ID and
        password).

    b. If you are giving away or selling your iPhone, simply click the **Eject**
        icon next to the iPhone, and you're done (see Figure 26–7).

Figure 26–7. *Ejecting the iPhone if you are giving it away or selling it*

    c.   Select **Restore from the backup of:** and verify that the pull-down menu is set to the correct device.

11. Finally, click **Continue** (see Figure 26–8).

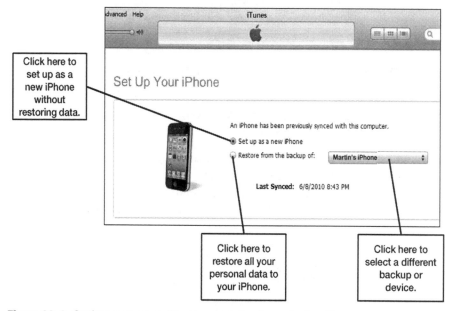

Figure 26–8. *Setting up as a new iPhone or restoring from a backup file*

12. If you chose to restore, then after a little while you will see a **Restore in Progress** screen on your iPhone and a status window in **iTunes** that says, "Restoring iPhone from backup..." This status window will also show a time estimate.

13. Next, you will see a little pop-up window saying, "The settings for your iPhone have been restored." In a few seconds, you will see your iPhone appear in the left nav bar under **DEVICES** in **iTunes**.

    a.   If you sync your information with **iTunes**, all data will be synced now.

    b.   If you use iCloud, Exchange, or another sync process, you will probably have to reenter passwords on your iPhone to get those sync processes back up and running.

Additional Troubleshooting and Help Resources

Sometimes you may encounter a particular issue or question that you cannot find an answer to in this book. In the following sections, we will provide some good resources that you can access from the iPhone and from your computer's web browser. The iPhone's on-device user guide is easy to navigate and can quickly provide you with the information you seek. The Apple knowledgebase is helpful if you are facing a troubleshooting problem that is proving especially difficult to resolve. The iPhone/iPod touch-related web blogs and forums are also good places to locate answers and even ask unique questions you might be facing.

On-Device iPhone User Guide

Follow these steps to access the on-device iPhone user guide:

1. Open your **Safari** web browser to view the online user guide for your iPhone.

2. Tap the **Bookmarks** button in the bottom row of icons.

3. Swipe to the bottom of the list and tap **iPhone User Guide**.

If you don't see that bookmark, then type this URL into **Safari**'s **Address** bar on your iPhone: http://help.apple.com/iPhone.

> **TIP:** To view the manual in PDF format from your computer, go to
> http://support.apple.com/manuals/iphone/.

Once you get to the user guide on your iPhone, you should see a screen similar to the one shown in Figure 26–9.

The nice thing is that you already know how to navigate the guide. Tap any topic to see more information about a topic—either another list of subtopics or more detailed information.

Read the topic or tap another link to learn more.

You can tap the button to the right of the screen to back out one level.

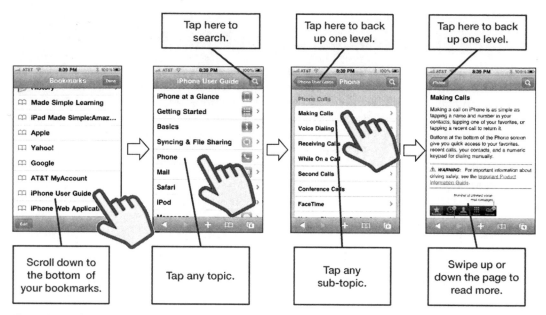

Figure 26–9. *Using the iPhone manual from **Safari** on your iPhone*

The Apple Knowledgebase

On your iPhone or computer's web browser, go to this web page:
www.apple.com/support/iphone/

Finally, click a topic in the left nav bar.

iPhone-Related Blogs

One of the great things about owning an iPhone is that you immediately join in the worldwide camaraderie of iPhone owners.

Many iPhone owners would be classified as *enthusiasts* and are part of any number of iPhone user groups. These user groups, along with various forums and web sites, serve as a great resource for iPhone users.

Many of these resources are available right from your iPhone, and others are web sites that you might want to visit on your computer.

Sometimes you might want to connect with other iPhone enthusiasts, ask a technical question, or keep up with the latest and greatest rumors. The blogs are a great place to do that.

Here are a few popular iPhone (and iPad or iPod touch) blogs:

- www.tipb.com
- www.iphonefreak.com
- www.gizmodo.com (iPhone section)

> **TIP**: Before you post a new question on any of these blogs, please do a search on the blog to make sure your question has not already been asked and answered. Also, make sure you are posting your question on the right section (e.g., iPhone) of the blog. Otherwise, you may incur the wrath of the community for not doing your homework first!

You can also do a web search for "iPhone blogs" or "iPhone news and reviews" to locate more blogs.

Index

■Special Characters and Numerics

"." shortcut, 87
+ (Plus Sign) button, 316, 476

■A

accessibility, 75–80
    Assistive Touch feature for, 53–54
    AssistiveTouch feature, 77–78
    magnifying entire screen with Zoom
        feature, 78–79
    options for Notification Center, 67
    setting Auto-Correction feature to
        speak aloud, 74
    Speak Selection and Speak
        Auto-text features, 77
    triple-click Home button options, 80
    TTY for deaf people, 235
    VoiceOver option, 75–77
    White on Black setting, 79–80
accessories, charging from, 40
Account screen, 269
Action button, 471, 477–478, 565
adapters, wall plug, 37
Add Event screen, 439
Add Playlist tab, 278
Airplane Mode setting, 146
Airplane Mode switch, 11–12
AirPlay, 157–167
    devices compatible with iPhone, 157
    Mirroring feature, 159, 548
    playing videos using, 334–335
    setting up, 157–159
    volume controls and, 182

AirPlay icon, 158, 166
Alarm widget, 186
albums
    for photos, 471
    viewing songs in, 280–282, 288–289
Albums icon, 277
Albums soft key, 8
Albums view, 280
Alert option, 441
alerts, 441
Allow Changes settings, 202
allowing changes, 202–203
Angry Birds, 543
AP Mobile app, 24
App Store, 18, 22, 523–539
    apps
        categories of, 531
        Details screen for, 527–528
        downloading, 534–535
        finding, 528–533
        Genius feature, 530–531
        maintaining and updating,
            535–537
        news and reviews about, 524
        searching for, 533
        Top Charts soft key, 532
    automatic downloads, 538
    Home page, 525–526
    network connection and, 525
    redeeming gift cards or iTunes
        codes, 535
    settings, 538–539
    starting, 525
App Store app, 30
App Store icon, 170
App Switcher bar, 4–5, 8

Apple ID, 46
Apple knowledgebase, 123, 580
Apple TV, viewing photos on, 480–481
Apply button, 465
appointments, 445–447
   events
      deleting, 447
      editing repeating, 446
      switching to different calendar,
        446
   meeting invitations, 447
   new, 438–439
   viewing and navigating, 433–434
apps
   AP Mobile app, 24
   App Store app, 30
   baseball app, 547–548
   Calendar app, 20, 431–458
      appointments, 445–447
      copying and pasting between
        email and, 443–445
      day and date on Calendar icon,
        433
      events, 438–443
      lists, 456–457
      multiple calendars, 436–437
      options for, 448–455
      reminders, 431–432, 455–458
      views, 434–436
   Camera app, 23, 460–466
      editing photos in, 465–466
      geo-tagging in, 461
      options for, 463
      switching cameras, 463–464
      using flash, 462
      viewing pictures from, 464
      zoom in, 462
   categories of, 531
   Contacts app, 20
   Details screen for, 527–528
   downloading, 534–535
   e-reader apps, alternative, 313–317
   Evernote app, 26
   FaceTime app, 20
   Fast App Switcher tool, 179–188
      accessing with Home button, 56

      apps, 180–181
      media controls and Portrait
        Orientation Lock feature, 181
      Siri app, 182–188
      volume controls and AirPlay
        feature, 182
   finding, 528–533
      viewing new apps, 529
      with What's Hot button, 529
   Folders app, 26
   Genius feature, 530–531
      Based On label, 530
      disabling, 531
      removing app suggestions from,
        531
   GoodReader app, 26
      connecting to Google Docs, 330
      PDF files in, 328–330
   Hulu + app, 30
   iBooks app, 22, 30
      downloading, 302
      downloading iBooks app, 302
      iBooks store, 302–305
      reading, 307–312
      Search button, 305
      syncing, 121–122
   iPod app, 8, 19, 22
   iTunes app, 505–521
      customizing soft keys in,
        507–508
      downloading content from,
        513–514
      in iCloud, 101–102
      Info tab, 109
      iPhone Summary tab, 107–108
      iTunes U section for educational
        content, 513
      media in, 508–513, 515–517
      navigating, 507
      and network connection, 506
      Ping social network, 521
      podcasts in, 518–520
      purchasing ringtones from,
        238–239
      redeeming codes in App Store,
        535

redeeming gift cards for, 520–521
searching, 514
setup with, 48–49
starting, 506
syncing, 105, 114–116, 118–119, 121–122
troubleshooting, 123–125, 573–574
updating iPhone operating system, 126–127
jumping between, 180
killing from Fast App Switcher bar, 180–181
Kindle app, 23
LinkedIn app, 25
LinkedIn social network, app for, 558–560
Mail app, 21
maintaining and updating, 535–537
Maps app, 21, 485–503
changing views in, 486–488
determining location, 486
Digital Compass feature, 503
getting directions with, 497–502
options for, 490–496, 502
searching, 488–489
Marvel Comics app, 23
Messages app, 21, 243–257
determining system currently in use, 244
iMessage service, 243–245
MMS, 253–257
text messages, 246–252
multiple accounts, in Notes app, 424–425
Music app, 276–279
changing view in, 280
editing soft keys, 277
playlists, 278–279
searching for music, 279
navigating inside, and settings screens, 55
New York Times app, 24, 322
news and reviews about, 524
Notes app, 26
NPR News app, 24

Pandora app, 22, 293–299
adjusting settings for, 298–299
main screen, 295–296
menu, 297
new stations in, 297–298
thumbs up or thumbs down, 296
Phone app, 20
Photos app, 23, 256
reference tables, 18
connecting and organizing, 20–21
entertainment, 22–23
information, 24
productivity, 26
social networking, 25
Reminders app, 431, 451, 456–457
restrictions for, 200–201
Rock Band app, 543
Safari app, 15, 20, 268
searching for, 533
Settings app, 9
settings screens, navigating inside apps and, 55
Siri app
capabilities of, 184–186
changing names and setting up relationships for, 186–187
enabling and configuring, 183
limitations of, 188
taking dictation, 188
Skype app, video calling with, 263–271
chatting, 269–270
on computer, 270–271
downloading, 264
finding and adding contacts to Skype app, 265–266
logging into Skype app, 265
receiving calls, 268–269
Skype account, 264
starting, 8
switching, 5
syncing
managing, 115–116
removing or reinstalling, 116
screen for, 114
Top Charts soft key, 532

Tweet Speaker app, 188
Twitter app, 25
Voice Control app, 20
Weather Channel app, 24
What's Hot button, finding apps
    with, 529
Wi-Fi option, Settings app, 12
Zinio app, 324–325
Arrow icon, 141, 564
Artists soft key, 8
Ask to Join Networks switch
    and Ask to Login switch on each
        network, 141
    main, 140
Ask to Login switch, Ask to Join
        Networks switch and, on each
        network, 141
Assign to Contact button, 478
Assistive Touch feature, for
        accessibility, 53–54
AssistiveTouch feature, 77–78
attachments, 385–391
    auto-open, 386–389
        opening docs in other apps, 388
        Quick Look mode, 386–387
        viewing video attachment, 389
    detecting, 385
    opening and viewing compressed
        .zip files, 389–391
Audio Source, 164
audiobooks, finding in iTunes app,
        512–513
Audiobooks icon, 277
Authentication feature, and SSL feature,
        403
auto-capitalization, auto-correction and,
        381
Auto-Capitalization option, 86, 197
auto-correction, and auto-capitalization,
        381
Auto-Correction feature, 72–74, 197
    setting to ON or OFF, 86
    setting to speak aloud, 74
Auto-Enhance button, 465
Auto-Lock feature, adjusting or
        disabling, 58

Auto-Lock menu, Settings app, 9
Auto-Lock option, Settings app, 9
auto-open attachments, 386–389
    opening docs in other apps, 388
    Quick Look mode, 386–387
    viewing video attachment, 389
AutoFill feature, 359–360
    enabling, 362–363
    entering usernames and passwords,
        359–360
    for personal information, 360
automatic-joining feature, 140–142
    Ask to Join Networks switch
        and Ask to Login switch on each
            network, 141
        main, 140
    Forget network option, 141–142

■ B

backups, restoring from previous, 49
Barnes and Noble reader, 301
baseball app, 547–548
Based On label, 530
batteries
    life of, 40–42
        charging battery, 41–42
        expected, 40–41
    packs, cases with external, 51
BCC (Blind Carbon Copy) recipients,
        377
blogs, as resource, 580–581
Bluetooth devices, connecting to
        headsets or car stereos, 208
Bluetooth technology, 160
    devices
        compatible with iPhone, 160
        disconnecting or forgetting, 167
        pairing with, 160–163
    headsets, 163–164
    Stereo Bluetooth, connecting to
        devices, 165–166
bookmarks, 491–492
    accessing and editing, 492
    in-page, 309–310
    new, 491

in Safari web browser, 350–354
  history and bookmarks, 351–352
  managing bookmarks, 352–354
  new bookmarks, 350–351
  Reading List bookmark, 354–355
syncing, 114
books, 301–317
  alternative e-reader apps, 313–317
    downloading, 314
    Kindle, 314–316
    Kobo, 317
  downloading iBooks app, 302
  iBooks store, 302–305
  moving and deleting, 313
  reading
    iBooks, 307–312
    PDFs, 306
  switching collections, 305–306
Bookshelf view, 304
Bottom Dock, moving icons to, 170–171
bottom icons, in YouTube, 340–341
brightness
  adjusting, 61
  and fonts, customizing for iBooks,
    307–308
Brightness icon, 308
Brightness slider, 308
buttons, 4
Buy pre-pay credit button, 269

C

Calendar app, 20, 431–458
  appointments, 445–447
    events, 446–447
    meeting invitations, 447
    viewing and navigating, 433–434
  copying and pasting between email
    and, 443–445
  day and date on Calendar icon, 433
  events, 438–443
    availability, 442
    calendars, 441–443
    new appointments, 438–439
    recurring, 440
    second alert, 441

lists
  moving and deleting, 457
  new, 456
multiple calendars, 436–437
options for, 448–455
  adding notes to task, 455
  changing default calendar, 449
  changing lists, 451
  reminders, 449–451
  setting due dates and locations,
    451
reminders
  completing, 455
  editing, 456
  options for, 457–458
  Siri assistant and, 431–432
  syncing and sharing your
    calendar and, 432
views, 434–436
Calendar button, 442, 446
Calendar icon, day and date on, 433
calendars
  adding notes to, 443
  changing default, 449
  choosing, 442
  multiple, 436–437
  sharing reminders and, 432
  switching events to different, 446
  syncing, 112, 432
Calendars button, 436
Call button, 267
call details, contact information details
    and, 215
Call Forwarding setting, 231–232
Call Waiting setting, 233
Caller ID, showing or blocking, 233
calling, video. See videos
Camera app, 23, 460–466
  editing photos in, 465–466
  geo-tagging in, 461
  options for, 463
  switching cameras, 463–464
  using flash, 462
  viewing pictures from, 464
  zoom in, 462
Camera icon, 564

Camera Roll album, 194
Camera Roll button, 272, 464
Camera Switch button, 271
cameras, quick access to, 54–55
Cannot Get Mail error, fixing, 370
Caps Lock feature, 85
car stereos, connecting to Bluetooth
    headsets or, 208
Carbon Copy (CC) recipients, 377
Carrier Services button, 236
carriers, wireless, 235
cases, 50
    with external battery packs, 51
    hard plastic and metal, 52
    leather and special, 52
    rubber and silicone, 51
    screen protectors, 52
    waterproof, 52
    where to buy, 51
Categories button, 303
categories, for videos, 332
Categories icon, 544
cautions, 31
CC (Carbon Copy) recipients, 377
cellular data networks, 142–143
chapters, for videos, 336
charging, 38–42
    from accessories, 40
    battery, 41–42
        extending life of, 42
        getting more out of, 41
        locations for, 42
    from computer, 39
    from power outlet, 38–39
Charts button, 303
chatting, with Skype app, 269–270
Checkmark icon, 136
Circle icon, 181, 457
closed captioning, for videos, 339
collections, switching, 305–306
comic books, 325–327
Compose button, in Twitter social
    network, 564
compressed files. See .zip files
computers, charging from, 39
conference calling, 228–230

    adding second caller, 228–229
    initiating, 228
    merging calls, 229–230
    talking privately with or
        disconnecting from individuals,
        230
Configure screen, 277
connections, 133–156
    Airplane Mode setting, 146
    benefits of, 133–134
    cellular data network, 142–143
    international travel, 144–150
        avoiding large bill, 144
        contacting phone company,
            144–145
        data-intensive activities, 146
        data roaming, 148–149
        international SIM card, 145–147
        local Wi-Fi networks, 149
        resetting data usage, 147–148
        time zone, 147–150
        turning off special rate plan, 150
    Personal Hotspot feature, 150–153
        connecting to, 153
        contacting phone company, 151
        enabling, 151–152
        setting up networking, 153
        vs. tethering, 150
    VPN, 153–156
        contacting help desk, 154
        setting up, 154–156
        switching networks, 156
        verifying connection, 156
    Wi-Fi network, 134–138
        advanced options for, 138–142
        connecting to, 135–138
Connections button, 560
Connectivity Status icons, reading,
    10–11
Constrain button, 466
contact information details, and call
    details, 215
Contact widget, 186
contacts
    adding new, 408–413
        creating new fields, 412–413

email addresses for, 411
from email message, 417–418
phone numbers for, 410
ringtones for, 411
street address for, 412
web site addresses for, 411
adding photo to, 413–414
assigning photos to, 478–479
assigning unique ringtones to, 237
composing text messages from, 250
finding and adding to Skype app,
265–266
Global Address List contacts
not showing up, 423
option for, 422
improving contact list, 408
linking to another app, 418
loading, 407
new from underlined phone number,
218
searching, 415–416
sending email message to, 420
sending picture to, 419
showing addresses on map,
420–421
sorting, 422
syncing, 110–111
with Google contacts, 110
with Yahoo! address book, 111
troubleshooting, 422–423
Contacts app, 20
Contacts list, 15
adding mapped locations to, 492
adding phone number from Recents
list to, 215
browsing, when on call, 222
placing calls from, 215–216
content, restrictions for, 204–206
controls
iPod, 8
in YouTube, 341–342
Copy and Paste feature, 90–94
App Switcher app and multitasking,
93
shaking to undo, 94

text
cutting or copying, 92
pasting, 93
selecting, 90–92
copying
and pasting from email, 395
photos, 477
saving and, text and graphics, 358
Cover Flow view, navigating albums
with, 281–282
Crop button, 466
cursors, placing, and editing text with
Magnifying Glass trick, 81
custom fields, for contacts, 412–413
customer reviews, in iTunes app, 516

D

data detectors, in notes, 429
data plans, texting plans and, 244
data roaming, 148–149
data usage, resetting, 147–148
Date and Time features, adjusting,
59–60
Day view, 433–434
deaf people, TTY for, 235
Default accounts, changing, 401
Default Calendar screen, 449
Default List screen, 458
definitions, in emails, 380
Delete Event button, 447
deleting
notes, 428
photos, 477–481
videos, 339
Details page, 451, 456
Details screen
for apps, 527–528
devices
Bluetooth technology
disconnecting or forgetting, 167
pairing with, 160–163
compatible with iPhone
AirPlay protocol, 157
Bluetooth technology, 160

pairing with
    headsets, 161–163
    turning on Bluetooth, 161
  Stereo Bluetooth, connecting to,
    165–166
dialing
  from Contacts list, 215–216
  from Favorites list, 213
  from keypad, 209
  person who left voicemail, 227
  from Recents list, 214
  underlined phone numbers, 217
  voice, with Siri assistant, 218
dictation, taking with Siri app, 188
dictionaries, built-in, 309
Digital Compass feature, 503
directions, getting with Maps app,
    497–502
  driving, transit, and walking
    directions, 501
  locations, 497–499
  routes, 501–502
Done button, 277
double-tapping, 17, 473
downloads
  automatic, 538
  of photos, 482–483
  viewing, 519–520
  of wallpapers, 193–194
drafts, saving to send later, 382
driving directions, and transit and
    walking directions, 501
due dates, setting locations and, 451

■E

e-reader apps, alternative, 313–317
  downloading e-reader apps, 314
  Kindle reader, 314–316
  Kobo reader, 317
Edit button, 277, 313, 436, 445, 456
editing notes, 427
educational content, iTunes U section
    for, 513

email, 32, 365–405
  accounts
    entering passwords for, 366
    new, 367–370
    syncing, 113
  adding new contact from message,
    417–418
  addresses, for contacts, 411
  attachments, 385–391
    auto-open, 386–389
    detecting, 385
    opening and viewing compressed
    .zip files, 389–391
  changing incoming server port, 404
  cleaning up and organizing inbox,
    393–394
    deleting, 393–394
    moving email to folder while
    viewing, 394
  composing and sending, 375–383
    addressing messages, 376–378
    auto-correction and auto-
    capitalization, 381
    changing email account, 378
    checking sent messages, 383
    keyboard options, 381
    message, 379–380
    saving draft to send later, 382
    subject, 379
  copying and pasting between
    Calendar app and, 443–445
  copying and pasting from, 395
  deleting
    removing messages after, 403
    from server, 403–404
  folders and mailboxes, 371–373
  Mailboxes screen, inboxes and
    accounts, 371
  messages
    inbox, flagged and threaded,
    373–374
    viewing individual, 374
  network connections and, 365
  reading, 383–385
    marking messages as unread or
    flagged, 384–385

zooming, 385
replying, forwarding, and deleting,
    391–393
    Forward button, 392–393
    Reply All option, 392
searching for messages, 396
sending
    from Contacts app, 420
    notes, 429
    photos, 476
    web pages, 357
settings for, 397–402
    adjusting, 399–400
    automatically retrieving email with
        Fetch New Data option, 397–
        398
    changing Default account, 401
    email signature, 400
    toggling sounds for receiving and
        sending email, 402
SSL and Authentication features,
    403
troubleshooting problems with,
    404–405
End location, Start location and,
    498–499
End Repeat button, 440
Enter Password screen, 136
entertainment, 22–23
EQ (Equalization) setting, for sound, 290
events, 438–443
    adding new appointment, 438–439
    availability, 442
    calendars
        adding notes to, 443
        alerts, 441
        choosing, 442
    deleting, 447
    editing repeating, 446
    recurring, 440
    second alert, 441
    switching to different calendar, 446
Evernote app, 26
Explicit option, 204

F

Facebook icon, 556–557
Facebook social network, 551–557
    app for, 553–555
        communicating with friends, 554
        navigating, 554
        uploading pictures with, 555
    connecting to, 552
    downloading and installing app, 552
    notifications, 556–557
FaceTime app, 20
FaceTime feature, 29, 260–262
FaceTime video calls, 223
factory defaults, resetting icon locations
    to, 174
Fast App Switcher tool, 179–188
    accessing with Home button, 56
    apps
        jumping between, 180
        killing from Fast App Switcher
            bar, 180–181
    media controls and Portrait
        Orientation Lock feature, 181
    Siri app, 182
        capabilities of, 184–186
        changing names and setting up
            relationships for, 186–187
        enabling and configuring, 183
        limitations of, 188
        taking dictation, 188
    volume controls and AirPlay feature,
        182
Fast Forward button, 181
fast-forwarding, videos, 333–334
Favorites button, 564
Favorites list, 210–213
    adding new favorites to, 210–212
    organizing, 212–213
Fetch New Data option, automatically
    retrieving email with, 397–398
fields, custom, for contacts, 412–413
first-person shooters (FPS), 543
flagged messages
    inboxes, threaded messages and,
        373–374
    overview, 384–385

flash, in Camera app, 462
flicking, 14, 416
folders, 175–176
    and mailboxes, 371–373
    moving, 176
    moving email to while viewing, 394
    new, 175
Folders app, 26
Following button, 564
fonts, brightness and, 307–308
Forget network option, 141–142
Forget this Device button, 167
formatting text, in emails, 380
Forward button, 392–393
four-digit passcode, passcodes,
        197–198
FPS (first-person shooters), 543
FREE button, 558

G

Game Center, restrictions for, 206
games, 541–548
    acquiring fun apps and, 543–544
    baseball app, 547–548
    online and wireless, 546
    precautions when playing, 545
    reviews for, 545
    trial or Lite versions of, 545
    two-player, 546
Games tab, 544
General button, Settings app, 9
General option, Settings app, 9
Genius feature, 530–531
    Based On label, 530
    disabling, 531
    removing app suggestions from, 531
Genius Playlist, 278, 289
Genres categories, 509
geo-tagging, in Camera app, 461
gestures, 13
Get a subscription button, 269
Get Skype for Mac button, 271
Get Skype for Windows button, 271
Get Skype link, 271

gift cards
    for iTunes app, redeeming, 520–521
    redeeming in App Store, 535
Global Address List contacts
    not showing up, 423
    option for, 422
GoodReader app, 26
    connecting to Google Docs, 330
    PDF files in, 328–330
Google contacts, syncing contacts with,
        110
Google Docs, connecting to with
        GoodReader, 330
Google Maps, 489
graphics, text and, 358
greetings, voicemail, 226
Grid option, 463
Gripper icon, 457
Groups screen, 266
groups, searching contacts using, 416

H

hard-resetting iPhone, 570
headsets, 36–37, 208
    Bluetooth technology, 163–164
        options when on call, 164
        pairing with, 161–163
    connecting to Bluetooth car stereos
        or, 208
Hide Sources, 163
highlighting, and notes, 310–311
history
    and bookmarks, in Safari web
        browser, 351–352
    in YouTube, 343
Hold button, 261
hold, putting caller on, 221
Home button, 3–5, 13, 19–20, 55–56
    accessing Fast App Switcher with,
        56
    double-clicking for media controls,
        285
    starting Siri assistant with, 56
    triple-click options for, 80
Home key, 172

Home page, for App Store, 525–526
home screen, 5
 adding web page icons to, 361
 wallpapers for, 189–193
Home Sharing, 291
hotspots, public Wi-Fi, connecting to
 network with web login,
 135–136
Hulu + app, 30

I

iBooks app, 22, 30
 downloading, 302
 downloading iBooks app, 302
 iBooks store, 302–305
 reading, 307–312
  built-in dictionary, 309
  customizing brightness and fonts,
   307–308
  highlighting and notes, 310–311
  in-page bookmark, 309–310
  search feature, 312
 Search button, 305
 syncing, 121–122
iBooks icon, 172
iCloud, 97
 buying more storage, 101
 on computer, 102–103
 iTunes In, 101–102
 managing, 99
 restoring phone with, 47–48
 setting up, 98–99
 setup with, 43–48
  configuring options for, 47
  free Apple ID, 46
  as new iPhone, 45
  restoring with, 47–48
 troubleshooting, syncing with, 574
icons, 169–176
 Connectivity Status, reading, 10–11
 deleting, 172–173
 moving
  to Bottom Dock, 170–171
  to different page, 171–172

resetting locations to factory
 defaults, 174
web page, adding to Home screen,
 361
I'm Reading button, 317
iMessage service
 enabling and adjusting settings, 245
 text messages and MMS vs.,
  243–244
 texting and data plans, 244
iMessages, 185
in-app notifications, 63
in-page bookmarks, 309–310
inboxes
 cleaning up and organizing, 393–394
  deleting, 393–394
  moving email to folder while
   viewing, 394
 and email accounts, 371
 and flagged and threaded
  messages, 373–374
incoming server ports, changing, 404
incoming servers, and outgoing servers,
 368–369
Infinity Blade game, 543
Info tab, in iTunes, 109
information, 24
Information icon, 548
international keyboards, 87–90
international SIM cards, 145, 147
international travel, 144–150
 avoiding large bill, 144
 contacting phone company, 144–
  145
 data-intensive activities, 146
 data roaming, 148–149
 international SIM card, 145, 147
 local Wi-Fi networks, 149
 resetting data usage, 147–148
 time zone, correcting, 147–150
 turning off special rate plan, 150
Internet connections, and Safari web
 browser, 346
invitations, to meetings, 447
iPhone Summary tab, in iTunes,
 107–108

iPod app, 8, 19, 22
iPod controls, 8
iPod icon, 8
iTunes app, 505–521
    customizing soft keys in, 507–508
    downloading content from, 513–514
    in iCloud, 101–102
    Info tab, 109
    iPhone Summary tab, 107–108
    iTunes U section for educational
        content, 513
    media in, 508–513, 515–517
        audiobooks, 512–513
        customer reviews, 516
        music, 509
        previewing, 515–516
        purchasing, 517
        TV shows, 511
        videos, 510
    navigating, 507
    and network connection, 506
    Ping social network, 521
    podcasts in, 518–520
        downloading, 518–520
        stopping and deleting, 519
    purchasing ringtones from, 238–239
    redeeming codes in App Store, 535
    redeeming gift cards for, 520–521
    searching, 514
    setup with, 48–49
    starting, 506
    syncing
        apps, 114–116
        bookmarks, 114
        calendar, 112
        contacts, 110–111
        email accounts, 113
        iBooks, 121–122
        movies, 118–119
        with multiple devices, 105
        music, 117–118
        notes, 114
        other options for, 105
        photos, 122–123
        Podcasts, 120–121
        requirements, 104

        ringtones, 117
        tv shows, 119–120
    troubleshooting, 123–125
        iPhone not recognized, 573–574
        iTunes locked up and will not
            respond (Mac computer), 125
        iTunes locked up and will not
            respond (Windows computer),
            124
        syncing with, 574
        using Apple knowledgebase, 123
    updating iPhone operating system,
        126–127

J

Join link, 270

K

keyboards, 86–87
    "." shortcut, 87
    Auto-Capitalization option, 86
    enabling Caps Lock feature, 87
    international, 87–90
    options for, 197, 381
    press and hold shortcut, 84
    setting Auto-Correction feature to
        ON or OFF, 86
keypads
    dialing from, 209
    when on call, 220
keys, 4
Kindle app, 23
Kindle books, 22
Kindle reader, 301, 313–316
Kobo reader, 301, 313–314, 317

L

Landscape mode, 30
Large Text feature, 80
Last.fm, 294
leather cases, 52
letters, typing uppercase, 83
Library button, 303, 307

LinkedIn app, 25
LinkedIn icon, 559
LinkedIn social network, app for, 558–560
    communicating with connections, 560
    downloading, 558–560
    logging in to, 559
    navigating, 559
links, activating from web pages, 350
List button, 280–281, 283, 435
List mode, music library, 14
List tab, 317
lists
    changing, 451, 458
    moving and deleting, 457
    new, 456
Lite versions, of games, 545
loading photos, onto iPhone, 466–469
Location option, 202
locations
    determining, 486
    directions from current, 497
    mapped, adding to Contacts list, 492
    setting due dates and, 451
    Start and End, 498–499
Lock screen
    notifications on, 62–63
    wallpapers for, 189–193
Lock Volume Limit button, 291

M

magazines, 323–325
Magnifying Glass search icon, 560
Magnifying Glass trick, editing text and placing cursor with, 81
Mail app, 21
Mail icon, 560
mailboxes, folders and, 371–373
Mailboxes screen, inboxes and accounts, 371
maintenance, 50–52
    cases, 50
        with external battery packs, 51

        hard plastic and metal, 52
        leather and special, 52
        rubber and silicone, 51
        screen protectors, 52
        waterproof, 52
        where to buy, 51
    cleaning screen, 50
Maps app, 21, 485–503
    changing views in, 486–488
    determining location, 486
    Digital Compass feature, 503
    getting directions with, 497–502
        driving, transit, and walking, 501
        locations, 497–499
        routes, 499–502
    options for, 490–496, 502
        adding mapped location to Contacts list, 492
        bookmarks, 491–492
        dropping pin, 494–495
        searching for nearby establishments, 493
        Street View, 496
        zooming, 494
    searching, 488–489
maps, showing contact addresses on, 420–421
Marvel Comics app, 23
media
    controls
        double-clicking Home button for, 285
        and Portrait Orientation Lock feature, 181
        showing when locked, 293
    in iTunes app, 508–513, 515–517
        audiobooks, 512–513
        customer reviews, 516
        music, 509
        previewing, 515–516
        purchasing, 517
        TV shows, 511
        videos, 510
    quick access to, 54–55
meetings, invitations to, 447
menus, 9

merging, conference calls, 229–230

Message viewing screen, deleting email from, 393–394

Messages app, 21, 243–257
  determining system currently in use, 244
  iMessage service
    enabling and adjusting settings, 245
    text messages and MMS vs., 243–244
    texting and data plans, 244
  MMS, 253–257
  text messages, 246–252
    composing, 246–250
    options after sending, 248–249
    replying to, 250
    tone and sound options for, 252
    viewing stored, 251

metal cases, hard plastic cases and, 52

Microphone icon, 184

MicroSIM, 147

Microsoft Exchange, troubleshooting, 574

MiniSIM, 147

Minus button, 316

mirroring, AirPlay Mirroring feature, 548

Mirroring feature, of AirPlay protocol, 159

MMS (Multimedia Messaging Service), 253–257
  pictures
    choosing from Photos app to send via Messages app, 256
    sending multiple, 257
    sending video and, 253–255
  and text messages vs. iMessage service, 243–244

Month button, 435, 451

Month view, 435, 451

More soft key, 8

More tab, 291

movies, syncing, 118–119

Multimedia Messaging Service. *See* MMS

multiple accounts, in Notes app, 424–425

multiple devices, syncing, 105

multitasking
  Fast App Switcher tool, 179–188
    apps, 180–181
      media controls and Portrait Orientation Lock feature, 181
      Siri app, 182–188
      volume controls and AirPlay feature, 182
  overview, 5

music, 275–299
  adjusting settings for, 289–293
    EQ for sound equalization, 290
    Home Sharing, 291
    showing media controls when locked, 293
    Sound Check feature for auto volume adjust, 290
    Volume Limit, 291
  finding in iTunes app
    Genres categories, 509
    Top Tens categories, 509
  Music app, 276–279
    changing view in, 280
    editing soft keys, 277
    playlists, 278–279
    searching for music, 279
  Pandora app, 293–299
    adjusting settings for, 298–299
    main screen, 295–296
    menu, 297
    new stations in, 297–298
    thumbs up or thumbs down, 296
  playing, 275, 283–289
    adjusting volume, 284
    double-clicking Home button for media controls, 285
    Now Playing option, 288
    pausing and, 283
    Shuffle option, 287–288
    songs, 284–289
  previewing, 515
  searching for, 279

syncing, 117–118
viewing songs in album, 280–282
Music app, 276–279
    changing view in, 280
    editing soft keys, 277
    playlists, 278–279
    searching for music, 279
Music Genome Project, 293
Music screen, 278
music videos, watching, 338
Mute button, 262
muting, when on call, 220

■N

Name field, 175
navigating, newspapers, 323
network connections
    and App Store, 525
    email and, 365
    iTunes app and, 506
networks
    Ask to Join Networks switch
        and Ask to Login switch on each
            network, 141
        main, 140
    Ask to Login switch, Ask to Join
        Networks switch and, on each
        network, 141
    cellular data networks, 142–143
    Compose button, in Twitter social
        network, 564
    Facebook social network, 551–557
        app for, 553–555
        connecting to, 552
        downloading and installing app,
            552
        notifications, 556–557
    Forget network option, 141–142
    hotspots, public Wi-Fi, connecting to
        network with web login, 135–
        136
    LinkedIn social network, app for,
        558–560
        communicating with connections,
            560

downloading, 558–560
        logging in to, 559
        navigating, 559
    network connections
        and App Store, 525
        email and, 365
        iTunes app and, 506
    Ping social network, 521
    profiles, in Twitter social network,
        564
    social networking, 25
    Social Networking category, 552
    Twitter social network, 560–565
        Compose button, 564
        profile in, 564
        tweets, 563, 565
    undiscoverable, 139
    undiscoverable networks, 139
    Virtual Private Networks. See VPNs
    VPNs, 153–156
        contacting help desk, 154
        setting up, 154–156
        switching networks, 156
        verifying connection, 156
    Wi-Fi networks, 134–138
        advanced options for, 138–142
        connecting to, 135–138
        local, 149
New and Notable section, 544
New Tweet screen, 564
New York Times app, 24, 322
newspapers, 321–323
    navigating, 323
    New York Times app, 322
Newsstand folder, 319–330
    comic books, 325–327
    magazines, 323–325
    newspapers, 321–323
        navigating, 323
        New York Times app, 322
    overview, 319–320
    subscribing to periodicals, 320
Next Song arrow, 284
Next Song control, 285
Next Track button, 181

notes, 31, 423–429
  adding new, 426
  data detectors in, 429
  deleting, 428
  editing, 427
  emailing, 429
  highlighting and, for iBooks,
      310–311
  multiple accounts for, 424–425
  printing, 429
  sorting of, 425
  syncing, 114–424
  titles for, 426
  viewing, 427
  voice dictation for, 428
Notes app, 26
Notification Center, 64–65
  accessibility options for, 67
  configuring, 65–67
notifications, 61–62
  in Facebook social network,
      556–557
  in-app, 63
  on Lock screen, 62–63
Now Playing icon, 288, 295
Now Playing option, 288
Now Playing screen, 288
NPR News app, 24
numbers
  rapidly typing single, 83
  typing symbols and, 82–84
    press and hold keyboard
        shortcut, 84
    touch and slide trick, 83

O

online games, and wireless games, 546
Open Pages button, 349
options
  for Camera app, 463
  for Global Address List contacts,
      422
  for keyboard, 197
  for passcodes, 199
  for videos, 338–339

  closed captioning, 339
  start playing option, 339
orientation
  portrait, locking screens in, 58
  Portrait Orientation Lock feature, 181
outgoing servers, incoming servers and,
    368–369

P

pairing, with Bluetooth technology
    devices
  headsets, 161–163
  turning on Bluetooth, 161
Pandora app, 22, 293–299
  adjusting settings for, 298–299
  main screen, 295–296
  menu, 297
  new stations in, 297–298
  thumbs up or thumbs down, 296
Paperclip icon, 565
Passcode Lock screen, 198
passcodes, 197–199
  complex password as, 198
  four-digit passcode, 197–198
  options for, 199
passwords
  changing for voicemail, 225
  entering for email accounts, 366
  entering for secure Wi-Fi network,
      136
  entering usernames and, for AutoFill
      feature, 359–360
  as passcodes, 198
pasting, and copying from email, 395
pausing, songs, 283
PDFs (Portable Document Format)
  in GoodReader, 328–330
  reading, 306
period shortcut, 87
periodicals, subscribing to, 320
Personal Hotspot feature, 150–153
  connecting to, 153
  contacting phone company, 151
  enabling, 151–152
  setting up networking, 153

vs. tethering, 150
personalization
    keyboard, 197
    sounds, 195–196
    wallpapers
        downloading through apps,
            193–194
        for home screen, 189–193
        for lock screen, 189–193
phone, 207–241
    companies
        contacting regarding international
            travel, 144–145
        contacting regarding Personal
            Hotspot feature, 151
    conference calling, 228–230
        adding second caller, 228–229
        initiating, 228
        merging calls, 229–230
        talking privately with or
            disconnecting from individuals,
            230
    features of, 207–217
        dialing from keypad, 209
        Favorites list, 210–213
        headsets, 208
        phone numbers, 207–217
        phone views, 210
        placing calls from Contacts list,
            215–216
        Recents list, 214–215
    functions while on call, 218–223
        browsing Contacts list, 222
        FaceTime video call, 223
        keypad, 220
        muting, 220
        putting caller on hold, 221
        speakerphone, 221
    new contact from underlined phone
        number, 218
    numbers
        adding to Contacts list from
            Recents list, 215
        for contacts, 410
        finding own, 207
        underlined, 217–218

options for, 231–236
    Call Forwarding setting, 231–232
    Call Waiting setting, 233
    Carrier Services button, 236
    security on SIM card, 233–234
    showing or blocking Caller ID,
        233
    switching between wireless
        carriers, 235
    TTY for deaf people, 235
ringtones
    assigning unique to contacts, 237
    custom, 239–241
    purchasing from iTunes app,
        238–239
    sounds, vibration and, 237
voice dialing with Siri assistant, 218
voicemail, 223–227
    changing password for, 225
    deleting messages, 227
    playing, 226–227
    setting up, 224–225
Phone app, 20
Phone icon, 560
phone voice, playback and, volume
        keys for, 57
Photo tab, 467
photos, 459–483
    adding to contacts, 413–414
    assigning to contact, 478–479
    Camera app, 460–466
        editing photos in, 465–466
        geo-tagging in, 461
        options for, 463
        switching cameras, 463–464
        using flash, 462
        viewing pictures from, 464
        zoom in, 462
    choosing from Photos app to send
        via Messages app, 256
    copying, 477
    deleting, 477, 480–481
    downloading, 482–483
    emailing, 476
    loading onto iPhone, 466–469
    moving between, 473

printing, 477
sending
    from Contacts app, 419
    multiple, 257
    video and, with Messages app,
        253–255
sharing, 477
shortcuts for taking, 459–460
syncing, 122–123
tweeting, 476
uploading with Facebook app, 555
viewing, 469–471
    albums, 471
    from Photos icon, 470
    slideshows, 475
viewing on Apple TV, 480–481
wallpaper as, 476
zooming, 473–474
    by double-tapping, 473
    by pinching, 474
Photos app, 23, 256
Photos icon, viewing photos from, 470
pictures. *See* photos
Pimp Your Screen icon, 193
pinching
    overview, 17
    zooming photos by, 474
Ping social network, 521
pins, dropping, 494–495
plastic cases, and metal cases, 52
Play/Pause button, 284
playback, and phone voice, 57
playing
    Now Playing option, 288
    Shuffle option, 287–288
        Shake to Shuffle feature,
            287–288
    songs
        moving to another part of, 286
        repeating, 286–287
        viewing others on album,
            288–289
    videos, 332–336
        changing size of video, 334
        fast-forwarding, 333–334
        rewinding, 333–334

using AirPlay, 334–335
using chapters, 336
using time scrubber bar, 334
in YouTube, 341
playlists, 278–279
Playlists view, 278
Plus Sign (+) button, 316, 476
Podcasts, 518–520
downloading
    overview, 518–519
    viewing downloads, 519–520
stopping and deleting, 519
syncing, 120–121
watching, 337
Portable Document Format. *See* PDFs
Portrait Orientation Lock feature, media
    controls and, 181
portrait orientation, locking screens in,
    58
Portrait Screen Rotation Lock, 8
Power button, 12
power cables, 37
power key, 19
power outlets, charging from, 38–39
Power/Sleep button, 4, 19, 190
powering, and Sleep mode, 53
press and hold keyboard shortcut, 84
Previous Song button, 284
Previous Song control, 285
Previous Track button, 181
Price button, 304
printing
    notes, 429
    photos, 477
    web pages, 357
privacy options, for Safari web browser,
    363
productivity, 26
profiles, in Twitter social network, 564
Purchases button, 303
Push Notifications warning message,
    553
push options, advanced, 398

Q

Quick Look mode, 386–387
quick start guide, 31
QuickMix, 295
quoting text, in emails, 380

R

Raise to Speak option, 183–184
Reader feature, 355
reading
    iBooks, 307–312
        built-in dictionary, 309
        customizing brightness and fonts,
            307–308
        highlighting and notes, 310–311
        in-page bookmark, 309–310
        search feature, 312
    PDFs, 306
Reading List bookmark, 354–355
Real Racing menu, 546
Recents list, 214–215
    adding phone number to Contacts
        list from, 215
    call and contact information details,
        215
    clearing all, 214
    placing call from, 214
recipients
    CC or BCC, 377
    deleting, 377
    moving, 378
recording
    video, 271–273
        focusing, 272
        sending, 273
        trimming, 272–273
Red-Eye button, 465
reference tables, 18
    connecting and organizing, 20–21
    entertainment, 22–23
    information, 24
    productivity, 26
    social networking, 25

reinstalling
    apps, in iTunes, 116
    iPhone operating system, 575–578
Reminder widget, 186
reminders, 449
    completing, 455
    details of, 451
    editing, 456
    new, 451
    options for, 457–458
    recurring, 451
    Siri assistant and, 431–432
    syncing and sharing your calendar
        and, 432
    views, 450–451
Reminders app, 431, 451, 456–457
removing apps, in iTunes, 116
Repeat symbol, 287
Repeat tab, 440, 451
Reply All option, 392
resources
    Apple knowledgebase, 580
    blogs, 580–581
    on-device user guide, 579
restoring
    with iCloud service, 47–48
    from previous backup, 49
restrictions, 199–206
    allowing changes, 202–203
    for apps, 200–201
    for content, 204–206
    for Game Center, 206
Restrictions button, 200, 204, 206
Rewind button, 181
rewinding videos, 333–334
ringers, volume keys for, 57
ringtones
    assigning unique to contacts, 237
    for contacts, 411
    custom, 239–241
        free approach to, 239–241
        syncing, 241
    purchasing from iTunes app,
        238–239
    sounds, vibration and, 237
    syncing, 117

roaming, data, 148–149
Rock Band app, 543
Rotate button, 465
routes
    looking at, 499–500
    reversing, 502
    switching between, 501
rubber cases, and silicone cases, 51

■ **S**

Safari app, 15, 20, 268
Safari web browser, 345–364
    adding web page icon to Home
        screen, 361
    adjusting settings for, 361–364
        changing search engines, 362
        enabling AutoFill feature, 362–
            363
        privacy options, 363
        security options, 364
    AutoFill feature, 359–360
        entering usernames and
            passwords, 359–360
        for personal information, 360
    bookmarks, 350–354
        history and, 351–352
        managing, 352–354
        new, 350–351
        Reading List, 354–355
    and Internet connections, 346
    launching, 346–347
    Open Pages button, 349
    Reader feature, 355
    saving and copying text and
        graphics, 358
    screen layout of, 347
    typing web address, 348
    watching videos in, 357–358
    web pages
        activating links from, 350
        emailing or tweeting, 357
        jumping to top of, 356
        moving through open, 348–349
        printing, 357
        zooming in, 349–350

saving, text and graphics, 358
screen protectors, 52
Screen Rotation Lock button, 8
screens
    cleaning, 50
    locking, in portrait orientation, 58
    Portrait Orientation Lock feature, 181
scrolling, 16
Search button, for iBooks store, 305
search engines, changing, 362
search feature, for iBooks, 312
Search window, 265, 558
searching
    for apps, 533
    contacts, 415–416
        by flicking, 416
        jumping to letter, 416
        using groups, 416
    iTunes app, 514
    with Maps app, 488–489
    for nearby establishments, 493
    Spotlight Search feature, 94–96
        activating, 95
        customizing, 96
        Search Web and Search
            Wikipedia options, 96
    videos, 332–333
    YouTube, 340
Second Alert option, 441
Secure Sockets Layer (SSL) feature,
        and Authentication feature, 403
security
    passcodes, 197–199
        complex password, 198
        four-digit passcode, 197–198
        options for, 199
    restrictions, 199–206
        allowing changes, 202–203
        for apps, 200–201
        for content, 204–206
        for Game Center, 206
    for Safari web browser, 364
    on SIM card, 233–234
server ports, changing incoming, 404
servers, deleting email from, 403–404
Set Home Screen button, 191

Set Lock Screen button, 191
Settings app, 9
Settings button, 317
Settings icon, 12, 135, 137, 141, 143,
        149, 151, 154, 156, 165
settings screens, navigating inside apps
        and, 55
setup, 43
    determining need for, 43
    with iCloud service, 43–48
        configuring options for, 47
        free Apple ID, 46
        as new iPhone, 45
        restoring with, 47–48
    with iTunes app, 48–49
        from previous backup, 49
Shake to Shuffle feature, 287–288
Shared tab, 291
sharing, photos, 477
Shelf view, 317
Shortcovers, 301, 314
shortcuts
    for taking photos, 459–460
    typing quick phrases with, 71
Shuffle option, Shake to Shuffle feature,
        287–288
Sign In button, 265
Sign In link, 268
signatures, email, 380–400
silicone cases, rubber cases and, 51
SIM (Subscriber Identity Module) cards
    international, 145, 147
    removing or installing, 37
    security on, 233–234
Simple Passcode option, 198
Siri app, 182–188
    capabilities of, 184–186
    changing names and setting up
        relationships for, 186–187
    enabling and configuring, 183
    limitations of, 188
    taking dictation, 188
Siri assistant
    and reminders, 431–432
    starting with Home button, 56
    voice dialing with, 218

size of video, changing, 334
Skype app, video calling with, 263–271
    chatting, 269–270
    on computer, 270–271
    downloading, 264
    finding and adding contacts to
        Skype app, 265–266
    logging into Skype app, 265
    receiving calls, 268–269
    Skype account, 264
Skype Credits, or monthly subscription,
        268–269
Skype icon, 170–171
Slacker Personal Radio, 294
Sleep mode, powering and, 53
Slide To Unlock screen, and quick
        camera and media access,
        54–55
Slideshow Play button, 475
slideshows, viewing, 475
SMS message, 179
social networking, 25
Social Networking category, 552
social networks, 551–565
    Facebook, 551–557
        app for, 553–555
        connecting to, 552
        notifications, 556–557
    LinkedIn, 558–560
    Ping, 521
    Twitter, 560–565
        Compose button, 564
        profile in, 564
        tweets, 563–565
soft keys, 8
    customizing, in iTunes app, 507–508
    editing, 277
soft-resetting iPhone, 570–571
songs
    locating for free custom ringtones,
        239–241
    moving to another part of, 286
    playing previous or next, 284
    repeating, 286–287
    viewing in album, 280–282, 288–289
Songs screen, 279

sorting
  contacts, 422
  notes, 425
Sound Check feature, for auto volume
    adjust, 290
sounds
  changing, 195–196
  EQ setting for, 290
  ringtones, vibration and, 237
  toggling for receiving and sending
    email, 402
  and tones for text messages, 252
Speak Auto-text feature, Speak
    Selection feature and, 77
Speak option, in emails, 380
Speak Selection feature, and Speak
    Auto-text feature, 77
Speaker icon, 163–164
speakerphone, when on call, 221
speakers, playing voicemail through,
    226
Spell Checker feature, 74
Spotify, 294
SSL (Secure Sockets Layer) feature,
    and Authentication feature, 403
Stanza reader, 301
Start location, and End location,
    498–499
start playing option, for videos, 339
Stereo Bluetooth, 158, 160, 165–166
storage, buying more for iCloud, 101
Store button, 302
street address, for contacts, 412,
    420–421
Street View, 496
subjects, email, 379
submenus, 9
Subscriber Identity Module cards. *See*
    SIM
subscriptions
  monthly, to Skype app, 268–269
  to periodicals, 320
swapping icons, 171
swiping, 15–17
  double-tapping, 17
  pinching, 17

scrolling, 16
Switch Camera button, 262, 464
switches, 4–9
switching apps, 5
switching cameras, 463–464
symbols, typing numbers and, 82–84
  press and hold keyboard shortcut,
    84
  touch and slide trick, 83
syncing
  apps
    managing, 115–116
    removing or reinstalling, 116
    screen for, 114
  bookmarks, 114
  calendar, 112
  contacts, 110–111
    with Google contacts, 110
    with Yahoo! address book, 111
  email accounts, 113
  iBooks, 121–122
  movies, 118–119
  with multiple devices, 105
  music, 117–118
  notes, 114–424
  other methods, 127–131
    setting up Exchange account,
      128–131
    setting up Google account,
      128–131
  other options for, 105
  photos, 122–123
  Podcasts, 120–121
  requirements for, 104
  ringtones, 117
  troubleshooting, 123–125, 574
    iTunes locked up and will not
      respond (Mac computer), 125
    iTunes locked up and will not
      respond (Windows computer),
      124
    using Apple knowledgebase, 123
    using iCloud, 574
    using iTunes, 574
    using Microsoft Exchange, 574
  tv shows, 119–120

T

Table of Contents button, 307
Take Photo or Video button, 555
tapping, 14
tasks, adding notes to, 455
tethering, Personal Hotspot feature vs., 150
text
  editing and placing cursor with Magnifying Glass trick, 81
  formatting, in emails, 380
  and graphics, saving and copying, 358
  quickly selecting and deleting or changing, 85
  quoting in emails, 380
text messages, 246–252
  composing, 246
    from contacts, 250
    from Messages app, 246–248
  and MMS vs. iMessage service, 243–244
  options after sending, 248–249
  replying to, 250
  tone and sound options for, 252
  viewing stored, 251
Text Telephone Devices (TTYs), for deaf people, 235
texting plans, and data plans, 244
threaded messages, inboxes, 373–374
time scrubber bar, for videos, 334
time zones, correcting
  on arrival, 147
  when returning home, 150
Title Page button, 311
titles, for notes, 426
tones, and sound options for text messages, 252
Top Charts soft key, 532
Top status bar, 10
Top Tens categories, 509
touch and slide trick, 83
  rapidly typing single number, 83
  typing uppercase letters, 83
touch screen, gestures, 13
traffic, checking, 488

transit directions, and driving and walking directions, 501
Trash Can icon, 480–481
trial versions, of games, 545
troubleshooting, 567–581
  cannot purchase from iTunes or app store, 573
  contacts, 422–423
  hard-resetting iPhone, 570
  iPhone stops responding, 567–569
  iTunes, 123–125
    iPhone not recognized, 573–574
    iTunes locked up and will not respond (Mac computer), 125
    iTunes locked up and will not respond (Windows computer), 124
    using Apple knowledgebase, 123
  no sound, 571–572
  reinstalling iPhone operating system, 575–578
  resources for
    Apple knowledgebase, 580
    blogs, 580–581
    on-device user guide, 579
  soft-resetting iPhone, 570–571
  syncing, 574
TTYs (Text Telephone Devices), for deaf people, 235
tv shows
  finding in iTunes app, 511
  previewing videos and, 516
  syncing, 119–120
  watching, 336–337
Tweet Speaker app, 188
tweets
  options within, 565
  photos, 476
  refreshing list of, 563
  web pages, 357
Twitter app, 25
Twitter social network, 560–565
  Compose button, 564
  profile in, 564
  tweets
    options within, 565

refreshing list of, 563
two-player games, 546
typing, 69–74
  Auto-Correction feature, 72–74
  Caps Lock feature, 85
  editing text and placing cursor with
      Magnifying Glass trick, 81
  keyboards, 86–87
    "." shortcut, 87
    Auto-Capitalization option, 86
    enabling Caps Lock feature, 87
    international, 87–90
    setting Auto-Correction feature to
        ON or OFF, 86
  numbers and symbols, 82–84
    press and hold keyboard
        shortcut, 84
    touch and slide trick, 83
  quick phrases with shortcuts, 71
  on screen with two thumbs, 70
  single number rapidly, 83
  Spell Checker feature, 74
  text, quickly selecting and deleting
      or changing, 85
  uppercase letters, 83

U

underlined phone numbers
  calling, 217
  new contact from, 218
undiscoverable networks, 139
Uniform Resource Locators (URLs),
    typing, 348
Universal Serial Bus (USB) to dock
    cables, 37
unread messages, 384–385
Upload button, 555
URLs (Uniform Resource Locators),
    typing, 348
USB (Universal Serial Bus) to dock
    cables, 37
user guide, on-device, 579
usernames, entering passwords and,
    359–360

V

vertical orientation, locking screens in,
    58
vibration, sounds, ringtones and, 237
Video Call button, 267
Video Recorder icon, 271
videos, 259–273, 331–343
  calling
    with FaceTime feature, 260–262
    with Skype app, 263–271
  categories for, 332
  deleting, 339
  finding in iTunes app, 510
  loading onto iPhone, 332
  music videos, 338
  options for, 338–339
    closed captioning, 339
    start playing option, 339
  playing, 332–336
    changing size of video, 334
    fast-forwarding, 333–334
    rewinding, 333–334
    using AirPlay, 334–335
    using chapters, 336
    using time scrubber bar, 334
  podcasts, 337
  previewing TV shows and, 516
  recording, 271–273
    focusing video, 272
    sending video, 273
    trimming video, 272–273
  searching, 332–333
  sending pictures and, with
      Messages app, 253–255
  tv shows, 336–337
  viewing attachments, 389
  watching in Safari web browser,
      357–358
  YouTube, 340–343
    bottom icons in, 340–341
    controls in, 341–342
    history in, 343
    playing videos, 341
    searching, 340
views
  in Calendar app, 434–436

changing in Music app, 280
on phone, 210
for reminders, 450–451
Virtual Private Networks. *See* VPNs
Voice Control app, 20
voice dialing, with Siri assistant, 218
voice dictation, for notes, 428
voicemail, 223–227
    changing password for, 225
    deleting messages, 227
    playing, 226–227
        adjusting greeting, 226
        calling back person who left
            voicemail, 227
        through speaker, 226
    setting up, 224–225
VoiceOver option, 75–77
volume, adjusting
    Sound Check feature for auto
        volume adjust, 290
    when playing music, 284
volume controls, and AirPlay feature,
    182
volume keys, 56–57
Volume Limit, 291
Volume slider bar, 283
Volume Slider control, 284
VPNs (Virtual Private Networks),
    153–156
    contacting help desk, 154
    setting up, 154–156
    switching networks, 156
    verifying connection, 156

▓ W, X

walking directions, and driving and
    transit directions, 501
wall plug adapters, 37
wallpapers
    downloading through apps, 193–194
    for home screen, 189–193
    for lock screen, 189–193
    using photo as, 476
waterproof cases, 52
Weather Channel app, 24

web addresses, typing, 348
web browser, Safari, 345–364
    adding web page icon to Home
        screen, 361
    adjusting settings for, 361–364
        changing search engines, 362
        enabling AutoFill feature,
            362–363
        privacy options, 363
        security options, 364
    AutoFill feature, 359–360
        entering usernames and
            passwords, 359–360
        for personal information, 360
    bookmarks, 350–354
        history and, 351–352
        managing, 352–354
        new, 350–351
        Reading List, 354–355
    and Internet connections, 346
    launching, 346–347
    Open Pages button, 349
    Reader feature, 355
    saving and copying text and
        graphics, 358
    screen layout of, 347
    typing web address, 348
    watching videos in, 357–358
    web pages
        activating links from, 350
        emailing or tweeting, 357
        jumping to top of, 356
        moving through open, 348–349
        printing, 357
        zooming in, 349–350
web page icons, adding to Home
    screen, 361
web pages
    emailing or tweeting, 357
    jumping to top of, 356
    moving through open, 348–349
    printing, 357
web site addresses, for contacts, 411
Week view, 434, 436
What's Hot button, finding apps with,
    529

White on Black setting, 79–80
Wi-Fi networks, 134–138
    advanced options for, 138–142
        automatic-joining feature,
            140–142
        undiscoverable networks, 139
    connecting to
        entering password for secure,
            136
        at public Wi-Fi hotspot with web
            login, 135–136
        switching to different, 137
        verifying connection, 138
    local, 149
Wi-Fi option, Settings app, 12
Wi-Fi switch, 12, 23
wireless carriers, switching between,
    235
wireless games, online games and, 546

Y

Yahoo! address book, syncing contacts
    with, 111

YouTube, 340–343
    bottom icons in, 340–341
    controls in, 341–342
    history in, 343
    playing videos, 341
    searching, 340

Z

Zinio app, 324–325
.zip files, opening and viewing
            compressed, 389–391
Zoom feature, magnifying entire screen
            with, 78–79
zooming
    in Camera app, 462
    email, 385
    in Maps app, 494
    photos, 473–474
        by double-tapping, 473
        by pinching, 474
    in web pages, 349–350
        by double-tapping, 349
        by pinching, 349–350